TIBETAN TALES

D1859445

TIBETAN TALES

DERIVED FROM INDIAN SOURCES.

TRANSLATED FROM THE TIBETAN OF THE
KAH-GYUR

BY

F. ANTON VON SCHIEFNER

DONE INTO ENGLISH FROM THE GERMAN, WITH AN
INTRODUCTION,

BY

W. R. S. RALSTON, M.A.

GYAN

Published by

Gyan Publishing House
5, Ansari Road
Daryaganj, New Delhi-110002
Phone: 011-47034999, 9811692060
E-mail: books@gyanbooks.com

Distribution Network
gyanbooks.com
India, USA, Canada, UK, Australia, France

© Publisher

All rights reserved. No part of this work may be reproduced, stored, adapted, or transmitted in any form or by any means, electronic, mechanical, photocopying, micro-filming, recording or otherwise, or translated in any language, without the prior written permission of the copyright owner and the publisher.

ISBN : 978-81-212-2911-1 (PB)
First Published, 1906

2nd Impression 2021

Printed at: Gyan Press, Delhi.

The book is sold subject to the condition that it shall not, by way of trade or otherwise, be lent, resold, hired out, or otherwise circulated without the prior publisher's written consent.

Tibetan Tales
Translated by: F. Anton Von Schiefner & W. R. S. Ralston

TIBETAN TALES

Derived from Indian Sources.

TRANSLATED FROM THE TIBETAN OF THE KAH-GYUR

BY

F. ANTON VON SCHIEFNER.

DONE INTO ENGLISH FROM THE GERMAN, WITH AN INTRODUCTION,

BY

W. R. S. RALSTON, M.A.

LONDON:
KEGAN PAUL, TRENCH, TRÜBNER & CO. LTD
DRYDEN HOUSE, GERRARD STREET, W.
1906.

CONTENTS.

INTRODUCTION.

In an Appendix to his "Buddhism in Tibet," Dr. Emil Schlagintweit has given "An alphabetical list of the books and memoirs connected with Buddhism." Although not completely exhaustive, it occupies thirty-five pages, and contains references to more than a hundred separate works, and a much larger number of essays and other literary articles. Of those books and articles, the titles of about sixty allude to Tibet. To them may be referred readers who wish for detailed information about that country, its literature, and its religion. All that it is proposed to do here is to say a few words about the Tibetan work from which have been extracted the tales contained in the present volume; to give a short account of the enthusiastic Hungarian scholar, Csoma Körösi, who had so much to do with making that work known to Europe; and to call attention to any features which the stories now before us may have in common with European folk-tales. To do more, without merely repeating what has been already said, would require a rare amount of special knowledge; and it may safely be asserted that remarks about Buddhism, made by writers who do not possess such knowledge, are seldom of signal value.

The tales contained in the sacred books of Tibet, it may be as well to remark at the outset, appear to have little that is specially Tibetan about them except their language. Stories possessing characteristic features and suffused with local colour may possibly live in the memories of the natives of that region of lofty and bleak table-lands, with which so few Europeans have had an opportunity of becoming familiar. But the legends and fables which the late Professor Schiefner has translated from the Kah-gyur are merely Tibetan versions of Sanskrit writings. No mention is made in them of those peculiarities of Tibetan Buddhism which have most struck the fancy of foreign observers. They never allude to the rosary of 108 beads which every Tibetan carries, "that he may keep a reckoning of his good words, which supply to him the place of good deeds;" the praying wheels, "those curious machines which, filled with prayers, or charms, or passages from holy books, stand in the towns in every open place, are placed beside the footpaths and the roads, revolve in every stream, and even (by the help of sails like those of windmills) are turned by every breeze which blows o'er the thrice-sacred valleys of Tibet;" the "Trees of the Law," the lofty flagstaffs from which flutter banners emblazoned with the sacred words, "Ah! the jewel is in the lotus," the turning of which towards heaven by the wind counts as the utterance of a prayer capable of bringing down blessings upon the whole country-side; or of that Lamaism which "bears outwardly, at least, a strong resemblance to Romanism, in spite of the essential difference of its teachings and of its mode of thought."[1] There is, therefore, no present need to dwell at length upon the land into which the legends and doctrines were transplanted which had previously flourished on Indian soil, or the people by whom they have been religiously preserved, but whose actions and thoughts they do not by any means fully represent. "At the present day," says Mr. Rhys Davids, "the Buddhism of Nepāl and Tibet differs from the Buddhism of Ceylon as much as the Christianity of Rome or of Moscow differs from that of Scotland or Wales. But," he proceeds to say, "the history of Bud-

[1] "Buddhism," by T. W. Rhys Davids (Society for Promoting Christian Knowledge), pp. 199-211 and 250.

dhism from its commencement to its close is an epitome of the religious history of mankind. And we have not solved the problem of Buddhism when we have understood the faith of the early Buddhists. It is in this respect that the study of later Buddhism in Ceylon, Burma, and Siam, in Nepāl and in Tibet, in China, Mongolia, and Japan, is only second in importance to the study of early Buddhism."[1]

With regard to the introduction of Buddhism into Tibet, Emil Schlagintweit[2] remarks that "the early history is involved in darkness and myth." Sanang Setsen, in his "History of the East Mongols,"[3] says that during the reign of King Hlatotori, who came to the throne in 367 A.D., four objects descended from heaven one day and lighted upon the golden terrace of his palace, "namely, the image of two hands in the position of prayer, a golden pyramid-temple an ell high, a small coffer with a gem marked with the six fundamental syllables (Om-ma-ni-pad-mè-hûm), and the manual called *Szamadok*."[4] As the king did not understand the nature of the holy objects, he ordered them to be locked up in his treasury. While they lay there, "misfortune came upon the king. If children were born, they came into the world blind; fruits and grain came to nothing; cattle plague, famine, and pestilence prevailed; and of unavoidable misery was there much." But after forty years had passed, there came five strangers to the king and said, "Great king, how couldst thou let these objects, so mystic and powerful, be cast into the treasury?" Having thus spoken, they

[1] "Lectures on the Origin and Growth of Religion, as Illustrated by some Points in the History of Indian Buddhism" (being the Hibbert Lectures for 1881), pp. 189–192.

[2] Whose statements are based upon those made by C. F. Köppen, in his standard work upon "Die lamaische Hierarchie und Kirche."

[3] "Geschichte der Ost-Mongolen: Aus dem Mongolischen übersetzt von Isaac Jacob Schmidt," pp. 25–27. St. Petersburg, 1829.

[4] According to Schlagintweit, "'Constructed Vessel,' a work on moral subjects forming part of the Kanjur."

suddenly disappeared. Therefore the king ordered the holy objects to be brought forth from the treasury, and to be attached to the points of standards, and treated with the utmost respect and reverence. After that all went well: the king became prosperous and long-lived, children were born beautiful, famine and pestilence came to an end, and in their place appeared happiness and welfare. With the date of this event Sanang Setsen connects the introduction of Buddhism into Tibet; but according to Tibetan historians, says Schlagintweit, "the earliest period of the propagation of Buddhism, which reached down till the end of the tenth century A.D., begins with King Srongtsan Gampo, who was born in the year 617 A.D., and died 698." This king is said to have sent a mission to India in the year 632 A.D., the result of which was the invention of a Tibetan alphabet, based upon Devanāgari characters, and the translation into Tibetan of Indian sacred books. In his introduction of Buddhism into his kingdom he is said to have been "most energetically supported by his two wives, one of whom was a Nepalese, the other a Chinese princess. Both of them, who throughout their lifetime proved most faithful votaries to the faith of Buddha, are worshipped either under the general name of Dolma (in Sanskrit Tārā), or under the respective names of Dolkar and Doljang." After making considerable progress during the reign of this monarch, the new religion lost ground under his immediate successors. "But under one of them, Thisrong de tsan, . . . Buddhism began to revive, owing to the useful regulations proclaimed by this king. He it was who successfully crushed an attempt made by the chiefs during his minority to suppress the new creed, and it is principally due to him that the Buddhist faith became henceforth permanently established."

Towards the end of the ninth century, continues Schlagintweit, Buddhism was strongly opposed by a ruler who "commanded all temples and monasteries to be demolished, the images to be destroyed, and the sacred books to be burnt;" and his son and successor is also said to have died "without religion;" but his grandson was favourably inclined towards Buddhism, and rebuilt eight temples. "With this period we have to connect 'the second propagation of Buddhism;' it received, especially from the year 971 A.D., a powerful impetus from the joint endeavours of the returned Tibetan priests (who had fled the country under the preceding kings), and of the learned Indian priest Pandita Atisha and his pupil Brom-*s*ton. Shortly before Atisha came to Tibet, 1041 A.D., the Kāla Chakra doctrine, or Tantrika mysticism, was introduced into Tibet, and in the twelfth and thirteenth centuries many Indian refugees settled in the country, who greatly assisted the Tibetans in the translation of Sanskrit books." It is probably from this period that the Kah-gyur dates.

In the fourteenth century arose the reformer Tsonkhapa, who "imposed upon himself the difficult task of uniting and reconciling the dialectical and mystical schools which Tibetan Buddhism had brought forth, and also of eradicating the abuses gradually introduced by the priests." Tradition asserts that he "had some intercourse with a stranger from the West, who was remarkable for a long nose. Huc believes this stranger to have been a European missionary, and connects the resemblance of the religious service in Tibet to the Roman Catholic ritual with the information which Tsonkhapa might have received from this Roman Catholic priest. We are not yet able to decide the question as to how far Buddhism may have borrowed from Christianity; but the rites of the Buddhists enumerated by the French missionary can for the most part either be traced back to institutions peculiar to Buddhism, or they have sprung up in periods posterior to Tsonkhapa."[1]

Mr. Rhys Davids has remarked that, "As in India, after the expulsion of Buddhism, the degrading worship of Siva and his dusky bride had been incorporated into

[1] Emil Schlagintweit, "Buddhism in Tibet," pp. 60–70.

Brahmanism from the wild and savage devil-worship of the dark non-Aryan tribes, so as pure Buddhism died away in the North, the *Tantra system*, a mixture of magic and witchcraft and Siva-worship, was incorporated into the corrupted Buddhism."[1] Of this change for the worse, evidence about which there can be no mistake is supplied by the Tibetan sacred books. Dr. Malan, who has made himself acquainted with the contents of some of their volumes in the original, says,[2] "There are passages of great beauty and great good sense, the most abstruse metaphysics, and the most absurd and incredible stories; yet not worse than those told in the Talmud, which equal or even surpass them in absurdity."

On New Year's day 1820, a traveller started from Bucharest on an adventurous journey towards the East. His name was Alexander Csoma Körösi (or de Körös),[3] and he was one of the sons of a Szekler military family of Eger-patak, in the Transylvanian circle of Hungary. In 1799, when he seems to have been about nine years old,[4] he was sent to the Protestant College at Nagy-Enyed, where he studied for many years with the idea of taking orders. In 1815 he was sent to Germany, and there he studied for three years, chiefly at the University of Göttingen, where he attended the lectures of the celebrated Orientalist Johann Gottfried Eichhorn. After his return from Germany, he spent the greater part of the year 1819 in studying various Slavonic dialects, first at Temesvar in Lower Hungary, then at Agram in Croatia. But he soon resolved to apply himself to less-known tongues.

[1] "Buddhism," p. 207.

[2] In a letter to the writer of the Introduction.

[3] In Hungarian his name would be written Körösi Csoma Sándor; in French, Alexandre Csoma de Körös; in English, he signed himself Alexander Csoma Körösi, the name Körösi being an adjectival form, meaning "of Körös."

[4] The exact date of his birth has not been ascertained, but one of his Hungarian biographers states that he was about thirty when he started eastward in 1820. Another asserts that he was born in the Transylvanian village of Körös, on the 4th of April 1784.

"Among other liberal pursuits," he wrote in 1825,[1] "my favourite studies were philology, geography, and history. Although my eclesiastical studies had prepared me for an honourable employment in my native country, yet my inclination for the studies above-mentioned induced me to seek a wider field for their future cultivation. As my parents were dead, and my only brother did not want my assistance, I resolved to leave my native country and to come towards the East, and, by some means or other procuring subsistence, to devote my whole life to researches which may be afterwards useful in general to the learned world of Europe, and in particular may illustrate some obscure facts in ancient history." Having no hope, he says, of obtaining "an imperial passport" for his journey, he procured "a printed Hungarian passport at Nagy-Enyed, to come on some pretended business to Bucharest," intending to study Turkish there and then to go on to Constantinople. But he could obtain neither instruction in Turkish nor the means of going direct to Constantinople. So he set forth from Bucharest on the 1st of January 1820, and travelled with some Bulgarian companions to Philippopolis. Tidings of plague forced him to turn aside to the coast of the Archipelago, whence he sailed in a Greek ship to Alexandria. Driven from that city by the plague, he made his way by sea to the coast of Syria, and thence on foot to Aleppo. From that city he proceeded to Bagdad, which he reached in July, travelling part of the way on foot, "with different caravans from various places, in an Asiatic dress," and the rest "by water on a raft." In September he left Bagdad, travelling in European costume on horseback with a caravan, and in the middle of next month he arrived at Teheran. In the capital of Persia he spent four months. In March 1821 he again started with a caravan, travelling

1 In a letter, containing a brief sketch of his life up to that time, which was published in 1834 in the first volume of the "Journal of the Royal Asiatic Society," and from which are taken the passages cited above as quotations.

as an Armenian, and, after a stay of six months in Khorasán, arrived in the middle of November at Bokhara. There he intended to pass the winter; but at the end of five days, "affrighted by frequent exaggerated reports of the approach of a numerous Russian army," he travelled with a caravan to Kabul, where he arrived early in January 1822. At the end of a fortnight he again set out with a caravan. Making acquaintance on the way with Runjeet Sing's French officers, Generals Allard and Ventura, he accompanied them to Lahore. By their aid he obtained permission to enter Kashmir, with the intention of proceeding to Yarkand; but finding that the road was "very difficult, expensive, and dangerous for a Christian," he set out from Leh in Ladak, the farthest point he reached, to return to Lahore. On his way back, near the Kashmir frontier, he met Mr. Moorcroft and returned with him to Leh. There Mr. Moorcroft lent him the "Alphabetum Tibetanum," the ponderous work published at Rome in 1762, compiled by Father Antonio Agostino Giorgi out of the materials sent from Tibet by the Capuchin Friars. Its perusal induced him to stay for some time at Leh in order to study Tibetan, profiting by "the conversation and instruction of an intelligent person, who was well acquainted with the Tibetan and Persian languages." During the winter, which he spent at Kashmir, he became so interested in Tibetan that he determined to devote himself to its study, so as to be able to "penetrate into those numerous and highly interesting volumes which are to be found in every large monastery." He communicated his ideas to Mr. Moorcroft, who fully approved of his plan, and provided him with money and official recommendations. Starting afresh from Kashmir in May 1823, he reached Leh in the beginning of June. From that city, he says, "travelling in a south-westerly direction, I arrived on the ninth day at *Yangla*, and from the 20th of June 1823 to the 22d of October 1824 I sojourned in Zanskár (the most south-western province of Ladákh), where I applied myself to the Tibetan literature, assisted by the Lámá."

With the approach of winter he left Zanskar, and towards the end of November 1824 arrived at Sabathú. In the letter which he wrote during his stay there, in January 1825, he says, "At my first entrance to the British Indian territory, I was fully persuaded I should be received as a friend by the Government." Nor was he disappointed. As at Bagdad and Teheran, so in India was the Hungarian pilgrim welcomed and assisted by the British authorities. In 1826 he seems (says Dr. Archibald Campbell [1]) to have paid a second visit to Western Tibet, and to have continued "to study in the monasteries of that country, living in the poorest possible manner," till 1831. In the autumn of that year Dr. Campbell met him at Simla, "dressed in a coarse blue cloth loose gown, extending to his heels, and a small cloth cap of the same material. He wore a grizzly beard, shunned the society of Europeans, and passed his whole time in study." It is much to be regretted that he has left no record of his residence in the monasteries in which he passed so long a time, in one of which, "with the thermometer below zero for more than four months, he was precluded by the severity of the weather from stirring out of a room nine feet square. Yet in this situation he read from morning till evening without a fire, the ground forming his bed, and the walls of the building his protection against the rigours of the climate, and still he collected and arranged forty thousand words in the language of Tibet, and nearly completed his Dictionary and Grammar." [2] Day after day, says M. Pavie,[3] he would sit in a wretched hut at the door of a monastery, reading

[1] Journal of the Asiatic Society of Bengal, vol. xiv., part 2, p. 824. A second article by Dr. Campbell, including a letter from Lieut.-Colonel Lloyd, was published in vol. xiv., part 2, pp. 823–827.

[2] Quoted by Dr. Campbell from an editorial article by Professor H. H. Wilson in the supplement to the Government Gazette of 9th July 1829. Journal of Asiatic Society of Bengal, vol. xi., part 1, p. 305.

[3] In an interesting article on Tibet in the *Revue des Deux Mondes*, vme série, tom. 19 (July 1847).

aloud Buddhistic works with a Lama by his side. When a page was finished, the two readers would nudge each other's elbows. The question was which of them was to turn over the leaf, thereby exposing his hand for the moment, unprotected by the long-furred sleeve, to the risk of being frost-bitten.

In May 1832 he went to Calcutta, where he met with great kindness from many scholars, especially Professor H. H. Wilson and Mr. James Prinsep, and, after a time, he was appointed assistant-librarian to the Asiatic Society of Bengal. At Calcutta he spent many years, and there his two principal works, the "Essay Towards a Dictionary, Tibetan and English,"[1] and the "Grammar of the Tibetan Language," were brought out at the expense of Government in 1834. "In the beginning of 1836," says Dr. Campbell, "his anxiety to visit Lassa induced him to leave Calcutta for Titalya, in the hope of accomplishing his design through Bootan, Sikim, or Nipal." Of his life in Titalya, where he seems to have spent more than a year, some account is given by Colonel G. W. A. Lloyd, who says, "He would not remain in my house, as he thought his eating and living with me would cause him to be deprived of the familiarity and society of the natives, with whom it was his wish to be colloquially intimate, and I therefore got him a common native hut, and made it as comfortable as I could for him, but still he seemed to me to be miserably off. I also got him a servant, to whom he paid three or four rupees a month, and his living did not cost him more than four more."

Towards the end of 1837[2] he returned to Calcutta. I have been favoured by a very accomplished linguist, the Rev. S. C. Malan, D.D., Rector of Broadwindsor, Dorset,

[1] "The work of Csoma de Körös is that of an original investigator, and the fruit of almost unparalleled determination and patience," says H. A. Jäschke, in the preface to his "Tibetan-English Dictionary."

[2] Colonel Lloyd says that he thinks Csoma Körösi remained at Titalya till November 1837. Journal of the Asiatic Society of Bengal, vol. xiv., part 2.

who was at one time secretary to the Asiatic Society of Bengal, with an account of his acquaintance with Csoma Körösi during the Hungarian scholar's second residence at Calcutta. Dr. Malan writes as follows:—

"As regards Csoma de Körös, I never think of him without interest and gratitude. I had heard of him, and seen his Tibetan Grammar and Dictionary before leaving England. And one thing that used to make me think a five months' voyage interminable was my longing to become acquainted with one who had prepared the way for the acquisition of a language of Asia, thought until then almost mythical. For neither Father Georgi's nor Abel Rémusat's treatises went very far to clear the mystery.

"One of my early visits, then, was to the Asiatic Society's house [in Calcutta], where Csoma lived as under-librarian.[1] I found him a man of middle stature, of somewhat strange expression and features, much weather-beaten from his travels, but kind, amiable, and willing to impart all he knew. He was, however, very shy, and extremely disinterested. Although I had to cross the river to come to him, I requested him at once to give me one lesson a week in Tibetan, and he agreed to do so most readily. But I could not make him consent to take any money. He told me to come as often as I liked, on the condition that his teaching was to be free, for the pleasure and love of it. Of course this prevented me from visiting him as frequently as I should otherwise have done, yet I went to him for a lesson as often as I dared to do so. Although I frequently asked him to come and stay in my house for change of air, I never could prevail upon him to come, owing to his shyness and retiring habits. But as I happened to be the only person who was troubling himself about Tibetan, he and I became very good friends during the whole of my (alas! too short) stay in India. And

[1] Dr. Malan is not certain about the date of his first interview with Csoma Körösi, but his Tibetan lessons began not later than August 1838.

when we parted he gave me the whole of his Tibetan books, some thirty volumes. I value such relics highly, and still use the same volume, containing his Grammar and Dictionary, which I used to turn over with him."

Speaking of Csoma Körösi's literary life at Calcutta, M. Pavie says, in the article which has already been cited, "These labours occupied his time for the space of nine years. He had turned his study into a sort of cell, from which he scarcely ever emerged, except to walk up and down the long neighbouring galleries. It was there that, during our stay in Bengal, we very frequently saw him, absorbed in a dreamy meditation, smiling at his own thoughts, as silent as the Brahmans who were copying Sanskrit texts. He had forgotten Europe to live amid the clouds of ancient Asia."

Early in 1842 Csoma Körösi left Calcutta, with the intention of revisiting Tibet, and of making his way, if possible, to Lhasa, where he was in hopes of discovering rich stores of Tibetan literature as yet unknown to the learned world. On the 24th of March he arrived at Darjíling, in Nepal, where the superintendent of the station, Dr. Archibald Campbell, did all he could to further his views. But on the 6th of April he was attacked by fever, and on the 11th he died, a victim, as Professor Max Müller has said, "to his heroic devotion to the study of ancient languages and religions." His wants, apart from literary requirements, appear to have been as few as those of any monk, whether Christian or Buddhistic. "His effects," says Dr. Campbell, "consisted of four boxes of books and papers, the suit of blue clothes which he always wore, and in which he died, a few shirts, and one cooking-pot. His food was confined to tea, of which he was very fond, and plain boiled rice, of which he ate very little. On a mat on the floor, with a box of books on the four sides, he sat, ate, slept, and studied; never undressed at night, and rarely went out during the day. He never drank wine or spirits, or used tobacco or other stimulants."

A few days before he died he gave Dr. Campbell "a rapid summary of the manner in which he believed his native land was possessed by the original 'Huns,' and his reasons for tracing them to Central or Eastern Asia." Dr. Campbell gathered from his conversation that "all his hopes of attaining the object of the long and laborious search were centred in the discovery of the country of the 'Yoogars.' This land he believed to be to the east and north of Lassa and the province of Kham, and on the northern confines of China; to reach it was the goal of his most ardent wishes, and there he fully expected to find the tribes he had hitherto sought in vain." On the way he hoped to make great literary discoveries, and he would dilate in the most enthusiastic manner "on the delight he expected to derive from coming in contact with some of the learned men of the East (Lassa), as the Lamas of Ladakh and Kānsun, with whom alone he had previous communion, were confessedly inferior in learning to those of Eastern Tibet." He was generally reticent about the benefits which scholars might derive from his contemplated journey, but "What would Hodgson, Tournour, and some of the philosophers of Europe not give to be in my place when I get to Lassa!" was a frequent exclamation of his during his conversations with Dr. Campbell before his illness.

The Asiatic Society of Bengal at once placed a thousand rupees at the disposal of Dr. Campbell for the erection of a monument above the remains of the Hungarian pilgrim. And the Government of India has since given instructions that the grave of this genuine and disinterested scholar shall be for all time placed under the care of the British Resident at Darjíling.[1]

To the Hungarian enthusiast may be fairly applied, with a slight change, the words which Professor Max

[1] For this piece of information I am indebted to Lieut.-Col. T. W. Lewin, who has himself been our Resident at Darjiling, and who availed himself of his stay in Sikkim to study the Tibetan language, of which he has published a Manual.

Müller[1] has written with reference to Hiouen-thsang, the Chinese pilgrim, who spent so much time "quietly pursuing among strangers, within the bleak walls of the cell of a Buddhist college, the study of a foreign language," that there was "something in his life and the work of his life that places him by right among the heroes of Greece, the martyrs of Rome, the knights of the Crusades, the explorers of the Arctic regions; something that makes it a duty to inscribe his name on the roll of the worthies of the human race."

Although the language and literature of Tibet occupied so much of Csoma Körösi's time and thoughts, yet the main object of his life was to work out the mysterious problem as to the origin of the Hungarian nation. According to M. Jules Mohl, it was a remark of Blumenbach's about the possibility of discovering in Asia the original home of the prehistoric ancestors of the Magyars, which first turned the attention to the subject of the young Hungarian, who was then studying medicine at Göttingen. According to Hunfalvy,[2] his fancy may have been fired by De Guignes's opinion, published a little before 1815, that the Huns had wandered from the western borders of the Chinese empire, first to the neighbourhood of the Volga, and then on to Pannonia. But the fact of Csoma Körösi being a Szekler by birth, says Hunfalvy, is regarded as one of the reasons for his looking for the origin of his nation and language in the seat of the ancient Huns. For the Hungarian chronicles had for centuries nourished in the Szeklers the belief that they were the direct descendants of the Huns of Attila. In a letter which he wrote home during his stay in Teheran, dated the 21st of December 1820, he said:—"Both to satisfy

[1] "Chips from a German Workshop," i. 278.

[2] "Die Ungarische Sprachwissenschaft," *Literarische Berichte aus Ungarn*. Budapest, 1877. Bd. i., heft i., pp. 54–97. For this and other references to Hungarian works and German works published in Hungary, I am indebted to Mr. E. D. Butler, of the British Museum, whose acquaintance with Hungarian literature has led to his being elected an honorary member of the Hungarian Academy of Sciences.

my own desire, and to prove my gratitude and love to my nation, I have set off, and must search for the origin of my nation according to the lights which I have kindled in Germany, avoiding neither dangers that may perhaps occur, nor the distance I may have to travel. Heaven has favoured my course, and if some great misfortune does not happen to me, I shall within a short time be able to prove that my conviction was founded upon no false basis." During his stay in Calcutta, between his expeditions, he experienced "the bitterest moments of his life," being conscious that up to that time he had fruitlessly looked for the origin of the Hungarians. It was that feeling, says Hunfalvy, which drove him forth upon the pilgrimage which proved fatal to him. "According to his conviction, the country inhabited by the Dsugur or Dzungar race, dwelling to the north-east of Lhassa, on the western frontier of China, was the goal which he had been seeking all his life, the region in which he might hope at length to discover the Asiatic descendants of the ancestors of his Hungarian forefathers." The foundation of his hopes, as expressed a few days before his death to Dr. Campbell, was as follows:—"In the dialects of Europe, the Sclavonic, Celtic, Saxon, and German, I believe, the people who gave their name to the country now called Hungary were styled Hunger or Ungur, Oongar or Yoongar; and in Arabic, Turkish, and Persian works there are notices of a nation in Central Asia resembling in many respects the people who came from the East into Hungary. In these languages they are styled Oogur, Woogur, Voogur, or Yoogur, according to the pronunciation of the Persian letters; and from the same works it might be inferred, he said, that the country of the Yoogurs was situated as above noted." His views, however, on this subject are not accepted by his countrymen. His opinion "was based upon a false foundation," says Hunfalvy, and consequently his labours in that particular field have remained without result. But as a scholar in general, as a specialist in everything which concerns Tibet, and as a single-minded, self-sacrificing student, he is held in high honour in his native land, as may be learnt from the oration which was delivered in his honour at Pest on the 8th of October 1843 by Baron Joseph Eötvos, who was at one time the Minister of Public Instruction for Hungary.

On this subject I have been favoured with a letter (in English) from the Hungarian linguist and explorer Professor Arminius Vámbéry. In it, after stating that scarcely anything is known in Hungary about the early years of Csoma Körösi, he proceeds to say:—"We only know that it was the study of Oriental languages in Germany which gave him the idea of the possibility of finding a people in Asia speaking our language, and closely connected with us. This, of course, was a mistake, for Hungarian, a mixed tongue consisting of an Ugrian and a Turko-Tatar dialect, has undergone two genetic periods—one in the ancient seat between the Urals and the Volga, and another after the settlement on Pannonia, where also large Slavonic elements inserted themselves. It was thus a sheer impossibility to discover in Asia a language similar to ours, although a considerable amount of affinity can be proved, partly in the Ugrian branch (the Ostyak and the Vogul), partly in the Eastern Turkish, unadulterated by Persian and Arab influence.

"This knowledge, however, is the result of recent investigations, and poor Körösi could have had hardly any notion of it. His unbounded love for science and for his nation drove him to the East without a penny in his pocket, and most curious is the account I heard from an old Hungarian, Count Teleky, regarding the outset of Körösi's travels. The Count was standing before the gate of his house in a village in Transylvania, when he saw Körösi passing by, clad in a thin yellow nankin dress, with a stick in his hand and a small bundle.

"'Where are you going, M. Körösi?' asked the Count.

"'I am going to Asia in search of our relatives,' was the answer.

"And thus he really went . . . undergoing, as may easily be conceived, all the hardships and privations of a traveller destitute of means, living upon alms, and exposed, besides, to the bitter deception of not having found the looked-for relatives. And still he went on in his unflagging zeal, until, assisted by your noble countrymen, he was able to raise himself a memorial by his Tibetan studies.

"I suppose that, when dying in Ladak . . . he always had his eyes directed to the steppes north of Tibet, to the Tangus country, where, of course, he would have again been disillusioned.

"Körösi was therefore a victim to unripe philological speculation, like many other Hungarian scholars unknown to the world. But his name will be always a glory to our nation, and I am really glad to hear that [some one] . . . has devoted time to refresh the memory of that great man.—Yours very sincerely,

"A. VÁMBÉRY.

"BUDAPEST, *February* 20, 1882."

About the time when Csoma Körösi was starting from Bucharest on his adventurous pilgrimage, another equally genuine and disinterested scholar, Mr. Brian Houghton Hodgson, was commencing his long residence in Nepal. Living continuously in that country for three-and-twenty years, and occupying from 1831 to 1843 the important post of British Resident at Kathmandu, he was able to succeed in making the immense collections of Buddhistic works which he afterwards, with a generosity as great as his industry, made gratuitously accessible to European scholars. "The real beginning of an historical and critical study of the doctrines of Buddha," says Professor Max Müller ("Chips," i. 190), "dates from the year 1824. In that year Mr. Hodgson announced the fact that the original documents of the Buddhist canon had been preserved in Sanskrit in the monasteries of Nepal." But there is no need to dwell here on the well-known fact that an immense amount of such Sanskrit literature was discovered by Mr. Hodgson in Nepal, and presented to the Royal Asiatic Society, the Asiatic Society of Bengal, and the *Société Asiatique* of Paris. We have at present to deal only with the stores of information which he extracted from Tibet. Mr. Hodgson not only established the fact, Professor Max Müller goes on to say, "that some of the Sanskrit documents which he recovered had existed in the monasteries of Nepal ever since the second century of our era," but he also showed that "the whole of that collection had, five or six hundred years later, when Buddhism became definitely established in Tibet, been translated into the language of that country." Of the sacred canon of the Tibetans, translated into their language from Sanskrit, Mr. Hodgson received a copy as a present from the Dalai Lama, and this he presented to the East India Company. As early as 1828 he printed in the "Asiatic Researches" (vol. xvi.) an article on Nepal and Tibet, in which he stated that "the body of Bhotiya [*i.e.*, Tibetan] literature now is, and long has been, a mass of translations from Sanskrit; its language native; its letters (like its ideas) Indian."[1] To that statement he in 1837 appended this note: "It is needless now to say how fully these views have been confirmed by the researches of De Körös. It is but justice to myself to add that the real nature of the Kahgyur and Stangyur was expressly stated and proved by me to the secretary of the Asiatic Society some time before M. De Körös's ample revelations were made. Complete copies of both collections have been presented by me to the Honourable East India Company, and others procured for the Asiatic Society, Calcutta: upon the latter M. De Körös worked." It was a fortunate combination which brought the special knowledge and the patient industry of Csoma Körösi into contact with the immense mass of materials obtained by Mr. Hodgson from Tibet.

[1] See, however, an account of Tibetan non-Buddhistic works in Journal of A. S. of B. 1881.

Of the sacred canon of the Tibetans the following description is given by Professor Max Müller, who refers to Köppen's "Religion des Buddha" as his authority:[1]—"It consists of two collections, commonly called the Kanjur and Tanjur. The proper spelling of their names is Bkah-hgyur, pronounced Kah-gyur,[2] and Bstan-hgyur, pronounced Tan-gyur. The Kanjur consists, in its different editions, of 100, 102, or 108 volumes folio. It comprises 1083 distinct works. The Tanjur consists of 225 volumes folio, each weighing from four to five pounds in the edition of Peking. Editions of this colossal code were printed at Peking, Lhassa, and other places. The edition of the Kanjur published at Peking, by command of the Emperor Khian-Lung, sold for £600. A copy of the Kanjur was bartered for 7000 oxen by the Buriates, and the same tribe paid 1200 silver roubles for a complete copy of the Kanjur and Tanjur together. Such a jungle of religious literature—the most excellent hiding-place, we should think, for Lamas and Dalai-Lamas—was too much even for a man who could travel on foot from Hungary to Tibet. The Hungarian enthusiast, however, though he did not translate the whole, gave a most valuable analysis of this immense Bible in the seventeenth volume of the 'Asiatic Researches,' sufficient to establish the fact that the principal portion of it was a translation from the same Sanskrit originals which had been discovered in Nepal by Mr. Hodgson."

The Sanskrit works which Mr. Hodgson so generously presented to the Asiatic Society of Paris were soon turned to good account. From them M. Eugène Burnouf drew the materials for his celebrated "Introduction à l'Histoire du Buddhisme Indien." But of the Tibetan sacred writ-

[1] "Chips," i. 193.

[2] M. Léon Feer has adopted the form *Kandjour* in his translation of Csoma Körösi's "Analysis" (*Annales du Musée Guimet*, tom. 2); but he says in a footnote to p. 143, "J'écris *Kandjour* contrairement à mes principes d'orthographe, parce que Kandjour est une forme qui imite la prononciation et n'est point du tout le calque du mot tibétain."

ings, which were also rendered available to European students, no great use has ever been made except by two scholars. Csoma Körösi, as has been already stated, published an "Analysis of the Tibetan Work entitled the Kah-gyur," and an "Abstract of the Contents of the *B*stan-*h*gyur;" and M. P. E. Foucaux brought out at Paris in 1847 his "Rgya Tch'er Rol Pa, ou Développement des Jeux, contenant l'Histoire du Bouddha Çakya-Mouni, traduit sur la Version Tibétaine du Bhahhgyour, et Revu sur l'Original Sanskrit (Lalitavistâra)." M. Foucaux's excellent work is too well known to require more than a passing notice here. But as Csoma Körösi's Analyses are probably less familiar, it may be well to extract from them a short account of the different sections of the colossal Tibetan collection.

The first of its two parts, he remarks, is styled Ká-gyur, or vulgarly Kán-gyur,[1] *i.e.*, "Translation of Commandments," being versions of Sanskrit writings imported into Tibet, and translated there between the seventh and thirteenth centuries, but mostly in the ninth. The copy on which he worked at Calcutta, consisting of 100 volumes, "appears to have been printed with the very wooden types that are mentioned as having been prepared in 1731." This first part comprises seven divisions, which are in fact distinct works. These he names as follows:—

1. *Dulvá* ("Discipline," Sanskrit *Vinaya*). This division occupies thirteen volumes, and deals with religious discipline and the education of persons who adopt the religious life. It is subdivided into seven parts as follows:—

1. "The Basis of Discipline or Education." 4 vols.
2. "A Sútra on Emancipation." 30 leaves.
3. "Explanation of Education." 4 vols.
4. "A Sútra on Emancipation for the Priestesses or Nuns." 36 leaves.
5. "Explanation of the Discipline or Education of the

[1] Written *b*kah-*h*gyur, the italicised letters not being sounded.

Priestesses or Nuns, in one volume with the preceding tract."

6. "Miscellaneous Minutiæ concerning Religious Discipline." 2 vols.

7. The chief text-book (or the last work of the Dulvá class) on education. 2 vols.

2. "*Shés-rab-kyi-p'ha-rol-tu-p'hyin-pa* (by contraction *Shér-p'hyin*, pronounced *Sher-ch'hin*), Sans. *Prajná páramitá*, Eng. 'Transcendental wisdom.'" This division occupies twenty-one volumes, which all "treat of speculative or theoretical philosophy, *i.e.*, they contain the psychological, logical, and metaphysical terminology of the Buddhists, without entering into the discussion of any particular subject."

3. "*Sangs-rgyas-p'hal-po-ch'hè*, or by contraction *P'hal-ch'hen*, Sans. *Buddhāvataṇsaka*, . . . Association of Buddhas, or of those grown wise." This division contains six volumes, the subject of the whole being "moral doctrine and metaphysics. There are descriptions of several *Tathágatas* or Buddhas, their provinces, their great qualifications, their former performances for promoting the welfare of all animal beings, their praises, and several legends. Enumeration of several *Bodhisatwas*, the several degrees of their perfections, their practices or manners of life, their wishes, prayers, and efforts for making happy all animal beings."

4. "D*kon*-m*ch'hog*-br*tségs-pa*, or by contraction D*kon*-br*tségs* (pronounced *kon-tségs*). In Sans. *Ratna-kúṭa*, the 'Jewel-peak,' or precious things heaped up, or enumeration of several qualities and perfections of Buddha and his instructions. The subject, as in the former division, still consists of morals and metaphysics, mixed with many legends and collections of the tenets of the Buddhistic doctrine."

5. "M*do*-s*dé* (Sans. *Sútránta*), or simply M*do* (Sans. *Sútra*), signifying a treatise or aphorism on any subject. In a general sense, when the whole *Káh-gyur* is divided

into two parts, Mdo and Rgyud, all the other divisions except the Rgyud are comprehended in the Mdo class. But in a particular sense there are some treatises which have been arranged or put under this title. They amount to about 270, and are contained in thirty volumes. The subject of the works contained in these thirty volumes is various. . . . The greatest part of them consist of the moral and metaphysical doctrine of the Buddhistic system, the legendary accounts of several individuals, with allusions to the sixty or sixty-four arts, to medicine, astronomy, and astrology. There are many stories to exemplify the consequences of actions in former transmigrations, descriptions of orthodox and heterodox theories, moral and civil laws, the six kinds of animal beings, the places of their habitations, and the causes of their being born there; cosmogony and cosmography according to the Buddhistic notions, the provinces of several Buddhas, exemplary conduct of life of any *Bodhisatwa* or saint, *etc.*" It is the second volume of this section which M. Foucaux has translated.

6. "*Mya-ñan-las*-h*das-pa*, or by contraction *Myang*-h*das* (Sans. *Nirváṇa*)," two vols. The title of these two volumes is in Sanskrit *Mahá parinirváṇa sútra*. . . . A *sútra* on the entire deliverance from pain. Subject, Shákya's death under a pair of *Sál* trees near the city of *Kusha* or *Kámarúpa*, in *Assam*. Great lamentation of all sorts of animal beings on the approaching death of Shákya, their offerings or sacrifices presented to him, his lessons, especially with regard to the soul. His last moments, his funeral, how his relics were divided, and where deposited."

7. "R*gyud*-s*dé*, or simply R*gyud*, Sans. *Tantra*, or the Tantra class, in twenty-two volumes. These volumes in general contain mystical theology. There are descriptions of several gods and goddesses, instructions for preparing the *mandalas* or circles for the reception of these divinities, offerings or sacrifices presented to them for obtaining their favour, prayers, hymns, charms, &c., &c., addressed

to them. There are also some works on astronomy, astrology, chronology, medicine, and natural philosophy."

Of the second great division of the Tibetan sacred books Csoma Körösi gives only a brief abstract, "without mentioning the Sanscrit titles of the works" from which its contents have been translated. It will be sufficient to quote the opening lines of his article.

"The B*stan*-H*gyur* is a compilation in Tibetan of all sorts of literary works, written mostly by ancient Indian *Pandits* and some learned Tibetans, in the first centuries after the introduction of Buddhism into Tibet, commencing with the seventh century of our era. The whole makes 225 volumes. It is divided into classes, the R*gyud* and M*do* (*Tantra* and *Sútra* classes in Sanscrit). The R*gyud*, mostly on *tantrika* rituals and ceremonies, makes 87 volumes. The M*do*, on science and literature, occupies 136 volumes. One separate volume contains hymns or praises on several deities and saints, and one volume is the index for the whole."[1]

In the year 1830, while Csoma Körösi was still pursuing his studies in the monasteries of Western Tibet, a Russian official, Baron Schilling de Canstadt, was beginning to look for Tibetan books in Eastern Siberia. His first visit, he says,[2] to the monastery of Tchikoï, twelve leagues from Kiachta, the town in which he was stationed, made him aware that it possessed a copy of the Kah-gyur, as well as other sacred books, which were ranged on either side of

[1] Csoma Körösi's analysis of the Tibetan sacred books has been translated by M. Léon Feer, and was published in 1881 under the title of "Analyse du Kandjour et du Tandjour," in the second volume of the "Annales du Musée Guimet," the sumptuous work due to the munificence of M. Guimet. M. Feer has appended to his translation a most useful "Vocabulaire de l'Analyse du Kandjour," giving all the names which occur in Csoma Körösi's Analysis, with the explanations it contains, together with an index and a "Table Alphabétique des Ouvrages du Kandjour," and several appendixes. The fourth volume of the "Annales du Musée Guimet" is to consist of "Extraits du Kandjour," translated by M. Léon Feer.

[2] In a very interesting paper printed in the "Bulletin Historico-Philologique de l'Académie de Saint Péterbourg," tom. iv., 1848, pp. 321–339.

the altar, wrapped in red and yellow coverings. As the Russian ecclesiastical mission to Pekin was then on the point of starting from Kiachta, he offered to obtain by its means from China such books as the priests might require. They gladly accepted his offer, and made out lists of Tibetan books, which proved of great service to him, especially after they had been supplemented by the additions which were made by a Lama who visited him at Kiachta. He still further ingratiated himself with the priests by presenting them with a *lo* or *tum-tum*, which he procured from the nearest Chinese town, as well as by the respect he showed for their sacred books. For when he was allowed to handle a volume of their copy of the Kah-gyur, he took care to touch the margins only of the leaves, not the holy printed part.

It happened that the chief of a tribe of Tsongols possessed a copy of a part of the Kah-gyur, and this he gave to the appreciative stranger, who rose still higher in the opinion of the natives when they found that he had ordered a silken wrapper to be made for each of the volumes presented to him. He himself was delighted, he says, at becoming "the proprietor of the first Tibetan work of any length which had up to that time passed into the hands of a European." After all this he was well received wherever he went. A prediction had been made a year before that a foreign convert to Buddhism, destined to spread that religion in the West, was about to visit Mongolia, and this prophecy was interpreted in his favour. The Buriat Lamas even looked upon him as "a Khoubilghan, an incarnation of an important personage in the Buddhist Pantheon." After a time he organised a band of copyists, sometimes twenty in number, who lived in tents in his courtyard, and frequently consumed as much as a hundred pounds of beef in a day, besides much brick tea, a caldron being kept always on the boil for their use. At the end of a year he possessed a collection of

Mongol and Tibetan books, containing two thousand works and separate treatises.

Happening to visit the temple of Subulin, he found that the Lamas were manufacturing an enormous prayer wheel. He offered to get the printing of the oft-repeated prayer done for them at St. Petersburg, whereby their machine would be rendered far more efficacious than if they trusted to native typography. They accepted his offer gladly, and to prove their gratitude, presented to him, in the name of the tribe, a complete copy of the Kah-gyur which they possessed, having obtained it from a Mongol Lama. Both parties to this transaction were equally pleased; for when the printed leaves came from St. Petersburg, it was found that each of them contained 2500 repetitions of the sacred formula, and the words were printed in red ink, which is 108 times more efficacious than black; and the paper itself was stamped with the same words instead of bearing the maker's name. So the Buriates were charmed, and so was the European bibliophile, who had got possession of what he had scarcely hoped ever to obtain, a copy of the Kah-gyur in 101 volumes, printed in the monastery of Nartang in Western Tibet. This copy, after the death of Baron Schilling de Canstadt, was purchased from his heirs by the Emperor Nicholas, and presented to the Academy of Sciences.

M. Vasilief, the well-known author of the "History of Buddhism," which has been translated from Russian into French and German, says[1] that when he was at Pekin he made inquiries about the Kah-gyur and Tan-gyur, and he was shown the building in which they used to be printed. But no edition, he was told, had been brought out for some time. Some of the wood blocks were lost, others had suffered injury. However, a copy of each work was procured by the Chinese Government and presented to

[1] In an account of the works, in the languages of Eastern Asia, belonging to the library of the University of St. Petersburg, printed in the "Mélanges Asiatiques" of the St. Petersburg Academy of Sciences, tom. ii., 1856.

the Russian mission. These copies are now in St. Petersburg. The Mongol Buriates of Russia, M. Vasilief states, are even more devoted to their religion, and look to Lhassa more longingly than their kinsmen in Mongolia itself. They read their sacred books, or hear them read, in Tibetan, and are edified, even though they do not comprehend. Any one who wishes to command a reading of the Kah-gyur or Tan-gyur addresses himself to one of the monasteries which possess those works, pays a certain price, and provides tea for the Lamas. A reading of the Kah-gyur, it seems, used to come to about fifteen pounds at one of the monasteries, exclusive of tea. At a given signal all the Lamas flock together, and take their places according to seniority. Before each are placed a number of leaves of the work, and off they set, all reading at once, so that the entire performance occupies only a few hours, after which each reader receives his share of the offering made by the orderer of the function.

Of the Russian scholars who availed themselves of the presence of the two editions of the Kah-gyur at St. Petersburg, the most enthusiastic and industrious was the late Professor Anton von Schiefner. From the Dulvā, the first of the seven divisions of that work, he translated into German the legends and tales, an English version of which is contained in the present volume. His German versions all appeared in the "Mélanges Asiatiques tirés du Bulletin de l'Académie Impériale des Sciences de St. Pétersbourg" (tom. vi.–viii.), with the exceptions of Nos. 2 and 5, which were published in the "Mémoires" of that Society (series vii., tom. xix., No. 6). Professor Schiefner, if he had lived another year, would have doubtless supplied a number of additional notes, and would have written an Introduction to the work. His lamented death on November 16, 1880, has deprived the present volume of what would probably have been one of its most interesting parts. It was at Professor Schiefner's express wish that the present translation was undertaken. It must be a subject of universal regret that he did not live to witness its appearance in print. The following tribute to his merits as a scholar was contributed, soon after his death, by Professor Albrecht Weber to "Trübner's Record."

"Professor F. Anton von Schiefner was a distinguished scholar of most various attainments. His specialty, however, was Tibetan, and more particularly the investigation of Buddhist legends of Indian and Occidental origin, a collection of which in English will soon be published by Messrs. Trübner & Co. He had, moreover, devoted himself with rare perseverance and disinterestedness to the utilisation and publication of the labours of two scholars whose own restless activity would, without him, have been almost entirely lost to the scientific world—namely, those of the Finnic linguist, Alexander Castrèn, and of the Caucasian linguist, Baron von Uslar. One might —*sit venia verbo*—almost say that both men had found in Schiefner their Homer. He edited the labours of Castrèn almost wholly from the posthumous papers of that brave and modest man, who, from 1838 to 1849, explored, under the greatest privations, the inhospitable regions of Norway, Lapland, and Siberia, where the tribes of the Finnic race are seated. Castrèn's *Reiseerinnerungen* and *Reiseberichte*, edited by Schiefner, present a vivid picture of the hardships Castrèn had to go through, and which finally caused his premature death, in 1852, at the age of thirty-nine. We have lying before us the twelve volumes of his Samoyedan and Tungusian Grammars and Vocabularies, as well as those of the languages of the Buryats, Koibals, Karagasses, Ostyaks, &c.; his ethnological lectures on the Altaic races, and those on Finnic mythology—all worked out by Schiefner's deft hand, and edited by him from 1835 to 1861. In connection therewith Schiefner also made a German translation of the Finnic national epos *Kalevala*, and also one of the Hero-Sagas of the Minussin Tatars. Schiefner was more advantageously situated in working up the collections of the estimable Caucasian linguist, Major-General von Uslar (1816 to 1873), written in the Russian language, with whom, until the General's death, he was always able to confer directly. While Schiefner's own and entirely independent work on the Thush language (1856), by the accuracy with which a hitherto quite uncultivated and altogether strange department was opened to linguistic investigation, had obtained for the author general appreciation, the united efforts of both scholars have furnished surprising results as regards these highly peculiar languages of the Caucasian mountaineers—the Avares, Abchases, Tchetchenzes, Kasikumüks, Kurines—which by their extraordinary sounds, as well as by their most singular grammatical structure, produce so very strange an impression. The personal intercourse with soldiers of Caucasian origin, garrisoned at St. Petersburg, was herein of high importance to Schiefner. His amiable and open manner in personal intercourse, characteristic of the whole man, bore him excellent fruit in this case. Science, and especially the St. Petersburg Academy of Sciences, has by Schiefner's death sustained a heavy, indeed a quite irreparable, loss."[1]

The edition of the Kah-gyur on which Professor Schiefner worked appears (says M. Vasilief, the author of the "History of Buddhism") to have been that in 108 volumes, printed at Pekin during the eighteenth century, and presented to the Asiatic Museum of the St. Petersburg Academy of Sciences by the Asiatic Department of the Ministry of Foreign Affairs, which had received it, about the year 1850, from the Russian Mission in China.

[1] A complete list of Professor Schiefner's writings is given in a memoir by F. Wiedemann, read at a meeting of the Imperial Academy of Sciences, December 11, 1879, and reprinted in the 10th volume of the "Russische Revue." From this it appears that he was born at Reval in 1817, the son of a merchant who had migrated thither from Bohemia; he studied in the University of St. Petersburg from 1836 to 1840, and then for two years in the University of Berlin. In 1848 he was appointed one of the librarians of the Imperial Academy of Sciences, of which he became a member a few years later.

The notes to the present volume signed S. are by Professor Schiefner. A few others have been added, consisting for the most part of extracts from Professor Monier Williams's Sanskrit Dictionary. The forms of Indian names adopted by Professor Schiefner have been retained in the English translation, with certain modifications—*y* being substituted for *j*, for instance, *ch* for *tsh*, and *j* for *dsh*. It ought to be stated that Professor Schiefner made several important corrections on the sheets which he prepared for the use of his English translator, and therefore the English version will sometimes be found to differ materially from the German text.[1]

[1] For special information about Tibet and Tibetan Buddhism the following works may be consulted:—Emil Schlagintweit's "Buddhism in Tibet," London, 1863; C. F. Köppen's "Die Religion des Buddha," Berlin, 1857–59, the second volume, entitled "Die lamaische Hierarchie und Kirche;" the "Souvenirs d'un Voyage dans la Tartarie, le Tibet, et la Chine, pendant les années 1844, 1845, 1846," Paris, 1853, by the French missionaries MM. Huc and Gabet, and "Le Christianisme en Chine, en Tartarie, et en Thibet," by the same authors; P. E. Foucaux's "Rgya Tch'er Rol Pa, or Dévellopement des Jeux, Traduit sur la version Tibétaine du Bhahhgyour, et revu sur l'original Sanskrit (Lalitavistâra)," Paris, 1848, containing an immense amount of valuable information in the Introduction and the Notes; Eugène Burnouf's "Introduction à l'Histoire du Buddhisme Indien," Paris, 1844, and "Le Lotus de la Bonne Loi," Paris, 1852; the "Narratives of the Mission of George Bogle to Tibet, and of the Journey of Thomas Manning to Lhasa, edited with Notes, an Introduction, &c., by Clements R. Markham," London, 1876, the Introduction containing a great deal of interesting information about Tibet and its explorers; Brian H. Hodgson's "Essays on the Languages, Literature, and Religion of Nepál and Tibet," London, 1874; General A. Cunningham's "Ladák," 1854; A. A. Georgi's "Alphabetum Tibetanum," Rom, 1762; Colonel Yule's "Cathay;" the "Travels in the Himalayan," by W. Moorcroft and G. Trebeck, London, 1841; Isaac Jacob Schmidt's "Forschungen im Gebiete der älteren religiösen, politischen und literarischen Bildungsgeschichte der Völker Mittel-Asiens, vorzuglich der Mongolen und Tibeter," St. Petersburg, 1824, his translation from the Tibetan of the "Dsanglun, der Weise und der Thor," St. Petersburg, 1843, and his "Index des Kanjur," St. Petersburg, 1845; T. D. Thomson's "Western Himálaya and Tibet," London, 1852; L. Torrens's "Travels in Ladâk, &c.," London, 1862; S. Turner's "Account of an Embassy to the Court of the Teshoo Lama in Tibet," London, 1800; G. T. Vigne's "Travels in Kashmír, Ladak, &c.," London, 1842; Col. Prjevalsky's "Mongolia, &c.," translated by E. D. Morgan, London, 1876; the French and German translations of V. Vasilief's Russian work on Buddhism; Anton Schiefner's "Tibetanische Studien," and a great number of articles in periodicals, the titles of which are given in the list by E. Schlagintweit, from which most of the foregoing references are

To European folk-tales the longer legends of the Kah-gyur bear but little resemblance, though many of the fables about animals, and other short stories towards the end of the present volume, have their counterparts in the West. Here and there, however, even in the long narratives of the legendary class, certain features may be recognised as being common to both Europe and Asia. The moral of King Māndhātar's story (No. 1), for instance, seems to be identical, different as is its machinery, with that of a story which is current in many Western lands. That monarch, after conquering the whole earth, ascends into the heavenly home of the thirty-three gods, and is allowed to share the throne of their chief, Śakra or Indra. But at last he wishes for too much. "He came to the conclusion that he must expel the king of the gods, Śakra, from his throne, and take into his own hands the government of both gods and men." As soon as he had conceived this idea, "the great King Māndhātar came to the end of his good fortune," and soon afterwards he died. The most familiar form of the European story, which inculcates a similar moral teaching, is the German tale of "The Fisherman and his Wife" (the 19th of Grimm's Collection). In it, a grateful fish for a long time accedes to every desire expressed by the fisherman. He and his wife become first rich, then noble, and eventually royal. But the fisherman's wife is not satisfied with being a queen. She wishes to be the Pope, and the fish fulfils her desire. Even then she is discontented, and at last she demands to be made God. When the fish is told this

taken. Among linguistic works may be mentioned Csoma Körösi's "Grammar of the Tibetan Language," Calcutta, 1834, and his "Essay towards a Dictionary, Tibetan and English," Calcutta, 1834; I. J. Schmidt's "Grammatik der Tibetanische Sprache," St. Petersburg, 1839, and his "Tibetisch deutsches Wörterbuch," St. Petersburg, 1841 (an adaptation for a German public, according to Jäschke, of Csoma Körösi's work); P. E. Foucaux's "Grammaire de la Langue Tibétaine," Paris, 1858; Col. T. W. Lewin's "Manual of Tibetan," Calcutta, 1879; and what is now the standard work on the subject, H. A. Jäschke's "Tibetan-English Dictionary," London, 1881.

by her husband, it replies, "Go back, and you will find her in her hovel." The fisherman's good fortune has come to an end. He and his wife are poor folks once more. In a Hesse variant the husband's final wish is, "Let me be God, and my wife the Mother of God."[1]

A curious parallel to one of the incidents in King Māndhātar's story is afforded by a Polynesian myth. On the crown of King Utposhadha's head, according to the Tibetan tale, "there grew a very soft tumour, somewhat resembling a cushion of cotton or wool, without doing him any harm. When it had become quite ripe and had broken, there came forth from it a boy, shapely and handsome." Mr. Gill tells us in his interesting "Myths and Songs from the South Pacific" (p. 10), that Tangaroa and Rongo were the children of Vātea, the father of gods and men, and his wife Papa. "Tangaroa should have been born first, but gave precedence to his brother Rongo. A few days after the birth of Rongo, his mother Papa suffered from a very large boil on her arm. She resolved to get rid of it by pressing it. The core accordingly flew out; it was Tangaroa! Another account, equally veracious, says that Tangaroa came right up through Papa's head. The precise spot is indicated by '*the crown*' with which all their descendants have since been born." Professor Schiefner mentions that a suggestion has been made to the effect that "the name of Utposhadha may be a transformation of the Greek Hephæstus, though the part which the latter plays in the Greek myth at the birth of Athene is of a different nature." But this seems to be going unnecessarily far.

The story of Kuśa, No. 2, may be linked with the numerous European variants of the tale which we know so well under the title of "Beauty and the Beast." The principal feature of that tale is the union of a beautiful maiden with a monster of some kind, whose monstrosity is eventually

[1] An account of the different classes of stories which turn upon wishes has been given by Benfey, "Panchatantra," i. 496–499.

cured by her love and devotion. The Beast with whom the Beauty is linked is generally a supernatural monster, and possesses the power of at times divesting itself of its monstrous or bestial envelope or husk, and appearing in its real form as a fairy prince or other brilliant being. It is, as a general rule, only at night in the dark that this transformation takes place. In some cases, as in the Cupid and Psyche story, the wife is forbidden to look upon her husband. He visits her only in utter darkness. But in many versions of the story she is allowed to see her pseudo-monster in all his brilliant beauty. He is often a deity, whom some superior divinity has degraded from the sky and compelled to live upon earth under a monstrous shape. One day the wife lays her hands on her husband's monstrous envelope or husk and destroys it. The spell being thus broken, the husband either flies away to heaven or remains living on earth in uninterrupted beauty.

In some of the European variants, the original idea having apparently been forgotten, the transformation appears not only grotesque but unreasonable. Thus in a Wallachian tale (Schott, No. 23), a princess is married to "a pumpkin," or at least to a youth who is a pumpkin by day. Wishing to improve her husband, she one day puts him in the oven and bakes him, whereupon he disappears for ever. In a German story (Grimm, No. 127), a princess who has lost her way in a wood is induced to marry an iron stove. But the disfiguring "husk" is in most cases the hide or skin of some inferior animal, an ass, a monkey, a frog, or the like, or else the outside of a hideous man. Sometimes it is a brilliant female being who is after this fashion "translated." Thus an Indian story[1] tells of a prince who was obliged to take a monkey as his wife. But when she liked she could slip out of her monkey skin and appear as a beautiful woman arrayed in the most magnificent apparel. She adjured her husband to take

[1] *Asiatic Journal*, New Series, vol. ii., 1833.

great care of her "husk" during her absence from it. But one day he burnt it, hoping to force her to be always beautiful. She shrieked "I burn!" and disappeared. In a Russian variant of the same story a prince is compelled to marry a frog, which is "held in a bowl" while the marriage service is being performed. But when it so pleases her, his frog-wife "flings off her skin and becomes a fair maiden." One day he burns her "husk," and she disappears. In the Tibetan story of Kuśa, the "Beast" is merely an ugly man disfigured by "the eighteen signs of uncomeliness."[1] On that account it was decided that "he must never be allowed to approach his wife by daylight." But she caught sight of him one day, and her suspicions were aroused. So she hid away a lighted lamp in her room, uncovered it suddenly when her husband was with her, shrieked out that he was a demon, and fled away. After a time, however, won by his military reputation, she said to herself, "As this youth Kuśa is excellently endowed with boldness and courage, why should I dislike him?" And straightway "she took a liking for him," just as the Beauty of the fairy-tale did for the Beast. It may be worth noticing that the conch-shell which Kuśa sounds with such force that the ears of his enemies are shattered, and they are either killed or put to flight, finds a Russian parallel in the whistle employed by the brigand Solovei, or Nightingale, whom Ilya of Murom overcomes. In the builmas, or Russian metrical romances, he often figures; and when he sounds his whistle his enemies fall to the ground, nearly or quite dead.

No. 3, which chronicles some of the wise judgments of King Ādarśamukha, comprises two different stories—the first narrating the ingenuity with which the king satisfied the demands of a number of complainants without injuring the man who had involuntarily given rise to their com-

[1] With the story of his birth may be compared the similar account of the birth of Śṛingabhuja in the Kathá Sarit Ságara. See Mr. Tawney's translation, vol. i. p. 355.

plaints; the second describing a journey made by a traveller who was commissioned by various persons, animals, or other objects, passed by him on his way, to ask certain questions on his arrival at his destination. The latter story is one which is familiar to Eastern Europe. In one of its Russian variants a peasant hospitably receives an old beggar, who adopts him as his brother, and invites him to pay him a visit. On his way to the beggar's home, he is appealed to by children, who say, "Christ's brother, ask Christ whether we must suffer here long." Later on, girls engaged in ladling water from one well into another beg him to ask the same question on their account. When he arrives at his journey's end he becomes aware that his beggar friend is Christ himself; and he is informed that the children he had passed on the way had been cursed by their mothers while still unborn, and so were unable to enter Paradise; and the girls had, while they were alive, adulterated the milk they sold with water, and were therefore condemned to an eternal punishment resembling that of the Danaides (Afanasief, "Legendui," No. 8). The judgments attributed in the Tibetan tale to King Ādarśamukha, and in another Tibetan work, the "Dsanglun" (as Professor Schiefner has remarked) to King *M*dges-pa, form the subject of a story well known in Russia under the title of "Shemyakin Sud," or "Shemyaka's Judgment." It exists there as a folk-tale, but it belongs to what may be called the chap-book literature of the country, and it is derived from literary sources. A variant given by Afanasief ("Skazki," v., No. 19) closely resembles part of the Tibetan tale. A poor man borrowed from his rich brother a pair of oxen, with which he ploughed his plot of ground. Coming away from the field he met an old man, who asked to whom the oxen belonged. "To my brother," was the reply. "Your brother is rich and stingy," said the old man; "choose which you will, either his son shall die or his oxen." The poor man thought and thought. He was sorry both for the oxen and for his brother's son.

At last he said, "Better let the oxen die." "Be it as you wish," said the old man. When the poor man reached his home the oxen suddenly fell down dead. The rich brother accused him of having worked them to death, and carried him off to the king. On his way to the king's court the poor man, according to the chap-book version ("Skazki," viii. p. 325), accidentally sat down upon a baby and killed it, and tried to commit suicide by jumping off a bridge, but only succeeded in crushing an old man whose son was taking him into the river for a bath. He had also had the misfortune to pull off a horse's tail without meaning it. When summoned into court for all these involuntary offences, he took a stone in his pocket tied up in a handkerchief, and stealthily produced it when he was had up before the judge, saying to himself, "If the judge goes against me I will kill him with this." The judge fancied that the stone was a bribe of a hundred roubles which the defendant wished to offer him; so he gave judgment in his favour in each case. The poor man was to keep his brother's horse until its tail grew again, and to marry the woman whose child he had crushed, and to stand under the bridge from which he had jumped and allow the son of the man he had killed to jump off the bridge on to him. The owner of the horse, the husband of the woman, and the son of the crushed man were all glad to buy off the culprit whom they had brought up for judgment. The satirical turn of the story and the allusion to bribe-taking are characteristic features of the Russian variants of this well-known Eastern tale. The Russian story takes its title from the notorious injustice and oppression of Prince Demetrius Shemyaka, who blinded his cousin, Vasily II., Grand Prince of Moscow, and for a time usurped his throne. To this day an unjust legal decision is known as a Shemyaka judgment. But in the Eastern versions of the story, which are numerous, there is no mention of injustice; stupidity, however, is sometimes attributed by them to the judge. Thus in the

Kathá Sarit Ságara[1] the story of Devabhúti tells how the excellent wife of the learned Brahman of that name "went into the kitchen garden to get vegetables, and saw a donkey belonging to a washerman eating them. So she took up a stick and ran after the donkey, and the animal fell into a pit as it was trying to escape and broke its hoof. When its master heard of that, he came in a passion and beat with a stick and kicked the Brahman woman. Accordingly she, being pregnant, had a miscarriage, but the washerman returned home with his donkey. Then her husband, hearing of it, came home after bathing, and, after seeing his wife, went in his distress and complained to the chief magistrate of the town. The foolish man immediately had the washerman, whose name was Balásura, brought before him, and, after hearing the pleadings of both parties, delivered this judgment: 'Since the donkey's hoof is broken, let the Bráhman carry the donkey's load for the washerman until the donkey is again fit for work, and let the washerman make the Bráhman's wife pregnant again, since he made her miscarry. Let this be the punishment of the two parties respectively.' When the Bráhman heard this, he and his wife in their despair took poison and died. And when the king heard of it, he put to death that inconsiderate judge."

As they deal with the subject of wise judgment, the seventh and eighth stories may be spoken of next. One of them describes the cleverness of a girl, the other that of a lad. Each of them is very popular in the East, and both of them find more or less complete counterparts in the West. There is a well-known group of folk-tales familiar to most European and Asiatic lands, the theme of which is the sharpness of a woman's wits. Just as there thrive among the common people of all countries many jeers and flouts against women, such as the proverbs

[1] Book xii. chap. 72, vol. ii. p. 180 of Mr. C. H. Tawney's most valuable translation, now being published in the "Bibliotheca Indica" by the Asiatic Society of Bengal.

"A woman's hair is long, but her mind is short," and "A woman is worse than a dog, for *it* does not bark at its master," or stories illustrative of a wife's obstinacy, folly, or perfidy, so there flourish by their side numerous popular arguments in favour of women, generally conveyed in the form of stories. In the Perso-Turkish story-book of "The Forty Viziers," a tale accusing women frequently alternates with one told in their defence. The framework of the collection is as follows:—A wicked queen calumniates her stepson as Phædra calumniated Hippolytus. His father sentences him to death. But the forty ministers intercede for him, each of them daily telling a tale of which the aim generally is to show how little reliance can be placed on a woman. Each night the queen tells a story which is usually of quite the opposite tendency, pointing out that men are miserable creatures, and that they are morally inferior to women. At the end of the forty days and nights, the prince is allowed to speak in his own defence (having been during that period prohibited by the astrologers from opening his lips), and all goes well. Among encomiums upon women, the story of Viśākhā (forming No. 7 of the present collection and a part of No. 8) is entitled to rank high. Her discretion, intelligence, and thoughtfulness for others, entitle her to an honourable place among the heroines of popular fiction. One of her decisions of a knotty legal point is specially interesting, as it belongs to the cycle of which Solomon's judgments in the case of the two disputing mothers is the best known example. The actual mother and the adopted mother of a boy dispute as to which is really his mother. The point is legally important, for with the possession of the boy goes that of his deceased father's homestead. The case is referred to the king, whose ministers investigate it, but in vain. At length Viśākhā is consulted. She replies, "What need is there of investigation? Speak to the two women thus: 'As we do not know to which of you two the boy belongs, let who is the strongest take the boy.' When each of them has laid hold of one of the boy's hands and he begins to cry out on account of the pain, the real mother will let go, being full of compassion for him, and knowing that if her child remains alive she will be able to see it again. But the other, who has no compassion for him, will not let go."[1] Professor Schiefner has called attention in a note to the article in "Ausland" by the late Professor Benfey on the somewhat similar tale of "Die Kluge Dirne," and to the variant of the Viśākhā story given in Mr. Spence Hardy's "Manual of Buddhism." There is a well-known folk-tale about a woman's intelligence, of which the Russian variant may be cited here. It is the 6th of Khudyakoff's collection of "Great Russian Popular Tales" (Moscow, 1860). A peasant girl was so intelligent that she solved all the problems proposed to her by a certain judge. Charmed by her cleverness, he married her. But he stipulated that if she ever found fault with any of his legal decisions she was to be divorced, and was bound to return at once to her father's cottage. Only she was to be allowed to take away with her whatever thing she liked best in her husband's house. All went well for some time with the judge and his clever wife. At length she heard him deliver a preposterous judgment in court, and she could not help protesting against it. Accordingly she was ordered to return to her father's hut. She obeyed, but she took with her the judge, to whom she had administered so much liquor before leaving, that she was able to drive him in a cart tranquilly sleeping. When he awoke, and found himself in his father-in-law's cottage, he naturally asked how he got there. "I brought you away with me," replied the divorced wife. "You know I was entitled to take away whatever I liked best in your house, and I chose you."[2] There is a very interesting story of the same kind in

[1] See Rhys Davids's "Buddhist Birth-Stories," pp. xiv, xlvi; and "Gesta Romanorum," No. 45.

[2] This story is to be found in divers places, the Talmud included.

Radloff's great collection of songs and tales from Central Asia ("Proben der Volkslitteratur der türkischen Stämme Sud-Sibiriens," vol. iii. pp. 347–354). There was once a choleric khan who understood the language of birds. He ordered his vizier one day to find out what two geese had said to each other as they flew past, threatening to put him to death if he failed to do so. The vizier applied for help to the khan's wise daughter, who gave him the information he required. He promised not to mention his informant, but he broke his promise. The khan was so angry with his daughter, when he found out that it was she who had told the vizier what the geese had said, that he gave her in marriage to the most miserable specimen of humanity he could find. She proved an excellent wife to her unsightly and poverty-stricken husband, and he and she prospered in consequence.[1]

The story of the cleverness of Mahaushadha (No. 8) forms the counterpart of that of Viśākhā, who herself plays a part in the tale, which is told at somewhat tedious length. Some of its incidents will be familiar to readers of Western folk-tales. Professor Schiefner has called attention (in a footnote to page 129) to several variants of the story of the mystic fowl—sometimes a cock, sometimes a hen or goose, a layer of golden eggs—the eater of which is destined to become a king. It forms the opening of the German story of "The Two Brothers" (Grimm, No. 60, vol. iii. pp. 102–107); but in it the peculiarity of the bird is stated to be that the eating of its heart and liver enables the eater to become rich. Three Russian variants of the story are given by Afanasief in his collection of "Russian Popular Tales" (v., No. 53, viii., No. 26, and pp. 464–7). In all of them the eater of the bird or a part of it becomes a king. Many mythologists[2] recognise

[1] The story of the suitors whom Viśākhā shut up in chests and put to shame occurs as a folk-tale in Miss Maive Stokes's "Indian Fairy Tales," No. 28, "The Clever Wife."

[2] See Gubernatis, "Zoological Mythology," ii. 311.

in the golden egg the Sun, which may be looked upon as a gleaming egg laid every morning by the brooding Night. But the king-making power attributed to the bird's eaten flesh remains a mystery. In the story of Mahaushadha, the boy Bahvannapāna, who has eaten the head of the mystic cock, is elected king by the ministers at a certain court on account of his good looks. Having gone forth in search of some successor to their deceased monarch, they find him sleeping under a tree, "the shadow of which never moved from his body," and they exclaim, "As he is extremely handsome, and is well provided with signs, we will invest him with the sovereignty." In the East-European variants the fortunate youth is frequently chosen as king because his taper, when he takes one to church, kindles of its own accord. One of the tasks which Mahaushadha is called upon to execute by way of proving his cleverness is "to supply some rice which had not been crushed with a pestle, and yet was not uncrushed, and which had been cooked neither in the house nor out of the house, neither with fire nor yet without fire," and to send it "neither along the road nor yet away from the road, without its being shone upon by the daylight, but yet not in the shade," by a messenger who should be "not riding, but also not on foot" (page 139). Similar tests frequently appear in European folk-tales. Thus, in one of the Lithuanian Tales (Schleicher, No. 1), a gentleman promises to marry a village maiden if she can fulfil certain conditions, saying, "If you come to me neither clothed nor bare, not riding nor driving nor walking, not along the road, nor beside the road, nor on the footpath, in summer and likewise in winter, then will I marry you." The abduction of the mule which was watched by five men (page 142), one of whom sat on its back while the others held its four legs, is evidently a reminiscence of an ingenious theft commemorated in many such stories as "The Master Thief" (Grimm, No. 192). But Mahaushadha's contrivances for making the dog talk and for keeping the sheep thin (page 175) are novel. The latter, as a plan of working on the body through the eye, may be compared with Jacob's use of the rods which he placed "in the watering-troughs when the flocks came to drink" (Genesis xxx. 38).

The "Clever Thief" (No. 4) is one of the numerous variants of the well-known story which we generally associate with the treasure of Rhampsinitos.[1] As Professor Schiefner has pointed out some of its Western parallels (pp. 37 and 43), it is not necessary to do more here than to add a few references to those which he has given. Professor Schiefner has himself written on the subject.[2] The most recent commentator is Professor G. Maspero, who has devoted to it four pages of the Introduction to his collection of ancient Egyptian tales.[3] The name of Rhampsinitos, he says, is a Greek form of the Egyptian name Ram-sis-si-nit, or Ramses the son of Nit. Two objections, he remarks, have been made to the supposition that the story is of Egyptian origin. One is the nature of the masonry employed by the builders of the treasury, which has been stated not to be in keeping with Egyptian architectural practice. The other is the shaving of the beards of the drunken soldiers who had been set to watch the corpse of the clever thief's comrade. This has been said to be an incident evidently not of Egyptian origin, seeing that in Egypt only barbarians wore beards. But Professor Maspero impugns both objections. He shows that some Egyptian temples did actually possess hiding-places resembling that described in the story; and as regards the shaving, he points out that in the first place Egyptians could wear beards, and did wear them when they felt inclined, and that in the second

[1] A good acount of the story is given by Sir George Cox in his "Mythology of the Aryan Nations," i. 111–121.

[2] "Ueber einige morgenländische Fassungen der Rhampsinit Sage," in the "Bulletin" of the St. Petersburg Academy of Sciences, tom. xiv. pp. 299–315.

[3] "Contes populaires de l'Égypte Ancienne." Paris, 1882. Pp. xxxvii–xli.

place the soldiers who guarded the corpse would belong "to a tribe of Lybian origin of the name of Matiou," and therefore be fully entitled, in their capacity of foreigners, to wear their beards. A modern Greek variant of the story has been lately discovered in Cyprus,[1] and Mr. Tawney has recently translated an Indian variant,[2] which offers a striking resemblance to the Gaelic tale of "The Shifty Lad."[3] The Tibetan tale, however, is more nearly akin to the Egyptian form of the story than to that which it takes in this Indian variant.

The story of Prince Sudhana (No. 5) has several points in common with Western folk-tales. One of these is the capture by the hunter Phalaka of the celestial maiden, the Kinnarī Manoharā, who becomes Sudhana's bride. This is effected by means of a "fast-binding chain" which the hunter throws around her when she is bathing in a lake. Her companions fly away heavenward, leaving her a captive on earth. This incident will at once remind the reader of the captures of "swan-maidens" and other supernatural nymphs, which so frequently occur in popular romance. It is usually the swan's feather-dress or bird-husk on which the liberty of the captured maiden depends. While she is deprived of it she must live on earth as a mortal's wife. But if she can recover it, she becomes a bird once more, and soars heavenward. Manoharā is captured by means of a magic chain. But her power of flying through the air depends upon her possession of a jewel. So long as she is without that, she remains a slave; when she recovers it, she becomes free and flies aloft.[4] Sudhana's visit to the palace of his supernatural wife's

[1] Sakellarios, "Cypriaques," iii., p. 157. Quoted by M. Émile Legrand in his "Recueil de Contes populaires grecs." Paris, 1881. Pp. 205–216.

[2] "Kathá Sarit Ságara," book x. chap. lxiii. The story occurs in vol. ii. part 7, of Mr. Tawney's translation. Calcutta, 1881.

[3] J. F. Campbell's "Tales from the West Highlands," No. 18, on which see the exhaustive notes by Reinhold Köhler in "Orient und Occident," ii. 303.

[4] For a full account of "swan-maidens" and the mediæval romance of "The Knight of the Swan," see Baring Gould's "Curious Myths of the Middle Ages."

father, and the task which is set him of recognising her amid her ladies, bear a strong resemblance to the adventures which befall the heroes of many tales current in Europe. A mortal youth often obtains, and then for a time loses, a supernatural wife, generally represented as the daughter of a malignant demon. He makes his way, like Sudhana, to the demon's abode. There tasks are set him, which he accomplishes by means of his wife's help. One of these is that he shall recognise her when surrounded by her numerous sisters, each of whom is exactly like her in appearance and dress. He calls upon her to step forth from among them; she does so, and the recognition takes place.

As a specimen of an European variant of the tale may be taken the Russian story of "The Water-King" ("Russian Folk-Tales," No. 19). In it a prince steals the dress of one of the water-king's twelve daughters while they are bathing. Her sisters become spoonbills and fly away, but she remains in his power till he restores her dress. Then she also flies away in spoonbill form. When he arrives after a time at her father's palace, she aids him to accomplish the tasks which are set him. At last the water-king says, "Choose yourself a bride from among my twelve daughters. They are all exactly alike in face, in hair, and in dress. If you can pick out the same one three times running, she shall be your wife; if you fail to do so, I shall have you put to death." The maiden whose dress he had stolen and restored enables him to succeed in this task also. The recognition of Sudhana by his wife, brought about by means of a ring, is an incident of which frequent use is made in folk-tales. When a demon's daughter, or a princess who has been enslaved by a demon, has enabled a hero to escape along with her from that demon's power, she often warns him that he will forget her if he, on his return home, kisses his mother (as in "Two Kings' Children," Grimm, No. 113), or does something else which he has been forbidden to do. He always neglects the warning and forgets his wife. But eventually she manages to remind him of her existence, usually by means of a ring. In the similar story of "The Mastermaid" ("Tales from the Norse," No. 11), the recognition is due to a golden apple and two golden fowls which the hero and heroine had carried off from a giant's palace. In "The Battle of the Birds" (Campbell's "West Highland Tales," No. 2), the prince forgets the giant's daughter after being kissed by "an old greyhound," but remembers her when he hears a conversation between a golden pigeon and a silver pigeon which spring out of a glass offered to his forgotten love. Similar parallels to this story will be found in most of the large collections of European folk-tales.

A curious feature in the story is the ablution to which Manoharā is subjected after her stay among mortals (p. 71), in order that "the smell of humanity" may be "washed off her." In a similar story in the "Kathā Sarit Sāgara,[1] a hero who has been deserted by his celestial spouse, Bhadrā, wanders long in search of her. At length he reaches a mountain lake to which come "to draw water many beautiful women with golden pitchers in their hands." He asks them why they are drawing water, and they reply, "A Vidyádharí of the name of Bhadrá is dwelling on this mountain; this water is for her to bathe in." Whereupon he slips into one of the pitchers the jewelled ring which his wife had given him. And so it comes to pass that when "the water of ablution" is poured over her, the ring falls into her lap. She recognises it, and all goes well.

The long history of "Prince Jīvaka, the King of Physicians" (No. 6), has little in common with Western folk-lore. The cures he performs, by either opening the skull and removing from the brain headache-producing centipedes, or else eliminating such similar intruders by a less heroic operation, may, however, be likened to somewhat similar

[1] Mr. Tawney's translation, i. 142.

kinds of surgical treatment mentioned in European folk-tales. Thus in a modern Greek story[1] a girl is relieved from the presence of a number of snakes which had taken up their abode within her by being suspended from a branch of a tree above a caldron of boiling milk, the vapour arising from which induced the reptiles to come forth. There is an English story also of a country clergyman who could obtain no rest from headaches, till at last he induced the village blacksmith to hit him on the head with his largest hammer. The ecclesiastic's skull cracked beneath the blow, and out came sufficient swarms of earwigs to account for his complaint. But this story requires verification. The cure effected at p. 103, to which no parallel is found in the variant of the legend in Mr. Spence Hardy's "Manual of Buddhism," though the skull-opening incident occurs in it (p. 242), resembles that brought about by Kīrtisenā in the case of King Vasudatta's headache in the Kathā Sarit Sāgara.[2] She learnt how to treat the malady from a Rākshasī, who gave the following instructions as to how the king might be cured, unaware that a human being was listening:—"First his head must be anointed by rubbing warm butter on it, and then it must be placed for a long time in the heat of the sun, intensified by noonday. And a hollow cane-tube must be inserted into the aperture of his ear, which must communicate with a hole in a plate, and this plate must be placed above a pitcher of cool water. Accordingly the centipedes will be annoyed by heat and perspiration, and will come out of his head, and will enter that cane-tube from the aperture of the ear, and, desiring coolness, will fall into the pitcher." Kīrtisenā carried out these instructions, and the result was that she "extracted from the head of that king, through the aperture of the ear, one hundred and fifty centipedes."

The lovely maiden Āmrapālī, the Dryad-like nymph

[1] E. Legrand, "Contes Populaires Grecs," Paris, 1881, pp. 228–230. The story is European by language only, not by domicile, for it was found at Smyrna.

[2] Mr. Tawney's translation, i. 265.

who emerges (p. 85) from the kadalī tree in the āmra grove, closely resembles the tree-maidens who figure in some European popular tales. In the 21st of Hahn's "Griechische Märchen," the stem of a laurel opens and forth comes "a wondrously fair maiden." In the sixth story of Basile's "Pentamerone," a fairy comes forth in the same way from a date spray, and in the second from a bilberry twig. The homes of the nymphs of this class are as often flowers as trees. In a Russian story (Afanasief, vi., No. 66), the heroine is transformed after death into a wondrous blossom. At midnight "the blossom begins to tremble, then it falls from its stem to the ground, and turns into a lovely maiden." In the same way the heroine of the German story of "The Pink" (Grimm, No. 76) becomes a flower at her lover's wish; and many other similar instances might be quoted. All such ideas as these appear to have been originally connected with the tree-worship which formed so important a part of the religion of our remote ancestors, and on which so excellent a work was written a few years ago by the late Wilhelm Mannhardt.[1]

Of special interest, as dealing with this kind of worship, is the opening of the Buddhistic legend of Mahākāśyapa and Bhadrā (No. 9). Tree-worship existed long before Buddhism was heard of, and it has succeeded in maintaining its existence in many lands up to the present day. There is no lack of stories relating to it; but it is not often that we obtain so clear an insight into the ideas of tree-worshippers, or are favoured with so detailed an account of the rites which they were wont to celebrate, as are afforded by the description of the childless Brahman's appeal to the Nyagrodha tree (p. 187). It serves to illustrate the confusion existing in the minds of tree-worshippers between the material tree and its spiritual tenant. The Brahman Nyagrodha, the tree's namesake, first caused the ground in its neighbourhood to be "sprinkled, cleansed,

[1] "Wald- und Feldkulte," 2 vols. Berlin, 1875–77.

and adorned." Then he set up flags and banners, and provided a profusion of perfumes, flowers, and incense. Finally, "he prayed to the tree-haunting deity," promising to pay that divine being due honour if a son should be born to him, but threatening, in case he should remain childless, to cut down the tree and split it into chips, destined to be consumed with fire. In another passage of the Kah-gyur (vol. vi., p. 280) Professor Schiefner remarks in a note appended to this passage, "Bhagavant gives directions that, in case it is absolutely necessary to fell a tree, the work-masters of the Bhikshus shall draw a circle around it seven or eight days before felling it, offer up perfumes, flowers, and oblations, recite *tantras* and utter spells, proclaim abhorrence of the path of the ten vices, and moreover say, 'Let the deity who inhabits this tree find another dwelling. With this tree shall a religious or ecclesiastical work be accomplished.' Seven or eight days after this the tree may be felled. But if any change be perceptible, it must not be felled. If none is perceptible, then it may be cut down."

One of the stories of the "Panchatantra" (the 8th of Book 5) may be compared with the opening of No. 9, so far as tree-worship is concerned, and with the already quoted (in illustration of No. 1) German story about a wife's unreasonable wishes. A weaver, who wanted timber for a new loom, was about to fell a tree, when the spirit which resided in it protested against the operation, and promised, if the tree was spared, to fulfil any wish the weaver might express. The weaver assented, but before specifying his wish he went home and consulted his wife. She recommended him to ask for an additional pair of hands and another head, for by their means he would be able to keep two looms going instead of one. The weaver took his wife's advice, and requested the tree-spirit to render him two-headed and four-armed. "No sooner said than done. In an instant he became equipped with a couple of heads and four arms, and returned home highly delighted with his new acquisitions. No sooner, however, did the villagers see him, than, greatly alarmed, they exclaimed 'a goblin! a goblin!' and between striking him with sticks and pelting him with stones speedily put an end to his existence."[1]

The greater part of No. 9, the account of the ascetic life led by Bhadrā and her husband, belongs to a different world from that of folk-lore, but in the "Acta Sanctorum," and in some popular legends derived from that source, parallels may be found equally conducive to edification.

In No. 10, also, we are taken away from the region of folk-tales, but this time into that of such literary fictions as form a part of the "Thousand and One Nights." It, also, is not of a very edifying nature; but it is valuable as showing what utter nonsense many of the corrupted Buddhistic legends contain, and illustrating the custom prevalent among literary Buddhists (one in which they were perhaps surpassed by the Christian compilers of such works as the "Gesta Romanorum") of appending an unexceptionable moral to a tale of an unsavoury nature. The rapidity with which the narrator, at the close of the story of Utpalavarṇā, passes from the record of her dissoluteness to the account of her conversion is somewhat startling. The same remark applies also to the close of the history of Kṛiśā Gautamī (No. 11). That narrative is as little edifying, for the most part, as the legend which precedes it. One of the tricks resorted to in it, the lengthening at will, by means of some magical substance, of the nose of an obnoxious individual, frequently figures in popular tales. In one of the stories from Central Asia (Jülg, "Mongolische Märchen," No. 14), the fairies elongate an intruder's nose to such an extent that they are able to tie seven knots in it. But they perform that operation by sheer force. In European folk-tales the abnormal growth of the nose, or the sudden appearance of horns or the like, is generally caused by the magical properties of some fruit or other apparently harmless substance

[1] Prof. Monier Williams, "Indian Wisdom," 3d edit., pp. 514–516.

(Grimm, No. 122, iii., 204, Hahn, No. 44). In the present case, the means employed for the lengthening of the nose is a piece of wood, and a piece of another kind of wood reverses the operation. In the folk-tales the magical substance which produces the wished-for result is generally discovered by accident. In the Tibetan legend its discovery is due to its employer's observation of a raven, which lengthened its beak by rubbing it on a piece of wood when it wanted to get at a corpse otherwise out of its reach, and afterwards reduced it to its normal proportions when it had finished its meal. The magic lute which plays so important a part in the story of Śusroṇī (No. 12) is of course closely related to all the musical instruments of magic power which both literature and folk-lore have rendered familiar, from the harp or lyre of Orpheus or Amphion to the pipe of the Piper of Hameln, the dance-inspiring fiddle of the German tales of "Roland" and "The Jew in Thorns" (Grimm, Nos. 56 and 110), the magic flute which an angel gives to the strong fool of the modern Greek story of Bakala (Hahn, No. 34), and a number of similar instruments capable of making trees and rocks reel and men and women wildly skip. In these dance-compelling instruments many mythologists recognise symbols of the wind.[1] One of the most interesting of the European folk-tales in which such instruments occur is the Esthonian story of "Pikne's Bagpipes," of which a full account is given by A. de Gubernatis in his "Zoological Mythology" (i. 159–161), taken from Dr. Löwe's excellent translation of Kreutzwald's collection (Ehstnische Märchen," No. 9). In it the thunder-god is robbed of his bagpipes (*toru-pil*, "Röhreninstrument") by the devil, who hides it away in hell, keeping it in an iron chamber guarded by seven locks. The consequence is

[1] "The same power of the wind which is signified by the harp of Orpheus is seen in the story of Amphion" (Cox's "Mythology of the Aryan Nations," ii. 249) "The pipe is a symbol of the storm-song (of the Maruts) which makes all things dance" (Mannhardt, "Germanische Mythen," p. 174).

that the clouds no longer yield a drop of rain. The thunder-god, under the form of a boy, obtains access to hell, and persuades the devil to let him play on the magic bagpipes. Thereupon "the walls of hell quaked, and the devil and his associates fainted away and fell to the ground as though dead." Returning home, the thunder-god "blew into his thunder-instrument till the rain-gates opened and gave the earth to drink." The termination of the history of Śusroṇī is closely akin to that with which all complete variants of the "Puss in Boots" story should end. They ought always to conclude with the ingratitude of the hero or heroine of the tale to the cat or fox or other animal which has made itself useful. The Marquis de Carabas ought to have proved ungrateful to the Booted Cat, just as Śusroṇī neglected to give her benefactor, the jackal, the daily meat which she had promised it. The asseverations of the king's wives in this story, and those of the hero and heroine of No. 18, may be compared with the similar affirmations of the heroine of the 26th of M. Legrand's "Contes Populaires Grecs." In it a king suffers from a strange malady, three branches having grown over his heart. His disguised sister tells him her story, and adds, "If I tell the truth, O my king, may one of the branches break which is over your heart!" By three such asseverations she breaks all three branches.

The story (No. 13) of the actor who dramatises the life of Buddha, and is punished for his audacity in making fun of the Six Bhikshus, soars high above the region of folk-lore. And there is but little in European popular fiction which can be likened to the legend of "The Dumb Cripple" (No. 14), who pretended to be unable to speak or walk, in order that he might not be made a king. reflecting that, "if he were to be invested with sovereign power, this would not be a good thing, seeing that in consequence of a sixty years' reign which he had accomplished in a previous state of existence, he had been born again in hell, and that he now ran the risk of going to hell a second time." The same remark holds good of the not very edifying history of Ṛshyaśringa or Gazelle Horn (No. 15), the ascetic who, out of spite, prevents rain from falling until his asceticism and his magic power collapse together.

The story of Viśvaṇtara (No. 16), the princely Bodisat, who not only gives away all his property and retires into the forest of penance, but even surrenders his two children to a cruel slave-owner, and finally hands over his wife to a stranger who demands her, has been already told by Mr. Spence Hardy in his "Manual of Buddhism" (pp. 116–124), under the title of "The Wessantara Játaka;" but as it is one of the most touching of the class of legends to which it belongs, having in it more of human interest than such narratives generally contain, and as the Tibetan variant is the more poetic and pathetic of the two renderings of the tale, Professor Schiefner has done good service by translating it. Such acts of renunciation as the princely Bodisat accomplished do not commend themselves to the Western mind. An Oriental story-teller can describe a self-sacrificing monarch as cutting slices of flesh off his own arms and plunging them into the fire in honour of a deity, and yet not be afraid of exciting anything but a religious thrill among his audience. To European minds such a deed would probably appear grotesque. And so the Eastern tales in praise of self-sacrifice do not seem to have impressed the lay mind of Europe. On ecclesiastical literature they probably exerted considerable influence. But folk-tales do not often deal with such heroic operations as were performed by Prince Viśvaṇtara in cutting himself loose from all worldly ties in order that nothing might prevent him from becoming the consummate Buddha. The sorrows of Madrī, the princely ascetic's wife, who is reduced by her husband's passion for giving everything away first to exile and poverty, then to bitter grief on account of the loss of her dearly loved little children, and finally to slavery, but who submits to all her husband's commands, may be compared with those of the patient Grisildes whose praises Chaucer has sung in "The Clerke's Tale." The Clerk states in his prologue that the story was one which he "lerned at Padowe of a worthy clerk," whose name was "Fraunces Petrark, the laureat poete;" Petrarch having freely translated it in the year 1373 from Boccaccio's "Decamerone." This story, however, appears to have been current in Italy for some time before. In folk-tales the similar sorrows of a wife who is condemned to a series of humiliations by a harsh husband are often described; but the husband's conduct is generally accounted for by the fact that his wife had at first rejected him with contumely, and he had made up his mind to retaliate. Patient Grissel's husband had absolutely no excuse to plead for his cruelty, nor can much be said in extenuation of that of such a husband as the German "King Thrushbeard" (Grimm, No. 52), the Norwegian "Hacon Grizzlebeard" ("Tales from the Norse," No. 6), or the Italian "King of Fairland," the husband of the proud Cintiella (Basile's "Pentamerone," No. 40). The Russian variant of "Patient Grissel's Story" (Afanasief, v. No. 29) seems worthy of mention, as not being likely to be familiar to Western Europe. A king marries a peasant's daughter on condition that she shall never find fault with anything he says or does. She makes him an excellent wife, and never opposes his will, even when he takes her children from her, pretending that they are to be put to death, in order that his neighbours might not laugh at them as being sprung from a peasant mother; or when he sends her back to her father's hut, and then recalls her from it as a servant, and orders her to get ready the room intended for his new bride. But the Russian story, as it stands alone (with the exception of the opening), is probably an echo from abroad.[1]

[1] The bibliography of the Griselda story is given at length by Dr. Reinhold Köhler, in an article fifteen columns long, in Ersch and Gruber's "Allgemeine Encyklopädie," section i., vol. xci. Leipzig, 1871.

In the Nidānakathā or "The Three Epochs" (translated in Mr. Rhys Davids's "Buddhist Birth-Stories," p. 33), there is an account of the great generosity of Mangala Buddha. "The story is, that when he was performing the duties of a Bodhisatta, being in an existence corresponding to the Vessentara existence,[1] he dwelt with his wife and children on a mountain." One day a demon named "Sharp-fang," hearing of his readiness to bestow gifts, "approached him in the guise of a Brahmin, and asked the Bodhisatta for his two children. The Bodhisatta, exclaiming, "I give my children to the Brahmin," cheerfully and joyfully gave up both the children, thereby causing the ocean-girt earth to quake. The demon, standing by the bench at the end of the cloistered walk, while the Bodhisatta looked on, devoured the children like a bunch of roots. Not a particle of sorrow arose in the Bodhisatta as he looked on the demon, and saw his mouth as soon as he opened it disgorging streams of blood like flames of fire; nay, a great joy and satisfaction welled within him as he thought, 'My gift was well given,' and he put up the prayer, 'By the merit of this deed may rays of light one day issue from me in this very way.' In consequence of this prayer of his it was that the rays emitted from his body when he became Buddha filled so vast a sphere." Another strange Indian story about self-sacrifice is that of the Dānava or Titan Namuchi,[2] who "did not refuse to give anything to anybody that asked, even if he were his enemy." Having practised asceticism for ten thousand years "as a drinker of smoke," he was allowed by Brahmā to become, like Balder, proof against all the ordinary forces of nature. After that he frequently made war against Indra, and often overcame him. When the gods and the Asuras churned the ocean of milk with the mountain Mandara, Namuchi received, as his share in the products

[1] *i.e.*, his last birth before attaining Buddhahood.

[2] Kathā Sarit Sāgara, vol. i. p. 444, of Mr. Tawney's translation.

of the churning, a horse which had the power of restoring to life, by a sniff, any Asura whom the gods had killed. This gave him great power. At length Indra went to Namuchi and asked for that horse as a gift. Namuchi gave it, and Indra, "as he could not be slain by any other weapon, killed him with foam of the Ganges, in which he had placed a thunderbolt." However, he was born again as "an Asura composed all of jewels," and he conquered Indra a hundred times. "Then the gods took counsel together, and came to him, and said to him, 'By all means give us your body for a human sacrifice.' When he heard that, he gave them his own body, although they were his enemies: noble men do not turn their backs on a suppliant, but bestow on him even their lives."

The story of a charitable monarch, whose uprightness and generosity are put to a severe test by a deity, occurs as a folk-tale in Miss Maive Stokes's "Indian Fairy Tales" (No. 13). It properly belongs to literature, in which it has assumed various forms, one of which has been made known to English readers by the late Sir Mutu Coomāra Swāmy in his "Arichandra, or the Martyr of Truth; a Drama translated from the Tamil." The story as told by an Indian ayah takes this form. There was a king named Harchand, who "used to pray a great deal to God, and God was very fond of him," but thought fit to test his goodness. So one day, when he had promised an ascetic "two pounds and a half of gold," all his wealth was turned into charcoal. In order to keep his word, Harchand was obliged to sell his wife and child for a pound and a half of gold, and then he sold himself for the other pound. Having become the property of "a Dom, that is, a man of a very low caste, who kept a tank into which it was his business to throw the bodies of those who died," he was charged with the care of the tank, and ordered to take a rupee in payment for each adult corpse, eight annas for a dead child, or a piece of cloth, in case the bearers of the body had no money. One day his wife arrived, bearing the corpse of his son, who had died. She had no money, but she said to herself, "I know that man is my husband, so he will not take any money for throwing his child into the water." But he was so honest, in the interests of his master, that he insisted upon a fee, which had to be paid at the expense of his wife's single covering. Eventually all went well, the dead boy was restored to life, and when the reunited royal family returned home, "the garden was in splendid beauty; the charcoal was turned back into gold, and silver, and jewels; the servants were in waiting as usual, and they went into the palace and lived happily for evermore."

The principal theme of "The Fulfilled Prophecy" (No. 17) is one that often occurs in popular tales, many of which are devoted to proving how impossible it is for a man, whatever crimes he may commit, to escape from his destiny. The "Two Brothers" (No. 18) is one of the great cycle of moral tales in which goodness is contrasted with badness, to the temporary advantage but eventual discomfiture of the latter. The blinding of the good brother by the bad is an incident suggestive of the opening of the well-known folk-tales of "True and Untrue" ("Tales from the Norse," No. 1), the "Two Wanderers" (Grimm, No. 107), and a great number of similar stories, to many of which references are given in vol. iii. p. 189, of Grimm's collection.

Stories about ungrateful wives are popular in Asia. In No. 21, "How a woman requites love," a husband twice saves his wife's life, once by rescuing her from his brothers, who proposed to feed upon her when destitute of other food in a desert, and again by supplying her with food and drink, much to his own inconvenience, when she was faint from hunger and thirst. "He sliced some flesh off his thighs," says the narrator, "and gave it to her to eat; and then he opened the veins of both his arms and gave her the blood to drink." In spite of which, she conspired against him with a handless and footless cripple.

In one of the Indian variants of the story ("Panchatantra," iv. 5), the husband's self-sacrifice takes a more poetic form. In the midst of a forest a wife suffered intensely from thirst. Her husband went to seek water. When he came back with some his wife was dead. A voice was heard saying that if he would give up half of his own life hers would be renewed. He immediately pronounced a formula by which he surrendered half of his life, and his wife was thereby resuscitated. Soon afterwards, being in a garden one day during the absence of her husband, she heard a cripple singing so beautifully that she fell in love with him at once. So she took an early opportunity of pushing her husband into a well. After which she led a wandering life, carrying about the cripple in a basket on her head. But her husband, who had not been killed by his fall, escaped from the well, and at length confronted her one day in the presence of a king, and demanded back the half of his life which he had given her. She uttered formal words of surrender and fell dead. The Indian variant of the story in the Daśakumāracharita is closely akin to the Tibetan, the husband assuaging his wife's hunger and thirst by means of his own flesh and blood, and being rewarded by being pushed into a well by his wife, who had fallen in love with a cripple whose hands, feet, nose, and ears had been cut off by robbers.[1] This story appears to be the original of a singular Mongol tale (Jülg's "Mongolische Märchen," p. 105). A man and his wife were walking along near a cliff, when they heard so lovely a voice resounding that the woman said to herself, "I should like to belong to the man who possesses so charming a voice," and she proceeded to push her husband into a well. Then she set off in search of the possessor of the voice. When she found him, he turned out to be a loathsome invalid, whose groans

[1] "Hindoo Tales, or the Adventures of Ten Princes." Freely translated from the Sanskrit of the Dasakumaracharitam, by P. W. Jacob," pp. 261–266.

had been rendered melodious by the echoing cliff. Full of remorse, she tried to make up for the murder of her husband by carrying away the invalid, under whose disagreeable weight she pined away and eventually died (Benfey, "Panchatantra," i. pp. 436-444). The form assumed by the story in the Kathā Sarit Sāgara[1] is almost identical with that in the Kah-gyur. The end, however, is more savage in the Indian than in the Tibetan variant. After the ungratefulness of the wife had been exposed, the king's ministers "cut off her nose and ears and branded her, and banished her from the country with the maimed man. And in this matter Fate showed a becoming combination, for it united a woman without nose and ears with a man without hands and feet." In the "Three Snake Leaves" (Grimm, No. 16), a wife who has been resuscitated after her death by her husband conspires against him with a ship-captain and has him flung into the sea. He is saved, however, and she and her accomplice are ultimately discovered and sentenced to be drowned.

The story of "The Grateful Animals and the Ungrateful Man" (No. 26) is one that is very widely spread throughout Asia, and has made its way into many parts of Europe. The merits of the lower animals were, in Eastern stories, frequently contrasted with the demerits of man, so far at least as gratitude is concerned, many centuries before such ideas as have in modern times led to the formation of societies for the protection of animals had exercised any influence over European thought. In the present instance a hunter, who draws out of a pit a lion, a snake, a mouse, a falcon, and a man, is rewarded by the two beasts, the bird, and the reptile, and by their aid is enabled to escape from prison, after having been thrown into it in consequence of the machinations of the man he had saved. In the "Panchatantra" (Appendix to Book i. story 2) a Brahman rescues a tiger, a monkey, a snake, and a man, with similar results. From the work of which

[1] Vol. ii. p. 101 of Mr. Tawney's translation.

the "Panchatantra" is the Sanskrit representative, the story made its way, about 750 A.D., into the Syriac "Kalilag and Damnag," and the Arabic "Kalilah and Dimnah," and thence, about 1080 A.D., into Symeon Seth's Greek translation from the Arabic, and the Latin translation (through the Hebrew) by Joannes of Capua in the second half of the thirteenth century, and so into the Spanish, German, French, Italian, and English translations of different versions of the Arabic work.[1] It occurs also in other works of Buddhistic origin. In a story from the Rasavāhinī, quoted by Spiegel in his "Anecdota Pālica," an inhabitant of Benares rescues from a hole a dog, a snake, and a man. The dog and the snake are grateful, and by their means their rescuer is enabled to escape the impalement to which he had been condemned in consequence of the malice of the ungrateful man he had rescued along with them. There can be little doubt that it was from Indian, and probably Buddhistic, sources that such grateful animals made their way into European folk-tales—as the ants, fish, and birds of the "White Snake" (Grimm, No. 17); the lions, bears, wolves, foxes, and hares of "The Two Brothers" (No. 60); the ants, ducks, and bees of "The Queen Bee" (No. 62); the horse, ducks, stork, and bees of "The Two Wanderers" (No. 107); and the bear, mouse, and monkey of "The Faithful Beasts" (Grimm, 104 of first edition, afterwards omitted); not to speak of the numberless counterparts of these grateful creatures in the folk-tales of every European land.

Of the rest of the stories, the greater part belong to the class of animal fables. Many of them are old acquaintances under a new guise. "The Ungrateful Lion" (No. 27), for instance, which tells how a woodpecker extracted a bone from a lion's throat, and was supposed by the lion to be sufficiently paid for his trouble by its escape from his jaws, closely resembles the fable of the wolf which paid

[1] For an account of this literature, see Mr. Rhys Davids's "Buddhist Birth-Stories, p. xxix.

in similar coin its long-billed benefactor. "The Wolf and the Sheep" (No. 29) is the familiar fable of "The Wolf and the Lamb," but the final argument of the wolf is different. The story of the ass which insists upon singing at the wrong time, and so is caught trespassing, and is punished (No. 32), has made its mark in European literature. The jackal which acts as arbiter between the two otters (No. 34), and takes as its share the main part of the fish they catch, leaving only the head and tail for them, closely resembles the well-known legal eater of the disputed oyster and presenter of the oyster-shells to the two claimants who had referred their dispute to his decision. The moral of the tale in which the lion is saved by the jackal (No. 35) is the same as that of the fable of the netted lion which the mouse rescued by gnawing its bonds. The blue-stained jackal (No. 36) is one of the disguised animals about which many fables are current in the West, such as the ass in the lion's hide, or the cat which fell into a shoemaker's tub, and afterwards played the part of a nun. And the monkeys which see the reflection of the moon in a well, and think that it has fallen out of the sky into the water, and form themselves into a chain whereby to draw it out (No. 45), are closely related to the foolish persons of the Wise Men of Gotham class, to whom various similar follies are attributed in many lands.

TIBETAN TALES.

I.

KING MANDHATAR.[1]

In olden days, when the life of man was of unlimited duration, lived King Utposhadha. On the crown of his head grew a very soft tumour, somewhat resembling a cushion of cotton or wool, without doing him any harm. When it had become quite ripe and had broken, there came forth from it a boy, shapely and handsome and gracious, perfect in every limb and joint, with a skin the colour of gold, a head like a canopy, long arms, a broad forehead, interlacing eyebrows, and a body provided with the thirty-two signs of a Mahāpurusha.[2] Immediately after his birth he was taken into the apartments of the women; and when King Utposhadha's eighty thousand wives saw him, milk began to flow from their breasts, and each of the women cried out, "Let him suck me! let him suck me!"[3] Wherefore he received the name of Māndhātar.[4] Some of them thought that, as he came into life out of the crown of a head, he ought to

[1] Kah-gyur, vol. ii. pp. 169-180. This Avadāna, of which Burnouf speaks in his "Introduction," p. 79, is contained in the eighteenth chapter of the Divyāvadāna. As there are many gaps in the Sanskrit MS. to which I had access, I have thought it best to keep to the more complete recension existing in the Kah-gyur.—S.

[2] Mahāpurusha is "a great man, eminent personage, great saint or sage, great ascetic, &c."

[3] *Mān dhāyatu, mān dhāyatu.*—S.

[4] A different account is given in the Vishnupurāṇa, on which see Lassen, Ind. Alt. (1st edition), Anhang I. p. v. note 7. The derivation of the name from the root

receive the name of Mūrdhaja (crown-born); consequently the name Māndhātar is known to some, and that of Mūrdhaja to others.

The young Māndhātar passed through a space of six Śakra-evanescences[1] during his boyhood, and an equal length of time after he was appointed crown prince. Once, while Prince Māndhātar was absent on a journey, King Utposhadha fell ill. As he became still worse, although he was treated with medicines from roots, stems, leaves, blossoms, and fruits, he ordered the ministers to invest the prince with sovereign power. In accordance with the king's orders, they sent word to the prince that King Utposhadha was ill, and had determined to summon him in order to invest him with sovereignty; it was meet, therefore, that he should come quickly. Soon after the messenger had set out King Utposhadha died. Thereupon the ministers sent another messenger with the tidings that the prince's father was dead, and that he ought now to come in order to assume the regal power. But Prince Māndhātar was of opinion that, as his father was dead, there could be no use in his going, and he remained where he was. The ministers again assembled and sent a minister as messenger. When he came to the prince and invited him to assume the sovereign power, Māndhātar said, "If in accordance with the law I acquire the power, the investiture therein ought to take place here."

The ministers sent to say, "O king, as there are many things which are needed for a regal investiture, such as a jewel-strewing,[2] a throne, a canopy, a fillet, and armlets, and as the consecration must take place in the palace, therefore it is necessary that the prince should come here."

dhā calls to mind the attempt to recognise in Athene "the unsuckled one." Cf. Eusthatius on the Iliad, p. 83 (p. 71 of the Leipsic edition), and Pott, Etymolog. Forschungen, Wurzelwörterbuch, I. i. p. 180.—S.

[1] An account of the duration of Śakra's life is given at the end of this tale.

[2] *Edelstein-streu* is Professor Schiefner's rendering of the Tibetan word which appears to represent the jewels which were to be scattered at the coronation.

He replied, "If the power comes to me in accordance with the law, then will all these things come here."

The Yaksha Divaukasa, who ran in front of Prince Māndhātar, brought the throne and the jewel-strewing, the inmates of the palace brought the canopy, the fillet, and the armlets. As the inmates of the palace came themselves, the place received the name of Sāketa.[1] When after this the ministers, the commander-in-chief, and the town and country people had drawn nigh unto the prince for the consecration, they said, "O king, be pleased to receive the consecration."

He replied, "Shall men, forsooth, lay the fillet on me? If I acquire the power according to law, the fillet shall be laid on me by demons."[2]

Thereupon the fillet was laid upon him by demons. Moreover the seven treasures were revealed,[3] namely, the treasure of the wheel, the treasure of the elephant, the treasure of the horse, the treasure of the gem, the treasure of the wife, the treasure of the householder, and, as the seventh, the treasure of the minister. Also there fell to his share fully a thousand sons, heroic, sturdy, endowed with the beauty of splendid bodies, victorious over hosts of foes.

In the neighbourhood of Vaiśālī there was a dense forest of a delightful aspect, in which five hundred hermits endowed with the five kinds of insight[4] had abandoned themselves to contemplation; and in this dense forest there dwelt also a great number of cranes. Now, as noise is a hindrance to contemplation, and the cranes made a noise as they flew, one of these Rishis

[1] See Böhtlingk-Roth on *Kati*. Sāketa is a name of Ayodhyā or ancient Oude.—S.

[2] *Amanushya*.—S.

[3] For a full account of these seven treasures, see Rhys Davids' Hibbert Lectures, pp. 130–134.

[4] *Klarsichten* is Professor Schiefner's rendering of the Tibetan equivalent of the Pāli word Abhiññā. Mr. Rhys Davids has kindly sent me the following explanation:—"There are five such Abhiññās, which are five kinds of insight or intuitive perception; that is, the intuitive perception of five classes of things."

became angry, and uttered a curse to the effect that the cranes' wings should be enfeebled. So, in consequence of the cranes having irritated the Rishis, their wings became feeble, and they took to going about, walking on their feet. The king, as he went afield, saw the cranes walking about in this way, and asked the ministers why the cranes went afoot. The ministers replied, "O king, as noise is a hindrance to contemplation, the Rishis in their wrath have cursed the cranes. On that account, in consequence of the anger of the Rishis, the cranes' wings have grown weak."

The king said, "Can they be Rishis who are so pitiless towards living creatures? Go to them, sirs, and tell them in my name that they shall not remain in my realm."

The ministers executed his commands. The Rishis reflected that the king had power over the four quarters of the world, and they determined to betake themselves to the slopes of Sumeru. So they went away and settled there.

As King Māndhātar's subjects were thinkers, scanners, and testers, and as in the course of thinking, scanning, and testing they took to cultivating various arts and industries, they obtained the designation of the Wise. Now they occupied themselves with field-labour. When the king, as he went afield one day, saw them engaged in field-labour, he asked the ministers what those men were doing. The ministers replied, "O king, in order that they may obtain refreshment, they produce corn and so forth." The king said, "What! do men practise husbandry in my realm? Let the deity send down a rain of seven-and-twenty kinds of seed." No sooner had King Māndhātar conceived this idea than the deity sent down a rain of twenty-seven kinds of seed. When the king asked the people of his realm to whose merits this occurrence was due, they replied, "To the king's merits, as well as also to our own."

Later on, men took to tilling cotton-fields. When

King Māndhātar saw this as he went afield, he asked the ministers what those men were doing. The ministers replied, "O king, they are tilling cotton-fields." The king asked what was the use of that. They answered that it was done for the purpose of producing clothes. Then said the king, "What! shall the men of my country till cotton-fields? Let the deity send down a rain of cotton." No sooner had King Māndhātar conceived this idea than the deity let a rain of cotton fall. When the king asked the people of his realm to whose merits this occurrence was due, they replied, "To the king's merits, as well as also to our own."

Afterwards these men began to spin cotton, and the king asked what they were doing. The ministers replied, "O king, they are spinning cotton in order to procure thread." The king said, "What! are the people in my realm spinning thread? Let the deity send down a rain of cotton thread." No sooner had King Māndhātar conceived this idea than the deity sent down a rain of cotton thread. The king asked to whose merits this occurrence was due. The answer was, "To the king's merits, as well as also to our own."

After this, when they gradually began to weave cotton, the king asked what they were doing. The answer was, "O king, they are weaving cotton in order to obtain raiment." The king said to himself, "What! shall the men of my realm weave cotton? Let the deity send down a rain of raiment." No sooner had King Māndhātar conceived this idea than the deity sent down a rain of raiment. The king asked to whose merits this occurrence was due. The answer was, "To the king's merits, as well as also to our own."

The king thought, "These men are ignorant of the power of my merits. I possess Jambudvīpa, the vast, rich, prosperous, fruitful realm, abounding in men and living creatures. I possess the seven treasures, the treasures of the wheel, of the elephant, of the horse, of the gem, of the wife, of the householder, and, seventhly, of the minister. I possess a complete thousand of bold, heroic sons, endowed with the beauty of splendid limbs, entirely victorious over opponents. Now, then, let a rain of precious stones fall within my palace, but not so much as a single piece of money outside."

Scarcely had this idea occurred to King Māndhātar when there began to fall within his palace a rain of precious stones which lasted for seven days, while outside not so much as a single piece of money fell. So King Māndhātar, like a being who has acquired great power and supernatural force by means of virtue and merit, enjoyed the fruits of his merits. The king asked to whose merits this was due. The reply was, "To the merits of the king." Then the king said, "Honoured sirs, ye have been in the wrong. If ye had said that all these things took place on account of the merits of the king, I should have caused a rain of precious stones to fall over the whole of Jambudvīpa, and each of you who wanted gems would have had as many as he wished."

During this inauguration of King Māndhātar's rule six Śakra-evanescences passed away. Then King Māndhātar asked his runner, the Yaksha Divaukasa, "Is there not some part of the world as yet unsubdued by me which I could subdue?"

Divaukasa replied, "O king, there is the dvīpa named Pūrvavideha, which is vast, rich, prosperous, fruitful, and replete with many men and living creatures. Thither might the king go and rule."

Then King Māndhātar reflected that he was in possession of the rich and so forth Jambudvīpa, that he possessed the seven treasures, that of the wheel and so forth, that he had a full thousand of heroic sons, that a rain of precious stones had fallen inside his palace for seven whole days, and that he now heard that there existed a part of the world called Pūrvavideha; so he determined that he would go thither and rule over it also. Scarcely had the king entertained this idea when, surrounded by his thousand sons, and accompanied by an army eighteen koṭi[1] strong, he rose heavenward and betook himself to Pūrvavidehadvīpa. There, like a being who has acquired great power and supernatural force by means of virtue and merit, he ruled, enjoying the fruits of his merits, for many years, many hundreds, many thousands, many hundreds of thousands of years. While he was ruling over Pūrvavidehadvīpa, six Śakra-evanescences passed away.

Afterwards King Māndhātar asked the Yaksha Divaukasa whether there existed any other dvīpas not as yet rendered subject to him. Divaukasa replied that there still remained a dvīpa called Aparagodānīya, vast, rich, prosperous, fruitful, replete with many men and living creatures, and that the king should go thither and reign therein. Then King Māndhātar reflected that he possessed the rich and so forth Jambudvīpa, that a rain of precious stones had fallen within his palace for the space of seven days, that he had come to Pūrvavidehadvīpa, and ruled there during many years, many hundreds, many thousands, many hundreds of thousands of years, and that as he now heard that there existed another dvīpa, called Aparagodānīya, he would go there also and rule over it too. Scarcely had King Māndhātar entertained this idea when he rose heavenward, surrounded by his thousand sons, accompanied by a host eighteen koṭi strong. Having reached Aparagodānīya, he tarried therein; and like a being who has acquired great power and supernatural force by means of virtue and merit, enjoying the fruits of his deserts, he ruled in Aparagodānīya for many years, many hundreds, many thousands, many hundreds of thousands of years. While he was ruling in Aparagodānīya, six Śakra-evanescences passed away.

Afterwards King Māndhātar asked the Yaksha Divaukasa whether there remained any other dvīpa not yet subjected to him. Divaukasa replied that there was

[1] A koṭi is equal to ten millions.

another dvīpa called Uttarakuru, vast, rich, prosperous, fruitful, replete with many men and living creatures, the inhabitants of which were still unsubdued and independent, and that he ought to go there and rule over his hosts. Thereupon King Māndhātar reflected that he possessed the vast, rich, and so forth Jambudvīpa, that a rain of precious stones had fallen within his palace for the space of seven days, that he had ruled in Pūrvavidehadvīpa for many years, many hundreds, many thousands, many hundreds of thousands of years, and that he had done likewise in Aparagodānīya, and that he now heard that there also existed a dvīpa called Uttarakuru, vast, rich, prosperous, fruitful, replete with many men and living creatures, the inhabitants of which region were as yet unsubdued and independent, and that it was meet for him to go there and rule his hosts. Scarcely had King Māndhātar entertained this idea when he rose heavenwards, surrounded by his thousand sons, accompanied by an army eighteen koṭi strong, his seven treasures having been sent on in front. On one side of Sumeru he saw several white spots. Having remarked them, he asked the Yaksha Divaukasa what those white spots were. "O king," replied the Yaksha, "what you see is the rice grown without ploughing or sowing by the inhabitants of Uttarakuru. As they enjoy this rice without having ploughed or sown, so will you, O king, when you have arrived there, enjoy this rice which grows without ploughing or sowing." King Māndhātar spoke about this to his ministers, saying, "Have ye, O chieftains, seen the white spots?"

"Yes!"

"O chieftains, they are formed by the rice which the inhabitants of Uttarakuru obtain without ploughing or sowing. As the inhabitants of Uttarakuru enjoy this rice which grows without ploughing or sowing, so will ye also enjoy it when ye have arrived there."

King Māndhātar afterwards saw from afar some

garland-like trees of various colours planted on one side of Sumeru. Having remarked them, he asked the Yaksha Divaukasa what were these garland-like trees of various colours. "O king, these are the wishing-trees of the inhabitants of Uttarakuru. The inhabitants of Uttarakuru clothe themselves with garments from the wishing-trees."

When King Māndhātar heard this, he said to his ministers, "O chieftains, have you seen the garland-like trees of various colours planted over there?"

"Yes!"

"O chieftains, those are the wishing-trees that bear the garments with which the inhabitants of Uttarakuru clothe themselves. Ye also, when ye have arrived there, will clothe yourselves with garments from off the wishing-trees."

King Māndhātar reached Uttarakuru, and there, enjoying the fruits of his deserts, like a being who has acquired great power and supernatural force through his virtue and merit, he ruled over his hosts for many years, many hundreds, many thousands, many hundreds of thousands of years. While he ruled over his hosts there, six Śakra-evanescences passed away.

Later on King Māndhātar asked the Yaksha Divaukasa whether there still remained anywhere a dvīpa as yet unsubdued. Divaukasa said, "No, there is none. However, there are the thirty-tree gods, who, long-lived, endowed with beauty, and replete with bliss, perpetually abide in the lofty Vimāna palace. Be pleased, O king, to go thither in order to look upon the thirty-three gods." Then King Māndhātar reflected that he possessed the vast, rich, prosperous, fruitful, and replete with many men and living beings Jambudvīpa, and that he possessed the seven treasures of the wheel and so forth, and that he had a full thousand of heroic sons, and that a rain of precious stones had fallen within his palace for the space of seven days, and that he had gone to Pūrvavidehadvīpa and had ruled there for many years, many hundreds, many thousands, many hundreds of thousands of years; and that he had gone on to Aparagodānīyadvīpa, and had there ruled for many years, for many hundreds, many thousands, many hundreds of thousands of years; and that he had moved forward to Uttarakurudvīpa, and there also had ruled over his hosts for many years, many hundreds, many thousands, many hundreds of thousands of years; and that inasmuch as there were thirty-three gods, long-lived, endowed with beauty, and replete with bliss, perpetually abiding in the lofty Vimāna palace, therefore he would make his way thither in order to visit the thirty-three gods. Scarcely had this idea occurred to King Māndhātar when he arose, surrounded by his thousand sons, accompanied by an army eighteen koṭi strong, and proceeded heavenwards, sending his seven jewels on in front.

Sumeru, the monarch of mountains, is surrounded by seven mountains of gold. King Māndhātar tarried on Mount Nemindhara, and while he ruled over his hosts on Mount Nemindhara six Śakra-evanescences passed away. Thence he betook himself to the golden mountain Aśvakarṇa. While he ruled over his hosts there six Śakra-evanescences passed away. From Mount Aśvakarṇa he went to the golden mountain Sudarśana, and while he ruled over his hosts there six Śakra-evanescences passed away. From Mount Sudarśana he went to the golden mountain Khadiraka, and while he ruled over his hosts there six Śakra-evanescences passed away. From Mount Khadiraka he went to the golden mountain Iśādhāra, and while he ruled over his hosts there six Śakra-evanescences passed away. From Mount Iśādhāra he went to the golden mountain Yugandhara, and while he ruled over his hosts there six Śakra-evanescences passed away.

When he left Mount Yugandhara, taking his course heavenwards, the five hundred Rishis, who now dwelt on one of the slopes of Sumeru, saw him coming, and they said, "Honoured sirs, here comes the worst of kings." The Rishi Durmukha poured water into the palms of his hands, and flung it towards the host in order to stop it. Then the treasure of the minister, which went in front of the host, said to the Rishis, "O Brahmans, cease to be angry. This is one who is everywhere victorious. This is King Māndhātar. It is not a case of cranes." Now when King Māndhātar came up to that spot, he asked who had stopped the army. The treasure of the minister replied that the Rishis had done so. The king asked what those Rishis delighted in. The minister replied, "In their matted hair."[1] The king said, "Then let it fall. And as for themselves, let them go on in front of me." Thereupon their matted hair fell, and they themselves began to move on in front of him, their hands grasping bows and arrows. Then the treasure of the wife said to the king, "O king, these Rishis are practising austerities; you ought to let them go free." So the king let them go free; and when they had again betaken themselves to their works of penance they became possessed of the five kinds of insight.

But King Māndhātar ascended higher together with his hosts. Now Sumeru, the monarch of mountains, plunged 80,000 yojanas[2] deep into the golden soil and soared aloft 80,000 yojanas above the waters, so its height was 160,000 yojanas. Each side also measured 80,000 yojanas, so that its circumference was 360,000 yojanas. Formed of four kinds of jewels, it was beautiful and splendid to look upon. On its summit dwelt the thirty-three gods. The five defences of the thirty-three gods were the water-inhabiting Nāgas, the dish-bearing Yakshas, the garland-wearing and the ever-elevated gods, and the four Mahārājas. The water-inhabiting Nāgas

[1] The word employed by Professor Schiefner is *Flechten*.

[2] "A yojana is four leagues."—Rhys Davids's "Buddhist Birth-Stories," p. 35.

stopped King Māndhātar's host. When King Māndhātar came up he asked who had stopped his host. The answer was, "O king, the water-inhabiting Nāgas have stopped it." The king said, "Shall animals wage war with me? These water-inhabiting Nāgas shall themselves be my advanced guard." Then the Nāgas marched along in front of King Māndhātar.

As the Nāgas marched along in front of the king they reached the abode of the dish-bearing gods, who said, "Honoured sirs, wherefore are ye on the move?" The Nāgas replied, "The king of men is coming here." Then the Nāgas and the dish-bearing gods turned round and stopped the host. When King Māndhātar came up he asked who had stopped his host. The answer was, "O king, these dish-bearing gods have stopped it." King Māndhātar said, "Let the dish-bearing gods themselves march in front of me." Thereupon they began to move onwards.

They and the Nāgas reached the abode of the garland-wearing gods, who asked them why they were on the move. They replied, "The king of men is coming here." Thereupon these gods and the Nāgas turned round and tried to stop the host. When the king came up he asked who had stopped his army. The answer was, "O king, the garland-wearing gods have stopped it." The king said, "Let these garland-wearing gods themselves march in front of me." Thereupon they began to move along in front.

As they proceeded they reached the abode of the ever-elevated gods,[1] who asked why they were on the move.

[1] An account of these various divinities is given by M. Eugène Burnouf in his "Introduction à l'Histoire du Buddhisme Indien" (1876, pp. 180, 535–557). With respect to the "ever-elevated" (or, to use Professor Schiefner's expression, "die stets betrunkenen") gods, he says (p. 538): "Le troisième étage est le séjour des êtres qu'on nomme, suivant Georgi, 'buveurs et stupides,' et qui ont en tibetain le nom de *Rtag myos*. Ces deux monosyllabes se traduisent littéralement par 'continuellement enivres,' et cette interpretation s'accorde bien avec la notion que Georgi nous donne de ces dieux."

They replied, "The king of men is coming here." Thereupon they turned round and stopped the host. When the king came up he asked who had stopped the host. He was told that the ever-elevated gods had stopped it. The king said, "Let the ever-elevated gods march in front of me." Thereupon they began to move onwards.

When they reached the abode of the four Mahārājas, and were asked by them why they were on the move, they said, "The king of men is coming here." The gods of the region of the four Mahārājas reflected that this must be a being endowed with great force of merit, and that they must not venture to impede him. Thereupon they informed the gods of the region of the thirty-three gods that the king of men was coming. The gods of the region of the thirty-three gods reflected that this must be a being endowed with great force of merit, and that, therefore, they ought not to repel him, but should receive him with honour. So the thirty-three gods received him with honour.

When king Māndhātar had ascended to the summit of Sumeru he saw a blue forest tract rising aloft like a tower of cloud, and he asked the Yaksha Divaukasa what it was. The Yaksha replied, "Those are the divine trees Pārijātaka and Kovidāra, under which the thirty-three gods, captivated and enchained by the five divine pleasures of sense, do sport, rejoice, and enjoy themselves throughout the four summer months. You also, O king, when you have arrived there, captivated by the five divine pleasures of sense, will sport, rejoice, and enjoy yourself." When King Māndhātar heard this, he asked his ministers if they had seen those tall blue trees which rose aloft like a tower of cloud, and when they replied that they had seen them, he said, "O chieftains, those trees are Pārijātaka and Kovidāra, the trees of the thirty-three gods, under which the thirty-three gods, captivated by the five divine pleasures of sense, do sport, rejoice, and enjoy themselves during the four summer months. Ye also, O chieftains, on arriving there, captivated by the five pleasures of sense, shall sport, rejoice, and enjoy yourselves."

Afterwards King Māndhātar perceived on the summit of Sumeru something white, which rose aloft like an accumulated mass of cloud, and he asked the Yaksha Divaukasa what it was. "O king," was the reply, "that is the meeting-place of the thirty-three gods, and it is named Sudharmā. There the thirty-three gods and the four Mahārājas meet together, and there they view, scan, and test the affairs of gods and men. Into that place you also, O king, will enter." On hearing this, King Māndhātar asked his ministers if they had seen the white mass which rose aloft like an accumulation of clouds, and when they had answered affirmatively, he said, "O chieftains, that is the meeting-place of the thirty-three gods and the four Mahārājas, Sudharmā by name. There the thirty-three gods and the four Mahārājas meet together, and view, scan, and test the affairs of gods and men. Thither, O chieftains, will ye also make your way."

Sudarśana, the city of the thirty-three gods, was 2500 yojanas in length and as many in breadth, and its circumference was 10,000 yojanas. It was surrounded by seven rows of golden walls, which were two and a half yojanas high. These walls had quadruple cornices of gold, silver, beryl, and crystal, and windows were set in them above and below. The space lying inside the city of Sudarśana was fair to see, pleasant, extensive, and copiously variegated with a hundred colours, and the ground was soft, extremely soft, like a cushion of cotton or wool, yielding to the pressure of the foot, rising again when the foot was lifted, and covered knee-deep with divine mandārava [or coral-tree] flowers; when a wind arose, the faded blossoms were swept away and a rain of fresh flowers descended. The city of Sudarśana had 999 gates, and at each gate were stationed 500 Yakshas arrayed in blue robes and coats of mail, and armed with bows and arrows, to serve as a guard and defence for the thirty-three gods, and also as an ornament. The market-place of Sudarśana, which was 2500 yojanas long and twelve broad, was fair to see, pleasant, strewn with golden sand, sprinkled with sandalwood water, covered over with gold trellis-work. On every side were to be seen water basins of various kinds, formed of cubes of four sorts, of gold, silver, beryl, and crystal. The steps of these basins were formed of four materials, of gold, silver, beryl, and crystal. The basins were surrounded by balustrades of four kinds, made of gold, silver, beryl, and crystal. The uprights, borders, and handles of the golden balustrades were made of silver; those of the silver balustrades were made of gold; those of the beryl balustrades were made of crystal, and those of the crystal balustrades were made of beryl. These basins were full of water which was cool and honey-sweet, were set thick with blue, red, and white lotuses, and replete with many water-haunting birds of beautiful form, which gave agreeable utterance to charming sounds. All around these basins grew blossoming and fruit-bearing trees of beauteous form and stately growth, adorned with wreaths, as when an adroit chaplet-maker or his pupil, in order to form an ornament for the ears, has deftly woven a garland of flowers. On land, likewise, birds of various kinds, all of beauteous form, agreeably uttered charming sounds.

In the city of Sudarśana were many wishing-trees, on which four kinds of raiment grew, blue, yellow, red, and white. Whatever garments were desired by the gods or the daughters of the gods were obtained by them as soon as the idea came into their minds. From the four kinds of ornament-trees came ornaments for the hand and foot, ornaments to be worn out of sight on the lower parts of the body, and ornaments intended for the eye. Whatever the sons or daughters of the gods wished for, that thing came into their hands as soon as they had expressed their wish. Four kinds of musical instruments, harps, pipes, guitars, and shells, did the gods and the daughters of the gods hold in their hands as soon as they wished for them. Four kinds of divine food, blue, yellow, red, and white, did the gods and the daughters of the gods obtain as soon as they wished for them. Storied houses provided with summer chambers, courts, windows, and peepholes, formed meeting-places for troops of women and Apsaras. There to the sound of music, with drink made of honey and from the kadamba tree, the thirty-three gods played, rejoiced, and took delight, enjoying the fruits of their merits. The meeting-hall of the thirty-three gods, Sudharmā by name, which was 300 yojanas long, 300 broad, and 900 in circumference, was beautiful, charming, exquisite to look upon, formed of crystal, and rising above the city to a height of 342 yojanas. In it were arranged the seats of the thirty-three gods, those of the thirty-two under-kings, and the seat of Śakra, the king of the thirty-three gods. King Māndhātar's seat was prepared for him at the end of all these seats. The thirty-three gods received King Māndhātar with a gift of honour. Then there entered in by ranks those beings who had acquired great power by the maturity of their merits, the others remaining without. King Māndhātar said to himself, "Of the seats which are here arranged, mine is undoubtedly the last." And he came to the conclusion that Śakra, the king of the gods, ought to give up to him half of his own seat. No sooner had he conceived this idea than Śakra the king of the gods gave up to him half of his seat, and King Māndhātar shared the seat with the king of the gods. Now when the great King Māndhātar and Śakra the king of the gods sat on the same seat, it was impossible to see in either of them, whether in length or breadth, in voice or in fulness of aspect, any difference from the other, any distinction or any pre-eminence, except that Śakra the king of the gods never closed his eyes. While King Māndhātar tarried among the thirty-three gods, thirty-six Śakra-evanescences passed away.

While he was there a war broke out between the gods and the Asuras. When the Asuras were defeated, they closed the gates of the Asura city and occupied the bulwarks round about. And when the gods were defeated, they in like manner closed the gates of the divine city, and occupied its bulwarks round about. Now it came to pass that the Asuras, having equipped a fourfold army, had already broken through the five defences, and were drawing nigh unto the king of the gods, Śakra, in warlike array. The Yakshas said to the king of the gods, Śakra, "Know, O Kauśika, that the Asuras have broken through the five bulwarks and are near at hand. Be pleased, therefore, to accomplish all that ought to be done and prepared." Now when Śakra, the king of the gods, had equipped a fourfold army and was setting out to wage war against the Asuras, King Māndhātar turned towards him and said, "Stay here; I will take the field myself." Śakra replied, "Let that be done." Then the king arose heavenward with an army eighteen koṭi strong, and caused his bowstring to clang. When the Asuras heard this sound, they asked whose bowstring it was that was thus clanging. Being told that the sound was the clang of King Māndhātar's bowstring, they were greatly astounded. King Māndhātar arrived, and the war-chariots of the contending gods and Asuras rose high into the air. As, in accordance with the ordering of things, no superiority or inferiority was to be found on either side, King Māndhātar soared behind all the Asuras towards heaven. The Asuras asked, "Who is this who has soared above us towards heaven?" Being told that it was Māndhātar, the king of men, they reflected that, as he had risen above their chariots, he must be a being who had attained to the glory of great power through the fulness of his merits: and overcome, full of fear and trembling, they turned their backs and withdrew into the stronghold of the Asuras.

When King Māndhātar inquired who had gained the day, the ministers answered that he was the conqueror.

Then King Māndhātar came to the conclusion that he was superior to the thirty-three gods. He reflected that he possessed the vast, rich, prosperous, fruitful Jambudvīpa, replete with men and living creatures; that he possessed Pūrvavidehadvīpa, Aparagodānīyadvīpa, and Uttarakurudvīpa; that he was the owner of the seven treasures, the treasure of the wheel, the treasure of the elephant, the treasure of the horse, the treasure of the wife, the treasure of the householder, and, seventhly, the treasure of the minister; that he had a full thousand of heroic, sturdy sons, endowed with the beauty of splendid bodies, victorious over hosts of foes; that a rain of precious stones had fallen within his palace for the space of seven days; that he had made his way to the abode of the thirty-three gods; that he had entered into Sudharmā, the meeting-place of the gods, and that the king of the gods, Śakra, had ceded to him the half of his seat; and he came to the conclusion that he must expel the king of the gods, Śakra, from his seat, and take into his own hands the government of both gods and men.

As soon as he had conceived this idea the great King Māndhātar came to the end of his good fortune. On his return to Jambudvīpa he was attacked by a violent illness, and amid intolerable agonies he drew nigh unto death. His ministers and other state officials, the astrologers and workers of cures by spells, betook themselves to him and addressed him thus: "When the king shall have passed away hence, it may be that the subsequent inhabitants of the kingdom will inquire what King Māndhātar said at the time of his death. What shall we say to them in reply?"

"O chieftains, when in time to come, after my departure, men shall draw nigh unto you and ask you that question, then shall ye give them this answer: 'O sirs, King Māndhātar, who possessed the seven treasures, who with a fourfold host of men acquired power over the four dvīpas, and made his way to the abode of the thirty-three gods, is said to have died before he had obtained satisfaction through the fivefold pleasures of sense.'"

Moreover he pronounced these ślokas:[1]—

"Even by a rain of gold pieces will wishes not be satisfied. The wise man, he who knows that wishes bring but little enjoyment and much sorrow, takes no delight even in divine enjoyments. The hearer of the perfected Buddha rejoices when desire fails. Even if a mountain of gold were like unto Himavant, yet it would not suffice for the wealth of a single individual; that the discerning one knows full well. He who observes sorrows, starting from this base, how can he take pleasure in enjoyments? He who is steady, who has learnt to recognise the thorn in the treasures of the world, will learn the essence of things to his own correction."

King Māndhātar ordered irresistible sacrifices to be offered, and he said in ślokas:—

"If one knows that the future lasts long but life is only brief, then ought one to acquire merits. If one does not acquire merits, then one has sorrow. Therefore must he who is acquiring merits offer sacrificial gifts, as is fitting. In this world and in the future will he, if he offer up gifts, obtain happiness."

The inhabitants of the town and country heard that King Māndhātar had fallen ill and was nigh unto death. Having learnt this, many hundreds of thousands of men assembled in order to see King Māndhātar. The king spoke to the multitudes upon the evil of lust and the ills of house-life, and then condemned desire. Thereupon many hundreds of thousands of men renounced house-life, retired from the world to the Rishis, and lived in the forest, fulfilling the four duties of Brahmans, and abandoning all striving after enjoyment. Persevering in this, they became participators in the world of Brahma.

While King Māndhātar was in his boyhood, while he was crown prince, while he exercised supreme power in Jam-

[1] Cf. Dhammapada, śl. 186, &c.—S.

budvīpa, while he lived in the dvīpas of Pūrvavideha, Aparagodānīya, and Uttarakuru, and on the seven golden mountains, and while he dwelt in the region of the thirty-three gods to which he went, eighty-four Śakra-evanescences passed away. The measure of life of Śakra, the prince of the five great kings, is as follows:—One hundred years of men represent one day of the thirty-three gods. If thirty such days are reckoned as one month, and twelve months as one year, then the measure of life of the thirty-three gods is a hundred divine years. According to human reckoning, that amounts to 3,600,000.[1]

[1] This number, in the German text, is given as 36,000; but that is probably a misprint. The German word which is here rendered by "evanescences" is *Schwunde*. It appears to define the period at the end of which Śakra's life comes temporarily to a close. For a different computation of the length of Śakra's life, see Hardy's "Manual of Buddhism," p. 25. "The déwalóka of Sekra or Indra, on the summit of Maha Méru, in which one day is equal to 100 of the years of men; and as they live 1000 of these years, their age is equal to 36,000,000 of the years of men."

II.

KUSA JATAKA.[1]

In olden times there was a mighty king named Śakuni, who was a beloved associate of the king of the gods, Indra. In spite of this he became absorbed in meditation, leaning his head upon his hand, reflecting that, inasmuch as he had neither a son nor a daughter, he would have to die, in spite of his riches and his power, without leaving behind him a son or a daughter, and that his family would become extinct. As he sat meditating in this wise, the king of the gods, Indra, saw him and said, "O friend, wherefore do you lean your head upon your hand, and wherefore do you sit there meditating in that manner?"

He replied, "O Kauśika, if I die without leaving a son or daughter, my family will become extinct, in spite of my possessing such wealth and power."

Indra said, "O friend, I will send you a medicine. Let your wives drink of it, and thereby you will obtain sons and daughters."

The king of the gods, Indra, betook himself to Mount Gandhamādana, brought away the medicine with him, and

[1] Kah-gyur, vol. ii. pp. 188–192. See "An Eastern Love Story. Kusa Jātakaya, a Buddhistic legend; rendered into English verse from the Singhalese poem of Alagiyavanna Mohoṭṭāla, by Thomas Steele." London, 1871. See also critical remarks on the work in the Göttinger Gelehrten Anzeigen, 1872, stück 31, pp. 1205–1225, by Dr. Reinhold Köhler, who has called attention to the previously overlooked redaction in chap. xiii. of the Dsanglun (p. 91 of the translation). In the Tibetan original, the king's name, Mahāśakuni, has been corrupted into Mahāschakuli. The name of his son, Woodblock, may be explained by the fact that *kuśa*, in the Chinese transcription *kiu-che* (or *keou-che?*) is a word of ambiguous meaning. In the Böhtlingk-Roth Sanskrit Dictionary, *kuśa* occurs in the sense of "wood."—S.

sent it to the king. The king sent it to his wives, with directions for them to drink it. The king's chief wife had just gone to sleep, but the other wives drank the medicine without waking her, and all of them became pregnant. When the queen awoke and perceived that they were pregnant, she said, "What have ye done to become pregnant?"

They replied, "The king gave us a medicine to drink."

"Why did you drink it without waking me? As this is so, tell me in what medicine-holder it was brought."

"It was contained in a kuśa box."

"Where is that?"

"Here it is."

The queen washed the kuśa box and drank the water, whereupon she also became pregnant.

After eight or nine months had passed by, all the wives gave birth to sons. The son to whom the chief wife gave birth possessed the eighteen signs of uncomeliness, a face like that of a lion, and an extremely strong body. His birth-feast was celebrated in great style, and the name of Kuśa was conferred upon him. When the king looked upon his other sons he rejoiced, but Kuśa's ugliness excited his wrath.

It came to pass that the subordinate kings said, "Honoured sirs, as King Mahāśakuni oppresses us all so greatly, let us go up and deprive him of his power."

So they came with a fourfold host and laid siege to his capital. As King Mahāśakuni could not venture to fight with them, he ordered all the gates to be closed and the walls to be occupied. Kuśa went to his mother and said, "Mother, why are all the gates shut?"

"As your father cannot venture to fight with the subordinate kings, he has shut the gates and remains within."

"Mother, as I wish to fight with them, let the king give me a chariot."

"My son, as you displease him and excite his wrath, how can he be expected to give you a chariot?"

"Do go to him, mother, and having gone, tell him that the youth Kuśa will fight with the enemy if a chariot is given him."

The king gave him a chariot, and Kuśa took two quivers, mounted the chariot, and prepared to start. The king of gods, Indra, said to himself, "As these subordinate kings are strong, this Bodisat of the Bhadrakalpa, the youth Kuśa, may fall into trouble, so I will lend him aid." And he gave Kuśa a shell, a disk, and a mace, and then said, "Bodisat, these things will save you."

Kuśa opened one of the gates and drove out. As soon as he sounded the shell, the hostile host was terrified at its sound; some were deafened by its clang, others fled away with shattered ears. Whenever he flung the disk or the mace, the enemy fell to the ground. He pressed into the midst of the host, and when he sounded the shell every ear cracked, and the enemy fled saying, "This man is a Rākshasa."

When the youth had overthrown the whole of them, he went to his father, and told him that he had conquered all the kings, and the land was at peace. On hearing this, King Mahāśakuni rejoiced, and said to himself, "The youth Kuśa is strong and remarkably brave. Why should I dislike him?" And he began to take delight in him.

After arranging marriages for all his other sons, the king set to work to find a wife for the youth Kuśa as well. But all men said, "We are ready to give our daughters, only not to Kuśa." Now a certain king desired to obtain another king's daughter in marriage, but did not succeed; and on her, by means of a trick, pretending it was for another of his sons, King Mahāśakuni laid his hands. And he gave her to Kuśa, and celebrated his marriage with her in consonance with the constellation, the epoch, and the moment.

Now the king had said, "Honoured sirs, let no one show the youth Kuśa a mirror. Moreover, he must not bathe in places where a man, in order to take a bath, must step into water. And he must never be allowed to approach his wife by daylight." But Kuśa's wife saw him playing with his brothers one day, and she said, "Who is that Piśācha [or demon] who is playing with the youths?"

"That is your husband."

"What! is my husband like that?"

When she had seen him another day sporting with the rest of the youths in the water, and had asked if her husband was really like that, she determined to clear the matter up. So she lighted a lamp and covered it over with a bowl. When Kuśa had approached his wife [by night], and she [had uncovered the lamp and] perceived that he had the eighteen marks of unsightliness and a face like a lion's jowl, she exclaimed, "Piśācha! Piśācha!" and fled away.

Now it came to pass that certain mountaineers rebelled against King Mahāśakuni. The king ordered the youth Kuśa to subdue those mountaineers, and sent him forth. When Kuśa had gone, his wife sent to say to her father and mother, "Is there no man left in the world, that ye have given me to a Piśācha? If I am to die, well and good. But if I am not to die, then will I take to flight." Thereupon her parents fetched her away. When the youth Kuśa returned home, after subduing the mountaineers, he asked his mother what had become of his wife.

"Her parents have taken her away," she replied.

"For what reason?"

"Because she took you for a Piśācha."

"Mother, I will go and bring her back."

"Do so."

He took the shell, the disk, and the mace, and set out on his way. It happened that at a certain hill-town a great number of men sat looking on one side, having closed their gates from fear of a lion. The youth Kuśa said, "What makes you sit there like that?"

"We do so from fear of a lion."

"Why do not you kill it?"

"We cannot."

"What will you give me if I kill it?"

"Half of our fourfold host."

The youth Kuśa drew near to the lion and sounded the shell. The lion's ears burst and it died. Kuśa took it and went to the hill-town and said, "O sirs, here is the lion."

"Then take the half of our fourfold host."

"I will leave it in your hands. Give it to me when I come back again," he said.

He betook himself to the hill-town where his wife was, and went to the house of a chaplet-maker, who said to him, "What are you?"

"I am the son of a chaplet-maker," he replied.

"What is your name?"

"Vṛiji."

As Bodisats are expert in all arts and accomplishments, he twined a splendid wreath, which the chaplet-maker gave to the king's daughter. The princess said, "How comes it that you have never before made me such a wreath as this?"

"It was my apprentice who made it."

"I should like to see your apprentice."

When the chaplet-maker brought him to her and she looked at the youth, she wondered where this demon could have sprung from, and she exclaimed, "Piśācha Piśācha!" Whereupon he fled. Afterwards he betook himself to the house of a cook, who said, "Who are you?"

"I am the son of a cook."

"What is your name?"

"Sugandhabhājana."

As he roasted and boiled excellently, the cook served up to the king's daughter the boiled and roasted meats which he had cooked. She said, "O friend, who prepared this food so excellently roasted and boiled?"

"My apprentice prepared it."

"I should like to see your apprentice."

This time also she cried out as before.

He next went to a doctor, who said, "Who are you?"

"A doctor's son."

"What is your name?"

"Ātreya."

The king's daughter fell ill with a disease of the brain, and the doctor could of himself do nothing to cure it. As he sat one day absorbed in thought on that account, Kuśa said to him, "Master, why are you so pensive?"

"The king's daughter is attacked by a disease of the brain, and I can do nothing to cure it."

"I will go and cure her."

So Kuśa went to visit her. When she saw him she thought, "Where can this demon have come from?" But she reflected that if she said that aloud he would not cure her, so she determined not to do so till he had cured her. When she became well she cried out, "Piśācha! Piśācha!" Whereupon he fled.

He betook himself to the ministers, who said, "Who are you?"

"I am Sahasrabala (Thousand-strength)."

They took him into their service.

Now it came to pass that the son of the before-mentioned king heard that the princess, whom Kuśa had formerly obtained, had been given up by him, and had returned home. So he sent to say that if the king would give him his daughter, all would be well; but if the king would not give her, he would despoil him of his sovereign power. The king replied, "I have given my daughter to the son of King Mahāśakuni. I cannot give her to another." So the prince came with a fourfold army and besieged the king's capital. The king could not venture to fight with him, so he ordered the gates to be closed and remained inside.

The youth Kuśa said to the ministers, "Sirs, wherefore are the gates closed?" They explained the whole matter to him. The youth Kuśa said to the ministers, "If the king's daughter is given to me, I will undertake to fight the enemy." The ministers laid the case before the king, who said, "I have given my daughter to the son of King Mahāśakuni. How can I give her to this man? The present complication is entirely due to this maiden." The ministers said, "As there is at present no other prospect of victory, let this man fight the prince offhand. We shall find out then which is the conqueror." The king said, "Let that be done by you." And the ministers said, "Thousand-strength, act according to your words."

Thereupon the youth took the two quivers, which held five hundred arrows, and also the shell, the disk, and the mace, and set forth. When he sounded the shell, the ears of the enemy were shattered, and they fled. The princess thought, "As this youth Kuśa is excellently endowed with boldness and courage, why should I dislike him?" So she took a liking for him, and said to the king, "What you promised, that fulfil."

"Daughter, I will give you to Kuśa."

"Father," she said, "this is the youth Kuśa himself."

"Go to him then, daughter, since that is so."

The king paid Kuśa great honour, gave him a fourfold host, and let him and the rest of his party go free.

Kuśa went to the other hill-town, and said to the inhabitants, "Honoured sirs, now give me the half of the fourfold army." They replied, "O youth, such a flood has taken place as has washed away the four divisions of the army." As there were sheep grazing at no great distance, the youth Kuśa uttered this saying, "Reflect and know that whither the sixty-year old bullock, whither the elephant has been brought, thither also will the cows and sheep be brought. If ye give me the army, good. If ye give it not, there will be a tussle for it."

After the army had been given to him he went down to

a river. Being wearied, he entered the water to bathe; and as he did so he saw the reflection of his face in the water, and thought, "As I have the eighteen signs of uncomeliness and a face like a lion, and as on that account the king's daughter takes no pleasure in me, it is needless that such a one as I should remain alive. I will go and put myself to death."

He entered into a copse, and was preparing to hang himself, when the king of the gods, Indra, reflected, "As this is a Bodisat of the Bhadrakalpa, and he is going to hang himself because he does not possess a beautiful appearance, I will fill his mind with hope." So Indra said to him, "Youth, despair not! And in order that you may not kill yourself, set this jewel upon your head, and your courage will be restored to you." Then Indra vanished.

When the youth Kuśa was going to enter into his house, the doorkeeper kept him back, saying, "Do not intrude here, for this is the house of the youth Kuśa." "I am Kuśa," he replied. As the doorkeeper would not believe him, Kuśa removed the jewel from his head. Then his appearance became what it had been before, so that the doorkeeper now believed him.

The youth Kuśa resolved to remain at that spot, and to let his father know. So he sent word to him saying, "I shall stay here."

The king of the gods, Indra, pointed out to him the locality of four treasures. Kuśa had a city built of the four precious stones, and it was named Kuśinagara, inasmuch as the youth Kuśa abode there. He became the mightily ruling Chakravartin Kuśa.

III.

ADARSAMUKHA.[1]

To King Ananda there were born five sons. The youngest of these, inasmuch as his face resembled a mirror, was named Ādarśamukha or Mirror-face. All five sons grew up. Prince Ādarśamukha was very gentle and modest, but the others were rash, rude, and hot-tempered. Their father called them together one day on a matter of business. The minds of the elder brothers were incapable of deciding the smallest of its points, but Prince Ādarśamukha answered with intelligence the difficult questions which were proposed to him.

Being attacked by illness, King Ānanda considered as to whom he should invest with the sovereign power. "If I invest one of my four elder sons with the power," he thought, "inasmuch as they are rash, rude, and hot-tempered, misfortunes will unduly increase among men; but if I invest Prince Ādarśamukha with the power, then my kinsmen will reproach me for having passed over my elder sons and given the power to the youngest. It is necessary, therefore, that I should devise some way of escape."

With that intention he decided in his mind on three

[1] Kah-gyur, book ii. pp. 198–201. We have here a simpler and at the same time more concrete recension of chap. xxxi. of the Dsanglun, with a continuation which includes chap. xxxix. of that work, with the latter of which Benfey's remarks in his introduction to the Panchatantra (i. 394) are to be consulted, as well as Sukhomlinof's account of "The Tale of Shemyaka's Judgment" in the *Zapiski* of the St. Petersburg Academy of Sciences, 1873, vol. xxii. book i. The decision in the second part of the continuation is attributed in the Dsanglun, chap. xxxix. to King Mdges-pa.—S.

precious things, and on a recognition by the women, and on six objects to be recognised by insight. Then he said to his ministers, "Give ear, O chieftains! After my death ye are to test each of the princes in turn. Him among them whom the jewel-shoes fit when they are tried on, under whom the throne remains steadfast when he is set upon it, on whom the diadem rests unshaken when it is placed upon his head, whom the women recognise, and who guesses the six objects to be divined by his insight, namely, the inner treasure, the outer treasure, the inner and outer treasure, the treasure of the tree-top, the treasure of the hill-top, and the treasure of the river shore—him by whom all these conditions are fulfilled shall ye invest with the sovereign power."

Then, according to the proverb which says that all which has been accumulated dwindles, and all that is high will meet with a fall, he died. Now when the ministers tried to place the jewel-shoes on the feet of the eldest prince, the shoes did not fit. When he was set upon the throne, it moved. When the diadem was placed upon his head, it shook greatly. Moreover the women did not recognise him. And when he was told the names of the six objects which were to be divined by his insight, he did not guess them. The fate of three of his younger brothers was just the same. But when the jewel-shoes were placed upon Prince Ādarśamukha's feet, they fitted him perfectly. When he was set upon the throne, it remained unmoved. When he was crowned with the diadem, his head looked forth from beneath it proudly. Moreover the women recognised him. Then the ministers said, "Now you must find out the six objects to be divined by insight, namely, the inner treasure, the outer treasure, the inner and outer treasure, the treasure of the tree-top, the treasure of the hill-top, and the treasure of the river shore." Ādarśamukha replied, "If the question is which is the inner treasure, that is the treasure which is inside the threshold. If the question is which is the outer treasure, that is the treasure which is outside the threshold. If the question is which is the treasure of the tree-top, that is the treasure which is at the spot on which the tree planted by the king casts its shadow at midday. If the question is which is the treasure of the hill-top, that is the treasure which is under the stone at the bottom of the tank wherein the king used to take delight. If the question is which is the treasure of the river shore, that is the treasure which is at the end of the channel by which the water flows out of the house." As all the problems were solved, the ministers made Ādarśamukha king, and he became a mighty monarch.

In a certain place among the hills there lived a Brahman named Daṇḍin, who borrowed a pair of oxen from a householder. After ploughing his land, he went with the oxen to the householder's dwelling. As the man was at his dinner, the Brahman Daṇḍin let the oxen go to their stall; but they went out again by another door. When the householder arose from his meal and found that the oxen had disappeared, he seized Daṇḍin and asked where the oxen were. Daṇḍin replied, "Did not I bring them back to your house?" "As you have stolen my oxen, give them back to me," said the other. Daṇḍin replied, "I have not stolen them." The other said, "King Ādarśamukha is wise. Let us go to him; he will settle this affair for us, separating the right from the wrong." So they both set out on their way.

A man from whom a mare had run away called out to Daṇḍin to stop it. He asked how he was to stop it. The man told him to do so in any way he could. Daṇḍin picked up a stone and flung it at the mare's head, the consequence of which was that the mare was killed. The man said, "As you have killed my mare, give me another one." Daṇḍin said, "Why should I give you a mare?" The man replied, "Come, let us go to King Ādarśamukha; he will settle our business for us." So they set off to go to him.

Daṇḍin tried to run away. As he sprang down from a wall, he fell on a weaver who was at his work below, in consequence of which the weaver died. The weaver's wife laid hands upon Daṇḍin and demanded that he, as he had killed her husband, should restore him to her. "Where am I to get your husband from for you?" he said. "Come, let us go to King Ādarśamukha," she replied; "he will settle our business for us." So they went their way.

About half-way they came to a deep river, which a carpenter was fording, his axe in his mouth. Daṇḍin asked him if the river was deep or shallow. The carpenter, letting his axe drop, said, "The river is deep." Then, as his axe had fallen into the water, he seized Daṇḍin and said, "You have flung my axe into the water."

"No, I have not."

"Come, let us go to King Ādarśamukha; he will settle our business for us."

By and by they who were leading Daṇḍin along came to a drinking-house. In it Daṇḍin sat down upon the landlady's new-born babe, which was lying asleep under a dress. "There's a child lying there! There's a child lying there!" cried the mother. But when she looked at it, the child was dead. She seized on Daṇḍin and demanded that he, who had killed her child, should give it back to her. He replied, "I did not kill it. Why should I give you a child?" She said, "Come, let us go to King Ādarśamukha." So they set out on their way.

At a certain spot a crow which sat on a withered tree saw Daṇḍin, and asked him whither he was going. He replied, "I am not going anywhere, but I am being taken by these people."

"Whither?"

"To King Ādarśamukha's."

"Then take charge of a commission from me, and say to King Ādarśamukha, 'At such and such a spot there stands a tree with dry leaves. On this tree sits a crow which wants to ask you what is the reason why it remains upon that tree, and takes no delight in other trees which are green and full of sap.' "

They went farther, and some gazelles saw Daṇḍin and asked him whither he was going. He replied, " I am not going anywhere, but am being taken by these people."

" Whither ? "

" To King Ādarśamukha's."

" Then take charge of a commission from us, and ask the king what is the reason why we find no pleasure in any other place than this, though other places possess meadows and green grass."

They went on farther. A partridge saw them and asked whither they were going, and all went on as above up to the words, " Then take charge of a commission from me also, and ask the king why I call like a partridge at one spot, and at another spot I have a different kind of voice."

Elsewhere they saw a snake, and just the same as before happened up to the utterance of the words, " Then take charge of a commission from me also, and ask the king why I creep out of my hole with ease, but creep back into it only with pain."

A snake and an ichneumon, which had quarrelled and were fighting with one another, likewise begged that the king might be asked on what account they, as soon as they saw each other, day by day became angry and began to fight. A young wife also commissioned them to ask wherefore she, so long as she lived in her father's house, longed after the house of her father-in-law, but now, since she entered her father-in-law's house, longed after the house of her father.

They went on and came to King Ādarśamukha's; then Daṇḍin wished the king long life and victory, and took a seat at a certain spot, and the others also seated themselves. After they had paid reverence with their heads to the king's feet, the king asked Daṇḍin, "Wherefore have you come?"

"O king, I have been brought hither."

"On what account?"

Daṇḍin related the whole story of why the householder had quarrelled with him. The king said to the householder, "Did you see the oxen, or did you not see them? Did Daṇḍin drive your oxen into the stalls?"

"Yes, O king."

The king said, "As Daṇḍin gave this man no information, his tongue shall be cut off. As this man did not tie up his oxen, his eyes shall be put out."

The householder said, "First I lost my oxen, in the second place my eyes are to be put out. Sooner than that, I prefer not to win my suit against Daṇḍin."

The owner of the mare said, "O king, Daṇḍin has killed my mare."

"How did he kill it?"

The man told the whole story in full. The king said, "As this man told him he might stop the mare by any means whatsoever, his tongue shall be cut off; but Daṇḍin shall have his hand cut off, because he thought it impossible to stop the mare except by throwing a stone at it."

The man said to himself, "First my mare died, now my tongue is to be cut off. Sooner than that, I prefer not to gain my suit against Daṇḍin."

The weaver's wife told her story in full, and the king said, "Then you shall receive this man as your husband." She said, "First of all this man killed my husband, and now he is to be my husband. Sooner than that, I prefer not to win my suit against Daṇḍin."

The carpenter fully explained his case. The king said, "As the carpenter spoke in the middle of the river and let his axe fall, his tongue shall be cut off; but Daṇḍin's eyes shall be put out, because he, although he saw that the river was deep, asked the carpenter about it." The carpenter said, "First I lost my axe, now my tongue is to be cut off. Sooner than that, I prefer not to win my suit against Daṇḍin."

The landlady told her story in full, and the king said, "As the landlady left her child sleeping with a dress completely hiding it, her hand shall be cut off; but Daṇḍin shall have his eyes put out, because he sat down on an unfamiliar seat without making any investigation."

The landlady said, "First my child died, now my hand is to be cut off. Sooner than that, I prefer not to win my suit against Daṇḍin."

Daṇḍin presented the crow's petition. The king said, "O Daṇḍin, say this to the crow: 'At that spot there is a treasure, which was hidden away under the withered tree by you when you were the head man of the village. Give it to some one or other and then go away, and you will fare well.'"

Daṇḍin executed the commission of the gazelles. The king said, "Tell the gazelles this: 'O gazelles, there stands a tree on that spot from the top of which honey drops down. Thereby are the meadows and the grass rendered sweet. But as the bees have now been driven out, do not tarry any longer on the spot, otherwise ye will suffer pain beyond measure.'"

Daṇḍin brought forward the request of the partridge. The king said, "Tell the partridge this: 'Where you possess a partridge's voice, there no treasure is to be found; but where you have a different voice, there a treasure is to be found. Point out this treasure to some one or other, and then, as it is not right that you should suffer pain beyond measure, betake yourself somewhere else.'"

Daṇḍin mentioned the request of the snake and the ichneumon, and the king said, "Tell both of them this: 'When ye were men, ye were born as two brothers. One of the two said, "Let us divide our property." But the other, overcome by envy, would not consent to the division. On that account the one, being too covetous, was born again as a snake; but the other, inasmuch as he was excessively covetous and clung to the property, was born as an ichneumon. Do ye then give these treasures to the Śramanas or the Brahmans, and then leave that spot. By that means will ye fare well.'"

Daṇḍin brought forward the snake's request, and the king said, "Say this to the snake: 'When hungry and in a state of collapse, you can easily creep out of your hole. But when you have partaken of copious food, then it is only with pain that you can creep back into the hole. If you can content yourself with so much food as is fit for you, you will fare well.'"

Daṇḍin mentioned the young wife's request, and the king said, "Tell the young wife this: 'In your father's house there is a friend. When you are in your father-in-law's house, you long after that friend; but when you are in your father's house, you long after your husband. As it is not right that you should suffer pain beyond measure, give up the one place of residence and take up your abode permanently in the other.'"

The young wife and the snake did what they were told to do. The snake and the ichneumon, as well as the crow, made over their treasures to Daṇḍin. The others likewise acted in accordance with the instructions given to them.

IV.

THE CLEVER THIEF.[1]

IN olden times there lived in a hill-town a householder, who married a wife of his own caste. When a son was born unto him, he said to his wife, "Goodwife, now that there is born unto us a causer of debts and diminisher of means, I will take merchandise and go to sea." She replied, "Do so, lord." So he went to sea with his merchandise, and there he died.

After his wife had got over her mourning, she continued to live, partly supported by her handiwork, and partly by her relatives. Not far from her dwelt a weaver who was

[1] Kah-gyur, iv. 132–135. One of the oldest of popular tales is the story told by Herodotus (bk. ii. chap. 121) of the treasury of Rhampsinitus, which its builder's two sons are in the habit of robbing, until one of the thieves is caught in the snares set for their feet, whereupon the other, to prevent a discovery, cuts off his brother's head and runs away. The king gives orders to expose the corpse, and to keep watch so as to see whether any one weeps and wails over it. The surviving son, forced by his mother's threats to look after his brother's burial, comes to the spot provided with skins of wine, makes the watchmen drunk, shaves off the right side of their beards, and carries away the dead body. Thereupon the king's daughter is obliged to yield herself to every one who will relate to her the cleverest and most scandalous trick he has ever played in his life. The doer of the deed comes and betrays himself. But when the princess tries to seize him, he leaves in her hold, not his own hand, but that of the dead man. At last the king promises his daughter's hand to the doer of this deed, so the thief reveals himself and receives the princess. As a like legend is connected with the treasury of Hyrieus in Orchomenus, where Trophonius cut off the head of his brother Agamedes (Pausan. ix. 37), and as according to Charax (Schol. ad Aristoph. Nubes, v. 508) the same story is told also of the treasury of Augeias at Elis, we can easily understand why some commentators, like C. O. Müller, wish to claim the legend for the Greeks, while Buttmann (Mythol. ii. 228) wishes to trace it to the East. See Liebrecht in his edition of Dunlop's "History of Fiction," p. 264, and Grimm, Kinder- und Hausmärchen iii. 260.—S.

skilled in his art, and who by means of adroitness succeeded in everything. Seeing that he, by means of his art, had become well to do, she came to the conclusion that weaving was better than going to sea, for when a man did the latter, he needlessly exposed himself to misfortune. So she said to the weaver, "O brother, teach this nephew of yours to weave." He replied, "As that is right, I will do so." The youth became his apprentice, and in a short time learnt the art of weaving, for he was sharp and quick.

As the weaver wore fine clothes, took good baths, and partook of delicate food, the youth said to him one day, "Uncle, how is it that although you and I are occupied in exactly the same kind of work, yet you have fine clothes, good baths, and delicate food, but I never have a chance of such things?" The weaver replied, "Nephew, I carry on two kinds of work. By day I practise weaving, but by night thieving."

"If that be so, uncle, I too will practise thieving."

"Nephew, you cannot commit a theft."

"Uncle, I can."

The weaver thought he would test him a little, so he took him to the market-place, purchased a hare there, and gave it to him, saying, "Nephew, I shall take a bath and then return home. Meanwhile, go on roasting this hare." While he was taking his bath, the youth hastily roasted the hare and ate up one of its legs. When the weaver returned from his bath, he said, "Nephew, have you roasted the hare?"

"Yes!"

"Let's see it, then."

When the youth had brought the hare, and the weaver saw that it only had three legs, he said, "Nephew, where is the fourth leg gone?"

"Uncle, it is true that hares have four legs, but if the fourth leg is not there, it cannot have gone anywhere."

The weaver thought, "Although I have long been a

thief, yet this lad is a still greater thief." And he went with the youth and the three-legged hare into a drinking-house and called for liquor. When they had both drunk, the weaver said, "Nephew, the score must be paid by a trick."

"Uncle, he who has drunk may play a trick; why should I, who have not drunk, do this thing?"

The weaver saw that the lad was a great swindler, so he determined to carry out a theft along with him.

They betook themselves to housebreaking. Once when they had made a hole into a house, and the weaver was going to pass his head through the opening, the youth said, "Uncle, although you are a thief, yet you do not understand your business. The legs should be put in first, not the head. For if the head should get cut off, its owner would be recognised, and his whole family would be plunged into ruin. Therefore put your feet in first."

When the weaver had done so, attention was called to the fact, and a cry was raised of "Thieves! thieves!" At that cry a great number of people assembled, who seized the weaver by his legs and began to pull him in. The youth, all by himself, could not succeed in pulling him out; but he cut off the weaver's head and got away with it.

The ministers brought the news to the king, saying, "Your majesty, the thief was himself arrested at the spot where the housebreaking took place; but some one cut off his head and went away with it." The king said, "O friends, he who has cut off the head and gone away with it is a great thief. Go and expose the headless trunk at the crossway of the main street. Then place yourselves on one side, and arrest whoever embraces it and wails over it, for that will be the thief." Thereupon those servants of the king exposed the headless trunk at the crossway of the main street, and stationed themselves on one side. Thinking it would be wrong not to embrace his uncle and moan over him, the other thief assumed the appearance of a madman, and took to embracing men, women, carts, horses, bullocks, buffaloes, goats, and dogs. Afterwards, all men thinking he was mad, he pressed the headless trunk to his breast, wailed over it as long as he liked, and then went his way. The king was informed by his men that a madman had pressed the headless trunk to his bosom, and while he held it there had wailed over it, and had then gone away. The king said, "O friends, this man of a surety was the other thief. Ye have acted wrongly in not laying hands upon him. Therefore shall hands be laid upon you."

The other thief said to himself, "If I do not show honour to my uncle, I shall be acting badly." So he assumed the appearance of a carter, and drove a cart up to the spot laden with dry wood. When he arrived there, he upset the cart with its load of dry wood, unyoked the oxen, set the cart on fire, and then went away. The headless trunk was consumed by the flames. The king was informed by his men that the corpse was burnt, and they told him all that had taken place. The king said, "O friends, the carter was certainly the thief. Ye have acted wrongly in not laying hands upon him. Therefore shall hands be laid upon you."

The thief said to himself, "I shall not be acting rightly unless I take soul-offerings to the burial-place for my uncle." So he assumed the appearance of a Brahman, and wandered from house to house collecting food. From what he collected he made five oblation-cakes, which he left at the burial-place, and then went his way. The king's men told him that a Brahman had wandered from house to house collecting food, and had then left five oblation-cakes on the spot where the body had been burnt, and had then gone away. The king said, "O friends, that was really the thief. Ye have acted wrongly in not laying hands upon him."

The thief thought, "I shall be acting badly if I do not

throw my uncle's bones into the Ganges." So he assumed the appearance of a Kāpālika,[1] went to the place where the corpse had been burnt, smeared his body with ashes, filled a skull with bones and ashes, flung it into the Ganges, and then went his way. When the king had been told by his men all that had happened, he said, "O friends, this was really the thief. Ye have acted wrongly in not laying hands upon him. In order to bring the matter to an end, do ye let it alone. I will lay hands on the man myself."

The king had a garden laid out at a spot where the Ganges formed a bay, and he set men to watch on both of its shores. In it he stationed his very beautiful daughter on the shore of the river, giving her orders to cry aloud in case any one tried to touch her. To the watchmen also he gave orders to repair to the park as soon as they heard any sound, and if any man was found there, to seize him and bring him before him. Now the thief thought that he must not allow the opportunity of enjoying the king's daughter to slip out of his hands. So he took an empty pitcher, went down to the shore of the Ganges, and began to draw water. As he was carrying the first pitcherful, the watchmen came running up, thinking that he was the thief, and hit him a blow, in consequence of which the pitcher was broken. As he was carrying the second pitcherful, his pitcher was broken in the same way. But after this had happened three times, the watchmen came to the conclusion that he was a water-carrier, and paid him no more attention. Then the thief covered his head with a pot, and swam down the stream to the bay. There he came ashore and said to the maiden, "If you utter a single cry you shall die." In her fright she remained silent. He tarried awhile with her, and then went his way. The watchmen did not know what to do, seeing that she had made no noise while the thief tarried with her, and had not begun to cry

[1] A skull-carrying Śiva-worshipper.

till he had satisfied himself and gone away; but they gave the king a full account of what had taken place. The king said, "It is a bad business that he was not caught."

The result of the thief's visit was that, after eight or nine months had elapsed, the princess bore a son. When the thief heard of this, he decided that he must not miss his son's birth-feast, so he assumed the appearance of a courtier [and betook himself to the king's palace]. As he was leaving the palace he called out to the royal servants, "O friends, by order of the king, plunder the merchants' quarter!" As the servants thought that the king had given permission for the plundering of the merchants' quarter in honour of his grandson's birth, they set to work thereat. In consequence of this a great outcry arose, and the king asked what was the meaning of it. When the ministers had supplied him with a full account, the king said, "If this be so, I also have been taken in by him. Wherefore, if I do not punish him, I shall lose my throne."

With this idea in view he caused an enclosure to be made, and, after some little time had elapsed, he ordered his ministers to make public through the realm a proclamation to the effect that all men who dwelt in the kingdom were bound to assemble within that enclosure; and that no excuse would avail, but if any one did not appear he should be punished. When the ministers had made this order public, and all the inhabitants of the realm were assembled together, the king gave the boy a wreath of flowers, and told him to give it to the man who was his father; and he gave orders to the watchmen to lay hands upon the man to whom the boy should give the wreath. As the boy walked with the wreath through the assembled crowds and closely observed them, he caught sight of the thief, and, in accordance with the incomprehensible sequence of human affairs, handed him the wreath. The king's watchmen seized the thief and brought him before the king. The king asked his ministers what ought to be done. They were of opinion that the thief must be put to death. But the king said, "O friends, so little does such a hero of a man deserve to be put to death, that he ought much rather to be carefully watched over." Thereupon he endowed his daughter with ornaments of all sorts, and gave her to the thief as his wife, and bestowed upon her the half of his kingdom.[1]

[1] Compare Loiseleur Deslongchamps, "Essai sur les Fables Indiennes" (Paris, 1838), ii. 124, and Reinhold Köhler in Benfey's "Orient und Occident," ii. 303-313. In the Gaelic tale of "The Shifty Lad," the thief is found out by having a golden apple given to him by a child. R. Köhler adds, "In the story of Dümmling, who wishes that the princess may have a child (Hahn, No. 8; Grundtvig, ii. 308; Müllenhof's "Sagen," p. 481; "Zeitschrift für Deutsche Mythologie," i. 38), the hero is discovered to be the father of the princess's child, inasmuch as it offers him a golden apple in preference to all the other men who have been invited. In the variant of the tale in Basile's "Pentamerone," i. 3, the boy embraces his father. In a Gaelic story (Orient und Occident, ii. 124), the princess recognises the father of her child among the men of Erin by the fact that a bird alights upon his head. —S.

V.

SUDHANA AVADANA.[1]

In olden times there were two kings in Panchāla, one in the north and the other in the south. The king of North Panchāla, whose name was Dhana, like a law-observing monarch, ruled according to the law in Hastināpura, a city which was endowed with wealth, health, fruitfulness, and greatness of extent and population, and which was free from disquiet, disorder, uproar, and robbery, in which disease had quite come to an end, and which was fully provided with rice, sugar-cane, bullocks, and buffaloes. Moreover in this city there was a great lake, full of blue, red, and white lotuses, and rendered pleasant and beautiful by ducks and geese of various kinds. As the Nāga Janmachitra,[2] who dwelt in this lake, sent down from time to time a torrent of rain, the land was very fruitful; and as the realm overflowed with food and drink, the inhabitants, intent upon gifts, sacrifices, and reverence, bestowed sustenance upon the Śramaṇas and Brahmans, and the poor and needy.

The king of South Panchāla, who paid no respect to the law, was haughty, choleric, passionate, and ill-natured. He did not rule in accordance with the law, and he

[1] Kah-gyur, ii. 202–209.

[2] What is said here about the Nāga is referred to an elephant (= nāga), as Professor Minayef reminds me, in a Pāli recension of the Viśvantara Jātaka. The king of Kalinga, in whose realms there was a famine due to want of rain, sent eight Brahmans to Jayaturā, the capital of Śibi, to obtain from Viśvantara the white elephant which had the power of producing rain. See Spence Hardy's "Manual," p. 116, and Köppen's "Religion des Buddha," p. 324.—S.

kept the inhabitants of his realm constantly in fear by penalties, blows, wounds, executions, arrests, and bonds, and by intolerance, inaccessibility, and malice of every kind. As he was overweening and did not rule according to law, the deity did not let rain fall from time to time, on which account men, full of fear and despair, deserted the country in troops, and betook themselves to the realm of the king of North Panchāla.

Some time after this, when the king of South Panchāla had gone to the chase and had set forth to inspect his domains, he remarked that all the towns and villages were deserted, and the parks and the temples of the gods had fallen into decay and ruin. Having observed this, he said to his ministers, "Honoured sirs, what is the reason of these towns and villages being deserted, and of the parks and the temples of the gods having fallen into decay and ruin? and whither have the people gone?" The ministers replied, "They have gone into the realm of Dhana, the king of North Panchāla."

"On what account?"

"Will your majesty accord impunity of speech?"

"Speak, for I accord you impunity."

Thereupon they said, "Your majesty, as the king of North Panchāla rules in accordance with the law, his land is great, rich, healthy, fruitful, densely peopled, free from disquiet, discord, disorder, uproar, and robbery; diseases have quite disappeared there, it overflows with rice, sugar-cane, oxen, and buffaloes; and its people, intent upon bestowing gifts, sacrifices, and reverence, offer sustenance to the Śramaṇas and Brahmans, and the poor and needy. But as you, your majesty, are choleric, passionate, and ill-natured, and have kept the inhabitants of the realm constantly in fear by means of penalties, blows, wounds, executions, arrests, and bonds, and by intolerance, inaccessibility, and malice of every kind, therefore have the people, full of fear and despair, gone into the land of the king of North Panchāla." The king of South Panchāla said, "O sirs, what would be a good way of making those people return and inhabit these towns and villages?" The ministers replied, "If your majesty, ruling after the fashion of the king of North Panchāla, will protect the land with gentle, benignant, and merciful mind, the people will soon return and inhabit these towns and villages." The king of South Panchāla said, "Sirs, since this is so, I will protect the land with gentle, benignant, and merciful mind, ruling after the fashion of the king of North Panchāla; but do ye take such measures that the people may come back again and inhabit these towns and villages."

"Your majesty, there is yet another cause for the state of things in Hastināpura. In that city there is a Nāga named Janmachitra, who dwells in a great lake filled with blue, red, and white lotuses of all kinds, and adorned with ducks and geese of divers species. As he sends down a torrent of rain from time to time, the harvest is always abundant and the soil is extremely fertile, and the land abounds in meat and drink." The king said, "Is there no means of summoning that Nāga hither?"

"Your majesty, as he can be conjured hither by men who are versed in charms and spells, let them perform the deed."

Thereupon the king fastened a golden basket to the end of a standard, and ordered proclamation to be made throughout the whole kingdom that he would give that golden basket to any one who could conjure the Nāga Janmachitra out of North Panchāla into South Panchāla, and would also heap upon him a profusion of great honours. After a time a serpent-charmer appeared before the ministers, and said that if the golden basket was given to him he would capture and bring in the Nāga Janmachitra. The ministers ordered the basket to be brought, and the serpent-charmer said, "I will leave this basket in the hands of a trustworthy man. Let him give it to me when I bring the Nāga Janmachitra." When this had been promised him, the serpent-charmer placed the golden basket in the hands of a trustworthy man and betook himself to the city of Hastināpura. Being well versed in signs, he perceived, after carefully observing the lake all round, that the Nāga Janmachitra must have his dwelling-place in a certain spot. So he went to fetch offerings and utensils, and said to the ministers, "Give me offerings and utensils, and within seven days I will capture and bring in the Nāga."

Now the Nāga had seen the serpent-charmer, and had said to himself, "This man has come to carry me off, and if at the end of seven days I am carried off, I shall suffer great distress on account of being severed from my parents. What shall I do? To whom shall I pray for protection?"

Now there lived in the neighbourhood of the lake two hunters, Masūraka and Phalaka. Living near the lake, they supported themselves by killing not only land animals, such as the hares, stags, boars, and so forth which came to that lake to drink, but also the fish, tortoises, and so forth which lived in the water. Of these two hunters Masūraka died, but Phalaka remained alive. As the Nāga Janmachitra came to the conclusion that there was no one except the hunter Phalaka to whom he could fly for refuge, he went, after assuming the form of a man, to the hunter Phalaka, and said to him, "O friend, if King Dhana's realm is vast, rich, healthy, fruitful, and populous, and overflows with rice, sugar-cane, oxen, and buffaloes (as was said above), do you know through whose power this has come to pass?" The hunter answered, "Well do I know that this takes place because that king rules in accordance with the law, and protects his land with gentle, benignant, and merciful mind." The Nāga said, "Does all this arise from that cause only, or from some other cause as well?" The hunter said, "There is another cause as well. In this lake lives the Nāga Janmachitra, who from time to time sends down a torrent of rain, in consequence of which the soil becomes extremely fertile, and is replete with food and drink." Janmachitra said, "If this Nāga were to be taken away from this land by any one, he would no longer be able to be of service, and he would be very wretched on account of being separated from his parents. What would the king and the inhabitants of the land do if he were to be carried off? what would you do?"

"We should perish."

"Do you know who this Nāga is?"

"No!"

"I am he, and a serpent-charmer from South Panchāla wishes to carry me off. He has gone back to fetch offerings and utensils, and will return in seven days. He will then drive pegs of Khadira-wood[1] into the shore of the lake at its four corners, will hang up various threads of different colours, and will recite spells. During that time you must remain hidden somewhere near. But when, as he is performing a ceremony of this kind, the waters of the lake begin to seethe and overflow, and I come forth from them, then you must bend your bow against the serpent-charmer, and run up to him quickly and say, 'Reverse the spell. If you do not do so I shall sever your head from your body and send it to the bottom of the lake.' But if he dies without reversing the spell, then, even after his death, I shall remain bound by its force all my life long." The hunter said, "As I would have done this of my own accord, were it merely for the sake of doing you a service, how much the more shall I be ready to protect you, inasmuch as I shall be doing a service to the whole kingdom. Say no more."

The Nāga then took up his abode in a lonely spot. When seven days had passed, the hunter hid himself near that place. The serpent-charmer came and began to prepare the offerings and utensils, driving in the pegs of

[1] See Tāranātha's "History of Buddhism in India," p. 70, where Nāgārjuna conjures the goddess Chaṇḍikā into the Manjuśri temple by the insertion of a wedge of Khadira-wood.—S. The Khadira is the *Acacia Catechu*.

Khadira-wood at the four corners, attaching various threads of divers colours, and reciting spells. When the water began to seethe, the hunter sped an arrow from his bow, and then drew his sword from its sheath and cried, "Will you carry off the Nāga who dwells in our land by means of spells? Reverse your spell. If you do not, I will sever your head from your body and send it to the bottom of the lake." The serpent-charmer, experiencing pain and grief induced by anguish and fear of death, reversed the spell, whereupon the hunter instantly killed him. When the Nāga was thus freed from the power of the spell, he came forth from the lake, embraced the hunter, and thus addressed him, "You are my mother, you are my father. In this wise am I, in that I trusted in you, spared the pain of being separated from my parents. Come, let us go to them." He led him to their abode, regaled him with meats and drinks of divers kinds, presented him with jewels, and then said to his parents, "This man has become my refuge, my friend, and my kinsman. Through his means I have been saved from separation from you." The parents also let him have all he wished for, and presented him with precious things of all kinds. These he took away with him, and then came forth from the lake.

Not far from the lake was a hermitage, rich in flowers, and fruits, and birds which uttered varied notes. Therein a Rishi abode, full of gentleness, mercy, and kindness towards living creatures. To this Rishi the hunter was wont to go daily, in the morning, at midday, and in the evening. To him he gave a full account of what had taken place between him and the Nāga Janmachitra. The Rishi said to him, "What need have you of jewels and gold? That habitation contains the Amogha-chain[1] (*i.e.*, that which holds fast). You must ask for that." As a desire for that Amogha-chain arose within the hunter's mind, he followed the advice of the Rishi, and again betook himself to the abode of the Nāgas. There

[1] In Sanskrit, Amoghapāśa.—S.

he saw the Amogha-chain at the entrance of the Nāgas' abode, and perceiving that it was the chain which he wanted, he entered into the abode. The Nāga Janmachitra and the other Nāgas were delighted, and they gave him jewels. But he said, "Jewels I want not; rather give me the Amogha-chain." Janmachitra replied, "What need have you of it? To us it is most needful. When the Garuḍa plagues us, it is to this chain that we are indebted for safety." The hunter said, "As ye are but seldom threatened with danger from the Garuḍa, therefore it is not so very necessary for you. But I am constantly in want of it. Therefore give it to me, if ye are mindful of the benefit conferred and the service performed." The Nāga Janmachitra said, "As this man has done me a great service, I will give him the chain, after I have asked my father and mother." After asking his parents, he give him the chain. Thereupon the hunter, as if he had recovered himself, returned home from the Nāga's abode with the Amogha-chain, full of happiness and joy.

King Dhana and his wife had neither son nor daughter. It happened once that he sat, resting his cheek upon his hand, absorbed by the thought that, since he had neither son nor daughter, his family would be extinct after his death, the treasures heaped up within his house would pass into other hands, and another king would rule over all that had been his. As he sat there thus absorbed in meditation, the Śramaṇas and Brahmans, his friends, companions, and kinsmen, asked him why he was so downcast. When he had fully explained the whole matter to them, they said, "Be pleased to pray to the gods. Then will a son be born unto you." As he had no son, but desired to have one, he prayed to Śiva and Varuṇa, to Kuvera and Vasudeva, and so forth, also to various other gods, to the gods of the parks, the gods of the forest, the gods of the crossways, the gods of the three ways, the gods who accept oblations, the ever-accompanying gods, and the gods like-minded and identical in date of birth. It is generally said that sons and daughters are born in consequence of such prayers, not otherwise; a thousand sons, for instance, may be born to a world-ruling prince when such prayers have been offered.

Praying in such a manner, Dhana obtained a hearing, and a Bodisat of the Bhadrakalpa entered into the womb of his good spouse. Some women who are endowed with insight possess five peculiar characteristics, one of which is that they know whether their child will be a boy or a girl. If it is a boy, it clings to the right side, and if a girl, to the left. Full of joy, spake the queen to her husband, "O lord, as the living being which has entered within me clings to the right side, and will certainly be a boy, therefore rejoice."

The king joyfully drew himself up, and stretched out his right arm, and said, "I shall behold the son whom I have long been desiring. As he will soon be born unto me, he will carry on my work, extend still more widely what has been acquired, and as my heir more widely propagate my race. And when we shall have died, whether we have presented many or few gifts and acquired much or little merit, it will follow after us in that place in which we shall both be born again, and our recompense will ripen through union."

Thus did he joyfully exclaim. As he knew that conception had taken place, he took care, in order that the existence in the mother's womb might be allowed to develop thoroughly, that there should be in his palace during the cold weather preservatives against cold, during the hot weather preservatives against heat. According to the directions of the physician, he provided food which was not too bitter, too sour, too salt, too sweet, too hot, or too acid — food which was without bitterness, sourness, saltness, sweetness, heat, or acidity. With strings of pearls of various kinds and with other ornaments he adorned the body of his wife, like unto an Apsaras wandering in the Nandana grove; and he made seats and seats, stools and stools, to prevent her from falling on the ground, and he ordered care to be taken that she should not hear the slightest unpleasant noise.

When eight or nine months had gone by, a boy was born of noble form and lovely aspect, fair and gleaming like unto gold in colour, with a head like a canopy, long arms, a brow of great width, interlacing eyebrows, a high-arched nose, and provided with the full complement of limbs and joints. When the joy-drum was beaten at the birth, the king heard it, and asked what that meant. His wives said, "Be of good cheer, your majesty; unto thee a son is born." Thereupon the king ordered all stones, gravel, and rubble to be cast forth from the city, the streets to be swept and sprinkled with sandal-water, standards and banners to be set up, extremely fragrant incense to be provided, flowers to be strewed, as though he had been delighted by various dreams, gifts to be bestowed upon the Śramaṇas, the Brahmans, the poor and the needy, and freedom to be given to all prisoners. After thrice seven days, on the twenty-first day, he appointed a great birth-feast. When the question was raised as to what name should be given to the boy, the ministers said, "As this boy is the son of King Dhana, he must be named Sudhana;" and so the name of Sudhana was given to him. The boy Sudhana was handed over to eight nurses, two to carry him, two to suckle him, two to cleanse him, and two to play with him. As these eight nurses fed him and brought him up on milk, both sweet and curdled, on butter, both fresh and clarified, on butter-foam,[1] and on the best of other things, he shot up rapidly like a lotus in a tank. By the time he was grown up he was acquainted with reading and writing, expert at the eight testings and distinguish-

[1] Butterschaum, perhaps a kind of clotted cream.

ings, and adroit in his manners; and he was skilled in the five arts, like a king who, coming of the Kshatriya caste and wearing the crown, zealously exercises over men power and might, and, if he rules over this orb, ought to be versed in the various divisions of knowledge and action, as was above mentioned.

His father bestowed upon him three wives—a first wife, a middle wife, and a last wife—and built for his use three separate palaces, for winter, spring, and summer; and in like manner he provided him with parks of three kinds, for winter, spring, and summer. There the young Sudhana, when he went alone, without any retinue, into the upper storey of the palace, diverted and enjoyed himself to the sound of musical instruments.

It happened once that the hunter Phalaka, as he roamed to and fro in search after game, arrived at a certain mountain, and at the foot of this mountain he perceived a Rishi's hermitage, rich in flowers and fruit. Around it fluttered birds of divers kinds, and there was near it a lake provided with red and white lotuses, and with geese and various kinds of ducks. As he was about to roam over this place of seclusion, he saw a Rishi with long hair on his head and body, and with long nails and a long beard, sitting in a grass hut under a tree. On seeing him he touched the Rishi's feet with his head, joined the palms of his hands, and said, "Venerable one, how long have you been in this place?"

"Forty years."

"While you have remained here, have you seen or heard anything strange or wonderful?"

The Rishi, calm of mood, deliberately replied, "Friend, do you see that lake?"

"Venerable one, I see it."

"That is the Brahmasabhā pool, filled with blue, red, and white lotuses, haunted by swarms of different kinds of birds, extremely rich in waters resembling silver, snow, and hoarfrost in colour. To this pool in the midst of the most fragrant flowers, there comes on the fifteenth day of the month Manoharā the daughter of Druma, the king of the Kinnarīs. Surrounded by five hundred Kinnarīs, she comes in order to bathe, after having washed and anointed her head. During the time of the bath they dance, sing, and make sweet music resound, such as enchants even the beasts of the forest. Even I myself, when I have heard these sounds, experience pleasure and delight for seven whole days. This maiden, O friend, I have seen."

The hunter Phalaka said to himself, "As I have obtained the Amogha-chain from the Nāga, I will cast it around the Kinnarī Manoharā. He came, accordingly, after a time, on the fifteenth of the month, bringing the Amogha-chain with him, concealed himself in a thicket not far from the lake, among fruits, flowers, and foliage, and kept watch. When Manoharā, surrounded by five hundred Kinnarīs, with befitting equipments, went into the Brahmasabhā lake to bathe, the hunter Phalaka straightway cast the Amogha-chain, and caught the Kinnarī Manoharā. Held by the chain, she began to bound and to run in the water and to utter shrieks of terror. Hearing these, the Kinnarī band broke up. Looking upon Manoharā, the Kinnarīs saw that she was taken prisoner, and they fled away terrified.

The hunter gazed at Manoharā, who was of an exquisitely proportioned figure and of a lovely countenance, and having gazed at her, he was about to draw near and lay hands upon her; but she said, "Man of low station, touch me not. I am not destined to marry you. As I am worthy of a king of goodly form, you must not lay hands upon me." The hunter said, "If I do not lay hands upon you you will flee away." She replied, "I will not flee away. If you will not trust me, take this head-jewel, by means of which I fly heavenwards." The hunter said, "Who can tell that?" She gave him the head-jewel and said, "I shall always be in the power of him whose hand holds this jewel." The hunter took the jewel, and led her away with him, just as if she had been secured by bonds.

About this time the youth Sudhana went forth to the chase one day. The hunter saw the youth Sudhana, who was handsome in form and of pleasant aspect; and having seen him he said to himself, "As this is Prince Sudhana, and as he is of goodly form and pleasant aspect, and as he, when he has looked upon this maiden, will take her to wife, I will of my own accord offer her to him as a present." So he led her, just as if she had been secured by bonds, to Prince Sudhana, and said, after touching his feet, "I offer unto you as a present this gem of a wife; be pleased to accept the gift." Prince Sudhana looked upon the Kinnarī Manoharā. She was of goodly form and pleasing countenance, with a complexion of remarkable brilliance and with all good properties, adorned with the eighteen signs of the woman, more beautiful than the children of men; the breasts wide apart, and arched like the tortoise Hiraṇyakumbha, firm, plump, extremely round and elastic; the eyes light blue, with small red veins and of elongated form, like young lotuses; the arch of the nose long and high; the lips like coral, gems, pearls, in form like the Bimba fruit; the chin ample and firm; the cheeks marked by very attractive moles; the eyebrows beautifully interlacing, black as a swarm of bees; the arms long and rounded like the spotless full moon; the belly a little overhanging with three deep folds; the upper part of the body a little bent from the down-hanging of the breasts, the under part beautifully formed like a disk; the hands like unto the pith of the banana tree; the legs beautiful from their delicacy and the rounding off of the calves; the veins scarcely visible and free from all crookedness, so that all the limbs were fair to see, proudly moving to the sound of the richly jewel-studded ornaments of the head, neck, and feet, and the many strings of pearls; the hair black and smooth, like unto Sachī, the feet adorned with ornaments; wearing a golden girdle, many strings of pearls hanging down at the belly, the complexion gleaming fair as gold.

No sooner had the youth set eyes on her than he was suddenly enchained by the bonds of passion—passion which, like the pure and spotless moon reflected in water, is, on account of its unstable nature, not easily to be grasped, and like a sea-monster in a billowy torrent, is not easily to be distinguished, which steps along like the Garuḍa or the flow of the wind, which flies about swiftly with a lightness resembling that of cotton, which, like a monkey, is always in motion, never resting in any place. When the arrow of passion, which is ever connected with woes and with longing to enjoy the bliss of love, without letting itself be warned off from the abyss of misfortune due to all those woes—when this arrow strikes the heart, shot from the careless bow with a scarcely audible sound arising from the longing after a meeting, then, completely befooled by senses which hang upon the fair one, a man falls, like a moth, into the flame. As in summer the lightning flashes from out of the rain-cloud, so did the dart of love strike Sudhana when he looked upon her whose countenance was like unto the moon. Then Prince Sudhana took Manoharā and brought her to the city of Hastināpura, and to the hunter he gave a splendid city. Ascending with Manoharā to the upper storey of the palace, the youth Sudhana spent his time with her in pleasure and sport; and by the hundredfold force of Manoharā's youth, beauty, and respect for him, the youth Sudhana was immediately and irresistibly captivated.

After a time two Brahmans wandered that way, one of whom attached himself to the king, the other to Sudhana. The Brahman who attached himself to the king was appointed a Purohita[1] by the king, who also bestowed much property upon him. But only a little

[1] "A family priest, a king's domestic chaplain, a priest who conducts all the ceremonials and sacrifices of the family, &c."

property was given to him who attached himself to Prince Sudhana. The prince's Brahman said to him, "O youth, what will you do for me when, after your father's death, you are made king?" The youth Sudhana replied, "As your companion has been appointed my father's Purohita, I will appoint you also to be a Purohita." As this conversation of theirs was passed on by one man to another, it came to the ears of the Brahman who was the Purohita. He said to himself, "If I can manage so that the youth does not acquire the sovereign power, there will no longer be any question as to the appointment to the Purohitaship."

It came to pass afterwards that the mountaineers of the king's realm rebelled. The king sent a general to subdue them, but he returned completely overcome and vanquished. Just the same happened to seven other generals whom the king sent out. The ministers said to the king, "Wherefore, your majesty, do you allow your forces to dwindle away and the power of the foe to increase? Be pleased to order out all who are capable of bearing arms within your realm." The Brahman who was the Purohita thought that this was the time for bringing about Sudhana's death, so he said to the king, "There can be no doubt that in that wise defeat will take place." The king said, "What am I to do then? Ought I to march out myself?" The Purohita said, "Your majesty, why should you go yourself? As the youth Sudhana has come to man's estate, and is proud of his strength and courage, you can send him out with the troops." The king said, "I will do so." Thereupon the king summoned the youth, and said to him, "O youth, march forth with the troops and subdue the mountaineers." "Your majesty, I will act in accordance with your commands."

Having thus spoken, Sudhana prepared to obey his father. On betaking himself to the zenana, he saw Manoharā there, and not only forgot all his other wives, but also, as soon as he saw her, forgot the commands laid upon him by the king. Thereupon the Purohita said to the king, "Your majesty, as there can be no doubt that the youth Sudhana is deeply in love with Manoharā, let the troops be drawn up, and order the youth, when he comes forth from the zenana, to set out on the march without going to see Manoharā again." The king said to the ministers, "Honoured sirs, equip the host." The ministers obeyed the orders of the king, and equipped the hosts, elephants, horses, chariots, and infantry, well provided with many kinds of weapons and appurtenances. Then they summoned the youth, saying to him, "O youth, as the troops are ready, come forth from thence." He said, "Your majesty, I will go forth when I have seen Manoharā."

The king said, "O youth, do not go to see her, for that would give rise to delay."

"If that be so, I will set out when I have seen my mother."

"O youth, your mother you may see."

Sudhana took Manoharā's head-jewel, went to his mother, touched her feet, and said, "O mother, as I am setting out to subdue the mountaineers, do you keep this jewel with the utmost secrecy, and do not give it to Manoharā except in a case of life and death." After saying these words to his mother, and taking leave of her, he set forth with the army to the sound of music. After gradually advancing for some time, he halted under a tree at no great distance from the mountaineers. Just at that time the Mahārāja Vaiśravaṇa was going to a Yaksha meeting, together with many Yakshas, many hundreds, many thousands, many hundreds of thousands of Yakshas. As he drove along, and was delayed upon the celestial road, he said to himself, "Often as I have driven along this road, yet has my chariot never once been delayed. What can be the cause of its being delayed now?"

Perceiving the youth Sudhana, he thought, "This is a Bodisat of the Bhadrakalpa, who has gone forth to war and will be in difficulty. I will assist him, and subdue the mountaineers without living creatures being exposed to danger." So he summoned Pānchika, the commander-in-chief of the Yakshas, and said to him, "Pānchika, come here.. Contrive so that the youth Sudhana may subdue the mountaineers without a battle being fought or injury being inflicted upon living creatures." The Yaksha commander-in-chief Pānchika listened to the orders of Vaiśravaṇa, and said, "I will act in accordance with your commands." Then he conjured up the four contingents of the divine host, men of the stature of palm trees, elephants of the size of mountains, horses as large as elephants, and chariots as bulky as the palace of the gods Vimāna. Together with his mighty host, spreading great alarm by means of all kinds of weapons, such as swords, mallets, javelins, lances, disks, maces, arrows, battle-axes, and so forth, and through the clang of all sorts of musical instruments, Pānchika moved onwards towards the mountaineers, whose walls gave way in consequence of the uproar made by the elephants, the horses, and the chariots, and of the clangings of all kinds, and of the power of the Yakshas. Seeing these hosts, and perceiving that their walls had given way, the mountaineers were greatly astonished, and asked the hosts whence they came. They replied, "Open the gates with all speed. The youth Sudhana is on the march behind us, and we are his army. If you do not open your gates with all speed, everything will be overthrown." The mountaineers said, "We did not rebel against the king. Moreover, the youth is judicious; but we have been reduced to fear and anxiety by the king's officials." Then they opened the gates, and went forth to meet the youth Sudhana, with banners and standards displayed, with full urns, and to the sound of all manner of instruments. After he had taken rest, he called them to him, nominated chiefs, fixed taxes, and took hostages. Then, having subdued the mountaineers, the youth Sudhana returned home.

That same night King Dhana dreamt this dream. A vulture came flying up, tore open the king's belly, seized his entrails, and wound them around the whole city. And the seven treasures came into the palace. Terrified by this dream, with creeping skin and unquiet mind, he rose swiftly from his couch, and sat down in his sleeping chamber, his head leaning on his hand, absorbed in meditation as to whether he was about to lose his sovereign power or whether he was about to die. In the morning he told his dream to the Purohita, who came to the conclusion that, as the king had dreamt such a dream, the youth must certainly have subdued the mountaineers, and that it was the Purohita's business to devise some means for his destruction, so he said to the king, "What your majesty has seen in this dream is not good. There is no doubt that either you will lose your sovereignty, or your life will be placed in danger. There is, however, a means of averting this evil. I have found it in the mystic lore of the Brahmans." "What is the means of averting it?" "Your majesty, let a tank be dug in the park, a man's height in depth, and let it be lined with mortar, and when all is smooth, let it be filled with the blood of young roes. Then, when you go there to bathe, you will enter the tank as far as the first step, and when you have descended to the first step you will go down to the second step, and after you have descended to the second step you will go on to the third step, and when you have descended to the third step you will go down to the fourth step. Then must four Brahmans, perfectly versed in the Veda and Vedānga, lick your feet with their tongues, and anoint them with the fat of a non-human being (*i.e.*, a demon). In this wise will all that is sinful in your nature become purified, and you will long retain your sovereignty." The king said, "All this may possibly be carried out, but yet demon-fat is very rare." The Purohita said, "Your majesty, is that a rarity which it is possible to find?" The king said, "What does that mean?" The Purohita said, "Your majesty, is Manoharā a human or a non-human being?" The king said, "O Purohita, speak not so; for the youth's life depends upon her." The Purohita said, "Your majesty, have you not heard that for the sake of the house should one of its inmates be given up, for the sake of the city should the house be given up, for the sake of the country should the city be given up, for the sake of one's own self should the country be given up?[1] If you, O king, are firm, you can bestow another wife on the discerning youth, and cause Manoharā to be put to death."

As the king, out of self-love, did not wish any means to be neglected, he acquiesced and ordered the preparations to be made according to the Purohita's directions, the tank to be dug, lined with mortar and glazed, and filled with the blood of roes and so forth. When Sudhana's wives saw these preparations, cheerfulness and joy sprang up within them. "As we also," they said, "shall acquire exquisite beauty if we avail ourselves of this, we shall be able to partake of great enjoyment with the youth Sudhana." As they spoke joyfully to this effect, Manoharā saw them, and asked wherefore they were so delighted. One of them explained the whole matter to Manoharā. Thereupon pain and displeasure sprang up within her, and she betook herself to Sudhana's mother, and touched her feet, and told her the whole story in words provocative of sympathy. The queen said, "As these things are so, ponder over them well, and I will ponder over them also."

When Manoharā had reflected and spoken, and the queen also had considered the matter, and had decided that it was right so to do, she gave Manoharā the head-jewel and a garment, and said, "Child, I was to give you this jewel only if your life was in danger. In the present circumstances I shall be beyond reproach."

[1] See Böhtlingk, "Indische Sprüche," 2d edit., No. 2627.—S.

After a time, all things having been prepared for the bath according to the command of the king, he entered the blood-filled tank and came forth from it again, and then the Brahmans licked his feet with their tongues. When, subsequently to this, all things had been set in order for the bath according to the commands of the king, and he had entered the blood-filled tank and emerged from it again, then the tongues of the Brahmans licked his feet. After that the supernatural being was brought forward. When Manoharā was ordered to draw nearer, she immediately rose heavenwards, saying, "After being seized and bound, after having laughed and played, like a cow freed from its bonds, will I flee away." When the king saw her sweeping through the air, fear came upon him, and he said to the Purohita, "How comes it that the Kinnarī Manoharā has flown away before our preparations were carried into effect?" The Purohita said, "Your majesty, the end is now attained, and your nature is made free from sin."

While Manoharā was wending her way through the air she said to herself, "The directions of the Rishi were the cause of my passing into this condition. Had he not given these directions I should not have been captured. So I will go to him for awhile." On reaching the Rishi's hermitage she touched his feet and said, "Great Rishi, in consequence of your directions, I have been captured and exposed to the touch of man, and have nearly lost my life. Now then, if the youth Sudhana should happen to come here in search of me, give him my ring, and say to him these words: 'O youth, turn back again, for the way is full of woe and hard to tread. But if you cannot turn back, it is right to show you the way. Thus, O youth, does Manoharā point it out. In the north there are three black mountains. When these are surmounted, there rise three more. When these three have been surmounted, there rise three more again. And when these three also have been surmounted, there remains the prince of mountains, Himavant. On its north side are the mountains Utkīlaka, Jalapatha, Khadiraka, Ekadāraka, Vajraka, Kāmarūpin, Kīlaka, Airāvata, Adhovāna, and Pramuchapa. Over these mountains you must make your way. Traverse Khadiraka, Ekadāraka, and Utkīlaka by the cavern. The king of the birds will carry you over Vajraka. In such a way will you traverse these mountains. You will overcome magic creatures, ram-like and goat-faced, and also a man having the form of the Rākshasa Pingalā. In the cavern is a huge snake, which rolls with the force of a foaming stream. This snake you must tame by force. When you see the black snake half coiling in the cavern, you must slay it, bending the bow and shooting the arrow. When you see two rams butting one another, break a horn off each of them, and you will find the way. If you see two iron men with fear-inspiring weapons, and you slay one of them, you will find the way. If you see an iron-lipped Rākshasī opening and shutting her mouth, you must fling a wedge at her forehead. Likewise must you spring across the fount with the wild whirlpool, which measures sixty fathoms. Bending your bow, you must slay Yakshas and Rākshasas with lion-yellow hair and eyes, difficult to resist and hard to approach. Many rivers, also, full of tens of thousands of alligators, must you cross. You will see the Crocodile, the Butterfly, the Sad, the Gay, the Weeper, the Laugher, a river full of snakes, and another full of reeds. In the Crocodile is Rākshasī-anger, in the Butterfly a demon, in the Sad are many water-monsters, in the Gay is a Vidyādhara, in the Weeper is a Kinnarī serving-maid, in the Laugher is a Kinnarī, in the snake-filled river are many snakes, in the river rich in reeds is Śālmali [the Seemul or silk-cotton tree]. In the presence of the Crocodile [river] you must stand firm, and be bold in that of the Butterfly. On reaching the Sad, you must bind the jaws of the water-monsters. With the Gay you will succeed by the help of some Nāgas, with the Weeper by means of courage, with the Laugher by means of silence.

The snake-filled river you must pass by means of snake-charms, and the reed-producing river by means of the charm of sharp weapons beaten together.[1] Having crossed all the rivers, you will come to a wild country wherein five hundred Yakshas dwell. Opposing these, overcome them. Then will appear the capital of the Kinnarī king. To him address yourself.'" Having spoken these words to the Rishi, Manoharā touched his feet with her head and went away.

Great was the joy when the king heard that the youth Sudhana had returned to Hastināpura with the army after subduing the mountaineers. As soon as the youth had rested, he went to his father, made obeisance, and took his place before him. The king began to speak with great joy, and said, "O youth, have you been successful?"

"Your majesty, through your grace have the mountaineers been overcome, hostages have been taken, and chiefs appointed. Tribute and taxes have also been levied. Be pleased to have all this taken into the treasury."

The king said, "O son, as you have done well, I will receive these things." Then the son made obeisance to his father, and was about to depart when the king said, "Stay, O youth, in order to take food with your father."

[1] This passage is extremely obscure. It is evident that Professor Schiefner was puzzled by it, for he has on the sheets prepared for the present translation made considerable alterations in his version as it originally appeared. There appears to be good reason for supposing that the Crocodile and the Butterfly, the Sad and the Gay, the Weeper and the Laugher, are names of rivers, but at present we must be contented with a hypothesis. The German text originally ran as follows: "Viele Flüsse, die mit zehntausend Alligatoren angefüllt sind, musst du überschreiten. Krokodile, Schmetterling, ein Betrübter, ein Bunter, ein Weinender, ein Lachender, Schlangenreicher und rohrreicher Fluss; im Krokodil ist Rākshasī-Zorn, im Schmetterling ein Dämon, in dem Betrübten viele Meerungeheuer," &c. As altered by Professor Schiefner it runs: "Krokodile, Schmetterling, eine Betrübte, eine Bunte, eine Weinende, eine Lachende, ein Schlangenreicher und rohrreicher Fluss," &c. The whole passage has been submitted to various experts, who are inclined to accept the fluvial hypothesis.

"Your majesty, as it is a long time since I saw Manoharā, I wish to go to her."

"O youth, put off going to her for to-day and go to-morrow."

"Father, I will certainly go to-day," said the youth, moving restlessly this way and that. Whereupon the king made no reply.

When the youth entered his house, and did not see the fair one at the door of the women's chamber, he was utterly cast down. As he did not see Manoharā, his mind became disordered, and he ran hither and thither, calling out, "Manoharā! Manoharā!" When the women had repeated these words to the winds, and he in his grief of heart had many times questioned them, they told him the whole story. Clouded over was his mind with grief. The women said, "Why should you be so cast down? In the band of women are those who are much more beautiful than she was."

When he had learnt how cruelly his father had acted, he went to his mother, touched her feet, and said, "O mother, as Manoharā is not here, Manoharā who was endowed with every virtue that could be wished for, and endowed with admirable beauty, where then has she gone? Thinking ever so rapidly, I am all confused in mind. On account of being separated from her my mind is exceedingly sad. As Manoharā dwells within my mind, pleasing to my mind and my mind's joy, as through separation from Manoharā my body is saddened, what is there that will make my pain diminish?" His mother said, "O son, as intolerable fear came upon Manoharā, I let her go away." "Mother, how did that come to pass?" His mother gave him a complete account of the matter. He said, "That was a cruel misdeed on my father's part." He said, moreover, "Mother, whither has she gone? which way lies the road?" His mother replied, "The road which Manoharā has taken is that of the mountains where Rishis and lions ever dwell, and which are the abode of the Dharma-rāja."[1] In his intolerable grief at being separated from Manoharā, the prince renewed his sad wailings, crying, "As Manoharā is not here, Manoharā who was endowed with every virtue that could be desired," and so on down to the words, "What is there that will make my pain diminish?" Then his mother said, "My son, as there are women in this band of wives who are more beautiful than she is, wherefore are you sad?" The youth replied, "Mother, how can I be happy if I find her not?"

Although his mother tried to console him, he still remained sad; but as he wandered hither and thither, looking for Manoharā and seeking for information as to her abode, a bright idea occurred to him. "Where I obtained her," he thought, "there will I go again and make inquiries." So he went to the hunter Phalaka, and asked him where it was that he had got possession of Manoharā. The hunter replied, "On the slope of such and such a mountain dwells a Rishi, in whose hermitage there is a pool, Brahmasabhā by name. Going there to bathe, I captured her according to the Rishi's directions." Sudhana said to himself, "I will go to the Rishi's abode, and there obtain information." Hearing that the youth was greatly depressed by his separation from Manoharā, the king said, "O youth, wherefore are you so depressed? I will now give you a much more beautiful wife." The prince replied, "Father, as she is not here, I shall certainly betake me to her tarrying-place." The king could not dissuade him from this, though he repeatedly attempted to do so. Then the king ordered watchers to be set at the gates and outlets from the walls, in order to prevent the youth from going forth. Thereupon the youth could not sleep the whole night long. Five are there who on their nightly couch are sleepless all night long, namely, the man whose mind is enchained by love for his wife, the wife who loves her husband, the red duck, the robber chieftain, the Bhikshu who studies zealously. The youth

[1] Dharma-rāja, "'king of justice,' an epithet of Yama."

said to himself, "If I go to the gate, the king's gatekeepers are harsh. As they would punish me, or even deprive me of life, I would rather depart by a road which has no watchers." So he went forth by night to a spot where no watcher was, having attached to a standard such blue lotus garlands as men bind around their heads. Just then the moon rose. When he saw the moon, he uttered this lament for his separation from Manoharā, "O full moon, king of the stars and illuminer of the night, thou who art dear to the eye of Rohiṇī,[1] excellent caravan-leader, hast thou seen the abiding-place of my loved one, the lotus-eyed Manoharā?"

Remembering the joys he had formerly experienced, he walked on, and when he saw a gazelle, he addressed it also, saying, "O gazelle, thou who enjoyest grass, water, and foliage, wander in peace and quiet, for I am no hunter. Hast not thou seen my deer-like, long-eyed, beautifully formed Manoharā?" Going on farther, and reaching another spot, he saw bees at work in the interior of a wood adorned with flowers and fruits, and to one of the bees he said, "O bee, thou who art blue, like unto the mountains, thou who abidest within hollow canes and upon lotuses, hast thou seen my Manoharā, her of the long hair, dark of hue, like unto bees?" Going still farther he saw a snake, and when he saw it he said, "O snake, thou who movest thy tongue as a forest tree its leaves, thou who emittest from thy mouth and eyes masses of smoke, hast thou seen her who is unlike thy poison-fire and the fire of passion? hast thou seen my Manoharā?" He went on still farther, and he heard a Kokila calling in the forest, and seeing it, he said, "O Kokila, thou who abidest on the magnificent trees of the forest, king of the troops of birds, hast not thou seen her who is endowed with the lovely, spotless eyes, like unto

[1] Rohiṇī, "name of the ninth Nakshatra or lunar asterism (personified as a daughter of Daksha, and the favourite wife of the moon, called 'the Red one,' &c.")

blue lotuses? hast not thou seen my Manoharā?" Going still farther on, he saw an Aśoka tree widely spreading forth its leaves, and when he saw it he said, "Thou who art called after happiness,[1] and who art the great king of the trees, troubled by grief for Manoharā, I clasp my hands. Do thou dispel my grief."

After this fashion, with troubled mind, he at length arrived at the hermitage of the Rishi. And when he had meekly paid reverence to the Rishi, he said, "O thou who art exalted through endurance, thou who art clothed in the bark of trees and the skins of wild beasts, thou who feedest on roots and sprouts, the Vilva tree and the Kapittha tree.[2] O Rishi, I pay thee reverence, bowing my head. Hast thou seen my Manoharā? Tell me quickly." Then the Rishi said to the youth Sudhana, "Welcome!" And after unfolding a carpet and making preparations for a friendly reception, he continued, "I have seen her who is endowed with smooth, interlacing eyebrows, who possesses a comely form, a face resembling the full moon, and eyes like unto blue lotuses. Take your seat upon the carpet, and partake of these different kinds of roots and berries. There is no doubt in my mind that you will obtain happiness in the future. Thus spake she of the beautiful eyebrows: 'I have learnt that the youth, rendered unhappy by longing, although a dweller in the forest, affected by great sorrow, will come to you.' Then she gave me this ring and said, 'As the way which leads to me is full of woe and hard to tread, he can turn back. But if he cannot bring himself to turn back, then you must direct him on his way.' And she spoke as follows: 'In the north there are three black mountains. When these are surmounted, there are three more on the other side; and when these three have been surmounted,

[1] The word *Aśoka* means "without sorrow: not feeling or not causing sorrow."

[2] "The tree *Ægle Marmelos* (commonly called Bel)," and "the elephant or wood-apple tree, *Feronia elephantum*."

there are again three more; and when these three also have been surmounted, there remains the king of mountains, Himavant. Here are certain remedies to be obtained. There is the remedy nectar.[1] When it has been boiled in melted butter, he who drinks it will feel neither hunger nor thirst, and will increase in memory and strength. There is also a monkey which must be carried away; there are spells which must be learnt; and there are also to be carried away a bow and arrows, a gleaming jewel, a deadly poison and a remedy, three iron wedges, and a lyre. On the north side of Himavant, king of mountains, is Mount Utkīlaka, and beyond are Mounts Jalapatha, Khadiraka, Ekadāraka, Vajraka, Kāmarūpin, Utkīlaka, Airāvata, Adhovāna, and Pramuchaka. These mountains you must climb, but to pass Khadiraka, Ekadāraka, and Utkīlaka you must traverse a cavern, and over Vajraka will the king of the birds convey you. In this way will you cross the mountains. Magic creatures, ram-like and goat-faced, and a man who has the form of the Rākshasa Pingalā, you must overcome. In the cavern is a snake which rolls with the strength of a foaming stream, and this you must overcome by force. Where there is a black snake, and you see half of it in the cavern, you must bend your bow and let fly your arrow and kill it. When you see two rams butting one another, break a horn off each of them and you will find your way. When you see two iron men holding fear-inspiring weapons, strike down one of them and you will find your way. When you see a Rākshasī with iron lips opening and shutting her mouth, fling a wedge at her forehead. Then you must leap across the fount with the wild whirlpool, which measures sixty fathoms. You must bend your bow and slay Yakshas and Rākshasas with lion-yellow hair and eyes, difficult to resist and hard to approach. Many rivers, also, filled with alligators, must you cross. There are the Crocodile, the Butterfly, the Sad, the Gay,

[1] The Sanskrit Sudhā, "the beverage of the gods, nectar, &c."

the Weeper, the Laugher, a river full of snakes, and a river rich in reeds. In the Crocodile is Rākshasī-anger, in the Butterfly is a demon, in the Sad are many water-monsters, in the Gay is a Vidyādhara, in the Weeper a Kinnarī serving-maid, in the Laugher is a Kinnarī, in the snake-filled river are many snakes, in the river rich in reeds is Śālmali. In the presence of the Crocodile you must stand firm, and you must be bold in the presence of the Butterfly. On reaching the Sad, you must bind the jaws of the water-monsters. With the Gay you will succeed by the help of some Nāgas, with the Weeper by means of courage, with the Laugher by means of silence. You will cross the snake-filled river by means of the charm against snakes, and the river rich in reeds by means of the magic of sharp weapons struck together. When you have crossed the rivers and reached a land rich in bushes, you must oppose and overcome five hundred Yakshas who dwell there. There stands the capital of the Kinnarī king. Go and speak with him.'"

Thereupon the youth Sudhana touched the Rishi's feet with his head, and went away in order to seek the remedies, spells, and antidotes indicated to him. When he had obtained all but the monkey, he came back with them to the Rishi. The Rishi gave him a monkey and said, "O youth, why do you trouble yourself so much? Wherefore is Manoharā so necessary to you. Alone, without companions, you will surely lose your life." The youth replied, "Great Rishi, I shall surely go, and why? Where has the heaven-traversing moon a companion? The king of the beasts, endowed with strength of tusks, and the fire which burns the forest—where are their companions? Wherefore should a strength like mine require a companion? What! shall not men trust themselves to the great ocean wave? Shall not one heal the hand which a snake has bitten? If a vigorous being struggles to the utmost, no blame can be found with the pains taken, even though they may not be successful."

Thereupon the youth Sudhana, provided with the various objects indicated by Manoharā, set forth. He passed in their turn the rivers, the caverns, and the abysses, assisted by the remedies, the spells, and the antidotes, and he came into the neighbourhood of the Kinnarī king, Druma. The youth gazed at the city, which was adorned by a park rich in flowers and fruits of various kinds, the haunt of all sorts of birds, provided with tanks, oblong and square lakes, and surrounded by Kinnarīs. He saw some Kinnarīs coming to draw water, and he said to them, "What are you going to do with all that water?" They replied, "The Kinnarī king has a daughter, Manoharā. As she has fallen into the hands of human beings, the smell of humanity has to be washed off her." The youth Sudhana said, "Are all these jugs to be emptied over her at once, or one after another?" They replied, "One after another." He thought, "Here is a good opportunity. I will drop this ring into one of the jugs." He chose the jug of one of the Kinnarīs, dropped the ring into it, and said to her, "Let your jug be the first to begin Manoharā's ablutions." Whereupon she thought, "No doubt he will be wanting something or other."

When this Kinnarī had been the first to empty her jug over Manoharā's head, the ring fell into Manoharā's lap, who said to her, "Has not a man come hither?" She replied, "Yes." "Go to him, and bring him to some retired spot." Accordingly the Kinnarī brought him in and took him to a retired spot. Then Manoharā touched her father's feet and said, "Father, if the youth Sudhana, who was my husband, were to come here, what would you do with him?" He replied, "As he is a man, and I have no need of him, I would cut him into a hundred pieces and scatter him on all four sides." Manoharā said, "Father, as he is a man, how could he be here? It was only my talk."

Afterwards, when the wrath of the Kinnarī king, Druma, was assuaged, he said, "If the youth comes, I will have you provided with all kinds of ornaments, and with many goods and treasures, and surrounded by Kinnarīs, and will give you to him as his wife." Thereupon Manoharā, full of great delight, clothed the youth Sudhana in divine array, and showed him to the Kinnarī king, Druma. When the Kinnarī king, Druma, saw the young Sudhana's stately form and pleasing aspect, his handsome face and brilliant complexion, he was greatly astonished. As he was desirous of having him as his son-in-law, he set in order seven golden stems, seven palms, seven kettledrums, and seven wild boars. Now the youth Sudhana was a Bodisat, and Bodisats are versed in all arts and in every kind of skill. Moreover, the gods take pains to remove all hindrances out of their way. The Bodisat stepped forth, surrounded by many thousands of Kinnarīs, amid dance and song, and to the sound of the harps, kettledrums, cymbals, lutes, drums, and the rest of the instruments of various kinds made by the gods. Before the eyes of the Kinnarī king, Druma, he drew nigh to the golden stems, wielding a sword which looked like the leaf of a blue lotus, and began to cut the stems in pieces as though he were slicing a plantain. Whereupon he broke them into fragments like grains of sesame. Moreover he shot an arrow uninjured through the seven palm-trees, the seven kettledrums, and the seven boars, and remained standing like Sumeru unremoved. Thereupon the heaven-inhabiting gods and many hundreds of thousands of Kinnarīs set up a cry of triumph with noise and shouting. When the Kinnarī king, Druma, saw and heard all this, he marvelled greatly.

After that the king placed Manoharā in the middle of a thousand Kinnarīs exactly like her, and said to the youth Sudhana, "Come hither, O youth, and recognise Manoharā." Then the youth Sudhana, in order that he might recognise her, uttered these verses, "Thou who art Druma's daughter, thou art also my beloved Manoharā; let it come to pass, in consequence of this truth, that thou, O

Manoharā, swiftly steppest to the front." Thereupon she immediately stepped forward, and the Kinnarīs said, "Your majesty, as this youth Sudhana is of excellent strength, manliness, and courage, and deserves to be Manoharā's husband, therefore please to be angry no longer, and to give Manoharā to him."

Then the Kinnarī king summoned the Kinnarī host, and the Kinnarī assembly paid great honour to the youth Sudhana. Holding Manoharā adorned with divine array with his left hand, and a jar full of gold-dust with his right hand, the king went up to the youth Sudhana and said, "O youth, I give you Manoharā as your wife, surrounded by a thousand Kīnnarīs. But men are of a fickle nature. Do not on any account desert her." "I will act, O father, in accordance with your words," said the youth Sudhana, and proffered obedience to the Kinnarī king, Druma. Then in a palace of the Kinnarī domain he and Manoharā, apart from men, revelled and enjoyed themselves to the sound of the musical instruments.

After a time, remembering his home, and being depressed by the pain arising from his separation from his parents, he informed Manoharā that he was overcome by the anguish caused by his separation from his parents. Thereupon Manoharā gave her father a full account of what had taken place. The king said, "Go with the youth, but act cautiously, seeing that men are deceitful." Then the Kinnarī king, Druma, let her go, after bestowing upon her jewels, pearls, gold and so forth in profusion.

Sudhana went his way with Manoharā, speeding onwards through the air by Kinnarī power, and at length arrived at the city of Hastināpura. In the city of Hastināpura, after all stones, gravel, and rubble had been swept away, and sandal-wood water had been sprinkled, and floral hangings, standards, and flags had been set up, and exceedingly fragrant incense had been provided, and flowers of all sorts had been strewn about, men gave themselves up to rejoicing. Then the youth, accompanied by Manoharā, surrounded by many thousands of leaders of men, made his entry into the city of Hastināpura.

When he had recovered from the fatigue caused by the journey, he took jewels of different kinds and went to his father, and remained standing beside the king, and gave him a full account of his journey to and from the Kinnarī city. As King Dhana had become aware that the prince possessed remarkable strength, manliness, and courage, he invested him with regal power. The youth Sudhana said to himself, "That I have met with Manoharā and obtained the might of kingly power is the special result of earlier deeds. Therefore will I now also bestow gifts and practise virtuous works."

And during the space of twelve years he without let or hindrance offered sacrifice in the city of Hastināpura.

VI.

PRINCE JIVAKA AS THE KING OF PHYSICIANS.[1]

In Videha, in a vast, rich, prosperous, fruitful, and populous land, reigned King Virūḍhaka. He had five hundred ministers, with Śakala at their head, and through his chief minister Śakala he ruled in accordance with the law, and transacted business according to justice. For this reason all men looked up to Śakala. After Śakala had taken to himself a wife of his own degree, and had lived with her, there was born unto him a son, to whom, on the twenty-first day after his birth, the name of Gopāla was given. After he had again lived with his wife, another son was born to him, to whom he gave the name of Siṁha.

When these two sons were grown up, it was with them just as it had been with their father, who from the very first surpassed all the other ministers in courage and superiority in the five arts. Now these ministers could not endure this. So they took counsel together, and betook themselves to the king, and asked him, when an opportunity presented itself, who really was king. The king replied, "Honoured sirs, what is the meaning of such a question? I am the king. Who else could there be?" They said, "O king, Śakala is king, not you. If he could manage it, he would deprive you of the regal power, set the diadem on his own head, and seize the regal power for himself." But the king saw quite clearly that they were hostile to Śakala because he was superior to them all.

[1] Kah-gyur, vol. iii. pp. 50*–67*. Spence Hardy has given in his "Manual of Buddhism," pp. 237–249, a portion of Jīvaka's wonderful cures, and also some varying accounts of his origin.—S.

On another occasion, the king was sitting surrounded by the band of ministers, while the first minister, Śakala, was detained in the king's palace, surrounded by eight thousand plaintiffs and defendants, so that the king's palace was quite full. But when the public business was brought to an end and the crowd had gone away, the palace was left quite empty. The king asked if all the crowd had left the palace. The ministers, trusting that they had found an opportunity, replied, "O king, what you wished to hear is evidently this: If Śakala could bring it about, he would deprive you of the sovereignty, set the diadem upon his own head, and seize the regal power for himself."

As kings, like crows, live in fear of death, he thought that what they said was doubtless true, and he began to find fault with Śakala. As every one finds in the world friends, foes, and indifferent persons, Śakala's attention began to be called to the fact that the king wanted to get up a quarrel with him, and that he must therefore take some precautions. After pondering over the matter, he considered whither he should betake himself. If he were to go to Śrāvastī, he would be in the same danger there, as that also was under regal power. Just the same would be the case if he were to go to Vārāṇasī, to Rājagṛha, or to Champā. Only in Vaiśālī did the people rule. There, if ten men were contented, twenty were discontented. He had better betake himself thither.

So he sent a messenger to the Liććhavis [1] of Vaiśālī to ask if he might take up his abode under the shelter of their power. They replied with all respect that he might come to Vaiśālī, and would be welcome there. Thereupon the first minister, Śakala, called his kinsmen together, and said to them, "Honoured sirs, I am about to move to Vaiśālī. Let those among you who are contented here remain here; but he who is not so, let him get ready

[1] For an account of the origin and history of these nobles, see Spence Hardy's "Manual," p. 235.

and go with me." He also ordered the herdsmen to drive the oxen and buffaloes to Vaiśālī, and told his servants to get themselves ready for the journey thither.

After having thus incited many men to get ready, he went to the king, touched his two feet, and said, "O king, as I have a little business to see to, allow me to go to the park." The king gave his consent. When Śakala had caused the park to be ransacked, he filled his waggons with treasures, which he covered over with food and liquor, and set off.

When the ministers heard that Śakala had absconded, they came in haste to the king and reported his flight. The king ordered them to recall him. They equipped a fourfold army, overtook him, and ordered him to turn back in compliance with the king's commands. He replied, "Honoured sirs, ye have long been considering whether I should die or take to flight. As the latter has now come to pass without much difficulty, think no more of it. I have escaped."

They shot some arrows in order to satisfy the king's expectations. Then they turned back and informed the king that Śakala had escaped. The king was displeased thereat and kept silence.

At that time there were three districts in Vaiśālī. In the first district were 7000 houses[1] with golden towers, in the middle district were 14,000 houses with silver towers, and in the last district were 21,000 houses with copper towers. In these lived the upper, the middle, and the lower classes, according to their position. The people of Vaiśālī had made a law that a daughter born in the first district could marry only in the first district, not in the second or third; that one born in the middle district could marry only in the first and second; but that one born in the last district could marry in any one of the three; moreover, that no marriage was to be contracted outside Vaiśālī, and that a woman recognised as a pearl

[1] Properly a house with a belvedere or small tower.—S.

among women should not be married to any one, but should appertain to the people for common enjoyment.

As Śakala was a man of position, he was allotted a house in the first district. When he began to live there, he could not be induced, although invited, to appear in the assembly of the people. The Liććhavis asked him why he did not appear. He replied, "As harm might come to me from the assembly, therefore I do not go to it." The inhabitants of Vaiśālī encouraged him to attend, saying that no harm could come to him. He then went to the assembly, but he never expressed any opinion. They invited him to do so. But he explained that he never did so, because if he did some evil might come upon him. They declared that he ought to do so, and that doing so would bring him into no trouble. So when he afterwards appeared in the public assembly, he expressed his opinion along with the rest.

Up to that time, the Liććhavis of Vaiśālī, whenever they sent a missive to any one, wrote it in a rude style. But after Śakala had given his advice they framed their missives in a friendly tone. They who received such friendly missives talked them over among themselves, and tried to find out the reason for this friendliness. Then some of them explained that it was since Śakala, the first minister of Virūḍhaka, king of Videha, came to Vaiśālī and took part in the councils, that letters of this kind, full of friendliness, had been issued.

After Śakala had arranged marriages for his two sons, Gopāla and Siṁha, there was born unto Siṁha a daughter, to whom the name of Vāsavī was given at her birth-feast. When the seers had inspected her, they declared that she would bear a son who would take his father's life, set the diadem on his own head, and seize the sovereignty for himself. After Siṁha had again lived with his wife, a daughter was born to him, whose birth also was celebrated in the most festive manner, and to whom the name of Upavāsavī was given. Her also the seers inspected, and they declared that she would bring into the world a son provided with excellent qualities.

Now it came to pass that Gopāla, who was fierce and of great strength, ravaged the parks of the Liććhavis of Vaiśālī. The park-keepers tried to prevent him from doing so, pointing out to him that the Liććhavis were fierce and of great power. As the keepers gained nothing thereby, they betook themselves to his father and besought him to restrain his son. Śakala sent for him, and made him aware of the danger which threatened him on the part of the Liććhavis. He replied, "Father, they have parks; we have none." Śakala said that he would ask the popular assembly for a park. He did so, and the assembly granted them an old park. In the park there was an ancient Sāla tree, out of which the one made an image of Bhagavant, and the other consecrated the same. The Sthaviras in the Sūtras also say that the Buddha Bhagavant went out from Vaiśālī into the Sāla forest of Gopāla and Siṁha.

When Gopāla had committed a thousand misdeeds, and the Liććhavis had blamed and reproved him and called him to account, Śakala sent for him, and commanded him, in order not to irritate the people, to retire to a certain hill district, and there to practise agriculture on his own lands. The son obeyed his father's commands.

Afterwards, when the commander of Vaiśālī died, the first minister, Śakala, was elected commander. After he had held this post for a short time, he also died. The people of Vaiśālī met together, and held counsel as to whom they should appoint commander. Then some of them said, "As the excellent minister, Śakala, has admirably protected the people, let us elect his son." Others said, "His son Gopāla is fierce and of great strength. If we appoint him as commander, discord will be sure to come upon the people. His younger brother, Siṁha, is good, accessible, and likely to render the people contented. If it so please the people, let us appoint him commander." As all acquiesced in this, the assembly waited upon Siṁha and offered him the post of commander. He answered, "Gopāla is my elder brother; therefore appoint him." They replied, "O Siṁha, is the post of commander hereditary in your family? If you are not inclined to take the post, we will appoint some one else commander." He reflected that it would not be well if the commandership were to pass to some other family from his own, so he decided that it would be better to accept it. Thereupon he was invested with the office in great state.

Previously to this, when the inhabitants of Vaiśālī sent a missive, they used to write, "Thus say the people, with Śakala at their head." A little after this a missive arrived at the place where Gopāla was practising agriculture on his lands. When Gopāla had opened it and perused it, he asked if his father was dead, seeing that the inhabitants of Vaiśālī had been in the habit of writing, "Thus say the people, with Śakala at their head," but now there was written, "Thus say the people, with Siṁha at their head." When he was told that his father was dead, he took offence, and went to Vaisālī, and asked Siṁha if it was right that he should have been made commander, although he himself, Gopāla, was the elder brother. Siṁha explained how the whole matter had come about. Full of displeasure against the Liććhavis, Gopāla determined, in consequence of this slight, to go to Rājagṛha. So he sent a messenger to King Bimbisāra to make known his desire to place himself under the king's protection. The king sent back word that he would be welcome. So he went to Rājagṛha, and King Bimbisāra made him his first minister.

Now after some time King Bimbisāra's chief wife died, and as he was sitting depressed, leaning his cheek upon his hand, Gopāla asked him what was the cause of his grief. He replied that his chief wife was dead, and he could not but be unhappy. Gopāla said, "O king, be not troubled in mind. My younger brother has two daughters, perfect in youth and beauty. They would be exactly suitable for you. One of them, according to predictions, will give birth to a son who will put his father to death. But the other will bring into the world a son possessing the most excellent characteristics. It will be well for you, O king, to have that maiden brought here, of whom it was predicted that she would bear a son with the most excellent characteristics."

Thereupon Gopāla informed his brother Siṁha that King Bimbisāra's chief wife was dead, and that he ought to send his daughter Upavāsavī, as she would in that case become the king's chief wife. Siṁha wrote to him in reply, "What this will come to I will not ask you. But you, who understand the measure of things, will know what ought to be done. As the people have made a law that no maiden of Vaiśālī may be given in marriage to an outsider, you must come yourself and wait in the park. I will go to the park with my daughter, and you can carry her off from there."

Thereupon Gopāla took leave of the king, mounted his chariot, and set off for Vaiśālī. Having arrived there, he waited in the park. At that time one of the gate-keepers of Vaiśālī had died and had been born again among the demons. He gave to the inhabitants of Vaiśālī the following instructions: "As I have been born again among the demons, confer on me the position of a Yaksha and hang a bell round my neck. Whenever any foe to the inhabitants of Vaiśālī appears, I will make the bell sound until he is arrested or has taken his departure." So they caused a Yaksha statue to be prepared and hung a bell round its neck. Then they set it up in the gatehouse, provided with oblations and garlands, along with dance and song, and to the sound of musical instruments.

Gopāla sent word to Siṁha to come to him, as he was waiting in the park. Taking the people of Vaiśālī into consideration, Siṁha went home and said to Upavāsavī, "You are to be given to King Bimbisāra as his wife, so take your ornaments and go forth to the park." When she began collecting her ornaments, Vāsavī saw her and asked why she was doing that.

"I am going to be married."

"To whom?"

"To King Bimbisāra."

Vāsavī said this could not be done, seeing that she was the elder sister.

"In that case do you take the ornaments."

While they were still discoursing the bell began to sound. The inhabitants of Vaiśālī were in great commotion, supposing that an enemy had come to Vaiśālī. Full of anxiety, Siṁha took with him his elder daughter, Vāsavī, under the impression that she was Upavāsavī, and went hastily to the park. There Gopāla, equally full of anxiety, received Vāsavī into his chariot and drove away.

The people of Vaiśālī set out in pursuit of him, overtook him, and began to fight with him. But as he was versed in the five arts of battle, he pierced five hundred Liććhavis to the heart, and said, "Honoured sirs, as I have pierced five hundred of your number to the heart, but am ready to leave the rest of you alive, do ye now turn back."

"No living being among us has been killed."

"Take off your armour."

When they had taken off their armour, five hundred of them fell to the ground and died. Thereupon the survivors thought that this man must be a Rākshasa, and they fled away full of terror. When they returned to Vaiśālī they began to take counsel together, and they said, "Honoured sirs, on this foe of ours we will let King Bimbisāra's sons take vengeance. Let us inscribe this on a tablet, place the tablet in a chest, seal up the chest, and put it away." All of which they did.

After a time Gopāla arrived at Rājagṛha and cried, "Upavāsavī, come forth."

She replied, "Uncle, I am not Upavāsavī, but Vāsavī."

"Why did not you tell me so before?"

She uttered no word in reply. Displeased and troubled, he went to the king, and the king, as soon as he saw him, said, "Have you come, Gopāla? You are welcome."

"I have come, O king."

"Have you brought Upavāsavī along with you?"

"O king! I have brought her and have not brought her."

"What does that mean?"

"I have brought Vāsavī, thinking that she was Upavāsavī."

"Bring her here, that I may see her."

Now when Vāsavī was brought, and the king saw her perfect youth and beauty, he was attracted by her to such an extent that he fell in love with her at first sight, and said, "Honoured one, a son who kills his father must do so merely for the sake of the sovereignty. Therefore, in case a son is born unto me, I will confer the diadem on him immediately after his birth."

Thereupon he took her as his wife. As she came from Videha, she received the name of Vaidehī.

Now there lived in a hermitage a Rishi endowed with five kinds of insight. One day when the king had gone to the chase, a gazelle terrified by the shooting of arrows took refuge in the Rishi's hermitage, and being seen there, was struck by the king's arrow. The Rishi said in his wrath, "Will you, O king of evil, kill the gazelle which had placed itself under my protection, when even beasts of prey respect my hermitage?"

While the Rishi was calling the king to account with such words as these, the king's troops came up and asked to whom these words were being addressed. The king said that they were levelled at him, and asked what ought to be the punishment for such a calling to account. The answer was that the proper punishment was that of death. "In that case," said the king, "I abandon the Rishi to it." When the preparations were being made for putting the Rishi to death, he formulated a curse, desiring that he, wheresoever he should be born again, might take the king's life, inasmuch as that king of evil had ordered him to be put to death without his having committed any fault or done any harm. Moreover, he reflected that as such kings keep very much out of the way, and are greatly watched over and guarded, he would scarcely be able to find a fit opportunity if he were born again anywhere else, and that he must therefore be brought into the world by this king's chief wife. By means of this curse he was brought into the world by Vāsavī.

On the day of his conception a rain of blood fell. Vāsavī was seized by a desire to cut flesh from the king's back and eat it. When she had told the king of this, he called the soothsayers together and consulted them about it. They decided that it was caused by the influence of a being which had entered into his wife's womb. The king sat absorbed in thought, meditating how he could satisfy her longing. Some sagacious persons advised him to have a cotton garment lined with raw meat, and to put it on, and then to offer the meat to his wife. Thereupon the king ordered a cotton garment to be lined with raw meat, and he put it on, and then offered Vāsavī the meat. She thought that it was the king's own flesh, and so ate it, whereby she was freed from her longing.

Afterwards a longing came upon her to drink of her husband's blood, and she told this to the king. The king had the veins opened in five of his limbs, and gave her the blood to drink, whereby she was freed from her longing.

When nine months had passed by, a fine, good-looking boy was born, and on the day of his birth there fell a rain of blood. The king called the soothsayers together and consulted them. They said, "O king, so far as we can learn from the words of wisdom, this son will undoubtedly deprive his father of life, and then set the diadem on his own head and seize the sovereignty for himself." The king thought, "As it could only be for the sake of the sovereignty that he would deprive me of life, he would surely not do so if I were myself to hand over the sovereignty to him."

At that time there lived in Vaiśālī a Liććhavi named Mahānāman. In his park there was an Āmra grove, in which the park-watchers saw that a Kadalī tree had suddenly grown up. As it immediately began to put forth blossoms, the watchers were greatly astonished, and they told Mahānāman. He sent for the soothsayers and consulted them. They decided that he ought to have the tree watched, for it would burst open at the end of seven days, and from within it a maiden would come forth. The householder Mahānāman, marvelling greatly at this decision, set careful watchers over the grove and kept count of the days. When seven days had elapsed, he caused the park to be cleared of all stones, gravel, and rubble, and to be sprinkled with sandal-water, very fragrant incense to be provided, many silken hangings to be set up, and flowers to be freely strewn around. Then he and his wife went out in great state to the park, surrounded by friends and acquaintances, to the sound of song and all kinds of music. After he had there sported, rejoiced, and enjoyed himself, the stem of the Kadalī tree burst, and there came into sight out of it a beautiful maiden, lovely to look upon, perfect in all parts of her body. Mahānāman handed her over to his good wife, who said, "My lord, be pleased to give her a name." Mahānāman said, "As this girl has been obtained from the Āmra grove, her name ought to be Āmrapālī. Mahānāman returned home and took charge of Āmrapālī.

She grew up, and there came to woo her, from the Krauncha land and the Śakya land and many other lands, many kings' sons, ministers' sons, merchants, traders, and caravan leaders. The householder Mahānāman reflected that those among them who did not obtain her would be offended, and that he had better ask the people for a legal decision. So when the people of Vaiśālī were gathered together he said, "Honourable Brahmans and householders, give ear! Having obtained a girl from my park, I have brought her up. As I am now thinking of giving her in marriage to some man of a family corresponding with my own, so let the people consider the matter." The men of Vaiśālī replied, "O householder, the people long ago passed a law that a pearl of a woman was not to be given in marriage, but should be placed at the disposal of the people. Therefore you must bring forward the maiden, in order that we may see what she is like."

After a time he came into the assembly with her. When the perfection of her youth and beauty was seen, all the people opened their eyes wide with astonishment, and when they had critically examined her, some of them cried, "O householder, this is a pearl of a woman, and therefore she belongs to the enjoyments of the people, and must not be married to any one."

When Mahānāman had returned home in displeasure, and was sitting absorbed in thought, his cheek leaning upon his arm, Āmrapālī saw him, and asked why he was so dejected.

"O daughter, you have been recognised as a pearl of a woman, and therefore you belong to the enjoyments of the people, so that my wishes will not be fulfilled."

"O father, are you dependent upon any one."

"O daughter, as the people formerly made a law that she who is really a pearl of a woman shall belong to the enjoyments of the people, and as you have now been recognised as a pearl of a woman, I am powerless."

Then she said, "If the people will grant five wishes of mine, I will belong to their enjoyments. A house must be allotted to me in the first district. When a man has entered my house, no one else must be allowed the right of entry. Whoever enters must bring with him five hundred Kārshāpaṇas. At the time when houses are searched, my house must not be searched till seven days have elapsed. And no heed is to be taken of those who enter or leave my house." Mahānāman laid Āmrapālī's proposal before the people, and they agreed to it, saying, "If she asks for a house in the first district, a house in the first district befits a pearl of a woman. If she asks that when one man has entered into her house, no other man should have the right of entry, that also is just; for as no wrath is so bad as wrath on account of a woman, in case one man entered in and another came in after him, assuredly one of them might kill the other. If she makes a stipulation that every one who comes in must bring with him five hundred Kārshāpaṇas, this likewise is reasonable; she doubtless requires the money for clothing and ornament. If she asks that her house shall not be searched till after seven days have elapsed, that also is reasonable; what danger can arise, whether the search takes place sooner or later? If she wishes no heed to be taken of the men who enter or leave her house, that again is just. As she is to be a courtesan, no man would enter her house if he knew that all who went in or came out would be watched." So when the people had granted her five wishes, she became the property of the people for enjoyment.

After a time,[1] Āmrapālī sent for painters living in various regions, and ordered them to paint on her walls the portraits of the kings, ministers, capitalists, merchants, traders, and caravan leaders whom they had seen. When the painters had completed the portraits, Āmrapālī put on ornaments of various kinds and inspected the portraits one after the other, asking the while, "Honoured sirs, who is this?"

"King Pradyota."

"Who is that?"

[1] A few lines have been omitted here.

"That is Prasenajit, king of Kośala."

"And this?"

"Udajana, king of Vatsa."

"And that?"

"Śreṇi Bimbisāra, king of Magadha."

In this way she went on asking, and the painters told her all the names. When she had looked at all the portraits, her eyes remained fixed on that of Bimbisāra, and she began to reflect whether a man of such port and stature would devote himself to love with her.

It happened one day that King Bimbisāra of Magadha went out on the roof of his palace, and there, surrounded by his band of ministers, he indulged in light talk, asking them what courtesans they had seen. Gopāla said, "O king, there are others besides, but in Vaiśālī there is one of exquisite youth and beauty, Āmrapālī by name. She is versed in the sixty-four arts of love, and deserves, O king, to be enjoyed by thee." The king replied, "If that be so, Gopāla, I will betake myself to Vaiśālī and enjoy myself with her." Gopāla called his attention to the fact that danger might threaten him on the part of the Liććhavis, who had long entertained hostile sentiments towards him. The king was of opinion that men who possessed manly hearts might always go anywhere. Gopāla said, "O king, if a man attaches importance to matters of small account, let him go." The king mounted his chariot and betook himself with Gopāla to Vaiśālī.

When they arrived there, Gopāla remained in the park, but the king went to Āmrapālī's house. Then the bell began to sound. The Liććhavis of Vaiśālī became greatly excited, thinking that as the bell had rung an enemy must have penetrated into the city. A great uproar arose, and King Bimbisāra asked Amrapālī what it meant.

"O king, the houses are being searched."

"On what account?"

"On your account, O king!"

"What is to be done, then? Shall I take to flight?"

"O king, be not troubled. As my house will not be searched till seven days have elapsed, you can go on enjoying yourself for seven days; therefore enjoy yourself. When seven days are over, you will know that it is time to go." So he enjoyed himself with her, and she became with child by him. When she informed him of that, he gave her a robe and a ring, and said, "If it be a daughter, let her remain with you. But if it be a son, put on him this robe, press the seal of this ring on his neck, and send him to me."

After leaving Āmrapālī's house, the king mounted his chariot and drove away with Gopāla. But the bell sounded. The Liććhavis, under the impression that an enemy had appeared, gave orders that he should be searched for, and sent after him five hundred men armed with arrows and spears.[1] When Gopāla saw them, he asked the king whether he would do the fighting or conduct the chariot. The king replied, "I am weary, so I will conduct the chariot, but do you fight with them." When Gopāla began to enter into combat with them, the inhabitants of Vaiśālī recognised him, and said, "Honoured sirs, this is a Rākshasa of a man, let us turn back." So they returned to Vaiśālī, and passed a resolution that they would let the children of Bimbisāra take vengeance on this foe of theirs.

Now when nine months had gone by, Āmrapālī gave birth to a fine, good-looking boy. While he was a growing lad, he was playing one day with the sons of the Liććhavis of Vaiśālī, and they addressed him with scoffing words, saying, "Son of a female slave, born from among the many hundreds of thousands, who is your father?" He went in tears to his mother. She asked him why he wept,

[1] Literally "having lizard-arrow-spokes" [Eidechsen-Pfeil-Speichen]. There is perhaps a connection between *godhana*, a kind of arrow with a broad point, and *godhā*. "an iguana, a very large sort of lizard" (Childers, p. 149).—S.

and he told her the whole story. She said to him, "If any one asks you that again, reply, 'There is not one among you who has such a father as I have.' If they inquire who he is, tell them that he is King Bimbisāra."

So when the children were again at play, and they questioned him as before, he replied that there was no one among them who had such a father as he had. "Who is he?" they cried. When he had mentioned the name of King Bimbisāra, they ill treated him all the more, because his father was their enemy. He told all this with tears to his mother, who reflected that the Liććhavis of Vaiśālī were very fierce and strong, and that they might find an opportunity of putting him to death.

After thinking over all this, she found out that a number of merchants were travelling with goods to Rājagṛha, so she said to them, "You and your packages will be able to pass in without paying duty if they are sealed with the seal of this ring. Take the boy with you to the king's palace, and place him, after stamping the seal of this ring on his neck, at the gate of Rājagṛha." The merchants promised to act in accordance with these instructions. Then she gave the boy a string of pearls, and said, "O son, betake yourself in the way of business to the king; lay the string of pearls at his feet and climb up to his breast. Should any one say, 'This is a boy who knows no fear,' ask whether a son has anything to fear from his father?"

When the merchants had arrived at Rājagṛha with the boy, they gave him a bath, stamped him with the seal, and took him to the gate of the palace. The boy made his way to where the king was, laid the string of pearls at the king's feet, and climbed up to his breast. The king said, "This boy seems to be without fear." The boy replied, "Has a son anything to fear from his father?"

As the king had in this way given utterance to the words "without fear," the boy was named Prince Abhaya [or fearless.]

King Bimbisāra, who was always longing after strange women, used to mount his elephant and roam through the streets of the city, turning his eyes this way and that. There lived at that time in Rājagṛha a very rich merchant, who told his wife one day that he was obliged to go into foreign parts with merchandise. After he had gone away, his wife, who fed delicately and dressed in fine raiment, was affected by desire. So when King Bimbisāra came riding on his elephant near her house, she seated herself at the window and threw him a wreath of flowers. The king caught sight of her and called on her to come down, but she said, "O king, I am afraid. It were better that you should come in here."

The king entered her house and took his pleasure therein; and as all things were propitious, she became with child. When she had made the king aware of this, he gave her a signet ring and a motley robe, and said to her, "If a son is born unto you, clothe him in this robe, stamp this seal on his neck, and send him to me. But if a girl is born unto you, she can remain with you." Having thus spoken, he went his way.

Now when the merchant had finished his business and had arrived in the neighbourhood of Rājagṛha, he sent a message to his wife saying, "Rejoice, good wife! I have arrived here after finishing my business, and I shall return home on such and such a day." Then she reflected that she had committed so great a fault, and she knew not what she was to do when her husband arrived. In her trouble she sent tidings thereof to the king. The king sent her back word that she should be of good cheer, for he would manage in such a way that her husband would not return home so soon. Accordingly he sent a messenger to the caravan leader, letting him know that such and such precious stones were required, and that he must not come back without bringing them. So the merchant was obliged to make a long journey on account of those precious stones.

When nine months had elapsed, the merchant's wife gave birth to a fine, good-looking boy. As women, even without receiving instruction, are full of knowledge, she fed the babe on butter and honey, stamped the seal of the ring on his neck, wrapped him in the robe, laid him in a chest, and ordered her serving-maid to deposit the chest at the gate of the king's palace, after having set lamps around it and lighted them, and then to keep watch till some one should take the child in.

All this the maid did. When the king had come out on the roof of his palace, and was standing there with Prince Abhaya, he perceived the lamps at the door of his palace. So he ordered his servants to find out what was the meaning of there being lamps burning at the palace door. The servants brought back word that there was a chest there. The king ordered it to be fetched, but Prince Abhaya besought the king to give to him whatever should be found within the chest. The king acceded to his request. When the chest had been fetched and laid before the king, he gave orders that it should be opened. When it was opened a boy was seen inside it. The king asked if the child was alive or dead. He was told that it was alive. Then the king recognised the seal and the robe, and he made over the child to Prince Abhaya. The prince brought him up, and as the king had asked if he was alive, and as Prince Abhaya had looked after his maintenance, the boy received the name of Jīvaka Kumārabhaṇḍa.[1]

When Jīvaka had grown up, he was sitting one day conversing with Abhaya. Abhaya said that it was incumbent on them to learn some craft, whereby they might

[1] Or Jīvakakumārabhṛtya, the first form in Burnouf, "Lotus de la Bonne Loi," 449. the second in Childers *sub voc.* *Komārabhacco.* See Böhtlingk-Roth under *Kumārabhṛtya,* a branch of the medical art ["care of a young child, care of a pregnant or lying-in woman, midwifery."—Monier Williams.] Both names are personifications of the healing art. See also Hardy, "Manual of Buddhism," p. 238.—S.

gain their bread later on. For even before the birth of Ajātaśatru it had been predicted that the sovereign power would appertain to him. When they two had considered this matter, a white-clad coachmaker, surrounded by a number of men clad in white, entered the king's palace. When Prince Abhaya saw him, he asked the king's people who that man was. They replied that he was a coachmaker.

"How much does he earn?"

"He earns his living."

Thereupon he thought that he too, after he had asked the king, would learn coachmaking. So he went to the king and told him that he wished to learn coachmaking. The king asked whether he desired to earn his bread in that way.

"Father, kings' sons are in the habit of learning all arts."

"In that case, O son, learn coachmaking."

So he began to study coachmaking.

Jīvaka also, having seen a white-clad physician, surrounded by several men clad in white, entering the king's palace, asked who that was.

"He is a physician," was the reply.

"What does he do?"

"He cures."

"What does he earn?"

"When he cures a patient he receives his fee; but if the patient dies, he receives nothing, for nothing is given."

Thereupon Jīvaka resolved to study the healing art. He went to his father and said, "O king, allow me to study the healing art."

"O son, you are a king's son. What do you want to do with the healing art?"

"O king, kings' sons are in the habit of learning all arts."

"In that case, O son, learn this art."

So Jīvaka began to study the healing art.

When he had studied it well, but had not as yet learnt how to open skulls, he had recourse to the king of physicians, Ātreya in Takshaśilā, of whom he had heard that he understood the art of skull-opening. Going to the king, he told him that he was about to journey to Takshaśilā.

"What for?"

"The king of physicians, Ātreya, lives there, who understands the art of opening the skull. It is in order to learn that art that I wish to go there."

"Do you desire, O son, to make a living thereby?"

"O king, a man must either not study the art of healing at all, or he must study it thoroughly."

"In that case, O son, go thither."

The king wrote a letter to King Pushkarasārin, saying, "My son is going to Atreya in order to study the healing art. Provide him with all things which he may require."

In the course of time Jīvaka arrived at Takshasilā, and Pushkarasārin, after reading the letter, handed him over to Ātreya, to whom he gave orders to instruct in the healing art the prince who had come there on his account. When Ātreya began to teach him, Jīvaka mastered everything excellently at the slightest intimation. Now Ātreya was wont, when he visited a patient, to take a young Brahman along with him. One day he took Jīvaka also, gave him directions to administer such and such remedies, and then went away. Jīvaka thought, "In the present case the master has made a mistake. If the patient takes this medicine, he will die this very day. As the remedy which the master has prescribed is not good, I will contrive an expedient. So he left the house along with Ātreya, and said when he came back again, "The doctor has told me not to give the medicine which he has prescribed, but such and such a remedy." When the patient had been treated in this way, he became better. The next time Ātreya visited the patient, after asking how he was getting on, he gave directions that the same medicine should be given to him on the following day. Being asked whether he meant the medicine which he had prescribed first or that which he had afterwards ordered, he said, "What did I prescribe first, and what afterwards?" He was told, "You prescribed the one when you were present here; about the other you gave orders to Jīvaka." He said to himself, "I made a mistake. Jīvaka is endowed with great insight." Then he said that the medicine which Jīvaka had prescribed was to be given.

Ātreya became well pleased with Jīvaka, and took him along with him wherever he went. The Brahmans' sons said, "O teacher, you are well pleased with him because he is a king's son, and you bestow instruction upon him, but none upon us." He replied, "That is not the case. Jīvaka possesses great intelligence, and he is able to comprehend intuitively whatever I indicate to him." They said, "O teacher, how do you know this?" He said to the Brahmans' sons, "Go and ask the price of various commodities, you of such a one, you of such another." And having so spoken he sent them off to the market. He also gave orders to Jīvaka to ask the price of a certain article. The Brahmans' sons did as they were bid. Jīvaka did likewise. But then he said to himself, "Suppose the master asks the prices of other wares, what shall I be able to reply? I will make myself acquainted with the prices of other commodities as well." When they had all returned to their teacher, they rendered an account of those things which they had been ordered to do. Then Ātreya began to ask the price of articles which he had not mentioned, saying, "O Brahman's son, what does this or that commodity cost?" He whom he questioned replied that he did not know. In like manner did the others make reply when he questioned them. But Jīvaka, when he was asked, told him the price of every kind of goods.

"O Brahmans' sons," said Ātreya, "have ye heard?"

"We have heard."

"Behold, this is the reason why I said that Jīvaka, as he is possessed of remarkable insight, intuitively comprehends any matter on a slight intimation being given to him. I will give you yet another proof of this."

Then he said to his pupils, "Go to the pine-hill, and fetch from it that which is no remedy." They went thither, and each of them brought away that which he thought was no remedy. But Jīvaka reflected that there is scarcely anything which is not a remedy, so he brought away only a knot from a reed and a morsel of stone. Halfway back he met a herd-girl, who was carrying a jug of curdled milk and a leavening pot, and who was intending to go to Ātreya, as she was suffering greatly with her eyes. Jīvaka asked her where she was going. When she had told him, he showed her a remedy which was near at hand. She applied it, and was cured at once. Full of joy thereat she said, "Take this pot and this jug of curdled milk." He accepted the pot, but he gave her back the jug of curdled milk. Then he went on his way carrying the pot.

Now the Brahmans' sons saw some elephant tracks in the middle of the road, and took to inspecting them. When Jīvaka came up with them, he asked what those marks were. "Footprints of an elephant," they replied. He said, "Those are the footprints of an elephant, not male but female, blind of the right eye, and about to bring forth young to-day. On it a woman was riding. She too is blind of the right eye, and she will bear a son to-day."

When they had all returned to Ātreya, each of them showed what he had brought away with him. Ātreya said, "O Brahmans' sons, all these things are remedies. This one is of use in such and such an illness, and the others in other illnesses." When Jīvaka was asked what he had brought, he said, "O teacher, all things are remedies; there exists nothing which is not a remedy. However, I have brought with me the knot of a reed, a morsel of stone, and a leavening pot."

"Of what use are these things?"

"If a man is stung by a scorpion, he can be fumigated with the reed knot and healed with the leavening pot, and with the morsel of stone can a pot of curdled milk be broken at harvest-time."

Ātreya laughed. The Brahmans' sons thought that the teacher was displeased with him, so they said, "O teacher, do you suppose that is all? We saw the track of an elephant in the middle of the road, and Jīvaka declared that the track was that of a female elephant, blind of the right eye and big with young, and that it will bring forth a young elephant to-day; and also that a woman had been seated upon it, who was also pregnant and blind of the right eye, and who will give birth to-day to a son."

Ātreya asked, "O Jīvaka, is this true?"

"Yes, O teacher."

"How did you know whether the footprints were those of a male or of a female elephant?"

"O teacher," replied Jīvaka, "how could I, who was brought up in a royal family, help knowing that? The footprints of a male elephant are round, those of a female elephant are oblong."

"How did you know that she was blind of the right eye?"

"Because she had eaten the grass which grew on the left side only."

"How did you know that she is big with young?"

"Because she had pressed hard with her feet."

"How did you know that she will give birth to a male foal?"

"Because she pressed hardest on the right side."

"How did you know that a woman had been riding on the elephant?"

"From her track in the road when she alighted."

"How did you know that she was blind of the right eye?"

"Because as she walked she plucked the flowers which grew on the left side only."

"How did you know that she was with child?"

"Because the heels of her feet had made the deepest impression. All this is so, but if the teacher does not believe me, let him send one of the Brahmans' sons to the inn."

Atreya sent some of them there, and all turned out to be just as Jīvaka had said. Then Ātreya said to the Brahmans' sons, "O Brahmans' sons, have ye comprehended? After such a fashion is Jīvaka's intelligence remarkable."

Jīvaka had learnt the whole art of healing, with the exception of the operation of skull-opening. Now a man who was afflicted by a cerebral malady came to Ātreya and asked him to treat him. Atreya replied that the man must dig a pit that day and provide it with dung, and that next day he would take the case in hand. When Jīvaka heard this, he went to him and said, "O friend, all that I have learnt have I learnt for the benefit of mankind. As I have not yet learnt the operation of skull-opening, hide me away so that I may see how you perform it." Atreya promised to do so, and showed him a place to hide in.

When Ātreya came, he placed the man in the pit, opened his skull, and was about to seize the reptile with his pincers, when Jīvaka cried out, "O teacher, be not hasty in seizing it; otherwise this son of a good family might die to-day."

"Are you there, Jīvaka?" asked Atreya.

"Yes, teacher," he replied.

"How then ought I to seize the reptile?"

"O teacher, warm the pincers and touch its back therewith. Then, if the reptile draws its arms and feet together, give it a toss out."

When all this had been done the man was cured.

Then Ātreya said, "O Jīvaka, go and bathe, and then come to me. As I am much pleased, I will communicate to you after what fashion the skull is opened."

Jīvaka bathed, and Ātreya showed him after what fashion the skull ought to be opened. Then Atreya said, "O Jīvaka, as I earn my bread thereby, do not practise the art in this country."

"O teacher, I will act accordingly."

With these words Jīvaka paid his respects to Atreya. Then he went to King Pushkarasārin, and informed him that, as he had now learnt the art of healing, he was about to take his departure.

Now there were in the borderland at that time some enemies of Pushkarasārin named Pāṇḍavas. Then said the king, "O Jīvaka, my enemies the Pāṇḍavas are in the borderland; bring them to discomfiture by the force of your intelligence, and afterwards come back here. Then will we proceed after the fashion of the world." Jīvaka promised to do so. As soon as a fourfold army had been equipped, he set out, discomfited the Pāṇḍavas of the borderland, took hostages and tribute from them, and then, having returned safely, handed over to the king what he had taken. The king was greatly pleased, and bestowed presents on Jīvaka, as Jīvaka did on Ātreya.

Jīvaka journeyed by degrees to Bhadraṃkara, and having arrived in that city, spent the summer there. After learning there the Śāstra, "Language of all Creatures," he departed from Bhadraṃkara. Seeing a man carrying a load of wood to the city, of whom nothing was left but skin and bone, and the whole of whose body was dropping sweat, he said to him, "O friend, how came you into such a plight?" The man replied, "I know not. But I have got into this state since I began to carry this load." Jīvaka carefully inspected the wood, and said, "Friend, will you sell this wood?"

"Yes!"

"For how much money?"

"For five hundred Kārshāpaṇas."

Jīvaka bought the wood, and when he had examined it, he discovered the gem which brings all beings to belief. The virtue of the gem is of this kind: when it is placed before an invalid, it illuminates him as a lamp lights up all the objects in a house, and so reveals the nature of his malady.

When Jīvaka had gradually made his way to the Udumbara land, he found there a man who was measuring with a measure, and who, when he had finished measuring, inflicted a wound upon his head with the measure. When Jīvaka saw this, he asked him why he behaved in that way.

"My head itches greatly."

"Come here and I will look at it."

The man lay down and Jīvaka examined his head. Then he laid on the man's head the gem which brings all beings to belief, and it immediately became manifest that there was a centipede inside. Thereupon Jīvaka said, "O man, there is a centipede inside your head." The man touched his feet and said, "Cure me." Jīvaka promised to do so, but he thought, "I will act according to the words of the teacher." So he said, "O man, dig a pit to-day and have dung in readiness. I will take your case in hand to-morrow." The man touched his feet and went away. Next day Jīvaka placed the man in the pit, opened the skull with the proper instrument, touched the back of the centipede with the heated pincers, and then, when the centipede drew its arms and feet together, he seized it with the pincers and pulled it out. Thereupon the patient recovered. The man gave Jīvaka five hundred Kārshāpaṇas, which he sent to Ātreya.

After this Jīvaka came to the Rohitaka land. A householder had died there who had possessed a park with beautiful flowers, fruits, and water, and who, as he had been excessively fond of the garden, had been born again there among the demons. When his son became master of the house, he appointed a certain man to watch over the park. The watchman, however, was killed by that demon, as was also a second watchman, after which the son of the deceased householder abandoned the park. Thereupon a dropsical man, whom all the doctors had given up, came to that park and took up his quarters there for the night, thinking that it would not much matter if the demon were to kill him. Now it happened that Jīvaka also spent the night in this park. The demon began to threaten the dropsical man. Then stepped forward the Dropsy and said, "As I have already taken possession of this man, wherefore do you threaten him? Is there no one here who will fumigate you with the smoke of goats' hair? That would make you fly twelve yojanas away?" The demon replied, "Is there no one here to give you radish-seed pounded and beaten up in butter? Thereby would you be broken to pieces." Jīvaka heard all this, and next morning he visited the householder, and asked him why he had abandoned the park which was so rich in flowers, fruits, and water. The householder told him all that had occurred. Then said Jīvaka, "O householder, fumigate the park with the smoke of goats' hair. Then will the demon fly twelve yojanas away." The householder did so, and the demon flew twelve yojanas away. This householder also gave five hundred Kārshāpaṇas to Jīvaka, who sent them as before to Ātreya.

Afterwards Jīvaka asked the dropsical man why he abode in the demon-haunted park. The man told him everything that had occurred. Jīvaka said to him, "Swallow radish-seed pounded and beaten up in butter, and you will recover." The man took the remedy and recovered his health. This man also gave five hundred Kārshāpaṇas to Jīvaka, who, as before, sent them to Ātreya.

Jīvaka gradually made his way to Mathurā, where he rested under a tree outside the city. Now it had come to pass there that a wrestler was smitten by an antagonist, and his bowels were displaced, so that he died and was carried out to be buried. A vulture and her little ones had their nest on a tree, and one young vulture said, "Mother, give us flesh." She replied, "Children, where is flesh to be found?" The young birds said, "Mother, as that Malla who was smitten in wrestling is dead and has been carried out, flesh is to be found there where he is."

"O children, the king of doctors, Jīvaka, has come here, and will set him to rights again."

"Mother, in what manner will he set him to rights?"

"By applying a certain powder to his bowels."

Jīvaka overheard all this. So he arose and went to where the corpse was, and inquired, saying, "Honoured sirs, whom have ye here?"

"A man who died after being struck down while wrestling," was the reply.

"Lay him down that I may look at him," said Jīvaka.

The dead man was laid down, and Jīvaka placed on his head the gem which brings all beings to belief. Perceiving that the man's entrails had been displaced, he blew some powder into the body through a hollow reed, and as soon as the powder had reached the entrails the man recovered. This man also gave five hundred Kārshāpaṇas to Jīvaka, who, as before, sent them to Atreya.

Now there was in Mathurā a householder who had a wife of consummate youth and beauty, whom he loved exceedingly. After his death he was born again as a reptile in the lower part of his wife's body. . . . When she heard that the physician Jīvaka had arrived, she went to see him, and said that she was ill, and that he must treat her. . . . He ordered her to lay aside her garments, and then he expelled the worm in the way in which, as will presently be described, he got rid of the centipede which had crept into a man's ear. Whereupon the patient recovered. As her desires were enhanced by passion, she made overtures to him, but he shut his ears and said, "You seem to me like a Rākshasī. I who have cured you am contented with having done so." She also gave him five hundred Kārshāpaṇas, which likewise he sent to Atreya.

After this Jīvaka went on by degrees and reached the shore of the river Yamunā. There he saw a corpse which, when the fish twitched the sinews of its heels, opened its eyes and smiled. Observing all this, he became aware of the connection which exists between the sinews and the rest of the body.

Having gradually made his way to Vaiśālī, he found there a wrestler the ball of whose eye protruded in consequence of a blow from a fist. Jīvaka paid him a visit, pulled the sinews of his heel, and restored the eye to its right place. This man also gave him five hundred Kārshāpaṇas, which he gave to Abhaya's mother.

At Vaiśālī there lived a man into whose ear a centipede had crept, and had therein given birth to seven hundred young ones. Tormented by his pains in the ear, this man went to Jīvaka and intreated him to cure him. Jīvaka said to himself, "Hitherto I have acted in accordance with my teacher's instructions, but now I will act according to my own intelligence." He said to the man, "Go and make a hut out of foliage, carpet it with blue stuff, place a drum underneath, and make the ground warm." The man provided everything as he was told. Then Jīvaka made the man lie down, sprinkled the ground with water, and beat the drum. Thereupon the centipede, thinking that the summer was come, crept out. Then Jīvaka placed a piece of meat on the ear. The reptile turned back, but presently came out again with its young ones, and they all laid hold of the piece of meat. Whereupon Jīvaka flung it into the flesh-pot, and the man recovered his health. He gave Jīvaka five hundred Kārshāpaṇas, and Jīvaka gave them to Abhaya's mother.

After a time Jīvaka came to Rājagṛha, and King Bimbisāra, hearing of his arrival, ordered Prince Ajātaśatru to go out to meet his elder brother. The prince set out on the way. But when Jīvaka heard that Prince Ajātaśatru was coming to meet him, he reflected that if he consented to this reception, Ajātaśatru, when he became king, might do him some harm. So he turned back, and entered the city by another gate.

On another occasion, when Jīvaka was strolling along surrounded by a great crowd, a Brahman who was afflicted with an eye disease accosted him, and begged him to prescribe a remedy. He replied angrily, "Sprinkle the eye with ashes." The man, who was of a simple nature, did as he was told, and he became well.

Another man, also afflicted with an eye disease, was on his way to visit Jīvaka, when the Brahman saw him and asked him where he was going. When the man had told him, the Brahman said, "What need have you of Jīvaka? Do what he told me to do." The man gave heed to the words of the Brahman, sprinkled his eye with ashes, and became blind.

At another time, a tumour formed on the crown of King Bimbisāra's head. He ordered his ministers to summon the physicians. The ministers did so, and the king told the physicians to treat the tumour. They said, "O king, as the great physician Jīvaka is here, why should we deal with it?" So the king ordered Jīvaka to be summoned. When he had been introduced, the king asked him to undertake the case. He consented to do so, on the condition that he should be allowed to give the king his bath. Then he anointed the tumour with myrobalan and with ripening substances, and he poured over it five hundred jugs of water in which such substances had been infused. When it was ripe he secretly touched it with a razor and squeezed it out. Then he applied healing remedies, and poured over it five hundred jugs of water in which such substances had been infused. Whereupon the wound healed so completely that the skin and the hair were perfectly even. When the king's bath was finished, he said that Jīvaka was now to begin the operation. Jīvaka replied, "O king, be pleased to partake of food." When the king had eaten, he again called upon Jīvaka to proceed. "O king," said Jīvaka, "the operation has been performed." The king would not believe this, but when he felt with his hand, he could not find the place where the hurt had been. Moreover, when he took a mirror and looked in it, he could see nothing. He asked his wife, but neither could she find the place where the hurt had been. The king was greatly astonished, and he said to his ministers, "Honoured sirs, appoint Jīvaka king of the physicians." But the man who had become blind said, "O king, is it from love towards your son or on account of his knowledge of things that you give him this appointment?" The king replied, "On account of his knowledge of things." The blind man said, "However this may be, he has not cured me." Jīvaka said, "O man, I have never seen you before; how, then, could I have cured you?" The blind man replied, "That is true; but he to whom you did prescribe a remedy taught me what to do."

"What did he teach you to do?"

"Such and such things."

"Your nature and that man's nature are different," said Jīvaka. "Now do this and that, and you will be made whole."

The man acted accordingly and was made whole. Then he said, "O king, be pleased to let Jīvaka be appointed king of the physicians." So Jīvaka was seated upon an elephant, and with great pomp was installed king of the physicians.

There lived in Rājagṛha a householder who suffered from a swelling of the glands,[1] and had been given up by all the physicians. He resolved to go to Jīvaka. If he could be cured by him, well and good; if not, then he was ready to die. He came to Jīvaka, and entreated him to

[1] See Böhtlingk-Roth under *gulma* ["any glandular enlargement in the abdomen, as that of the mesenteric gland, &c, so as to be seen externally," &c.—Monier Williams.]—S.

cure him. Jīvaka said that the remedies which his case required were hard to find. Thus the man thought, "As even Jīvaka has given me up, what is there for me to do? As my time has come, I will die of my own accord." So he went away to the cemetery. Now a corpse was being burnt there, and an ichneumon and a lizard, which were fighting with one another, fell into the fire. Being tormented by hunger, he devoured them both. Then he drank some rain-water which he found in the cemetery, and afterwards he betook himself to a cattle-shed in the neighbourhood of the cemetery, where he fed upon kodrava[1] porridge and sour milk mixed with butter. Thereupon the tumour gave way, and he, after it had discharged upwards and downwards, was restored to health.

At another time Vaidehī suffered from a tumour in the groin. She communicated the fact to the king, who ordered Jīvaka to cure his stepmother. Jīvaka undertook the case, prepared a poultice, and asked her to sit down upon it. After examining the poultice on which she had sat, he perceived where the diseased spot was. Then he applied maturing means, and when he saw that the tumour was ripe, he concealed a lancet in the poultice, and gave directions to the queen-mother as to how she was to sit down upon it and rise up again. She acted accordingly, and the tumour gave way as soon as it was pricked by the lancet. He then caused it to be washed with bitter water mixed with healing substances, and applied healing substances to it, after which she became well.

Jīvaka went to the king, who asked him if he had healed his stepmother. He replied that he had done so.

"But you have not looked upon her without her clothing?"

"No!"

"How then did you manage?"

When Jīvaka had described what he had contrived, the

[1] *Kodrava*, "a species of grain eaten by the poor, *Paspalum Scrobiculatum.*"

king marvelled greatly, and gave orders to the ministers to install Jīvaka a second time as king of the physicians.

But the man with the swelling of the glands, to whom Jīvaka had said that it would be difficult to find a remedy for his ailment, asked the king whether he had ordered Jīvaka to be installed as king of the physicians out of love for his son or on account of that son's knowledge of things. The king replied, "On account of his knowledge."

"However this may be, he has not cured me."

"O man," said Jīvaka, "I did not undertake your case. I merely said that it would be difficult to find you a remedy."

"What is the remedy in my case?" asked the man.

"If on the fourteenth day of the waxing moon," replied Jīvaka, "a fair-haired man dies and is burnt at the cemetery; and if at that time an ichneumon and a lizard are fighting with one another and fall into the fire; and if you eat both of them, and then drink of the water of the rain poured down by Mahesvara on the cemetery; and if you afterwards partake of kodrava porridge and curdled milk mixed with butter, in that case you will recover. It was because I thought of all this that I told you that the remedy would be a difficult one to find."

Then the man said, "Your knowledge is excellent, for these are the very things of which I have partaken." And he joyfully exclaimed, "O king, as Jīvaka deserves to be king of the physicians, let him be appointed to that office."

And so Jīvaka was for the second time installed as king of the physicians.

At the time when Ajātaśatru, impelled by Devadatta, the friend of vice, deprived of his life his father, the lawful king, he fell ill with an internal tumour. He called upon the physicians to cure him. They replied, "O king, as your elder brother is here, Jīvaka, the king of the physicians, wherefore should we cure you?" So the king told his ministers to call in Jīvaka. This was done, and the king charged him to remove the tumour, which he undertook to do.

Jīvaka reflected that the tumour might yield to one of two influences, either that of excessive joy or that of excessive wrath. And that as it would be impossible to arouse excessive joy within so sinful a man, it would be necessary at all risks to excite in him excessive wrath. So he told the king that he could heal him, provided that the king would feed on Prince Udajibhadra's flesh.

When the king heard this he became furious, and cried, "Very good! I have killed my father, and you want to put Udajibhadra to death. Then if I die of this complaint you will be king."

Jīvaka replied, "Such are the means of effecting a cure; in no other way can I restore you to health."

When the king had given his consent, Jīvaka brought Prince Udajibhadra before the king, robed in all stately array, and said, "O king, take pains to look well at Prince Udajibhadra, for after this you will not be able to see him again." Having thus exhibited him, he took him to his own house and there hid him away.

He then went to the cemetery of Śitavana in search of human flesh. There was no lack of corpses there, and from one of these corpses he took some flesh and carried it away with him. This he prepared with the most excellent materials, and then he served it up to the king at dinner-time. When King Ajātaśatru had received the bowl of flesh-broth, and was preparing to partake of it, Jīvaka seized it, hit him over the head with it, and said to him, "O evil-doer, you have taken the life of your own father, and now you want to feed on the flesh of your own son."

The king cried in his wrath, "If this be so, why have you put him to death?"

As he thus broke out in anger, his tumour gave way, and discharged upwards and downwards, its contents coming to light mixed with blood from the wound.

When the king saw that, he fell fainting to the ground. But after he had been sprinkled with water he came to himself, and then, when he had bathed and partaken of strengthening nourishment, he recovered his health.

After that, Jīvaka brought before the king Prince Udajibhadra arrayed in all state, and touched the king's feet and said, "O king, here stands Prince Udajibhadra. I would not deprive an ant of its life, not to speak of the prince. But as it was only by this contrivance that the king's life could be saved, therefore did I contrive it." The king marvelled greatly, and gave orders to his ministers to install Jīvaka for the third time as the king of the physicians. The ministers set him upon an elephant and with great pomp installed him for the third time as king of the physicians.

VII.

VISAKHA.[1]

Mṛgadhara, the first minister of King Prasenajit of Kośala, after he had married a wife of birth like unto his own, had seven sons. To six of these he gave names at his pleasure, but the youngest one he called Viśākha.

After his wife's death he arranged marriages for his six elder sons, but they and their wives gave themselves up to dress, and troubled themselves in no wise with household affairs.

The householder Mṛgadhara was sitting one day absorbed in thought, resting his cheek upon his arm. A Brahman, who was on friendly terms with him, saw him sitting thus absorbed in thought, and asked him what was the cause of his behaviour. He replied, "My sons and their wives have given themselves up to dress, and do not trouble themselves about household affairs, so that the property is going to ruin."

"Why do you not arrange a marriage for Viśākha?"

"Who can tell whether he will make things better, or bring them to still greater ruin?"

"If you will trust to me, I will look for a maiden for him."

The minister consented, and the Brahman went his way. In the course of his researches he came to the land of Champā. In it there lived a householder named Balamitra, whose daughter Viśākhā was fair to see, well pro-

[1] Kah-gyur, iii. 71*-80*. Cf. Benfey, *Ausland*, 1859, p. 487, "Die kluge Dirne;" Spence Hardy, Manual of Buddhism, pp. 220-227, 364.—S.

portioned, in the bloom of youth, intelligent and clever. Just as the Brahman arrived, she and some other girls who were in quest of amusement were setting out for a park. On seeing the girls, he thought that he would like to look at them a little. So he followed slowly after them, occupied in regarding them. The girls, who were for the most part of a frivolous nature, sometimes ran, sometimes skipped, sometimes rolled about, sometimes laughed, sometimes spun round, sometimes sang, and did other undignified things. But Viśākhā, with the utmost decorum, at an even pace walked slowly along with them. When they came to the park, the other girls undressed at the edge of the tank, entered into it, and began to sport. But Viśākhā lifted up her clothes by degrees as she went into the water, and by degrees let them down again as she came out of the water, so circumspect was she in her behaviour. After their bath, when the girls had assembled at a certain spot, they first partook of food themselves, and then gave to their attendants to eat; but Viśākhā first of all gave food to the persons in attendance, and then herself began to eat.

When the girls had finished their eating and drinking and had enjoyed the charm of the park, they went away. As there was water to be waded through on the road, the girls took off their boots and walked through it, but Viśākhā kept her boots on. They went a little farther and came to a wood. Into this Amra wood she entered, keeping her parasol up, though the others had discarded theirs. Presently a wind arose together with rain, and the other girls took shelter in a temple, but Viśākhā remained in the open air. The Brahman, who had followed her, and had noted her characteristics and her behaviour, marvelled greatly and began to question her, saying—

"O maiden, whose daughter are you?"

"I am Balamitra's daughter."

"O maiden, be not angry if I ask you a few questions."

She smiled at first, and then said, "O uncle, why should I be angry? Please to ask them."

"While these girls, as they went, were all running, skipping, rolling, turning round, singing, and doing other undignified things, you wended your way slowly, decorously, and in a seemly manner, reaching the park together with them."

Viśākhā replied, "All girls are a merchandise which their parents vend. If in leaping or rolling I were to break an arm or a leg, who then would woo me? I should certainly have to be kept by my parents as long as I lived."

"Good, O maiden; I understand."

He said to her next, "These girls took off their clothes at a certain place, and went into the water and sported in it unclothed, but you lifted up your clothes by degrees as you went deeper into the water."

"O uncle, it is necessary that women should be shamefaced and shy, and so it would not be well that any one should look upon me unclothed."

"O maiden, who would see you there?"

"O uncle, you would have seen me there yourself."

"Good, O maiden; that also I comprehend."

He said to her further, "These girls first took food themselves and then gave to the persons in attendance; but you first gave food to the persons in attendance, and then took your own."

"O uncle, that was for this reason: we, reaping the fruits of our merits, constantly have feast-days; but they, reaping the fruits of their trouble, very seldom obtain great things."

"Good, O maiden; I comprehend this also."

He asked her, moreover, "While all the world wears boots on dry land, why did you keep yours on in the water?"

"O uncle, the world is foolish. It is precisely when one is in water that one should wear boots."

"For what reason?"

"On dry land one can see tree-stems, thorns, stones, prickles, fragments of fish-scales or shells of reptiles, but in the water none of these things can be seen. Therefore we ought to wear boots in the water and not upon dry land."

"Good, O maiden; this also I understand."

Then he asked her this question: "These girls kept their parasols up in the sun; you kept yours up in the wood under the shade of the trees. What was the meaning of that?"

"O uncle, the world is foolish. It is precisely when in a wood that one must keep a parasol up."

"For what reason?"

"Because a wood is always full of birds and monkeys. The birds let fall their droppings and pieces of bones, and the monkeys their muck and scraps of the fruit they eat. Besides, as they are of a wild nature, they go springing from bough to bough, and bits of wood come falling down. When one is in the open this does not happen, or, if it takes place, it is but seldom. Therefore a parasol must be kept open in a wood; in the open it is not necessary to do so."

"Good, O maiden; this also I comprehend."

Presently he said, "These girls took refuge in a temple when the wind arose with rain, but you remained in the open air."

"O uncle, one certainly ought to remain in the open air and not take refuge in a temple."

"O maiden, what is the reason for that?"

"O uncle, such empty temples are never free from orphans, bastards, and sharpers. If one of them were to touch me on a limb or joint as I entered such a temple, would not that be unpleasant to my parents? Moreover, it is better to lose one's life in the open than to enter an empty temple."

Full of delight at the demeanour of the maiden, the Brahman betook himself to the dwelling of the householder Balamitra and said, desiring to obtain the maiden, "May it be well! May it be good!"

The people of the house said, "O Brahman, it is not yet the time for asking; but what do you ask for?"

"I ask for your daughter."

"On whose behalf?"

"On behalf of the son, Viśākha by name, of Mṛgadhara, the first minister of Śrāvastī."

They replied, "It is true that we and he are of the same caste, but his country lies too far away."

The Brahman said, "It is precisely in a far-away country that a man should choose a husband for his daughter."

"How so?"

"If she is married in the neighbourhood, joy increases when news comes that she is prosperous; but if a misfortune occurs, a man's property may be brought to nought, he being exhausted by gifts, sacrifices, and tokens of reverence."

They said, "This being so, we will give our daughter."

Thereupon the Brahman, having uttered a wish for a happy result, returned to Śrāvastī, and there, after recovering from the fatigue of the journey, went to see the minister, Mṛgadhara, and described to him the maiden's youth, beauty, and intelligence, as well as her demeanour and manner of eating. Then he said, "With great toil have I wandered through many lands and cities, and with much trouble have I found her. Now go and fetch her."

The first minister, Mṛgadhara, took note of the day and hour, and found that the stars were propitious. Then he set forth and fetched away Viśākhā with great pomp as his son's spouse. The mother gave her daughter, when she was leaving for her husband's land, the following counsel: "O daughter, always honour the sun and the moon, pay attention to the fire, wipe dirt off the mirror, and wear white clothes. You shall take but not give. You shall keep your word. When you rise up, you shall yield your place to none. You shall partake of savoury food. You shall sleep tranquilly. You shall apply a ladder."

When Mṛgadhara heard this, he thought that the girl had received a quite wrong piece of advice, and that he must dissuade her from following it and give her proper directions. The loving mother, with troubled heart and eyes full of tears, embraced, her daughter, and said with sorrowful voice, "O daughter, this is the last time that I shall see you."

Viśākhā replied by way of admonition, "O mother, were you born here? Is not the maiden rather born in the house of her relatives? Is that house your home? Is it not rather this one here? Although I was born here, I shall live there. As that which unites undoubtedly underlies separation, be pleased not to wail but rather to keep silence."

After that Mṛgadhara went his way.

Viśākhā and her husband with the attendants from her house went on board a ship. Soon afterwards a mare which had thrown a foal was to be brought on board the ship. As it felt that its foal would be restless on land, it resisted, and could not be got on board. This gave rise to much noise. When Viśākhā heard it she asked what was the cause. Being told how it arose, she gave directions that the foal should be brought on board first, in which case the mare would follow of its own accord. Her orders were obeyed, and the mare went on board. Mṛgadhara asked the men why they had come so late.

"Because the mare would not come on board."

"Then how was it induced to come?"

"It did so after the Champā maiden had told us how to manage, and we had embarked the foal before the mare."

"The Champā maiden is wise."

On their way, the travellers had on one occasion chosen their quarters for the night, and Mṛgadhara's tent was pitched under the projecting part of a hill. When Viśākhā saw it she asked to whom it belonged. "To Mṛgadhara," was the reply. "Move it away from there," she said. "Why should it be moved?" "Because," she replied, "if the projecting part of the hill were to fall while he was asleep, he would certainly be crushed to death. Then I should all my life be exposed to the annoyance of having people say that my husband married a wife, whose father-in-law died on the way before she entered his house."

After the bed had been moved away the projecting mass of the hill fell down. A great crowd came running together, full of anxiety lest the householder should have been crushed. But he exclaimed, "Honoured sirs, here am I; be not afraid, but look after my bed." "It has been removed," was the reply. "Who did that?" he asked. "Viśākhā," they replied. He said, "The Champā maiden is wise."

Later on, when they had taken up their quarters in an old park, and Mṛgadhara's couch had been prepared in an empty temple, Viśākhā saw it and asked whose it was. "That is the master's couch," was the reply. "Move it away," she said. "Why so?" "Because," she replied, "if the temple were to fall down he would be crushed to death, and trouble would come upon me."

After the couch had been removed the temple fell down, and people came running up, and so forth as before.

By and by they reached Śrāvastī, and after they had recovered from the fatigues of the journey and presented ornaments to friends, relatives, and connections, Viśākhā began to attend to the domestic affairs of the family. As Mṛgadhara's daughters-in-law took it in turns to look after the food for the household, Viśākhā received instructions to provide it on the seventh day. As the time drew near for her turn to come, she daily rolled into pellets and desiccated what remained over of the perfumes used by her husband and his parents. Of the powder which she thus each day obtained she took some out of the box; the rest she mixed with oil and divided it into equal portions. When her turn came next day, she took care that spirituous liquors were prepared, and she renewed the freshness of her own and her husband's faded garlands. When the morning came, she bestowed upon the labourers oranges, perfumes, flowers, and meat and drink. They were greatly pleased, and thought that, after a long time, the householder's old wife had looked after them. And in the course of the day they did a double amount of work.

When Mṛgadhara inspected the work towards evening and saw that much had been done, he asked if additional day-labourers had been employed. Being told that this was not the case, he asked what the reason was that a double amount of work had been accomplished. The reply was, "O master, as is the food so is the labour." "What is the meaning of that?" he asked. Whereupon a full account was given to him of how everything had come to pass.

Mṛgadhara's sons spoke about this to their wives, who said, "If we, like Viśākhā, were to steal things from the house and thereby give pleasure to the day-labourers, the master and the labourers would be pleased with us too." Whereupon Mṛgadhara said to Viśākhā, "O daughter, in what manner did you prepare the food?" She told him all about it. Mṛgadhara was much pleased, asked her to manage the affairs of the household, and ordered all the people of the house to perform, according to Viśākhā's wishes, whatsoever tasks she might allot to them. She thus became the mistress of the house, and as she was excellent in her behaviour and in her whole nature, all the people of the house rejoiced.

At another time it happened that some geese from Uttarakurudvīpa flew over the house, carrying rice which had grown without any ploughing or sowing having taken place. The geese in Rājagṛha saw them and cackled, and they in their turn cackled, not being able to subdue the force of instinct, so that some of the ears of rice fell on the roofs of Rājagṛha. The king distributed them among the ministers, and Mṛgadhara gave his share to Viśākhā. She placed them in a box and afterwards handed them over to the husbandmen. They were greatly pleased, and prepared a small field for them. And after it had been sowed with their seed at the fitting time and the deity had sent down rain, there grew up splendid rice, answering to the seed. Next year, moreover, they had a very abundant harvest, and in the following year a still more abundant one. Consequently all the granaries were filled with the rice brought by the geese.

When it came to pass that Prasenajit, the king of Kośala, was attacked by an illness, and all the physicians were summoned and consulted, they gave it as their opinion that if some of the rice brought by the geese could be found, and soup were to be made of it, and the king were to partake thereof, in that case he would recover. So the king called the ministers together, and asked them what they had done with the ears of rice which the geese had brought, and which he had given to them. Some of them said, "O king, we gave them to the temple;" and others, "We threw them into the fire;" or others, "We fastened them up in the vestibule." But Mṛgadhara said, "I gave them to Viśākhā. I will inquire what she has done with them." When he asked Viśākhā she replied, "O master, does some one wish to partake of the geese-brought rice?"

"As the king is ill, the doctors have prescribed for him the rice which the geese brought hither."

Then Viśākhā filled a golden vase with the geese-brought rice and sent it to the king. The king ate thereof and recovered.

On another occasion some country folks came bringing a mare and her foal. As they could not tell which was the mare and which the foal, the king ordered the ministers to examine them closely, and to report to him on the matter. The ministers examined them both for a whole day, became weary, and arrived at no conclusion after all. When Mṛgadhara went home in the evening, Viśākhā touched his feet and said, "O master, wherefore do ye return so late?" He told her everything that had occurred. Then Viśākhā said, "O master, what is there to investigate in that? Fodder should be laid before them in equal parts. The foal, after rapidly eating up its own share, will begin to devour its mother's also; but the mother, without eating, will hold up her head like this. That is the proper test."

Mṛgadhara told this to the ministers, who applied the test according to these instructions, and after daybreak they reported to the king, "This is the mother, O king, and that is the foal." The king asked how they knew that.

"O king, the case is so and so."

"How was it you did not know that yesterday?"

"O king, how could we know it? Viśākhā has instructed us since."

Said the king, "The Champā maiden is wise."

It happened that a man who was bathing had left his boots on the bank. Another man came up, tied the boots round his head, and began to bathe likewise. When the first man had done bathing and came out of the water, he missed the boots. The other man said, "Hey, man, what are you looking for?"

"My boots."

"Where are your boots? When you have boots, you should tie them round your head, as I do, before going into the water."

As a dispute arose between the two men as to whom the boots belonged to, they both had recourse to the king. The king told the ministers to investigate the case thoroughly, and to give the boots to the proper owner. The ministers began to investigate the case, and examined first the one man and then the other. Each of the men affirmed that he was the owner. While these assertions were being made, the day came to an end, and in the evening the ministers returned home wearied out, without having brought the matter to a satisfactory conclusion. Viśākhā questioned Mṛgadhara, and he told her all about it, whereupon she said, "O master, what is there to investigate? Say to one of them, 'Take one of the boots, and to the other man, 'Take the other boot.' The real owner will say in that case, 'Why should my two boots be separated?' But the other, the man to whom they do not really belong, will say, 'What good do I gain by this if I only get one boot?' That is the proper test to apply."

Mṛgadhara went and told this to the ministers, and so forth, as is written above, down to the words, "The king said, 'The Champā maiden is wise.'"

It happened that some merchants brought a stem of sandal-wood to the king as a present, but no one knew which was the upper end of it and which the lower. So the king ordered his ministers to settle the question. They spent a whole day in examining the stem, but they could make nothing of it. In the evening they returned to their homes. Mṛgadhara again told Viśākhā all about the matter, and she said, "O master, what is there to investigate? Place the stem in water. The root end will then sink, but the upper end will float upwards. That is the proper test."

Mṛgadhara communicated this to the ministers, and so forth, as is written above, down to the words, "The king said, 'The Champā maiden is wise.'"

There was a householder in a hill-village who, after he had married in his own rank, remained without either son or daughter. As he longed earnestly for a child, he took unto himself a concubine. Thereupon his wife, who was of a jealous disposition, had recourse to a spell for the purpose of rendering that woman barren. But as that woman was quite pure, she became with child, and at the end of nine months bare a son. Then she reflected thus:

"As the worst of all enmities is the enmity between a wife and a concubine, and the stepmother will be sure to seek for a means of killing the child, what ought my husband, what ought I to do? As I shall not be able to keep it alive, I had better give it to her."

After taking counsel with her husband, who agreed with her in the matter, she said to the wife, "O sister, I give you my son; take him." The wife thought, "As she who has a son ranks as the mistress of the house, I will bring him up."

After she had taken charge of the boy the father died. A dispute arose between the two women as to the possession of the house, each of them asserting that it belonged to her. They had recourse to the king. He ordered his ministers to go to the house and to make inquiries as to the ownership of the son. They investigated the matter, but the day came to an end before they had brought it to a satisfactory conclusion. In the evening they returned to their homes. Viśākhā again questioned Mṛgadhara, who told her everything. Viśākhā said, "What need is there of investigation? Speak to the two women thus: 'As we do not know to which of you two the boy belongs, let her who is the strongest take the boy.' When each of them has taken hold of one of the boy's hands, and he begins to cry out on account of the pain, the real mother will let go, being full of compassion for him, and knowing that if her child remains alive she will be able to see it again; but the other, who has no compassion for him, will not let go. Then beat her with a switch, and she will thereupon confess the truth as to the whole matter. That is the proper test."

Mṛgadhara told this to the ministers, and so forth, as is written above, down to the words, "The king said, 'The Champā maiden is wise.'"

After a time Mṛgadhara fell ill. One day the physician gave him a remedy and he obtained relief. The next day the physician gave him something which was not a remedy, and he was the worse for it. Viśākhā thought, "Why does the minister find relief one day and on the next day feel worse?" So she examined the remedy which brought relief, and employed it again. Then she closed the door to the physicians and treated the patient herself. Whereupon he recovered. Mṛgadhara considered why it was that he had felt better one day and worse the next, and that now that no physician came he had recovered, so he asked Viśākhā, and so forth as before.

Prasenajit, king of Kośala, had an overseer of elephants named Śrīvardhana. The king reprimanded him one day. When Viśākhā heard of that she said to Mṛgadhara, "O master, it is right that Śrīvardhana should be pardoned." He replied, "O daughter, do you bring about the pardon." Thereupon she said to the king, "O king, Śrīvardhana has been guilty of an error. Be pleased to forgive him. The king forgave him.

"O king, if you forgive him, be pleased to restore him his position."

The king did so. Śrīvardhana knew that he had Viśākhā to thank for his pardon, and he resolved to make a return for that.

At another time Mṛgadhara was attacked by a disease of the private parts, and he was ashamed to let Viśākhā treat him for it. She said to herself, "Wherefore is the master ashamed? May not a daughter nurse her father? Still he is ashamed." Then she thought that, as he would not let himself be nursed by her, he must take to himself a wife. So she betook herself to Śrīvardhana's house, and there, after a greeting, took a seat. Śrīvardhana, who had one daughter, bade her touch Viśākhā's feet, but Viśākhā said, "Rather ought I to touch your feet." And she added thereto, "May it be well! may it be well!" Thereupon Śrīvardhana inquired what it was she asked for.

"For your daughter."

"On behalf of whom?"

"Of my father-in-law."

He said nothing in reply.

Śrīvardhana's wife asked what there was to prevent her being given to him.

"O good wife, as we owe a debt of gratitude to Viśākhā, let her be given."

"Such being the case, we will give her."

Thereupon Mṛgadhara, with great pomp, took her to himself as his wife. After which she, and not Viśākhā, nursed him.

Mṛgadhara once said to Viśākhā, "Answer, O daughter." She said, "O master, have I done anything wrong?"

"O daughter, have you not utterly neglected to obey the directions which your mother gave you?"

"O master, I have obeyed them all. Inasmuch as the words, 'Honour the sun and the moon,' signify that the father-in-law and the mother-in-law must be considered by the daughter-in-law as the sun and the moon, therefore have I testified my respect for those relatives. Inasmuch as the words, 'Pay attention to the fire,' signify that the husband ought to be valued by the wife like fire, impossible to be too well cared for and fostered, therefore have I taken care of my husband as one would of the fire. Inasmuch as the words, 'Wipe the mirror clean,' signify that the house ought to be swept and cleansed like a mirror, therefore have I cleansed the house every day. The words, 'Wear white clothes,' signify that when one is engaged in housework one wears other clothes, but must put on white clothes for a sacrifice or when about to pass into the husband's presence; to all this I have paid attention. The words, 'You shall take but not give,' signify that one should never say a bad word to any one. In this matter also I have followed my instructions. The words, 'Take heed to your speech,' signify that no secret ought to be divulged. To this also I have adhered. The words, 'When you stand up, yield not your place to any other person,' amount to this: 'As you are a becoming daughter-in-law, you must sit in a special place.' And I have sat apart. The words, 'Eat savoury meats,' mean that one should eat when one has become very hungry. I have never taken any food until after giving theirs to the household. The words, 'You shall sleep softly,' mean that at night, after all the household work is finished and all implements put away, as there is no need of staying up, one should sleep. I have acted accordingly, always reflecting that this thing was well done and that thing badly. The words, 'You shall apply a ladder,' have this meaning. Like as one who, having in an earlier state followed the path of the ten virtuous works, has arrived among the gods, so must you, born here in the human world, attain to that by deeds, bestowing gifts, gaining merits, and avoiding sins. This treasure-ladder is like unto a staircase to heaven. All this also have I followed as well as I could."

"Excellent, Viśākhā, excellent! Your mother is a wise mother; and as you have guessed the meaning of what your mother said enigmatically, you are still wiser than she."

Then Mṛgadhara thought, "If Bhagavant allows it, I will call Viśākhā my mother." Going to Bhagavant, he touched his feet and said, "O worthy of reverence, is it allowable for a man to call his daughter-in-law his mother?" Bhagavant replied, "If she has five qualities. If she is a nurse to the sick, if she lives in wedlock as a decorous wife, if she protects living creatures, if she is a good guardian of property, and if she has inherited wisdom—in that case she may be called mother."

Thereupon Mṛgadhara went to King Prasenajit of Kośala and asked for leave to call Viśākhā his mother. The king said, "As Viśākhā has taken care of me also, I will, after consulting my grandmother, call her my sister."

So he asked his grandmother, and she said that he might justly call Viśākhā by that name.

King Araṇemi Brahmadatta had become attached to the daughter of a servant-maid, and that attachment had resulted in the birth of a son, to whom the name of Balamitra was given. Balamitra was banished from the country by his grandfather on account of an offence, and he went to Champā. As Viśākhā was his daughter, she might well be called Prasenajit's sister.

The king gave orders that Viśākhā should be set upon an elephant, and that public proclamation should be made that she, Viśākhā, was Mṛgadhara's mother and King Prasenajit's sister. In what had been a park she built a monastery, and made it over to the community of Bhikshus of the four parts of the world. Accordingly it is stated by the Sthaviras in the Sūtras that the Buddha Bhagavant abode at Śrāvastī in the palace of Mṛgadhara's mother Viśākhā, in what had been the park (Pūrvārāma).[1]

At another time Viśākhā produced thirty-two eggs. When Mṛgadhara heard of it, he sat for some time absorbed in meditation, resting his head upon his hand. He was inclined to throw away this mass produced by the fairest in the land. But Viśākhā said, "O master, throw them not away, but ask Bhagavant." He did so, and Bhagavant said that they were not to be thrown away, but that thirty-two cages were to be made and filled with cotton, and that an egg was to be placed in each of the cages, and was to be daily stroked three times with the hand, and that on the seventh day thirty-two sons would come to light. When Viśākhā had done all this, thirty-two boys made their appearance on the seventh day. All of them, when they grew up, were sturdy, very strong, and overcomers of strength.

One day when they had gone out to drive in their

[1] See Spence Hardy, Manual, p. 227.—S.

chariot and were returning home, they came into collision with the chariot of the Purohita's son, who had also driven out and was on his way back, so that the poles of the two carriages clashed. The Purohita's son called out to them to make way, but they bade him do so himself. Then, as the Purohita's son began to use abusive language, Viśākhā's sons seized the pole of his chariot and upset him on a heap of rubbish. When he had come to his father, with his robe drawn over his head, he said with tears, "O father, thus have Viśākhā's sons treated me."

"O son, wherefore have they done so?"

The son gave a full account of the matter. Then said his father, "O son, as this is so, we must contrive some means for making these men keep their mouths shut and not complain." So he carefully sought for a pretext for calumniating them.

After a time the hillmen rebelled against King Prasenajit, who sent a general against them, but he was beaten by the rebels and he turned back. After the king had in this way sent out the general seven times, and the general was always beaten and obliged to retire, the king determined to take the field himself with a fourfold army. Viśākhā's sons, as they came into the city, saw the king, and asked him whither he was going.

"To subdue the hillmen."

"O king, stay here. We will go forth."

"Do so."

The king let them go forth with the fourfold army, and they overcame the hillmen, took from them hostages and tribute, and then came back. Then the Purohita said, "O king, as these men are of remarkably great strength, reflect that they will accomplish what ought to be done only at the king's command."

As kings are afraid of being killed, the king took this to heart, and once more asked the Purohita what was to be done. The Purohita said, "What is to be done, O king? If these men desire it, they can deprive you of your regal power and exercise it themselves." The king, greatly incensed, considered how, if that was going to be the case, he could put them to death. He wished to contrive a means of doing so, but was anxious that the secret should not be betrayed, and so he resolved to undertake the affair without asking any one about it.

Having come to this conclusion, he determined to invite them to his palace and rid himself of them. He informed Viśākhā that her sons would eat with him on the following day. Viśākhā thought, "As my sons are to eat to-morrow at their uncle's, I will entertain Bhagavant and the clergy."

So she betook herself to Bhagavant and touched his feet. He gratified her with discourse regarding the doctrine. When Viśākhā rose from her seat, she invited Bhagavant and the clergy into her house.

The king's messenger invited her sons to come to the palace. Now the king had caused a strong poison to be put into the food. When they were stupefied thereby, he ordered their heads to be cut off.

VIII.

MAHAUSHADHA AND VISAKHÂ.[1]

In olden times Janaka ruled as king in the land of Videhā. He took unto himself a beautiful spouse, who bore him a son, to whom, as food and drink were abundant in the land, the name of Annapāna [Food-Drink] was given. When he had grown up, he proved strong, resolute, and irascible. The queen became arrogant on account of her son, and no longer complied with the king's wishes. This greatly troubled the king, and he, by the advice of his ministers, determined to choose another wife. The ministers called his attention to the daughter of the king of Aparāntaka. Although he was not on friendly terms with that king, his ministers gave him encouragement, and undertook to arrange the matter. The king of Aparāntaka granted his daughter, on the condition that if she gave birth to a son, that son was to be recognised as the heir to the throne. Her loveliness made her very agreeable to the king, and he promised her the fulfilment of her wishes. So she likewise demanded that the son whom she expected should enjoy the succession to the throne. To the king this was as it were a stab in the heart, and he suffered great disquiet at the thought of how he should pass over Annapāna, his bold and comely son, the fruit of a marriage with one of equal birth. The ministers remarked his anxiety, and he informed them of its cause. They stated that as the king of Aparāntaka had granted his daughter only on this con-

[1] Kah-gyur, vol. xi. fol. 53–87.

dition, and as it was as yet uncertain whether she would give birth to a son or a daughter, King Janaka ought to grant her the desired promise.

A son was born, to whom the name of Rājyābhinanda was given, on account of the longing for royal power which had been entertained even before his birth. He grew up, but still his father did not proclaim him his successor. At length the youth's grandfather sent a message to King Janaka, and threatened to make his appearance with a mighty army. The ministers recommended that Rājyābhinanda should be proclaimed successor, and that Annapāna should be put to death. Janaka refused to comply with such a demand. Murderers of fathers, it was true, had been met with, but it was an unheard of thing that a father should kill his son. Nor would he consent to his being mutilated, that being equivalent to death. As little would he agree to his being banished; but he invested the younger prince with the right of succession.

When Annapāna heard of this, he went to his mother, informed her of the evil tidings, and told her that he was about to go to Panchāla. And thither he went. With wearied limbs he lay down to rest in the shade of a tree. There the king's people found him. Astonished by his beauty, they brought him to the king, to whom he told the story of his fortunes. The king gave him the hand of his daughter, and bestowed lands upon him. The son who was born of this marriage was named Bahvannapāna.

Annapāna fell ill and died, and the king gave his daughter, along with her son, to the Purohita, with whom she lived happily. One day a cock crowed near the house. A Brahman who happened to be there, and who was skilled in omens, heard it crow and said, "He who eats the flesh of this cock will become king."[1] The

[1] Cf. Gaal, *Märchen der Magyaren*, Wien, 1882, p. 196. *Der Vogel Goldschweif*, especially p. 213: Hahn, Gr. und alb. Märchen, Leipzig,

Purohita heard these words, and, after asking the Brahman some questions, took the cock and killed it. Then he said to his wife, "Have this cock cooked immediately. I will eat it when I come back from the king's palace." Then he betook himself to the palace.

While he was there, the boy Bahvannapāna came back from school hungry, and could not find his mother. He said to himself, "What has been cooked for us? what sort of food?" In his mother's absence he looked about, and saw the cock in a saucepan with its head uppermost. So he cut off the head and ate it. His mother came in presently and said, "Who has eaten the head?" The boy replied that he had eaten it. His mother gave him some food and sent him to school.

After a time the Purohita also came and asked for food. When he saw that the cock's head had disappeared, he asked where it was. His wife said, "The boy has eaten it." He ate up the rest of the cock, but remained in doubt as to which of the two would become king, he who had eaten the bird's whole body, or he who had eaten only a bird incomplete as to the parts of its body. In order to remove this doubt, he called in for the second time the Brahman who was skilled in omens. The Brahman asserted that he who had eaten the head would become king, but that he also would become king who should kill him who had eaten the head, and should eat his head.

Therefore the Purohita determined to put the boy to death. But as he saw that he could not do this without the boy's mother remarking it, he resolved to take her opinion about the matter. With many friendly words he addressed her in a cajoling manner: "O good one, is it better that your husband or your son should become king?" Quickly recognising the complicated nature of

1864, i. 227. *Das goldene Huhn:* Haltrich, "Deutsche Volksmärchen." Berlin, 1856. "Der seltsame Vogel:" Miklosich, *Ueber die Mundarten der Zigeuner*, IV. No. vi., *Die Diamenten legende Henne.*—S.

the situation, she reflected that if she said it would be better for her son to become king, she would be at variance with her husband. So she said, in accordance with his view of the matter, that it would be better for her husband to become king. But as she was very shrewd and intelligent, she perceived that he wished to kill her son on account of the cock's head, and she determined to save her son at any rate. So she told her son that, as he had acted wrongly in eating the cock's head, he must leave the country with all speed, and betake himself to his grandfather's land, where he had relatives. The son fled to Videha, and there, tormented with hunger and thirst, he lay down one day in order to sleep under a tree in a park.

A little before that time Rājyābhinanda had been attacked by a malady of which, in spite of the efforts of the physicians, he could not be cured. He succumbed to it, and thereby was the reigning family brought to an end.

Now it was part of the royal statutes that until a new king had been chosen the corpse of the late king could not be honoured with funeral ceremonies. Accordingly the ministers, the other officials of the court, the Brahmans, and the interpreters of signs, set out to look for a person distinguished by the force of his virtuous merits. Under a tree outside the city, a tree the shadow of which never moved from his body, they found an extremely handsome youth with a lion-like breast. When the six ministers had looked at him, they exclaimed in astonishment, "Never have we seen any one who equalled this man in force of virtuous merit. As he is extremely handsome, and is well provided with signs, we will invest him with the sovereignty." Having thus spoken, and having agreed thereupon, they aroused him from his sleep. He awoke and asked, "Why must I get up?" They replied, "In order to be proclaimed king." He said, "Ought a slumbering king to be awakened in this manner?" The ministers said, "How then ought he to be awakened?" The youth replied, "He ought to be awakened with song and cymbals and beat of drum." On hearing this, they came to the conclusion that he truly sprang, not from an inferior, but from a noble family, and they asked him, "Who are you? whose noble son are you?" Then the youth rose up lion-like and said, "Annapāna was the son of Janaka, king of Videha, and I am Annapāna's son, Bahvannapāna." Thereupon the six ministers smiled and said, "We have actually lighted upon our own prince."

In the midst of a great multitude, with conjurations, and with song and cymbals and beat of drum, they conducted him into the city, and there they consecrated him as king. As the extinct royal family was renewed in him, he also received the name of Janaka, and his former name of Bahvannapāna fell into disuse. After they had thus invested him with the sovereignty, they came to the conclusion that he was of a simple nature, and they despised him to such a degree that he had no power at all.

King Bahvannapāna once went forth in order to inspect his realm. Whenever he asked to whom villages, towns, and hill-places belonged, he was always told that they belonged to the six ministers. Thereupon he perceived that he could command only food and clothing, but that beyond that he had no power. When he had plunged into a sea of thought, trying to think out what he should do, a deity consoled him, saying that he ought not to be sorrowful. In his own country, in the hill-village Pūrṇakatshtshha, a son named Mahaushadha was about to be born to the head-man, Pūrṇa. This son he ought to make his minister, who would gain possession of the realm and restore it to him, and turn out fortunate and advantageous to him. The king sent forth men to seek out this Pūrṇa, and to learn whether his wife had a son or not. The men returned with the information that the village head-man really existed, and that his wife was with child. Then the king wrote to him and made him come to him, conferred upon him the village, and bade him henceforth carefully watch over the child, which was as yet in its mother's womb, so that none of its limbs might suffer any injury. When the boy came into the world and his birth-feast was celebrated, the name of Mahaushadha (Great Remedy) was given to him at the request of his mother, inasmuch as she, who had long suffered from illness, and had been unable to obtain any relief from the time of the boy's conception, had been cured by him.

As the boy was sitting on his father's shoulder one day, and was being carried for a bath from the middle of the street to a tank, the father saw a piece of fish lying before him. Taking it for a precious stone, he tried to lift it up with his toes. Then said Mahaushadha, "Dear father Pūrṇa, you think that a precious stone has been dropped here. Gazing with open eyes at the piece of fish, you fancy that it is a precious stone. Test it, dear father Pūrṇa. It is no precious stone; only a piece of red fish crushed underfoot. Vaiśravaṇa[1] is not accustomed to be so careless."

When they had come to the tank, and Pūrṇa and Mahaushadha had laid their clothes on the bank and had gone into the water to bathe, the father wanted to lay hold of a crane which was resting on a lotus, but when he drew near the bird flew away. Then Mahaushadha said, "From the lotus flew the crane away. The crane flew away, the lotus remained. Only see, father dear, how the crane flies away from the lotus."

[1] "Vaiśravaṇa, 'son of Viśravas,' epithet of Kuvera, the god of wealth."

On another occasion the father went to the river Ganges to bathe, carrying his son as before on his shoulder. When they had left their clothes on the shore and had gone into the water, they saw a metal basin floating on the water with a goose sitting upon it. Then said Mahaushadha, "The river Ganges supports the metal basin, on the metal basin rests a goose. Look, O father dear, at the metal basin with the goose carried along by the river Ganges."

Another time, when Mahaushadha had gone to the shore to bathe, he saw how a pot, on which was a water-hen, was borne along by the current of the river Ganges. Then he said, "The river Ganges bears along the pot, on the pot sits a water-hen. Only look, father dear, at the pot with the water-hen and the Ganges."

Again, on another occasion, he saw a ram carried along by the current of the river Ganges with a heron standing upon it, and he said, "The river Ganges bears along a ram, and likewise the heron which stands upon it. Look, father dear, at the ram and the heron borne along by the river Ganges."

After this it happened one day that Mahaushadha was at play with the children, and they chose him as their king.[1] He named some of the boys as his ministers, and they went on playing together. There came along the road an old Brahman with his young wife, on their way to another country. The Brahman stepped aside for a time, and during his absence a rogue, full of desire for the wife, came up to her and said, "Good woman, whither has your father gone?"

"Who?" said the wife.

"He is apparently your grandfather," replied the rogue.

"What do you mean?" she said.

[1] Cf. "Ardschi-Bord chi-Chān" in Jülg's *Mongol. Märchensammlung* Innsbruck, 1868, pp. 197, *et seq.*—S.

"He is apparently your great-grandfather," said the rogue.

"He is not my father, nor my grandfather, nor yet my great-grandfather, but my husband," said the wife.

Thereupon the rogue said with a smile, "O foolish woman, are you not ashamed to say in the presence of your friends or any other decorous person that this man is your husband? Have you not on this stately earth seen men of divine beauty?"

"Such men are no more to be found."

"Take me as your husband, and we will live together. Should the old Brahman put in a claim for you, then say to the great assembly, 'This man is my husband.'"

After the rogue had said this she went off with him. When the Brahman came back, he could not see his wife. He climbed a height, and saw her walking off with another man. He ran after her, and seized one of her hands, the rogue holding on to the other. The Brahman said, "Why are you taking away my wife?"

"She is my wife; do not trouble yourself about her," replied the rogue.

As the Brahman persisted in saying that she was his wife, a quarrel arose between the two men on the highway, and they pulled the woman this way and that way. But as the rogue was younger and stronger than the Brahman, he dragged her away from him. Being overcome, the Brahman called out in that lonely place for help. At that time Mahaushadha and the other children were at play in the forest, and they heard his cries for help. The children said to Mahaushadha, "As you wish to be called the king, and that Brahman is shouting for help, why do not you save him from danger?" So he bade the children bring the parties before him, and he asked them what had occurred. The Brahman said that the other man had forcibly torn away his wife from him, the weaker of the two. On the other hand, the rogue declared that the Brahman lied, and that the woman was his own wife. The woman herself affirmed that the rogue was her husband. Mahaushadha, who perceived that the Brahman had not become excited without due cause, determined to apply a test.[1]

"Say, O man, where do you come from along with your wife?"

"From my father-in-law's," replied the rogue.

"What did you eat and drink there?"

"We had meat, cakes, sorrel, and wine," replied the rogue.

"Vomit then, if that be so," said Mahaushadha; "we shall see then if that be true or not."

The rogue put his finger down his throat and vomited, but no such food came to light. Then Mahaushadha asked the Brahman whence he had come.

"From my father-in-law's," replied the Brahman.

"What did you eat there?"

"Curdled milk, porridge, and radishes."

Him likewise Mahaushadha ordered to bring up what he had eaten, and the result was that he produced the food in question. As Mahaushadha now perceived that the rogue had deluded and carried off the Brahman's wife, he gave orders that he should be chastised by blows from sticks and fists, and that he should then be set fast up to the neck in a hole a man's stature in depth, and that there should be written on his forehead with peacock's gall these words—

"He who thus steals a wife, him does Mahaushadha punish in this wise. He who, like unto the wife-stealer, has stolen a child, an ox, a coverlet, yarn, or the like, such thieves as this shall be arrested up to the number of five hundred, and shall be chastised by blows from sticks and fists, and shall be set up to their necks in a

[1] Cf. "Śukasaptate," in the Greek version of Galanos, 4th night, p. 10.—S.

pit, and their names shall be written on their foreheads with peacock's gall, indicating that Mahaushadha will thus punish others also who shall commit thefts."

Now, when the six ministers had exhausted the land, and the king became aware of the fact, the idea came into his mind of finding out of what nature Mahaushadha really was. He told the ministers that he was going to the chase, and he went with a great following to the hill-villages. When the five hundred rogues who had been set in the pit saw the king, most of them cried out, "O king!" The king heard the cry, and looked around on all sides, but he saw no man, though the cry again resounded. One of the rogues perceived this, and repeated it. The king caught sight of him, and read on his forehead the words written with peacock's gall: "Whoever has stolen a wife, a child, an ox, a coverlet, and so forth, him does Mahaushadha punish in this wise." When Mahaushadha and the other children heard that the king had seen these things, his heart rejoiced within him, and he thought that although Mahaushadha was a child, yet in regard to such deeds he had done no wrong. However, he ordered the rogues to be drawn out of the pit, and set them at liberty.

When Pūrṇa heard that the king had come to Pūrṇakatshtshha, he went to meet him, bearing a jar full of water, a canopy, banners, and standards. The king said to him, "Pūrṇa, be not afraid. Bring hither your son that I may see him." Pūrṇa replied, "O king, as the boy is still very young, I will not bring him before the face of the king." However the king ordered the father to fetch his boy. Then the king gazed upon the exceedingly handsome and spirited boy; but as he was still a child, and had not come to man's estate, the king let him go back to his father's house.

Some time later King Janaka wished to test the nature of Mahaushadha's intelligence. So he sent a messenger to Pūrṇa, the head-man of the hill-village Pūrṇakatshtshha, with an order to send a rope made of sand one hundred ells long. When the messenger had arrived and communicated the order, Pūrṇa was greatly alarmed. From his birth upwards he had never seen or heard of such a thing, and he would therefore have to expect a reprimand. He became so depressed that Mahaushadha asked him why he was so ill at ease. The father replied that he was not sure that the king did not mean to punish him, the demand being of such an unheard of kind. Mahaushadha asked him to send for the messenger, saying that he would reply to the king. Thereupon he said to the messenger, "Make known to the king this my request, without forgetting it. As the people of our country are slow-witted, unintelligent, and stupid, may it please the king to send an ell of that kind of rope as a pattern, like unto which we will twine a hundred, nay, a thousand ells, and will send them to him." When the messenger had reported this to the king, the king asked whether it was Pūrṇa or his son who had given this answer. The messenger said that it was Mahaushadha. The king was astonished, and perceived that the commands of the deity were being executed, and that Mahaushadha would re-establish his power.

As the king wished to put Mahaushadha a second time to the test, he sent to Pūrṇa, and ordered him to supply some rice which had not been crushed with a pestle, and yet was not uncrushed, and which had been cooked neither in the house nor out of the house, neither with fire nor yet without fire; sending it neither along the road nor yet away from the road, without its being shone upon by the daylight, but yet not in the shade, not together with a woman, but also not with a man, by one not riding, but also not on foot. The messenger came to Pūrṇakatshtshha, sent for Pūrṇa, and, after holding merry converse with him on various subjects, informed him of the king's orders. Pūrṇa was greatly discomfited. But Mahaushadha, having found out the cause of his dejection, comforted him, declaring that he would manage the whole affair himself.

Having dried some rice in the sun, he sent for a number of women, and made a man give each of them a handful of grains. These they shelled with their nails, picking out the kernel of each grain without breaking it. When the women had done this, he threw the rice into a pot, and cooked it on the threshold of the house. As he was to cook it without fire and yet not without fire, he cooked it in the sun. In order that it might be conveyed neither along the road nor yet away from the road, he ordered the man who carried it to walk with one foot on the road and the other foot by the side of the road. As it was to be brought neither in the sunlight nor in the shade, he bade the man fasten the pot which held it to the end of a stick, and cover it over with a thin cloth. As the bearer was neither to ride nor to go afoot, he told him to put a shoe on one of his feet and leave the other unshod. And as the bearer was to be neither a man nor a woman, he sent a hermaphrodite.

When the messenger presented himself before the king, and, on being questioned by King Janaka, gave him a full account of the whole matter, the king was greatly pleased, and asked if he had been sent by Pūrṇa or by Mahaushadha. The messenger replied that he had been sent by the latter, whereupon the king said, "Mahaushadha is clever, resolute, sharp-witted, and ingenious."

Some time afterwards the king sent to Pūrṇa, and ordered him to supply a park with kitchen-gardens, fruit-trees, and tanks. When the messenger came to Pūrṇa and told him what were the king's orders, Pūrṇa again fell into very low spirits. Mahaushadha begged his father not to distress himself, promising to arrange everything to the king's satisfaction. Then he sent for the messenger, and told him to give the following reply to the king:—

"As no one among the mountains knows anything about a park of that kind, and therefore no one can construct one, may it please the king to send hither one of the parks belonging to his palace. When my father has seen it, and learnt of what nature it is, he will send one like unto it."

When the messenger returned with this reply, the king was highly pleased, and when he learnt that it was again Mahaushadha who had sent it, he perceived that he was very intelligent.

Some time later the king again sent a messenger to Pūrṇa, ordering him to plant a tree, and to send it to him at the end of a year, bearing blossoms and fruits. When the messenger had executed his commission, Pūrṇa again became dejected, but Mahaushadha comforted him, saying that the matter would not be a difficult one to manage. And he sent a Ricinus shrub, which at the end of a year bore blossoms and fruits. When the king saw it, he asked whether the idea was Pūrṇa's or Mahaushadha's. The messenger named the latter, and the king found nothing more to say in the matter.

Some time later the king sent five hundred oxen to Pūrṇa. These he was to feed and to milk, and he was to send to the king milk, curdled milk, butter, cream, and cheese. When the messenger came to Pūrṇa with these orders, Pūrṇa was greatly troubled, and said to the villagers, "Surely in this matter the king wishes to punish me, seeing that he requires me to milk oxen." When Mahaushadha perceived his distress, he comforted him, saying that he would contrive a reply with which the king would be pleased without this thing being accomplished. Then Mahaushadha gave full directions to a father and son, ordering them to betake themselves to the capital, near the king's palace. He told the father to wrap up a wooden bowl in a cloth and fasten it over his belly, and then to roll to and fro on the ground and pretend to be crying. And he told the son to utter fervent prayers, to scatter flowers, food, and incense towards the ten parts of the world, and to cry aloud, "May this, my father, propitiously bring forth his child!"

When the father and son, in accordance with these instructions, had drawn nigh unto King Janaka, they did all that they had been told to do. When the king heard the words, "May he who in the world protects the world preserve my father, and let him propitiously give birth to his child!" he sent some of his men to find out what that meant. They came, and saw a big-bellied man rolling to and fro on the ground and crying, and his son invoking Yama, Vaiśravaṇa, Vasu, and the other kings of the gods. The men reported this to the king, and he sent for the father and son. The son begged that his father might be allowed to bring forth his child. Thereat the king laughed, and said that he had never seen or heard of a man who gave birth to a child.

Then said the youth, "Are things as you say they are?"

"Yes!"

"In that case, I ask you wherefore you sent five hundred oxen to Pūrṇakatshtshha, with orders that milk, sour milk, curdled milk, and fresh butter should be obtained from them. Have you ever seen or heard of oxen big with young and producing calves?"

Then the king laughed, and asked who was the originator of this idea, Pūrṇa or Mahaushadha, or some one else. When the messenger stated that it was Mahaushadha, the king and his ministers were greatly astonished.

Some time later, the king, in order to apply another test, sent a messenger to Pūrṇakatshtshha with a mule, and ordered Pūrṇa to keep watch over it without tying it up, and to feed it without placing it under a roof. The messenger brought the mule to Pūrṇa, and warned him that he would forfeit his life and limbs in case the mule escaped. When Pūrṇa heard that, he was terrified and fell into very low spirits, as he did not think he was equal to the task. But Mahaushadha bade him be of good cheer. By day the mule was to be allowed to graze at its will, but at night it was to be guarded by twenty men, five of whom were to look after it during each of the night-watches, one of them sitting on its back, the others holding a leg apiece. After this fashion the twenty men watched it without taking it under a roof.

After a time King Janaka sent a messenger to see how Pūrṇa was treating the mule. He reported to the king the precautions which had been taken. The king perceived that the mule could not escape while it was guarded in that way, so he said that he wished one of the men to be sent for. The minister asked which man was to be summoned. The king said that they were to send for the man who was sitting on the mule's back. For while the others were asleep he could ride off with the mule. So the king had the watcher sent for who sat on the mule, and the man came away together with the beast.

When Pūrṇa was told next morning that the mule had gone off, he saw that his life was forfeited, and he took to wailing from fear. When Mahaushadha saw how miserable Pūrṇa was, he began to reflect that hitherto he had found a means of escape on each occasion, but that this time there was none. Of this, however, he said nothing. Although he was much alarmed, yet he devised a plan, and said to his father, "There is still one expedient left for settling this business." His father asked what it was, and Mahaushadha replied that he could manage the affair provided Pūrṇa could endure being jeered at. Pūrṇa declared that he was ready to do anything which would prevent his life being taken. Thereupon Mahaushadha cut the hair of his father's head so as to form seven strips, and he daubed the head itself with red, black, brown, white, and other paints. Then he and his father mounted an ass and betook themselves to the capital.

When they arrived there, the news spread abroad that Mahaushadha had come riding upon an ass, and that he had cut his father's hair into seven strips. When the king and the ministers heard this, they asked, "Why has he, who has the reputation of being so discreet and intelligent, performed so unbecoming an action?" The king and the ministers went out to see if Mahaushadha had really come in the manner alleged, or if the report was false. When the king and his followers saw that it was really so with him, the ministers said, "Wherefore is Mahaushadha praised for his judgment, intelligence, and wisdom? In spite of all that, how unbecomingly he has acted!"

The king asked Mahaushadha why he had thus dishonoured his father. He replied, "I have not dishonoured him, but have honoured him. As I stand much higher than my father on account of my great knowledge, I have shown him honour."

The king asked, "Are you the better of the two, or is your father the better?"

He replied, "I am the better, my father is the worse."

The king said, "Never have I seen or heard that the son is better than the father. As it is the father through whom the son becomes known, while the mother feeds him, takes care of him, and brings him up, therefore we hold that the father is altogether the better of the two."

Then said Mahaushadha to the king, "Test the matter thoroughly to see if the father is really so or not."

As the king and the ministers affirmed that it was so, and not otherwise, Mahaushadha fell at the king's feet and said, "O king, this being the case, as the mule which you sent us to watch over has run away, but as according to the testimony of the king and the ministers the father is considered better than the offspring, and the father of the mule is the ass, accept this ass as a set-off."

When the king and the ministers had heard his speech, and perceived the cunning contrivance which it carried out, they were astonished. Whether he had acted becomingly or unbecomingly, it was clear that he was clever. Having thought the matter over, the king was much pleased, and he arrayed Mahaushadha in fine robes of various kinds, and bestowed upon him the power of a minister, and on the father he conferred that village.

After Mahaushadha had been appointed a minister, his fame spread abroad throughout the whole city as that of a wise and intelligent man.

Now a very learned Brahman had gone abroad in order to increase his property, after he and his wife had spent all that she had brought along with her; and he returned home with five hundred gold pieces of ancient date. Before entering his house he was desirous of disposing of his money, for none could tell whether his wife might not have taken up with another man during his absence. His wife was of remarkable beauty, and therefore he considered that she might have found favour in the eyes of other men during his absence. So in the evening twilight he went to the cemetery, dug a hole under a Nyagrodha tree, put the money into it, and then went to his home.

Now the wife had a lover, the Brahman Mahākarṇa (Great Ear). The pair had about that time partaken of delicate food, and she had anointed herself with fragrant ointment, and was reposing upon the couch of enjoyment. Just then came the Brahman and called to her to open the door. The woman asked who was there. When he had pronounced his name, she uttered a joyful cry, aroused Mahākarṇa, and hid him under the bed, and then went to open the door. With thorough dissimulation she wept and flung her arms round her husband's neck, showed him honour and respect, and placed savoury food before him. After partaking of it, he came to the conclusion that the reason of her having provided such a supper must certainly be that she had given herself up to another man. As he was of an ingenuous nature, he asked her, "O good wife, how comes it that you have such food, seeing that this is not a holiday, a festival, or day of public rejoicing?" She replied, "A deity made me aware that you were coming to-day, so I provided this meal on your account." The Brahman said, "Then it is not I alone who am fortunate. My wife also, it seems, receives tidings from the deity in dreams."

After he had eaten and washed, he lay down upon the bed to rest, and conversed with his wife about her welfare. Presently she asked him if he had brought anything with him. He said that he had. Thereupon the wife intimated by signs, "Mahākarṇa, let thine ear listen to what is being said." Then she said, "Where have you put the five hundred gold pieces, as you have not shown them to me?" He replied, "I will show them to you to-morrow." Then said the wife, "Why have you kept the matter from me, though I am the half of your body?" The honest Brahman said, "I have hidden the money outside the city." The wife said, "Hear, O Great Ear, where the money has been put." The Brahman said that he had hidden the money under a Nyagrodha tree in the cemetery. Then said the Brahman's wife, "As you, my lord, are fatigued and exhausted by the journey and on my account, now go to sleep."

When she saw that he had gone to sleep, she bade Mahākarṇa act in accordance with what he had heard. Mahākarṇa slipped quietly out of the house, went to the cemetery, dug up the money, and then betook himself to his own house.

When the Brahman went to the cemetery the next day, and found that his money was no longer there, he beat himself on the head and breast, and returned home. His wife, his friends, his brothers, and his relatives asked him what had happened, and he told them everything. They advised him to have recourse to Mahaushadha. Then the Brahman went wailing to Mahaushadha, his face streaming with tears, and told him his misfortune. Mahaushadha remained silent for a moment. Then he asked, "Brahman, at what spot and at what time did you hide the money? Did any one see it? or have you talked about it to any one?" The Brahman gave a full account of the whole affair. Mahaushadha came to the conclusion that the Brahman's wife had some other man as a lover, and that what had taken place was due to that man's contrivance. But he spoke words of comfort to the Brahman, saying that if the money was not found he would pay it to him out of his own purse. Then he asked him if there was a dog in his house. The Brahman replied that there was. Then said Mahaushadha, "Go and invite eight Brahmans to your house. Invite four of them yourself, and let your wife invite the other four. Tell her that you have made a vow to the god Śiva that if you should accomplish your return prosperously you would entertain eight Brahmans."

The Brahman followed these instructions, and when the Brahmans had been invited, he went to Mahaushadha in order to acquaint him with the fact. Then said Mahaushadha, "When you are about to receive the Brahmans into your house, call this man of mine, and station him at the door when they enter. And during the meal let him stand inside without being occupied in any way." And to his man he said, "Take note of everything significant. When the Brahmans come in, see which of them the dog barks at, and before whom it wags its tail; for such is the nature of dogs." Moreover, he ordered the Brahman not to set the food before his guests with his own hands, but to leave that to his wife. He told his man also to pay heed to the Brahman's wife while she was serving the food, and see to whom she made a sign, at whom she gazed without changing countenance, whom she addressed with a smile, and to whom she served the best fare, and to make him acquainted with all this.

These instructions having been given, the Brahman took the servant home with him and stationed him at the door. Then he told his wife to summon the guests whom she had invited, while he summoned those whom he had invited. As the other guests entered the house one after another, the dog barked. But when Mahākarṇa came in, the dog looked at him, drooped its ears, wagged its tail, and followed after him. When he had entered in and called the dog, the servant learnt that he was Mahākarṇa. Afterwards the servant saw the food distributed, and remarked that the Brahman's wife, while taking part in the distribution, made a sign with her eyebrows to Mahākarṇa, smiled slightly, fixed her eyes upon him, and supplied him with the best of the food. All that he saw he afterwards reported to Mahaushadha.

As soon as Mahaushadha heard these things, he sent for Mahākarṇa, asked him if it was a Brahman's business to lay hands on the property of others, and ordered him to restore what he had stolen. Makākarṇa said he thought that Mahaushadha ought to make himself easy, as he, Mahākarṇa, knew nothing at all about the matter. Thereupon Mahaushadha gave orders that the evil-doer should be thrown into prison, and left there until his bones became visible. At this threat Mahākarṇa was so terrified that he begged for mercy with a contrite heart, promising to repay all. Going home, he fetched the money, tied up just as it had been, and handed it over to Mahaushadha, who gave it to the Brahman. The Brahman rejoiced greatly, and seeing that his having recovered what he had lost was entirely due to Mahaushadha's powerful assistance, he wished to make manifest his gratitude to him, so he brought him half of the money as a present. Mahaushadha accepted the present and then returned it to him. When the news of all this became spread throughout the city, the king, the ministers, and the citizens praised Mahaushadha highly on account of his wisdom, and esteemed themselves fortunate in having such a minister.

After a time it happened that a certain man who had gone on business into another land came back to his own country. Having come to the edge of a tank, he opened his meal-pouch, took out some of the meal, and mixed it with water and partook thereof. After feeding he tied up his pouch and went his way. Now while he was sitting there a snake had crept into the pouch, one of those snakes which emit poison when disturbed. But when the man turned to his pouch after his repast, he tied it up without examining it. Then he flung it across his shoulder and went on to the capital. There a soothsayer informed him that he was in imminent danger of losing his life.

Some time after he had received this information, he regretted that he had not asked the soothsayer on what ground it was based. Having thus reflected, he determined not to go home till he had consulted the minister Mahaushadha. When he had gone to him and had told him the whole story, Mahaushadha came to the conclusion that the soothsayer must certainly have given him this piece of information because his pouch contained one of the snakes which emit poison when disturbed. Therefore he bade him open his pouch with a piece of wood, in the presence of witnesses, but in some retired place. In that case he would soon learn the ground in question. The man did so, and when the poisonous snake lifted up its head, breathed furiously, and made its outstretched tongue vibrate, Mahaushadha said, "That is the danger by which you were threatened."

After a time Mahaushadha equipped a complete army and went out to take a survey of the land. Whenever he asked to whom the different villages, towns, and cities belonged, the inhabitants replied that they belonged to this or that minister. Then Mahaushadha perceived that the six ministers had in this manner taken possession of the whole country, and that King Janaka's rule was restricted to his own food and drink. He asked the king who really was the master of the villages, hill-towns, and cities. The king related to him how the merciful gods had informed him that in the village Pūrṇakatshtshha a son named Mahaushadha was about to be born to Pūrṇa, and that he, the king, would make Mahaushadha his first minister, who would recover for him all his power, by which means he would become possessed of complete regal authority.

"Therefore [continued the king] have I provided you with all things necessary while you were still in your mother's womb, and from that time forth, and have raised you to the rank of first minister. Now by the force of your intelligence shall you fulfil the words of the deity and help me to gain my supremacy."

Thereupon Mahaushadha paid honour to the king, and bade him take courage, saying that he would act in such a way that the king would be well pleased. Accordingly he sent for the head-men of the villages, towns, and cities one after another, and assured them that he would arrange matters in such a way that they would be satisfied with him. Much harm had been done to them by those ministers, who had levied out of covetousness immoderate rates and taxes. If they would act in accordance with his instructions, he would be mindful thereof, and would fix moderate taxes, set all other things in order, and help them to secure their welfare. In any case, they ought to revolt, and when the king came with the other ministers, they ought to say that they would not submit until the minister Mahaushadha should come, but that when he came, they would obey him but no one else.

When he had given them these instructions, and had stirred up the people in all those parts and instigated them to rebellion, so that they recalled their allegiance, the other ministers petitioned the king, and King Janaka sent forth those six ministers together with a great army; but they did not succeed in getting possession of a single village or hill-town. So they sent a messenger to the king with the statement that they could not enforce submission unless the king came himself; but the king also could not obtain the submission of a single hill-town. So, as many men had fallen in battle, the king and the ministers became dejected. Then said the inhabitants of the hill-villages, "If the first minister Mahaushadha were to come, we would obey him and submit ourselves to him. We have not rebelled against King Janaka, but we have behaved as we have done because the ministers have wrought us injury."

Thereupon the king sent a messenger to Mahaushadha, saying, "As we cannot reduce the land to submission, do you come hither." When Mahaushadha had looked at the king's letter, he went at once to the king. When the people of that land saw him, they all paid reverence to him, and he spoke words of encouragement to them, and fixed their taxes according to law, and succoured the poor and lowly and helpless. To the townspeople and the country-folk he gave presents, greeting and embracing them as if they were his parents, brothers, and kinsmen. The old men of the land, and the young people and the women, looked upon him as a son or a brother. To all of them he gave great satisfaction; and then, after he had finally united all the lands together, he went back to the seat of royalty, together with King Janaka. By means of these deeds he gained an honoured reputation among other kings also. King Janaka was so highly pleased that he gave his daughter in marriage to Mahaushadha, who lived with her happily.

After a time there came unto King Janaka a king[1] who had lost his possessions. As King Janaka did not care for him, he betook himself to Mahaushadha, who received him with compassion and supplied him with means of subsistence.

Some time afterwards a Brahman came to Mahaushadha and asked him for a measure of barley. Mahaushadha promised it to him, but intrusted the delivery of it to the overseer of the granary, who kept putting the matter off from day to day and gave nothing.

Now it came to pass one day that the king was sitting surrounded by the ministers and the town and country folk at a certain spot where many people paid reverence to him. He asked the ministers to what person a secret might be intrusted, on whom it might be safe to rely. The ministers began to consider. One of them said that a man might intrust a secret to his friend; another, to his wife; a third, to his mother; a fourth, to his sister; a fifth, to his brother. When Mahaushadha was asked by the king why he did not in his turn express an opinion, he replied, "O king, my opinion is that a man ought not to intrust a secret to any one, but least of all to his wife. This will I prove unto you, O king."

Some time after this the king's peacock was missing.

[1] Properly speaking a Kshatriya, as will be seen farther on.—S.

Mahaushadha found it but hid it away. Then he took another which resembled it and said to his wife, "Have you heard that the king's peacock up at the palace is missing?" She replied that she had heard about it. Then Mahaushadha said to her, "Say nothing about it to any one, but cook it quickly, and I will eat it."[1] She said to herself, "See now, this man from the hill-village wants to eat the king's peacock. My father places the utmost confidence in him, and he acts to the king's hurt."

Some time afterwards, Mahaushadha dressed in full array a courtesan who bore a likeness to one of the king's wives, and brought her to his wife. And he said to his wife, "This is such and such a wife of the king's. As I am very intimate with her, and you are dear to me, do not mention it to any one." Thinking that she and Mahaushadha were living together, the king's daughter became very angry. And she considered that as he was dishonouring her father, who was quite unaware thereof, it was not right to appoint as first minister a man sprung from a lowly family in a hill-village, and to intrust the whole of the king's affairs to him, the shameful one. So with a view to seeing that he was put back again into his former place, she went to her father and said, "O father, you have unadvisedly appointed this miscreant first minister, and you placed reliance upon him in an unbecoming manner. He has sinned against the king's wife, having had to do with such and such a wife of yours. And besides, it is he who has eaten the king's peacock. Moreover, he has received in a friendly manner and has supplied with all necessaries men coming from a foreign land. But you, O father, have always held him dearer than all others, and no one save him has pleased you."

[1] As regards the king's peacock, see the Śukasaptati, 21st night, in Galanos's translation, p. 34.—S.

In order to sift this matter thoroughly, the king ordered his executioners to put Mahaushadha to death. Accordingly these men of low caste fastened a karavīra wreath around his neck, beat a drum, the sound of which resembles the voice of an ass, abused him with coarse language and threatened him. Like unto the servants of the god of death, with sharpened weapons in their hands, they led him away to the cemetery. But no man believed that he would be put to death. The towns-people and villagers had their eyes full of tears, and they uttered cries of sorrow and despair, and prayed to the gods, just as if a child of their own were going to be killed; and the poor Kshatriyas whom Mahaushadha had received kindly and provided with means of subsistence said to the king's men, "As we will put this man to death, do ye turn back."

As he passed out of the city, the Brahman's wife Ātmavīrā laid hold of the skirt of his robe and said, "You who were to have given me the measure of barley, give it and go." But Mahaushadha uttered this śloka: "A king does not become a friend, a hangman has no acquaintances; to women ought no secret to be intrusted; peacock's flesh ought no one to eat; to the Brahman's wife Ātmavīrā a man ought not to admit that he possesses a measure of barley."

As he walked along uttering these words, the executioners said, "Have you, who are endowed with knowledge and excellent wisdom, anything to set forth?"

Mahaushadha replied, "O king, I have nothing to set forth; but in the despair of anguish I said what was needful."

"What is that?"

He replied, "A king does not become a friend," and so forth. And he continued, "O king, I beseech you to listen to me a little. When I said, 'A king does not become a friend,' could you not perceive that I said so with reference to earlier times, when you had absolutely no influence over villages, towns, and cities ?"

When they had gone somewhat farther, it was suggested to King Janaka that he should again ask Mahaushadha what he had to set forth. Then the king called to him and questioned him. He replied, "O king, from being one who had merely food, drink, and service, you have by my means become a king ruling the earth, with a realm, an army, and treasures. But you, without recognising what I did for you in early days, are sending me to death, on which account I uttered the words, 'A king does not become a friend.' I said also, 'A hangman has no acquaintances.' This hangman, if he were to go without bed and clothing to the king in order to obtain the means of living from the king, when he had drawn nigh unto the king, would not be received by him; but I have bestowed land on the hungry fugitive, by means of which he has by this time become prosperous. Now he conducts me to my death, on which account I said, 'A hangman has no acquaintances.' As regards the words, 'To women ought no secret to be intrusted,' I uttered them for the following reason. When you, O king, sitting one day in the midst of your court, asked whom one might venture to trust, and the ministers replied one's father, or mother, or sister, or comrades, but you, O king, said that a man should intrust a secret to his wife, because a man's wife is the half of his body, then did I entertain the idea of bringing the whole matter before the eyes of the king. In order to provide a test, I hid away the king's peacock, and took another peacock, which I ate. Then I took from the chamber of the women the ornaments belonging to a certain woman, and hung them around the neck of a certain courtesan, and led her into my house. Be pleased, O king, to look upon that courtesan."

When the king had placed side by side the courtesan

and the designated inmate of his women's chamber, and had looked upon them both, and had found that there was a remarkable similarity in their appearance, figure, behaviour, and characteristics, so that it was impossible to distinguish one from the other, then the king, after some consideration, perceived that Mahaushadha was innocent.

"As to the words [continued Mahaushadha], 'To the Brahman's wife Ātmavīrā a man ought not to admit that he possesses a measure of barley.' I uttered them for this reason. When you had sentenced me to death, and the executioners were leading me away, she called out, 'Give me the measure of barley,' and on its account seized me by the skirt of my robe."

When all this was made clear to the eyes of the king, he rejoiced, and gave orders that Mahaushadha should be released, and he heaped upon him tokens of honour. Mahaushadha made obeisance to the king, and then said, "O king, have you learnt what the secrecy of wives is? I have no longer any need of your daughter. I will seek me a wife like unto myself in race, beauty, character, and wisdom."

When the king had granted him permission, he went to the mountain forest Kaksha,[1] in order to find for himself a maiden. He had put on the dress of a Brahman, and carried a water-jug in his right hand, his body being adorned with the string of sacrifice and covered with the skin of a gazelle, and his face marked with three lines of ointment. When he had gone half-way, darkness came on. A Brahman asked him whence he came.

"From the Videha land," he replied.

"Whither do you intend to go?"

"To the Kaksha forest."

[1] Among the explanations of *kaksha* given in Monier Williams's Sanskrit Dictionary are "the interior of a forest, a forest of dead trees, a dry wood, &c."

"Do you know any one in whose house you can find shelter?"

Mahaushadha said that he did not. Then the Brahman took him into his own house and entertained him in a becoming manner. But Mahaushadha suspected that his host's wife, who loved another man, was a worthless woman. When he took his departure next day the Brahman said to him, "Consider this house as your own when you come here on your journeyings to and fro."

"That will I do," replied Mahaushadha, and went his way.

About half-way there was a barley-field, and in it he saw a very beautiful maiden, of high race and of great modesty.

As soon as he saw her a longing after her entered into his mind.

"Good maiden," he asked, "who are you? Whose daughter are you? What is your name?"

"I am Viśākhā," she replied.

"Whose daughter are you?"

"His who works in wood for all the village."

Then thought Mahaushadha, "Her form is fair, but I will now test her intelligence a little."

He went into a wheat-field, lifted up his hands, and while he flourished his hands on high, he trampled on the wheat with his feet. Then said Viśākhā, "O Pundit, as you have flourished your hands on high, so also ought you to flourish on high your feet."

"This maiden is clever," he thought. Then he said with a smile, "You are very brilliant, O maiden, seeing that you have earrings and armlets."

"The reason is, O Pundit, that both have little oxen," said Viśākhā.[1]

1 "This seems to refer to the shape of the earrings," says Professor Schiefner; but the repartee still remains obscure. The same remark may be made about several of Viśākhā's wise sayings.

Then said Mahaushadha, "The maiden is of fair form and charming appearance."

"That is through the favour of the village elder," replied Viśākhā.

"Where has your father gone?" he asked after a time.

"He has gone to make two roads out of one. After collecting the twigs of the thorn-bushes, he uses them for making the road. In this manner he gives men two roads."

"Where has your mother gone?"

"To fetch seeds from the fruits of the field."

"Maiden, shall I take you to be my wife?"

"If the head of the village gives permission," said the maiden.

"Show me the way," he said, "by which one can go straight and safely to the Kaksha forest."

She pointed out to him a crooked road, and then set out herself along another road. There she took off her clothes beside a tank, shut one eye, and while waiting to see if he would recognise her or not, bowed down upon one side and said, "In the direction of the hand which is used in eating should one go. From the direction of the hand which is not used in eating should one deviate, and so go to the Rice-Soup forest."

When Mahaushadha had gone some way along the road indicated to him, he perceived her from afar off, and said, "Fair one with the roguish eyes, having on no garment woven of cotton, but being clothed with the unspun and unweaved, show me how it is possible to go to Kusumagrāma."

Thereupon said the maiden, slightly smiling, "Here leave on one side the left-hand road, where there is corn and the palāsa blossoms display themselves; there, O Brahman, must you take your way." [1]

[1] The obscurity of some of the allusions in this conversation is probably due to the fact that they involve a play upon words which could not always be fully rendered by the translator of the Tibetan text.

He set forth. Coming to the house of Viśākhā's father, he found that her parents were not at home. So he said to the village head-men, "If you allow it, I will take this woman to be my wife."

When the head-men of the village heard these words, they immediately with one accord began to upbraid him, saying, "You wretched mendicant Brahman, are not you ashamed to want such a maiden as our Viśākhā? Get away with you at once from this spot. Or must we hand you over to be devoured by fierce dogs?"

Driven away by them, he returned to Viśākhā. While he was still at a distance, she bade him welcome. When he told her of his interview with the village head-men, who had been on the point of beating him, she said, "How and in what manner did you speak?"

When he had told her everything, Viśākhā said to him, "O Brahman, you are not expert in such matters. Have you behaved in the way in which a man ought to propose for a maiden?"

"How else, then, ought one to act?" asked the Brahman.

"First of all," replied the maiden, "the man must draw near. Then he must gain favour. And if that is granted, he must offer hospitality and organise an entertainment, after which he may bring forward his desire."

He went away and acted in accordance with this advice, entertaining the village head-men at an excellent banquet. Then he arose and asked for Viśākhā. This time they gave their assent. Just as this point was reached her parents arrived. Then Mahaushadha and the village head-men asked her parents for her. The parents were of opinion that the matter required consideration.

Then said the village head-men, "What is there to consider about? He is a young, shapely, handsome, learned Brahman, perfectly versed in the Vedas and Vedāngas. So give him your daughter without further consideration."

Thereupon Mahaushadha offered hospitality to the Brahmans, and he received the maiden as his wife. The next day he invited his wife's parents, paid them honour, bestowed upon them raiment and gifts in return for the bride, and then went his way to King Janaka in Videha.

On the way a Brahman entertained him at the festival of the fourteenth day of the half-moon, and gave him as a present a measure of barley, which he poured into a corner of his robe. When he came to the house of his friend he knocked at the door. The Brahman's wife said, "Who is there?" He replied, "It is I, your husband's friend." She replied, "My husband is not at home, and as there is no one else here, I cannot admit any man during his absence. Seek for shelter elsewhere."

Soon afterwards, while Mahaushadha was considering how it was that she did not admit him, he saw another man admitted. Then said Mahaushadha, "There was a reason for my not being admitted."

While he was still thinking the matter over, the Brahman himself came up from a village and called aloud at the door. When his wife heard her husband's voice, she considered what she should do, and with some misgivings hid her visitor away in a basket.

After this the two men who were outside entered in and sat down. Then said Mahaushadha to the Brahman's wife, "Where shall I put this barley?"

"On the floor," she replied.

The Brahman said, "Mice might come and eat it."

He looked under the bed and searched all the ends and corners of the house, but nothing came to light. All at once he saw a basket laid aside, into which he thought the corn might be put.

"Into this basket will I pour the barley," said Mahaushadha.

"That basket contains a treasure of mine," said the Brahman's wife. "How can barley be put into it?"

"Set aside the treasure in some pot," said the husband, "then we can pour the barley in here."

Mahaushadha also said, "In order that the mice may not render the barley useless, it must be poured in here."

Then said the Brahman's wife, who became terrified at the thought of the consequences, "The basket is damp; the barley will get spoilt inside it."

"You need not be uneasy," replied Mahaushadha to the Brahman's wife. "I will take care that no dampness remains in it, and that the barley is not spoilt."

Then he stood up, reversed his gazelle skin, and tied the string of sacrifice twice round his neck. Then he went out to fetch wood and water, with the intention of cleansing the basket.

The Brahman's wife, experiencing the pain of parting from her lover, and fearing that he would be killed, sent a messenger with all speed to his house, in order that, things being so, some one might come from thence immediately. As soon as his father heard the news, he came to Mahaushadha and said, "I want to purchase this basket."

"Be of good cheer and take it," was the reply.

"On what terms?"

"On payment of five hundred gold pieces, not otherwise."

While thus speaking, Mahaushadha lighted a lamp close by the basket. But the father, thinking that it would not be well to let the matter become known, opened the door of the house, and had the basket taken up by a strong man and conveyed to his own house.

On the following day Mahaushadha gave a hundred gold pieces to the man to whom the house belonged, told him what his wife's character was like, and advised him, after such an occurrence as this, to be on his guard. The remaining four hundred pieces he made over to that Brahman, in order that he might go with them to the Kaksha forest, and present them to Viśākhā, the maiden whom he had asked in marriage.

"Tell them [he said] that I am no Brahman, but Mahaushadha, the chief minister of the king of Videha, and that I came in that guise only to carry out my quest. Therefore must they watch carefully over the maiden."

Having in this way sent the gold pieces and a missive along with them, he himself went to King Janaka.

The Brahman went to the Kaksha forest, and delivered to Viśākha the missive and three hundred of the pieces of gold. When Viśākha perceived that she had not received the fourth hundred, she at once began looking under the bed.

"What are you looking for there?" he asked.

"Men have come from the court of the king," she replied, "with orders to seize the malefactor, and have gone away. Therefore do I look for him who has not gone."

Then she took some clay and said to that Brahman, "As I do not know who it is who has thus come here, I should like to try if a foot can go in here or not. So put your foot in here for a while."

When the Brahman, to avoid being suspected, had inserted his foot into the clay, she suddenly drove a peg[1] into it.

"Why do you arrest me?" asked the Brahman.

"Because that man sent me four hundred pieces, but you have abstracted a hundred of them," she replied.

The Brahman was astounded, and thought: "This

[1] The German text runs: "Als der Brahmane . . . . einen Fuss hineinsteckte, schlug sie rasch einen Pflock hinein." The sense appears to be doubtful.

woman and Mahaushadha are two demons. Two great demons have combined together." And he paid her the residue. Then her parents came in, and he said, showing them the gold, "The man is no Brahman. He is the king of Videha's principal minister, Mahaushadha."

When the maiden's parents and kinsmen heard that, they said that they were allied with a man of power, that they were in that respect very fortunate, and that their family would be made famous by means of Mahaushadha.

When Mahaushadha arrived in the city, and the king heard of that, he and the old ministers were greatly pleased.

"How have you fared?" asked the king.

"I have chosen me a wife," he replied.

"What kind of wife?"

"A very beautiful one," replied Mahaushadha, "of perfect intelligence, suitable for me."

And he asked the king if, as she was of such a nature, he might now marry her.

"Except me," said the king, "is there any man equal to you? And why? Because you are my chief minister. Therefore marry her to my great pleasure."

"O king, I will do so."

Surrounded by the band of ministers, Mahaushadha invited the Brahmans, householders, and populace to be his guests. Collecting together the rest in great numbers, the elephant-drivers, the horse-drivers, the chariot-drivers, and the goers on foot, he went to the house of his father-in-law in the mountain forest Kaksha. Having arrived there, he celebrated a great wedding-feast, and after a time he returned to the city with his wife, and lived with her there in love's delights.

After this there came from the north to King Janaka in Videha five hundred merchants with goods and horses.

In that city lived many courtesans, who were wont, by means of their wiles, to despoil of their goods the merchants who came thither. As soon as they heard that merchants had come from the north, they fastened upon them. But the chief of the merchants was very cautious. The most attractive of the women took him in hand, but with no success. Then she called the merchants together, and requested them to render their chief well disposed towards her. But although the merchants and the women took great pains day after day, yet he did not yield to enticement. Then that courtesan went to the chief and joked and laughed.

"Why do you trouble yourself?" said the chief. "You will not entice me."

"What will you give me," she asked, "if I do entice you?"

"I will give you five of our best horses. But if you fail to entice me, and you have no money, then you must follow after me."

Thus ran their talk. But in spite of all her efforts she could not attain her end.

One day the merchants said to their chief, "Do as other people do?"

"I have enjoyed the woman by night in a dream," replied the chief.[1]

The merchants repeated this to the woman, who called upon the king's men to arrest the merchant, saying, "As you have enjoyed my love, pay me five first-rate horses."

"You lie, disreputable female," replied the merchant.

So they two carried up their dispute to the palace.

The king and his court attempted to settle the question. Evening came, but still they did not succeed. Worn and fretted by hunger, they resolved to postpone the decision of the question, and went to their homes.

[1] Compare Benfey, Pantschatantra, i. 127, and Liebrecht in Jahrbuch für rom. und engl. Literatur, iii. 147, and in Pfeiffer's Germania, v. 53.—S.

When Mahaushadha came home that evening, Viśākhā said, "My lord, why have you tarried so long to-day?"

He gave her a full account of the whole question which they had not been able to settle.

"If a question remains unsettled by all of you," she said, "after being thus considered and discussed, how comes it that you hold such a position?"

"Such being the state of affairs," said Mahaushadha, "can you, perchance, decide the question?"

"I can," she replied. "See how great is my judgment! Go and order the five good horses to be placed at the edge of a piece of water. Then let the king and the ministers meet together at that place and give their opinions on the matter. If it turns out that, as the woman says, the merchant has really enjoyed her, then let the five good horses be given to her. But if it be proved that he did so only in a dream, then let her be shown the image of the horses in the water. If she says that she can neither grasp nor use them, then let her be told that, just as it is impossible to grasp that image, so is it also with the fruition of love in a dream."

All this was carried out. All were astonished at this decision, and the king asked who had been the discoverer of this way of escape. Whereupon Mahaushadha replied that Viśākhā had discovered it. Then all perceived that the carpenter's daughter was exceedingly clever, and her fame spread abroad throughout all lands.

After that a merchant from the north made a present of two mares[1] to the king, and said, "These two mares, O king, are dam and foal, but which the dam is and which the foal, nobody knows." When in this case also the king and his court were in difficulties, the carpenter's daughter Viśākhā settled the question as before, saying

[1] Cf. Śukasaptati, 37th Night, in the translation of Galanos.—S.

that the thick-haired mare was the dam and the soft-haired the foal.

Another time a snake-catcher brought two serpents, one of which was male and the other female, but nobody knew which was which. When Mahaushadha consulted Viśākha, she laughed, and wondered how it was that the king's ministers were unable to solve such a problem. What was needed was to fasten the leaf of a cotton plant to the end of a reed, and to stroke the backs of the serpents with the cotton. The serpent which was unable to endure that stroking would be the male.

On another occasion, a merchant from the south brought a stem of sandal-wood,[1] of which no one knew the upper end from the lower. Mahaushadha again consulted his wife, who told him to throw the stem into a pool. The root end would then sink downwards.

Once King Janaka was pleased to try which of his ministers was capable of recognising precious stones. With this intent he caused a gem to be fastened to the top of a standard upon the belvedere, underneath which was a tank. The king promised to give the gem to him who should recognise it; but no one who went into the water, intending to grasp at the light he saw there, was considered entitled to obtain it. When Viśākhā was consulted by her husband, she said that he must look upwards, for that light was only the reflection of the gem attached to the standard, and that it was necessary to go in the direction of the standard in order to obtain the gem.

As Viśākhā was very handsome, the six ministers tried, by means of all sorts of presents of gold, silver, and precious stones, to entice her into making an assignation, but they could not succeed in doing so. As they did not desist, she asked her husband if it was really the

[1] Cf. Śukasaptati, 38th Night.—S.

custom of the country that every young and handsome woman should be cajoled by other men. He replied that this took place everywhere, for men were greedy after all women, and they were instructed by the women themselves; but that if a woman was prudent, she did not give her consent. Then said Viśākhā, "If I were to bring a man of that kind to harm or disgrace, would any danger arise out of it?" Mahaushadha said, "Do so, and fear not." So she told him that he was to feign an illness, and she would turn it to good account. He did so. Then she sent messengers to inform the ministers, who had become acquainted with his indisposition, that she would grant them the fulfilment of their desires. Having caused an image of Mahaushadha to be made of wood, she dressed it and laid it in his bed. To each of the ministers she sent word to come to her at a certain hour, without letting the others know anything about it. She had also caused six chests to be made, and had distributed them in six of her rooms. Each of the ministers, on his arrival, she hid away in one of the chests. Next day she let the report spread abroad that Mahaushadha was dead. Thereupon the king and his court, as well as the rest of the people, broke forth into lamentation. But Viśākhā locked the chests and took them to the king, and said, "Now that Mahaushadha is dead, here are his treasures of gold, silver, and precious stones, sealed with his own signet." While the king was grieving that these presents should have been made to him on the very day of their owner's death, Mahaushadha came into the palace by another way, laughing and adorned with flowers. Having made obeisance to the king, he said, "Do you mean now to take possession of my property, O king, although you have never shadowed me with the canopy of your grace?"

"I have not taken it," said the king. "It was brought here from your own house."

"Great king and Mahaushadha," said Viśākhā, "there is another world besides this. These are precious stones from it. Take them as a pledge. Great king, these are the men who have dishonoured me, the widow separated from her husband, and have stolen from me my treasure."

Thereupon Mahaushadha pointed out the excellent intentions in the minds of the first ministers. When the king had looked in, and had seen the six ministers with their hair and beards shorn, and their hands and feet drawn together, he laughed and said to Mahaushadha, "Tell me, whose contrivance is this?"

"It is Viśākhā's contrivance," he replied, and then he proceeded to tell the whole story. The king marvelled at the acuteness and resolution shown by Viśākhā, and the cleverness of the carpenter's daughter Viśākhā obtained praise in all lands.

The king resolved that Mahaushadha should try to find him a wife of similar discretion, in which case everything would be placed on a good footing both at home and as regards affairs exterior to the palace.

"Where shall I look for her?" asked Mahaushadha.

"The king of Panchāla has an exceedingly beautiful daughter called Aushadhī," replied King Janaka. "She is endowed with knowledge and memory, and I have heard that in acuteness she resembles Viśākhā. Obtain her for me as my wife."

"O king," said Mahaushadha, "in this matter must some stratagem be employed, for there is enmity between you and him."

Then King Janaka sent his ministers and his Purohita in order to make proposals of marriage. The king of Panchāla called his ministers together and asked them what he should do. They said, "As King Janaka formerly refused to listen to your orders, we must manage so that they may fall into our power. Tell them that you will give your daughter, and that an appointment must be made for the purpose of receiving her, at a certain hour, on such and such a day of the half-moon, at such and such a place."

Having thus spoken, they went forth and announced that King Janaka was to receive the Princess Aushadhī.

"When and where?" asked the envoys.

"On such and such a day, at an appointed hour," was the reply.

Thereupon the king of Panchāla sent forth invitations to the wedding. And he prepared food and drink, and infused into it divers kinds of poisons. When all was ready, he sent out messengers to the people to come forthwith.

When Mahaushadha heard that, he said to King Janaka, "It is not fitting that we should act hastily."

"For what reason?"

"This king is a neighbour who has always been opposed to us, at variance with us. We must send a spy in advance."

"Whom shall we send?" said the king.

"O king," said Mahaushadha, "be at ease. I have a parrot called Charaka,[1] who is clever and honest. Him will I send. He will return after he has held converse with all."

"Do so," said the king.

The parrot flew off, and considered to whom he should draw nigh, with whom he should make friends and hold converse. In spite of looking around on all sides, he could detect nothing, and he had to consider how he should begin the usual style of business. Entering the palace, and there looking about him, he saw a maina[2] sitting on some timber-work, and flew up to her, and the two birds took pleasure in each other's company.

[1] This appears to be a correct restoration of the Sanskrit name, though the parrot's name is given further on as Māṭhara.—S.

[2] *S'ārikā*, *Gracula religiosa*, *Prediger krähe*.—S.

She asked him where he came from. He replied, "I come from King Śibi in the north. I was the guardian of a park, and I had as wife an excellent, beautiful, clever, devoted, and sweet-spoken maina. Having flown to a distance one day, she was carried off by a falcon. Full of grief and trouble on this account, I have gone wandering hither and thither, and so have come to where you are. Will not you, O good one, be my wife?"

"Never has it been heard or seen," she replied, "that a maina became the wife of a parrot. I have heard that really the wife of a parrot is a parrot too."

Thereupon the parrot tried by other flights in this and that direction to draw nigh unto her, and to render her well disposed towards him, whereby he entered into loving relations with her.

When the parrot saw in the king's palace many kinds of food, such as honey-puffs and other dainties, being cooked in pans, and many cates made of sugar, he said to the maina, "Wherefore are these things being cooked? Is it likely that we shall get any?" Then he said to the maina in verse, "Of this plentiful fresh oil which is being cooked in the pan, shall we partake? Answer softly, O maina."

"That which is being cooked in the pan," replied the maina, "shall not be your food, O clever parrot Charaka. With this food is poison mixed for the benefit of Janaka."

Then the parrot, employing wisdom, artfully said to the maina, "As it is said that the king of Panchāla is about to give his daughter to Janaka, and the news of this has been spread abroad in all the land, I ask whose words are truthful? on whose words can reliance be placed?"

"Clever parrot Charaka," said the maina, "this evil one is not going to give him his daughter. The men of evil purpose seek only to slay him."

When the parrot Charaka had heard this, having seen and heard, sought and learnt, he returned home, like a merchant who has succeeded in obtaining gains. But to the maina he said, referring to King Śibi, "Now must I go, O good one, in order to let King Śibi know that I have found a soft-spoken maina like unto my wife."

"O lord," said the maina, "when you have gone away, and have informed King Sibi, let it be made known after a space of seven days, after no longer lapse of time. Let King Śibi know what are my descent, my family, and my means. For my sake be not lost."

The parrot flew away, and gave a full account of all these things to Mahaushadha, who made King Janaka acquainted therewith.

When the king of Panchāla saw that Janaka was not coming, he equipped a complete army, and went forth against King Janaka, and besieged his capital. The first minister, Mahaushadha, perceived that there was no withstanding him in fight, so he considered how he could excite discord. By means of sending divers presents to King Śibi's five hundred ministers he produced dissension. When this had been brought about, Janaka sent envoys to the king of Panchāla with a message to the effect that, although he was in a position to fight the king of Panchāla, yet he wished to be reconciled with him, and not to fight with him who was his father-in-law. The king of Panchāla should know that in King Janaka's hands lay life and death. But though he could fight with him, yet he would rather not do so. If the king of Panchāla was in doubt, let him consider that Janaka had sent such and such presents to such and such ministers.

The king of Panchāla laid hands on those ministers with the presents, and that same evening he returned home. On his arrival there, he ordered the five hundred ministers to be executed, and made their sons ministers in their stead, and he became reconciled with King Janaka.

When Mahaushadha learnt that the ministers had been put to death, he rejoiced at having brought this about. They being dead, he said to the king, "Now will I go myself to see if I can obtain the princess or not."

When he had arrived in the land of Panchāla, the king invited him to enter the city. But he replied that he would stay where he was in the park, or in case he entered the city, he would go to the house of a certain minister. The king of Panchāla was alarmed at these words, thinking that Mahaushadha might be wishing again to sow discord between him and his ministers, so he sent to tell him that he might stay where he was if he wished it.

Now the ministers reflected that Mahaushadha had deprived their fathers of life, and they thought, remembering the old grudge, that if they brought the matter energetically before the king, Mahaushadha would never return home. So, after they had met together, they said to the king, "It is Mahaushadha in whom King Janaka has such a source of mental power. When he is at home by the king's side, no one can injure the king, but while he is here, we might well go forth again to attack King Janaka."

The king consented thereto, and they set out for King Janaka's capital with a fully equipped army. King Janaka also made himself ready. Now Mahaushadha learnt that the king of Panchāla had invaded King Janaka's country by such and such a road. After remaining a little longer where he was, he learnt that the treasures of the king of Panchāla were kept in a certain place, and that the king's daughter, Aushadhī by name, lived there also. So he went thither with a small troop of trusty adherents and surrounded the treasury. Entering therein, he emptied it of its contents and carried off the princess along with the gold and precious things. Then he got his army ready, and entered King Janaka's country from a different side. Thereat King Janaka rejoiced, and so did the ministers, the villagers, and the rest of the people, saying that he had accomplished a great work, and they made him many demonstrations of honour.

When the king of Panchāla's ministers heard that Mahaushadha had arrived with the maiden and the treasure, they abandoned the siege of the capital and returned to their own country; and King Janaka, having obtained the maiden as his wife, lived with her in happiness and love.

After a while, the king of Panchāla sent a messenger to his daughter, and asked for information as to who it was by whose coming the matter had been found out, and who it was who had brought about the dissensions. She sent word back that it was Mahaushadha's parrot named Charaka, which, being endowed with human speech, had spied the matter out. Then the king of Panchāla desired that it should at any rate be delivered up to him. So with great difficulty she contrived to catch it in a net, and she sent it to her father. The king flew into a passion, upbraided the bird in divers ways, and then ordered it to be killed. The parrot Charaka fell at the king's feet, and besought him to allow it to die as its father and grandfather had died. The king gave his consent, and asked in what manner its father and grandfather had been put to death. When its tail had been wrapped in cotton and drenched with mustard-oil, and when all this had been set on fire, and the bird was let go to fly up into the air, it set the whole of the royal palace in a blaze,[1] and then dived under water. When it had returned home, and King Janaka and Mahaushadha asked

[1] Cf. Pabst, "Bunte Bilder, d. i. Geschichten in Ehstlands, &c.," Reval, 1856, i. 14, and Mannhardt's "Germanische Mythenforschungen," Berlin, 1858, p. 39.—S. Also the burning of Lankā in the Rāmāyana, due to the attempt to punish the monkey-general Hanumat by setting his tail on fire.

it whence it came, it gave them a full account of everything which had taken place, whereat they rejoiced. But the king of Panchāla, being full of wrath, sent a letter to say that as the parrot had after such a fashion brought about injury, it must be again sent to him without fail. His daughter laid hands on the bird and sent it. The king of Panchāla in his rage plucked it quite bare, made a mere lump of flesh of it, and with the words, "Go and get eaten," flung it out of the window. Thereupon a falcon snapped it up. But it besought the falcon, saying, "If you eat me, you will have food for one day only; but if you will let me go, I will take care that you shall receive every day much food and whatever else you need."

The falcon gave heed to its words, and after the parrot had confirmed them by an oath, it was released. Charaka said, "At such and such a spot is the king's temple, convey me thither." The falcon did so. The parrot went inside and crept into a hole.

Next day the Brahmans came to offer sacrifices to the deity. As they were preparing to offer perfumes, incense, food, gifts, and oblations, Charaka cried out, "O Brahmans, to the sinful king of Panchāla shall ye convey these words of mine: 'As you have committed such and such a sin, I have inflicted injury upon you. If you do not act in obedience to my words, I will do the same again. You must bring day by day as an offering of food a whole measure full of red raw meat, sesamum, and rice porridge. After that I will consider what is to be done.'"

The Brahman went to the king and told him this. Thereupon the king ordered food-offerings and oblations to be prepared, and came every day with the ministers and the Purohita in order to beseech the deity to say if he were forgiven or not, and to promise that he would act in accordance with the divine commands.

When, after some time, the wings of the parrot Charaka

had grown again, it became capable of flying, and felt a desire to take to flight. Then it said, "You, O king, together with the commander of the army, the queen, the prince, and the ministers, must appear before me with heads shorn as smooth as pestles. If ye do so, then will I vouchsafe forgiveness."

The king took this to heart and behaved accordingly, and the whole party, with heads shorn like pestles, proceeded to the abode of the deity, fell at its feet and begged for pardon. Then the parrot flew aloft, uttering this verse:—

"The doer of the deed is requited. See how the plucker in his turn is plucked! Now he who by himself was plucked has thoroughly well plucked the enemy and all the rest."

Having thus spoken, Charaka flew away to Mahaushadha, who asked it whence it came, as he had not seen it for so long a time. It gave a full account of what kind of trick it had played. Mahaushadha was delighted therewith, and he reported it to King Janaka, who likewise rejoiced greatly, and considered himself fortunate in having so intelligent a minister.

At another time the king, in order to see which of his ministers was the cleverest, took it into his head to summon them, and to give to each of them a dog, with directions to train it to speak with a human voice within a given time. The ministers took the dogs home with them, and managed to rear them properly, but not to teach them to speak.

Mahaushadha took his dog home, and gave it a place at a little distance from the table, fastening it to a peg. The dog was accustomed to see various kinds of meats, drinks, and soups prepared for Mahaushadha, but could not get at them. By means of giving it little food and that bad, Mahaushadha brought it about that the dog was neither dead nor alive, and was lean and gaunt with exhaustion.

After a time the king ordered the dogs to be brought, whether instructed or not instructed. The other ministers, who were not versed in the sciences, had not been able to teach their dogs to speak. Then the king ordered Mahaushadha to bring the dog which had been handed over to him. When the gaunt, famished dog appeared before the king, he asked why it was so thin. Mahaushadha replied, "O king, I have given it the same kind of food that I ate myself." But the dog exclaimed, "O king, that is not true. I am all but dead with hunger." Thereupon Mahaushadha said, "After this fashion have I taught the dog to speak." Whereat the king was highly pleased.

Another time, when the king wished to make a similar trial, he ordered each of the ministers to feed and water a sheep in such a manner that the sheep should become strong without waxing fat.[1] Five hundred of the ministers were unaware how to set about this matter. They reared their sheep, but the sheep became fat. But Mahaushadha, while he placed delicate food before his sheep, set up in front of it a wooden wolf which he had provided for the purpose. The sight of the wolf frightened the sheep so much that it grew up strong without becoming fat. When the king saw that the sheep of the other ministers were flourishing and very fat, but that Mahaushadha's sheep had become strong without growing fat, he highly commended his wisdom.

On another occasion the king was again desirous of finding out who was possessed of wisdom. The five hundred sons of the ministers were holding a feast in the park. As they sat there eating and drinking, they took to describing marvellous things, each one being called upon to state whatever wondrous thing he had

[1] Cf. "Les Avadānas, trad. par Stan. Julien," Paris, 1859, ii. 48.—S.

either himself experienced or had heard described while tarrying at home. Then out of friendship they told one another the marvels they had witnessed at home and elsewhere. Along with the rest Mahaushadha's son was called upon by the young men to relate something. He said that there was a stone in his father's house which, although it formed the base of a column, would yet, if thrown into water, swim to and fro, and lend itself to rubbing and kneading, and so forth. The youths expressed their opinion that no such marvel existed in any of their houses. As he would not give way, and they doubted his word, he said that he would stake upon it five hundred pieces of gold. He told this to his father, who said, "Son, do not show them the stone." So when the youths came, he did not show them the stone, and his five hundred gold pieces were forfeited.

After a time Mahaushadha took some monkeys and gave them a musical training. Then he said to his son, "Go to your comrades and tell them, in reference to your former undertaking about marvels seen at home, that you are willing to stake twice as much money as before on the fact that you can show in your house musical monkeys, capable of dancing and singing and playing on the drum." In accordance with these instructions the young man, after speaking of other things, passed on to that subject, and said that he had seen such creatures. They declared that they had never either seen or heard of monkeys which performed musically. "What will you give me if I show you some?" he said. They replied, "You have already lost five hundred pieces of gold, and now you will lose a thousand if you cannot show us these monkeys, but have been talking nonsense as before. But if you do show them to us, then we will pay you that sum." When they had settled this wager, the monkeys were brought into the royal palace, where they played and sang and danced before the king. So the young men were obliged to pay the thousand pieces of gold. The king was greatly astonished; he had never seen or heard of anything like it before. Thereupon the king, the ministers, and the inhabitants of the city all paid great honour to Mahaushadha, in that he was wise and clever above all other men.

It happened that there was born unto a very learned Brahman in the land of Videha a very beautiful daughter, whom he determined he would give in marriage to him only who equalled himself in acuteness and knowledge. She received the name of Udumbarikā.

Unto another Brahman there was born a bad-looking son, unlike his father, and marked with eighteen signs of ugliness. On account of his ugliness his parents, at the time of his birth, gave him the name of Virūpa. As he was so hideous, and his parents were ashamed of his ugliness, they thought it would be of no use to have so bad-looking a creature educated. But when he had grown up, being desirous of instruction, he determined to go to another country in order to study. There he was accepted as a pupil by a Brahman, and he soon made himself master of all the knowledge his teacher possessed.

In consequence of this, Udumbarikā's father determined, in spite of Virūpa's ugliness, to give him his daughter to wife. However Virūpa did not dare to draw nigh unto her, but resolved to go back to his own home, in order to live with her there.

When Udumbarikā set eyes upon this paragon of ugliness, she being herself beautiful, she felt ashamed of him. Virūpa set out with her for his own country. On the way their stock of travelling provisions came to an end. Arriving at the edge of a piece of water, they threw themselves down upon the ground, feeling very hungry. A fellow-traveller, having stirred up some meal and water with a bit of wood, began to partake of it, and the woman, tormented by hunger, begged to have some too. Then Virūpa took a handful of meal and partook of it by himself.

"As I also am sorely tormented by hunger," said Udumbarikā, "I would fain partake of that water."

"As the early Rishis and law-teachers have forbidden women to partake of such water, I will not give you any," replied Virūpa.

While they were suffering from hunger in a desert during a time of drought, Virūpa found some dog's flesh, which he roasted and ate. When Udumbarikā wanted some too, he would not give her any, because the Rishis had forbidden women to partake of such food. Thereupon she gave way to all kinds of wailing, lamenting that she, unhappy one that she was, should be tormented by the pangs of hunger, and asking wherefore, on account of what fault of hers, had her parents wedded her to such a man.

They proceeded farther, and saw a ripe Udumbara tree. Virūpa climbed it and feasted on its fruit. Udumbarikā said he ought not to eat it all himself, but ought to give some to her also. He ate the ripe fruit and threw down to her only what was unripe. She told him he ought not to fling her the unripe fruit only, but ought to give her the ripe fruit also. He replied, "If you want ripe fruit, climb the tree yourself and pluck and eat."

Tormented by hunger, she climbed up into the tree with difficulty, and there ate some fruit. But Virūpa thought, "What can such a wretched man as I am do with such a wife—I, who can scarcely support myself? She will not so much as look at me."

Coming down from the tree, he surrounded it with thorns and then went his way.

Now it happened that just at that time King Janaka went out hunting, and he heard in the forest the wailing of Udumbarikā deserted by her husband. Following the sound, he caught sight of the bright-eyed one, who seemed to him like a goddess of the forest. When she had come down from the tree he reposed by her side, and then set her in his chariot, conveyed her to the city, and gave himself up to pleasure with her.

Meanwhile Virūpa, as he walked along by himself, repented of having deserted his wife. So he returned to the Udumbara tree, but found that his wife was not there, and learnt that King Janaka had taken her away with him, and had made her one of his wives. Thereat he was sorely grieved.

He went to the gate of the palace, but he was not admitted within. Then he saw that there were men at work in the courtyard of the palace, and he resolved to carry stone along with them. By this means he gained access to the palace, where he saw his wife and the king in loving converse. He hit upon a plan of speaking with his wife, and he and she discoursed in verse as follows :—

He. "Golden is the corner-stone. Dost thou rejoice in blaming? Fair one, lovest thou me not? Take, O carpenter, the stone!"

She. "At that spot did I beseech thee. In my memory dwell the words, 'To women meat is forbidden.' Me didst thou forsake."

He. "Beside the Udumbara tree, O fair one, hast thou asked me, born beside the river Ganges. Take, O carpenter, the stone."

She. "When I asked for meal and water, thus was I answered: 'It is not right that a woman should partake thereof.' Therefore have I hither come."

He. "Much has the learned mouth spoken. Speak of the countless golden glitter. Fair one, lovest thou me not? Take, O master, the stone!"

She. "Unripe was what thou didst give me. The ripe didst thou eat thyself. Mindful of harsh speech do I now sit dallying here."

He. "Down from the mountain will I dash, poison also will I drink, O Brahman woman. Wailing for thee am I here. Take, O carpenter, the stone!"

She. "Dash thyself down from the mountain, drink thy poison, O Brahman! In love's time thou didst not love. At home must dalliance take place."

While they two thus held converse, the king became suspicious, and said, "O queen, as I do not understand what ye are saying to each other, speak to me without fear, that I may hearken to your words." As the king was completely under her influence, she gave him a full account of everything. The king asked her if she wished to go away with her husband. She did not like to say openly that her husband was repulsive to her, for she was afraid that he, as he was a Brahman, might bring a curse upon her by means of evil spells. Then the king asked Mahaushadha what was to be done. Mahaushadha promised to arrange so that the king would not have to part with her.

"How so?" asked the king.

"As this Brahman," replied Mahaushadha, "is a man of very small means, but these women are exceedingly grand, I will speak to him after such and such a fashion. If I suggest it to him, he will look for his wife among your women, without identifying her."

The Brahman was summoned, and was asked what he was looking for, and why he had entered the palace. He replied that he was looking for his wife, whom the king had brought there.

"Shall you be able to identify your wife?" asked Mahaushadha.

"Yes," replied Virūpa.

"I will bring the five hundred women before you," said Mahaushadha. "If you pick out from among them one who does not belong to you, your body shall be cut to pieces with weapons."

Then the king ordered all his wives to appear arrayed in all their bravery, and to make the greatest possible display of ornaments. And the king caused Udumbarikā to be placed at the head of all the women, looking like the spouse of Indra, and surrounded as it were by Apsarases, and situated on a highroad, where sacrifices were brought. Mahaushadha called the Brahman to the front, and told him to take away his wife if he recognised her. But when Virūpa saw Udumbarikā and the other women adorned with all their bravery, he stood still like a snake charmed by a spell. Like one unable to gaze at the light of day looked the Brahman at the women. Then he saw a female slave, a carrier of water, like unto a Piśāchī [or female demon] in appearance, standing at the back behind one of the king's wives, and he seized her by the hand and said, "This is my wife."

"If that be so, then take her away with you," said Mahaushadha.

The Brahman took her and said, "The excellent loves the excellent, and the mediocre the mediocre; to the crooked one is my heart attached. O fair one, I am like unto a Piśācha, and you too are a Piśāchī. Come unto me, O Piśāchī. As I am like unto a Piśācha, we will take pleasure together."

Therefore King Janaka forgave Mahaushadha all the faults which he had ever committed.

One day the king went into the park with his wives, and enjoyed himself there together with them. One of them took off a string of pearls worth a hundred thousand pieces of money and hung it on a spray of an aśoka tree. While sporting with the king she forgot about it and left it there. At midnight, after she had gone back to the palace with the king, she remembered that she had left her necklace in the forest. Meanwhile it had been carried off to the top of a tree by a female monkey.

The king ordered his men to hasten to the forest and bring back the necklace. They went there, but they did not find it. Now a beggar had gone there in search of the remnants of the food of which other men had made a meal. As he came forth from the forest after partaking of such food, the king's men arrested him. As no one else was to be seen there, they called on him to render up the necklace. Although he protested that he had not taken it, had not even seen it, yet he was beaten with fists and stakes, and then thrown into prison.

Tormented by hunger, he reflected that, unless he contrived some cunning way of escape, he would die there of starvation. So he said to the jailer that he had, it was true, taken the pearl necklace, but that he had given it to such and such a young merchant. Him also the king's men summoned, and the two men were set fast connected by wooden fetters.

The merchant used to receive from home dainty food. While he was partaking of it the beggar asked him for some. But the merchant reviled him, saying, "It is all very well for you to accuse me of theft in order that I may nourish you with my food. I will give you none of it." And having thus spoken, he ate it all up.

After this, when the merchant wished to change his place, and said, "Let us stand up and move," the beggar replied, "I will not listen to your words; I shall not get up." Then said the merchant, "Henceforward will I behave so that you will be contented." Thus with friendly words and with an oath he won over the beggar, and was able to do as he wished.

The next day the merchant sent home orders to provide in future food enough for two persons. Thereat the beggar was highly pleased, and he reflected that in former times he used to wander about the whole city without being able to find the means of filling his belly, but now food and drink in plenty were at hand, and it would be well to call in a courtesan. Accordingly, he accused one of a share in the theft, and the king's men set her also in the prison. When the beggar was sitting in company with these two prisoners and enjoying food and drink, he said, "Good is it if we get free from here after the space of a dozen years."

While they so enjoyed themselves a further desire arose within them. They thought that in order to have still more pleasure they must call in a lute-player. So the beggar accused a lute-player also of having taken the string of pearls. Then the king's men cast him also into the prison.

After some time the others besought the beggar to find some means whereby they might become free, saying that in that case he should want for nothing. He promised to do so, and bethought himself that no one could be of use except Mahaushadha. So he told the king's men that Mahaushadha's son had likewise taken part in the affair, and they sent for him also.

When Mahaushadha heard that his son had been imprisoned, he felt that he must certainly go to the palace, for if he did not do so his son would fret himself. On arriving there, he asked the king what offence his son had committed. The king replied that he had been imprisoned on the testimony of the beggar with respect to the stolen pearl necklace. When Mahaushadha had become fully acquainted with the contrivance of the captives, he said to the king, "The theft has not been committed by any of these people. Let them all go free on my word." So they were released.

After this he went out to the park, and came to the spot, to the very tree, where they had been before. When he looked closely at the tree, he perceived a female monkey sitting at the top of it. Then he felt sure that this animal had taken the string of pearls, and that it must be enticed to come down by some artifice. So he asked the king to go there with his wife, and when there, to hang a necklace round her neck. When that was done, the monkey, as it sat on the tree-top, hung the pearl necklace round its neck. Then Mahaushadha told the king's wife to dance. When she did so, the monkey on the tree-top also began to dance; but still the string of pearls did not fall from off its neck. In order to bring that about, Mahaushadha asked the king to make his wife, as she danced, hang down her head. Then the monkey also began to dance about with its head hanging down, whereupon the string of pearls fell down from off its neck. Full of joy, the king embraced Mahaushadha and bestowed much property upon him.

After a time the six ministers assembled together and held counsel as to what was to be done, seeing that whereas they had formerly been esteemed, honoured, and exalted by the king, they had now lost their credit on account of a half-starved, gross-witted upstart. Then some of them said, "Inasmuch as we have hitherto been at variance one with another, therefore have we become destitute of power. Now let us go into the park, and when we have gone there, let us take an oath and bind ourselves by a vow. By that means shall we once more recover our power."

Mahaushadha saw them going thither, and reflected that, as they had gone somewhere as if by common consent, they probably had in hand something never seen before. Having suspected this, he sent the parrot Māṭhara[1] after them, in order that it might find out what they were about, what they said and did.

When they had reached the park and there met together, they began to communicate to each other their

[1] See note on p. 168.

faults and secrets, saying, "Now will we lend each other support."

"I ate the king's peacock," said one.

"I sinned with the king's wife," said another.

"I will do likewise," said a third.

After all six of them had revealed their secrets to each other, they partook of food out of the same vessel.

But the parrot Māṭhara reported all it had heard to Mahaushadha, and he reported it to the king, who banished those ministers from the country.

IX.

MAHAKASYAPA AND BHADRA.[1]

WHILE Bhagavant was dwelling in the region of Tushita, there lived in the city of Nyagrodhika a highly respectable Brahman named Nyagrodha, whose means were so great that he rivalled Vaiśravaṇa in wealth. He possessed sixteen slave villages, thirty agricultural villages, sixty vegetable-garden villages, nine hundred and ninety-nine pair of plough oxen, six hundred millions of gold pieces, and eighty golden earrings capable of vying with those of King Mahāpadma. He had married a wife of birth like unto his own, but their union remained childless. In order to obtain offspring he appealed to all the gods, but without result.

As he sat one day sorrowing, his mother advised him to go to the park and have recourse to the deity of the thick-foliaged Nyagrodha tree from which the city took its name, a tree provided with wide-spreading branches and a splendid crown.

"Your father also remained childless [she said], although he had appealed for offspring to many hundreds of thousands of gods. At length he betook himself to that Nyagrodha tree, and after he had implored its aid you were born, and for that reason was the name of Nyagrodha bestowed upon you."

So Nyagrodha also betook himself to that tree, and caused the ground around it to be sprinkled, cleansed, and adorned. He then filled the space with perfumes, flowers, and incense, and set up flags and standards.

[1] Kah-gyur, vol. ix. pp. 26-42.

Then, after having entertained eight hundred Brahmans and bestowed upon them materials for robes, he prayed thus to the tree-haunting deity:—

"Be pleased to bestow upon me a son. If a son is born unto me, I will pay thee boundless honour after this fashion for the space of a year. But if no son is born unto me, then will I cleave thee down to the level of beard-grass [1] and split thee into chips. These will I burn, when they have been dried by the wind and the sun, and their ashes will I scatter to the storm-wind or cast into the rolling stream."

The deity, who was one of but small power, was well pleased with the prayer, and moreover was afraid of being possibly driven away from that haunt. So, being in favour with the four Mahārājas, the deity went to the Mahārāja Rāshṭrapāla, and besought him to fulfil Nyagrodha's request. Rāshṭrapāla considered that he could not do this, inasmuch as the birth of sons and daughters takes place only in consequence of former actions. So he betook himself, along with the deity of the tree, to Virūḍhaka, to Virūpāksha, and to Vaiśravaṇa. But they likewise declared their incompetency. Then the four Mahārājas betook themselves to Śakra, the prince of the gods, and said, "O Kauśika, a deity belonging to our company is in danger of being driven from home. Be pleased on that account to bestow a son on Nyagrodha, the respected Brahman of the city Nyagrodha."

Śakra replied that it did not lie in his power to bestow a son or daughter, seeing that sons and daughters are born as a result of their own [previous] merits. Just then the court of the gods was illuminated by a great radiance, at the sight of which Śakra begged the four Mahārājas not to go away yet, for Mahābrahma was doubtless about to appear. Then appeared Mahābrahma in youthful perfection, and took his place on Śakra's

[1] Andropogon muricatus.—S.

bosom. He it is who fulfils all things which shall be accomplished. Then Śakra, the prince of the gods, laid the palms of his hands together, and thus prayed to Mahābrahma:—

"O Mahābrahma, art thou not Brahma, Mahābrahma, the ruler, the worker, the bestower, the spell-wielder, the lord, the most high, and, as father of the worlds, the creator of all beings? Lo, a deity belonging to our court, a dweller upon the earth, is in danger of being driven away from a tree-habitation. Be pleased, therefore, to bestow a son upon the respected Brahman Nyagrodha of the city of Nyagrodhika."

Mahābrahma reflected that he really could not confer on any one a son or a daughter, but that, if he stated that he could not do so, then all the designations would be discredited which it was customary to apply to him, such as Brahma, Mahābrahma, the ruler, the worker, the bestower, and the spell-wielder. In case he should say that he would bestow a son or daughter, inasmuch as he had no power to do so, it would be requisite for him to take heed as to how he should accomplish that bestowing. With that end he said privately to Śakra, the prince of the gods, "O Kauśika, neither has the world made me, nor I the world."

Śakra replied, "O Mahābrahma, since this is so, inspect thy region, and if a being is found there in the act of being subjected to the law of death, induce it to enter into the womb in the house of the respected Brahman."

Brahma asked him why he did not inspect his own region. Śakra replied, "In the region of Brahma the gods are known to be powerful, but those of this region are considered powerless, and on account of their feebleness they would not venture to make their entry."

When Brahma had given his consent, and had returned into his own region, he perceived that the life of a certain god was coming to an end, five prognostics thereof being visible. To him he spake thus :—

"O friend, as it appears that thou art departing from thy pleasant abode, and art making a change, be so good as to enter into the womb in the house of the respectable Brahman Nyagrodha in the city of Nyagrodhika. I will see that nothing shall be wanting in the way of appointments."

The god replied in displeasure, "O Mahābrahma, release me from this obligation. Wherefore this stress? Brahmans are addicted to perverse doctrines. He who wishes to come into existence in the house of a Brahman is like unto one who from love of golden fetters sets his own feet in bondage. Now will the Bodisat, after having thrice accomplished the purification of the Kāmāvaćara gods, descend from the region of the Tushita gods, and at midnight, as a snow-white elephant like unto the Airāvaṇa, with six tusks and seven splendid limbs, enter the womb of Mahāmāyā, the wife of King Śuddhōdhana, in that monarch's Śakya seat, not far distant from the hermitage of the Rishi Kapila, on the shore of the Ganges, in the neighbourhood of the Himalaya. There will he be born, after the lapse of ten full months, and, having become possessed of the highest and most consummate wisdom, will set up the pillars of doctrine, will strike the drum of doctrine, and will offer the sacrifice of doctrine. Therefore will I too, departing from here, make my entry into some house of no account. Then going forth from it, renouncing the world, I will enjoy in doctrine the drink of the gods. But were I to be born in the house of a rich Brahman, and were to be his only son, no one would permit me to enter into the clerical state. This being so, I do not hold it needful for me to be born of a Brahman family."

"Even if this be so," replied Mahābrahma, "thou wilt make thy entry there at my request. At the fitting time will I, in that case, instruct thy parents aright."

Thereupon the god's son gave his consent and entered the womb of Nyagrodha's wife. After the lapse of eight or nine months a fine boy was born and his birth-feast was solemnised. In the city of Nyagrodha all stones, gravel, and rubbish were swept aside, sandal-water was sprinkled, flowers of all sorts were strewn, incense was burnt in censers filled with perfumes, standards, flags, silken ribbons and streamers were hung out, markets for goods were provided, gifts were bestowed and benefits conferred at the four gates and the cross-ways inside the city, food being bestowed upon those who wanted food, drink upon those who desired drink, clothes upon those who needed clothes, and garlands, perfumes, and ointments upon those by whom garlands, perfumes, and ointments were required.

After many gifts had been given and benefits conferred in this way during the space of thrice seven, consequently of twenty-one days, the kinsmen assembled together, and bestowed upon the boy the name of Nyagrodhaja, inasmuch as he had been obtained in consequence of the prayer addressed to the Nyagrodha tree; but the Brahmans named him Kāśyapa, as his father was of the Kāśyapa race.

When he had grown up, and had partaken of instruction in all Brahman learning, his father intrusted him with the instruction of five hundred Brahmans' sons. Afterwards his father reflected that it was the custom for Brahmans to live for forty-eight years in chastity, and only in advanced life to enjoy their wives. But he wished to choose a wife for his son betimes, in order that the great and rich race might be transmitted. So he said to his son, "O son, as this is the law of the world, a wife must be taken for the maintenance of the race."

"O father," replied the son, "what shall I do with a wife? I will go into the forest of penitence."

However, as his father repeatedly maintained that the race must be transmitted, Kāśyapa hit upon a means whereby he would seem not to be opposing the demands of his parents, and yet would avoid consorting with his wife. He said to his father, "O father, order gold from the river Jambu [1] to be given to me." His father sent for the treasurer, and ordered him to give his son Nyagrodhaja as much Jambu-river gold as he required. The treasurer promised to act in accordance with this command. Thereupon Nyagrodhaja called in an experienced smith, and ordered him to make out of this gold the likeness of a woman. Then he gave this image to his father, and said, "O father, if a maiden can be found resembling this image, she shall become my wife. No other can I take as my wife."

As his father sat sorrowfully reflecting that it would be hard to find a maiden whose appearance was like that of even ordinary gold, the young Brahmans saw him, and asked what was the cause of his depression. He explained to them that it arose in consequence of his son's desire, one which his parents had never anticipated. They bade him be of good cheer. A man thus disposed must be treated by similarly framed wise measures. As he had caused an image of that kind to be prepared, his father ought to have three others prepared in addition. With these four images they ought to be sent out into the four quarters of the world. There could be no doubt that they would discover the maiden.

The Brahman followed their advice, and caused three additional images to be prepared. The young Brahmans took the four images, and began wandering through villages, market-towns, cities, and other places, and in them as they went they played upon divers musical

[1] Jambu: "Name of a fabulous river, said to flow from the mountain Meru, and to be formed by the juice of the fruits of an immense Jambu-tree on that mountain."

instruments. The Brahman Nyagrodha had given them directions not to choose a likeness to the image out of an inferior caste and family. As they considered it would be impossible for them to go from house to house, they determined to find out some other way of proceeding. In the villages, market-towns, cities, and other places at which they arrived, they always set up the image in the central point, and paid it reverence, offering up incense, perfumes, flowers, and so forth, and letting music resound, and they gave notice that it was the Goddess of Virgins who had arrived. To virgins who paid her honour would she grant five wishes: birth in an exalted race, marriage into an exalted race, residence in a fully provided house, submission on the part of the husband, and the possession of children. When these words of theirs had become known, crowds of maidens arrived, and with sacrifices and testimonies of honour they addressed their prayers to the image.

After some time, the young Brahmans who had gone towards the east, the north and the south, came back without having met with any success. When the Brahman Nyagrodha saw them return, he remained sitting where he was absorbed in thought. But his son Nyagrodhaja was exceedingly joyful and said, "It is good that ye have found nothing."

Meanwhile the young Brahmans who had travelled westwards went on wandering through villages, towns, lands, and capitals, till at length they came to the city of Kapila, situated in the land of Kapila. In it lived a very rich Brahman named Kapila, to whom there had been born, after he had married in his own degree, an extremely beautiful daughter. To her, in accordance with the custom prevailing in Madhyadesá, the name of Bhadrā was given on account of her beauty; and so, as her father's name was Kapila, she was called Kapilabhadrā. She had grown up by the time when those young Brahmans happened to arrive with their image, and set it up with all marks of honour in the middle of the market-place, and the maidens of Kapila drew near to the Goddess of Virgins, and prayed to her and brought her offerings. Among others, the wife of the Brahman Kapila heard of this, and told her daughter to go and make an offering to the Goddess of Virgins. She replied, "Of what use will it be if I make an offering to the Goddess of Virgins?"

"If you beseech her," said her mother, "five kinds of things may be vouchsafed: birth in an exalted race, marriage into an exalted race, residence in a fully provided house, submission on the part of the husband, and possession of children."

To these words spoken by her mother Kapilabhadrā replied, "O mother, I come of an exalted race and I am endowed with beauty. As I have no longing after any kind of love, I do not see what I have to desire."

However, as her mother repeatedly urged her to go, Kapilabhadrā, in order to fulfil her mother's wishes, set out to visit the Goddess of Virgins, taking with her flowers, incense, powders, robes, and the like. As she drew near to the image it became less and less brilliant, so that by the time when she came up to it, it seemed as if it were made of iron. When the young Brahmans had considered the question as to what sort of change it was that had taken place, and by whose power it had been brought about, they perceived that the brilliance [which had caused the change] proceeded from that maiden. So they inquired of her whose daughter she was. "The Brahman Kapila's daughter Bhadrā," she replied.

Having learnt this, they betook themselves to the Brahman Kapila's house, and remained standing at its door asking for the bestowal of a gift. The Brahman Kapila thought they were asking alms, so he gave orders that the young Brahmans should be presented with meal of the colour of māluta flowers, oil, grapes, pomegranates, and tamarinds. Now it is the custom in Madhyadeśa for gifts from a father's house to be distributed by his daughters. This is done because people suppose that they obtain what is costliest by means of the gift from the father's house. So Kapilabhadrā came with the gifts to the spot where the young Brahmans were begging, and offered them the gifts. But the young Brahmans refused to accept them. Hearing this, the Brahman Kapila asked the young Brahmans what it was they desired. They replied, "You should give us your daughter; we do not want the gift of meal." Then the Brahman Kapila angrily told those young Brahmans that he would not give them his daughter. They explained that it was not for themselves that they had requested the bestowal of his daughter. Thereupon the Brahman Kapila declared that he could not understand the matter. Then the young Brahmans asked him if he had never heard of the extremely rich and respected Brahman Nyagrodha, and his exceedingly handsome and intelligent son, versed in all sciences, and said that it was in that son's behalf that they had asked for the daughter's hand. Kapila replied that he had in truth heard a full account of the virtues and attributes of the respected Brahman, but that he did not see how an alliance could be entered into at such a distance. The young Brahmans said in reply to this, "Honoured sir, have you never heard what men are wont to say, 'Fire, wind, a horse, a poison that runs along the veins, and a Brahman of firm resolution, do not allow themselves to be stopped.' That Brahman is very rich, and you too are the same. You both have men and beasts for coming and going. Moreover, enduring is the friendship which is contracted afar off."

When the Brahman youths had succeeded in rendering the Brahman Kapila well disposed towards the Brahman Nyagrodha, he bestowed upon all of them towels, bricks powder, sesamum-oil, combs, and other things used in bathing. The youths set out with these things for the bathing pools outside the city of Kapila.

While they were bathing, the Brahman Kapila bethought himself of taking counsel with his friends and relations. So he went back into his house and told these things to his wife and his kinsmen. They said, "This Brahman is highly distinguished, and therefore we should be ready to take great pains in order to give him the daughter, even if he had no desire to obtain her. All the more unreservedly, therefore, ought she to be given to him now that he himself asks for her. If he enters into an alliance with us and becomes her husband, the daughter also will be fortunate."

Thereupon the parents betrothed their daughter to the Brahman youth Nyagrodhaja, having previously bathed and put on white garments, and the prayers for good fortune and happy results having been uttered by the Brahmans. The Brahman youths then informed the maiden's parents of the month, day, hour, and constellation at which the youth would appear; and then, having completely attained their end, they joyfully set out for Nyagrodhika.

When they arrived there, the Brahman youth Nyagrodhaja, who had descried them from afar, perceiving that they were joyful, said to himself that they had doubtless found just such a maiden as he had thought of. The young Brahmans betook themselves to the Brahman Nyagrodha, paid him reverence, and sat down. He welcomed them and asked, "Have ye, O Brahman youths, obtained that which we proposed and hoped?"

"O Pandit," they joyfully replied, "be of good cheer; we have obtained what is far more excellent than what you imagined. You instructed us to pay attention, not to the maiden's caste, family, and descent, but to her beauty. We have obtained one who is endowed with beauty, caste, family, descent, and property."

The Brahman youths then gave a full account of all the questions which had arisen, and of how the name, day, hour, and constellation had been settled, adding, "As we, O Pandit, have accomplished everything, and have returned back, now know, O Pandit, that the time has arrived." When the Brahman Nyagrodha had heard this report, he rejoiced greatly, and bestowed upon the Brahman youths food, drink, clothes, and ornaments of the very best kind.

But when the Brahman youth Nyagrodhaja heard of the beauty and great brilliance of this maiden, he was greatly disturbed, and he reflected that if her beauty was so great, great also no doubt would be her passions. So he resolved to go and inspect her beforehand. He said to his parents, "O my parents, I will bathe first at a bathing-place, and will get married afterwards." His parents gave their consent. Thereupon Nyagrodhaja, accompanied by one young Brahman, set out from the city of Nyagrodhika for the city of Kapila.

When he had arrived there, and had recovered from the exertions of the journey, he took the leaf of a tree, and began collecting alms throughout the city. Going from house to house, he came to the door of the Brahman Kapila's house. Thereupon Kapila's daughter Bhadrā came forth with a gift, and the Brahman youth Nyagrodhaja looked upon her, and guessed that it was she.

"Whose daughter are you?" he said to the maiden.

"I am Kapila's daughter," she replied.

"Are you betrothed to any one?"

"I have heard," she replied, "that my parents have given me in marriage to the son, Nyagrodhaja by name, of the respected Brahman Nyagrodha, who dwells in the city of Nyagrodhika."

"O Bhadrā," said Nyagrodhaja, "what need have you of such a husband? Know that she whose husband he will be will be just as if she had no husband."

"How so?"

"What can be done," he replied, "with such a man as he, seeing that he has no craving for any kind of love?"

"Oh, sir, that is excellent," she said. Then, after thinking awhile, "You have given me back my life, you have entertained me with Amṛita," she said aloud, "I too, O Brahman youth, have no craving for any kind of love." Moreover she said, "Your appearance has become such a delight to me as is produced by neither delicious sandal nor rohiṃī ointment, being great as is the distance between the rich man and the pauper. But as I am powerless, and my parents have betrothed me, I know not what can be done."

Then said the Brahman youth Nyagrodhaja to Kapila's daughter Bhadrā, "O Bhadrā, be of good cheer! I myself am the Brahman youth Nyagrodhaja."

When Kapila's daughter Bhadrā heard this, she was greatly comforted, and she said to Nyagrodhaja, "O Brahman youth, enter in and confirm the vows. The virtuous keep their vows."

After Nyagrodhaja and Kapila's daughter Bhadrā had held counsel together thereon, he went back to Nyagrodhika.

After this, when the Brahman Nyagrodha had set his house in order, according to the laws of householders, Nyagrodhaja married, and he and his wife were housed by his parents in one and the same habitation, and in it two beds were provided for them. Then said Nyagrodhaja to Kapila's daughter Bhadrā, "O Bhadrā, remember the previously taken vow." And just the same did Bhadrā also say to Nyagrodhaja. After they had thus admonished one another, they lived together like a mother and a son.

The Brahman Nyagrodha and his wife asked the women-servants on what terms were their son and his wife. They replied, "On those of a mother with her son, a son with his mother." When the Brahman and his wife heard this, he said, "That is our fault, not the fault of those two. Why did we provide them with two beds?" Then he gave orders that only one bed and one stool should be provided. Nyagrodhaja saw that his parents had taken this step, which was antagonistic to the vow that had been taken, and Kapila's daughter Bhadra perceived the intention of the parents. Then she said to Nyagrodhaja, "O lord, on our account have these steps been taken; but be mindful of the previously taken vow." He replied, "Be of good cheer, and have no fear." Then during the first part of the night, Kapila's daughter Bhadrā slept in the bed, and Nyagrodhaja sat on the stool. During the second night watch, Nyagrodhaja slept while Bhadrā occupied the seat. In the last watch Bhadrā again slept, but Nyagrodhaja remained awake sitting on the stool.

The old people next took away the stool too. Then Kapila's daughter Bhadrā again admonished Nyagrodhaja as before. He replied, "Be without fear or care, and remain mindful of the vow." Thereupon Bhadrā slept during the first night-watch, but Nyagrodhaja walked up and down. During the middle watch Nyagrodhaja slept, but Bhadrā walked up and down; and in the last watch Bhadrā again slept, but Nyagrodhaja walked up and down.

Thus for the space of twelve years they occupied the same single-bedded room without an amorous thought ever arising in their minds. Then the king of the gods, Śakra, thought, "As it is a very wonderful thing to see such a freedom from passion, I will put these two to the test." With this purpose he assumed the form of a snake, which glided into their bedroom and coiled itself up under the bed. When Nyagrodhaja caught sight of the black snake with terrible poison fangs under the bed, he feared that it might do some harm. Now in her sleep

Bhadrā had let one of her hands hang down. Nyagrodhaja considered what could be done, and lifted up her hand with the jewelled handle of the fly-flapper. Awakened and alarmed by the touch of the handle, Bhadrā cried out in displeasure, "My lord, what means this touch? Surely you have not touched me with amorous intent!"

"Oh no, Bhadrā!" he replied, "but because I feared that this poisonous snake might bite you did I lift up your hand."

"With what did you do so?" she asked.

"With the jewelled fly-flapper's handle," he replied.

"My lord," she said, "better would it have been that the snake should have bitten me than that you should have touched me with the jewelled fly-flapper's handle."

"Why so?" he asked.

"As a fair tree clasped by the māluta creeper perishes," she replied, "so do men go to ruin from a woman's touch. Therefore is it better that one should be swiftly bitten by the snake of death than that the hand of a man should touch an honourable woman. In consequence of the contact of the king's daughter's body was the great ascetic Ṛishyaśringa long ago deprived of the power he had gained by penance. On the path of the storm-wind did he approach the king's palace. He went back to the forest on foot."

After the young couple had gone on living for some time in this fashion, the two old people died. Then the Brahman youth Nyagrodhaja thought, "So long as my parents were alive we had no cares, but now that they are dead we must manage the affairs of the household ourselves." So he told Bhadrā that she must take heed to the indoor affairs, but that he would go and look after the fields.

Now when he regarded the work done afield, he saw how the nine hundred and ninety-nine pair of plough-oxen were tormented by small insects, how the oxen had their nostrils bored through, their shoulders worn, their loins torn by the iron, and how the labourers, long-haired and long-bearded, attired in garments of hemp, had wales on their hands and feet, and, with bodies covered with dust, were like unto burnt-out tree-stumps, and how, looking like Piśāchas, they abused and struck one another for the sake of a plough or a ploughshare, on account of the use of the oxen or the goad. So he went up to them and asked them to whom they belonged. They replied that they were the labourers of the Brahman youth Nyagrodhaja. He asked by whom they had been taken into service. They replied that they had been engaged, not by him, but by his father, for the cultivation of his estate. Then said Nyagrodhaja to these labourers, "O sirs, if ye were engaged by Nyagrodhaja's father for the cultivation of his estate, wherefore do ye labour with blows and abuse? If ye commit such misdeeds with your bodies and your speech, are ye not afraid of suffering in a round of long pains through the maturing of such conduct?"

Then Nyagrodhaja resolved that he, sinning neither with the body nor in speech or thought, would acquire merit. So when he had returned home, he said to Bhadrā, "O Bhadrā, manage the household with care."

"O lord, what are you going to do?" she replied.

"I am going into the forest of penance," he said. Then he added the following verse:—

"A small measure of cooked rice, a lonely couch, ensures bliss. A cotton double garment is to be worn. All else is tinged with gloom."

For some time Bhadrā took charge of the household. Seeing the slave-women with wales on their hands and feet, clad in hempen garments, with dishevelled hair, striking each other with pestles on account of mortars, pestles, cooking-pits, and the like, she asked them to whom they belonged. They replied, "To Kapila's daughter,

Bhadrā." Being asked if Bhadrā had chosen them herself, they replied that it was not she but her mother-in-law who had taken them for the work of her household. Then she also was moved; and, as at that time the Buddha was not yet born, she bestowed gifts upon the Tīrthakas, Mimāṁsakas, Parivrajakas, Nirgranthas, Ājīvakas, Ash-bearers, and so forth, and upon the poor and needy, and the askers for alms; so that the poor were not poor, and the slave-women, the day-labourers, and the servants had no more to cook.

After dividing all his property among ministers, friends, relations, and connections, Nyagrodhaja entered his house and inspected the clothes-room, with the intention of choosing a humble garment. He took out from thence a large cotton robe worth a hundred thousand pieces of money, and he gave a similar robe to Bhadrā, but the house he made over to his kinsmen.

Then said Nyagrodhaja to Bhadrā, "O Bhadrā, whither will you go?"

"I will go together with you into the forest of penance," she replied.

"It is not allowable for me to live in the penance forest with a wife," he said.

"In that case," replied Bhadrā, "let me be the first to go forth from the house."

"Why so?" he asked.

"If you are the first to go forth from here," said Bhadrā, "many men will long after the wife, as after rice-soup that is ready for the table. It is not becoming that, if you go away, other men should long after me."

Then the Brahman Nyagrodhaja thought, "This damsel is very discreet and of well-ordered intelligence." And he said to Bhadrā, "Bhadrā, come here; we will go forth from the house together."

Thereupon they two went away from the house together. After they had journeyed for a short time together, the husband said to the wife, "O Bhadrā, go and live in whatever way pleases you."

At that time there lived in Rajagriha the Nirgrantha Pūraṇa, who asserted that he knew all that is unknown, and who was surrounded by many Nirgranthas[1] and Nirgrantha students. To him Bhadrā betook herself and said, "Reverend sir, I wish to be received by you into the clerical order." He received her, and she entered among the Nirgranthas. When the Nirgranthas saw Bhadrā's exquisite beauty, they said to each other, "All we who have entered the clerical order have done so by reason of the five powers of divine love. Now Kapila's daughter Bhadrā looks like unto a divine being, but we know not whether she has acquired the powers of divine love or not. So we desire to enjoy the company of Kapila's daughter Bhadrā." Betaking themselves to the Nirgrantha Pūraṇa, they explained the whole matter to him, and asked for Kapila's daughter Bhadrā. As a favour to his pupils he granted her to them. Thereupon the five hundred Nirgranthas, in consequence of former actions, enjoyed her company every day. Disquieted, she consulted Pūraṇa. He said, "Whom the lot betokens, with him have to do."

At that time Bhagavant, after enjoying himself in love as the Bodisat for twenty-nine years, and then gazing upon age, disease, and death, had risen up at the midnight hour, and betaken himself on the good steed Kaṇthaka to the forest, and, after enduring for six years a penance of no avail, bathing in the river Nairañjanā, partaking of the milk-food sixteen times purified by Nandā and Nandabalā, had been praised in verse by the Nāgarāja Kāla, had received the Svastika

[1] Nirgrantha, "Freed from all ties or hindrances; a saint, a devotee, who has withdrawn from the world, &c."

grass from the grass-seller, had betaken himself to the Bodhi tree without allowing himself to be disturbed, and had without fear strewed the litter, taking his seat with crossed legs as the sleeping Nāgarāja coils himself together, and there had remained in this position till purification was attained, and had uttered words stirring his soul. After he had there overcome Māra and a host of thirty-six tens of millions of demons, he attained to the most complete insight, and became the perfect Buddha. Admonished by Brahma, he betook himself to Vārāṇaśī, and after he had set in movement the wheel of faith, he confirmed Ājuāna Kauṇḍinya and eighty thousand gods in the truth, also he converted the troop of the Five, and the followers of the Five, and fifty village youths. Having reached the cotton-tree forest, he converted the sixty Bhadravargiyas; having reached Senānī, he confirmed in the truth the two maidens Nandā and Nandabalā; having reached Uruvilvā, he converted Uruvilvā-Kāśyapa and five hundred others by means of the eighteen magic transfigurations; having reached Gāyā, he converted Nadīkāśyapa and a thousand wearers of matted hair by means of three metamorphoses; having reached the Yashṭi forest, he converted King Bimbisāra with his son and his court, eighty thousand gods, and many hundreds of thousands of Brahmans and householders of Magadha. From Veṇuvana Bhagavant betook himself at that time to Bahuputrachaitya. There Kāśyapa saw Bhagavant under a tree, and was received by him. Kāśyapa gave him the costly cotton robe, and received the Buddha's robe in return.

At the time of the festival of the meeting of the Nāgarājas Girika and Sundara, many Nirgranthas came to Rājagṛiha. When Kāśyapa perceived Kapila's daughter Bhadrā, as he remarked that her appearance was altered, he asked her whether she had preserved her chastity.

After she had informed him of what had taken place, he invited her to turn her mind towards the teaching of Bhagavant. As she hesitated, he assured her that this teaching contained in it nothing sinful, for its followers experience no desire for the love of gods, not to speak of that of men. He sent her to Mahāprajāpatī, who received her.

When she next met him as she was collecting alms, she complained that, like a fat sheep, she attracted universal attention on account of her beauty. Thereupon he told her that she need not go out collecting alms in future; he would give her every day half of what he himself collected. Thereat the Six scoffed. At length Bhadrā became an Arhantin, and Mahākāśyapa gave her back her liberty to collect alms for herself.

Now, when Ajātaśatru had killed his father, and nothing sufficed to rouse him from his sorrow, an evil minister, who remarked the beauty of Bhadrā, conceived the idea that she might be able to gladden his heart. So he caused her to be seized while she was out in quest of alms, and had her washed in one of the royal bath-houses, and provided with royal perfumes, flower chaplets, raiment, and brilliant ornaments. Then he conducted her to the king, who fell passionately in love with her as soon as he saw her, and enjoyed himself with her.

As Bhadrā was not present at the fifteenth Upavasatha,[1] Mahāprajāpatī ordered Utpalavarṇā to see after her. Utpalavarṇā introduced herself into the palace through a window by means of magic, and instructed Bhadrā in magic. Then Bhadrā betook herself, adorned with all her ornaments, to the summer residence of the Bhikshuṇīs, where the Twelve mocked at this magnificent array. Mahāprajāpatī ordered her to give the ornaments back to the king and to put on again the brown clerical

[1] "A fast-day, day of preparation for the Soma sacrifice, &c"

robe. When she reappeared at the palace, and the king, aroused from sleep, wished to embrace her, she raised herself heavenward by magic means. When he saw her thus soaring, fear came upon him. He uttered cries of anguish, and asked her whether she was a goddess, a Nāgī, a Yakshiṇī, or a Rākshasī. At his request she swept down again. He fell at her feet, and she granted him the forgiveness for which he prayed.

X.

UTPALAVARNA.[1]

THERE lived in Takshaśilā a very rich householder, to whom his wife bore a daughter of great beauty. As the child's eyes were like blue lotus blossoms, and as she exhaled a lotus-like fragrance, while the colour of her body resembled that of the lotus stamen, her relations gave her the name of Utpalavarṇā.[2] As her father had no son, he determined that, when his daughter was grown up, he would give her in marriage only to one who, on becoming his son-in-law, would take up his abode with him.

There was also in Takshaśilā another householder, who died leaving a son behind him. This son, while wandering about after the death of his parents, entered the house of Utpalavarṇā's father, who proposed to him that he should take up his residence with him as his son-in-law, whereto he consented.

After the death of Utpalavarṇā's father, her mother, who had food and clothing in plenty, experienced amorous desires. But she had scruples about inviting a stranger into the house, so she determined to allure her own son-in-law. Understanding the hints she gave him, he complied with her desires.

Being just on the point of being confined, Utpalavarṇā told her maid to call her mother. But when the maid came to the mother's chamber, she found her and her son-in-law alone together, so she determined to wait

[1] Kah-gyur, vol. viii. pp. 216–273.
[2] From *utpala*, the blue lotus, *varṇa*, colour, &c.

awhile. When the mother came forth from the chamber, the maid told her that Utpalavarṇā had ordered her to be called. When the maid got back, she found that her mistress had given birth to a daughter, and she was asked what had detained her. The maid replied, "May your mother and your husband remain well!" Being asked what she meant by that, the maid related what had taken place. Utpalavarṇā imagined that the maid calumniated her husband and her mother; but the maid said that, as she was not believed, she would make the matter manifest to her; so when the mother and her son-in-law were alone together, the maid called in Utpalavarṇā. When Utpalavarṇā saw those two together she thought, "Has this wretched woman seen no other man in Takshaśilā, that she keeps company with her son-in-law? And has this wretched man seen no other woman in Takshaśilā, that he keeps company with his mother-in-law?" Full of wrath, she cried aloud to her husband, "Wretched man, henceforth do what you please with her!" With these words she flung her new-born daughter to her husband. The babe glanced off from the father's body and fell on the threshold, whereby its head was wounded. But Utpalavarṇā veiled herself and left the house.

Seeing a caravan starting for Mathurā, she joined it. The caravan-leader, becoming ardently enamoured of her on account of her beauty, asked her to whom she belonged. She replied that she belonged to him who gave her food and clothing. So he took her to wife, and when they at length came to Mathurā, he left her there.

When he had sold his goods, and had returned to Takshaśilā with the money, the other merchants exchanged hospitable invitations and entertained one another. As the caravan-leader offered no such entertainment, the merchants asked him why he did not do so. He replied, "Ye who have your housewives with you are indeed able to entertain, but as I have no one who could undertake the trouble for me, I do not know how I can entertain." The merchants were of opinion that, under these circumstances, he ought to look out for a damsel. He replied, "If I can find a damsel like my wife, I will marry her." They begged him to describe his wife's appearance. He did so, and they perceived that he had a jewel of a wife, but they said that they would bestir themselves to discover one like her. Perceiving that Utpalavarṇā's own daughter answered to that description, they asked for the maiden's hand on behalf of the caravan-leader. Her relatives said, "Honoured sirs, we are ready to give her; but in case he discovered anything to find fault with in her after you have received her from us, he might send her back and go away." The merchants gave an assurance that this would not be the case, and then the girl was made over to them, and the caravan-leader married her.

Having disposed of his goods, he set off with the proceeds for Mathurā. Coming to a certain rock not far from the city, he left his goods there, together with the girl, saying that he was obliged to go for a short time to Mathurā.

There Utpalavarṇā greeted him and asked after his welfare. He began to complain that he had been robbed. She was delighted that he himself had arrived in safety, and said that the god of wealth would assist him later on. After some time he said, "O fair one, I must go to look for the goods of which I have been robbed." She gave her consent. Scarcely had he gone when one of the friends of his youth arrived and asked Utpalavarṇā where he had gone. She told him that he had gone to look for the goods which had been stolen from him. Thereupon he informed her that her husband had never completed a journey with such freedom from loss as on this occasion, and that he had deceived her. Moreover, he related to her how her husband had brought with him from Takshaśilā a Gandhāra [1] woman whose feet she was not worthy to wash. When the friend had affirmed the truth of his assertions she remained sitting in silence.

When the caravan-leader came back she passed over the slight and asked him if he had recovered his goods. He replied that he had. Then she said, "O master, you have deceived me. Your goods have not been stolen. I have heard that you have brought with you a Gandhāra woman from Takshaśilā. Bring her here. For soon come to an end the means of him who resides in two places."

"O fair one," he replied, "that is true, indeed; but have not you heard that in the house of a man who has two wives the soup is often cold, and therefore cannot be relished, and that in that house are found strife, discord, and bickering?"

"O master," she said, "pay no heed to that. It shall not be so. Only bring her here. If she is like a younger sister, I will look on her as a sister. If she is like a daughter, as a daughter will I regard her."

The caravan-leader complied with her request and fetched the girl, and on her appearance Utpalavarṇā conceived affection for her. One day, when she was dressing the girl's hair, she perceived a scar on her head, and asked her what had caused it.

"I know nothing about it," replied the girl, "except that my grandmother has told me that my mother once tossed me to my father in a fit of passion, and I fell upon the threshold, and that was how the scar was produced."

"What is your grandmother's name?"

"So and so."

"And your mother's?"

"Utpalavarṇā."

[1] Takshaśilā was "a city of the Gandhāras, the Ταξιλα of Ptolemy in the Pañjāb."

Then Utpalavarṇā thought, "As there I was mother and joint-wife, and here my daughter is joint-wife, I must anyhow depart." So she veiled her head and went away from the house.

Seeing that a caravan was starting for Vaiśālī she attached herself to it, entered into intimate relations with the merchants, and arrived at Vaiśālī together with them. When the courtesans residing in Vaiśālī asked why the merchants from Mathurā had nothing to do with them, one of their number said, "Is it not because they have brought with them a Gandhāra woman of such beauty that we are not worthy to wash her feet?" Then they all assembled and betook themselves to Utpalavarṇā and invited her, as her vocation was the same as theirs, to enter among them. Utpalavarṇā laid aside her head-dress and straightway went unto them.

As they sat one day at the drinking-board they discoursed about the various merchants whom they had relieved of divers sums. Now there lived in Vaiśālī a young grocer named Anishtaprāpta, whom none of them had as yet been able to allure. They said, "Whoever amongst us succeeds in alluring the young grocer, her will we style a capable woman." Utpalavarṇā asked whether in case she succeeded in alluring him, they would recognise her as their mistress. They replied that they would; in return for which she promised that if she failed she would pay sixty Kārshāpaṇas.

Having hired an apartment near the grocer's dwelling, she gave her maid instructions to buy perfumes from him every day. In case he asked her for whom she bought them, she was to reply that a young man of good family had come to Utpalavarṇā's house, and that it was for him that they were intended. The maid acted in accordance with these instructions. After a time, Utpalavarṇā told her maid to procure from the same young man, bitter, acid, and tart drugs. If he asked for whom they were intended, she was to say that the young man of good family was ill, and that she had bought the drugs for him. If he asked whose money it was that was paid, she was to say that Utpalavarṇā paid it. The maid did as she ordered. When the grocer saw that Utpalavarṇā was providing for the invalid out of her own means, he conceived a liking for her, and told her maid to let her know that he wished to pay her a visit. She executed the commission, but Utpalavarṇā told her to say to him that the young man of good family was not yet cured.

As the grocer repeatedly inquired on what day he might come, Utpalavarṇā perceived that he had conceived a strong passion for her, and she resolved to carry out an elaborate piece of deceit. She made a man's figure of grass, and had it taken to the cemetery and there burnt. Then she went, wailing and with dishevelled locks, close by the shop of that grocer, where he was able to see her. According to the words of Bhagavant, women enchain men in eight ways; by dancing, singing, playing, laughing, weeping, and by their appearance, their touch, and their questions. Excited by strong passion, the grocer said to the maid, "O maiden, now will I go." The maid asked her mistress, who replied, "Go, maiden, and say to him, 'The young man of good family died to-day, and the mourning is not yet over. How then can you pay me a visit?'"

When the maid had executed her commission, the young man's longing to see Utpalavarṇā increased. Then she sent to tell him he was not to visit her in her house. But she made an appointment with him at a spot in the park. The grocer went to the park, taking with him quantities of food, drink, raiment, and garlands. After he had eaten and drunk for a while with Utpalavarṇā, and was no longer master of his senses, being overcome by the power of wine, she determined that she would let him be seen by the public. So she set a wreath on his head, threw her arms round his neck, and convoyed him home. When the courtesans saw this, they were astonished and said, "This Gandhāra woman has splendidly beguiled the young grocer," and they named her their mistress.

After having for some time led a life of pleasure in the company of the other courtesans, she became in the family way. Now there were two gate-keepers at Vaiśālī, one for the east gate, the other for the west gate. As they were on very friendly terms with each other, and they wished this state of things to be continued as much as possible, even after their death, they agreed that their children should be united in marriage. When at the end of nine months Utpalavarṇā had given birth to a son, she reflected that women who had young children were avoided by men. So she said to her maid, "Go, maiden, take this child and a lamp, and deposit them both at a certain spot by the roadside, and then wait till some one takes up the child." The maid took the child, and laid it down at a spot near the abode of the eastern warder. Then she placed the lamp beside the child, and remained on the watch. When the eastern warder saw the lamp, he suspected what had taken place, and betook himself to the spot. Seeing the child, he took it up in his arms, and carried it to his wife, saying, "Good wife, there is a son for you." Thereat she was greatly pleased. When the morning came, and found sounds of rejoicing still continuing, the neighbours asked one another why there was such rejoicing in the eastern warder's house. Some said that a child had been born therein, others asked where the child could have come from, seeing that his wife had certainly not been in the family way. When the western warder heard of it, he reflected that, if a daughter should be born to him, the eastern warder's son would become his daughter's husband; so he sent a present of raiment and ornaments. As for the boy, he throve apace, and when he was grown up he entered an association.

Some time after the birth of her son, Utpalavarṇā again became in the family way, and at the end of nine months bore a daughter, with whom she dealt just as she had done with the boy. Her maid abandoned the child by the roadside near the western warder's house, and he took it to his wife, who received it joyfully. And the eastern warder, seeing in the girl the future wife of his son, sent her raiment and ornaments. The girl throve apace, and when she grew up also entered an association.

It happened one day that five hundred associates were going to visit a park, and as they took counsel together the idea occurred to them of taking a courtesan along with them, and they resolved to invite the Gandhāra woman, stipulating that if any of their number would have nothing to do with her, he should pay the associates sixty kārshāpaṇas. When they had agreed with Utpalavarṇā for five hundred kārshāpaṇas, and had taken her to the park, only the eastern warder's son had no inclination towards her. Then Utpalavarṇā said to him, "Sir, take your pleasure, else must you pay the sixty kārshāpaṇas." The fear of this penalty induced him to surrender himself to enjoyment. Afterwards an affection for Utpalavarṇā arose within him, and he made her his concubine. Thereat the Liććhavis were greatly angered, and they wanted to put him to death for having made a courtesan his concubine. Every one possesses in the world friends, foes, and persons indifferent to him. He betook himself to the eastern warder, and told him what had occurred. The eastern warder was terrified. He went to the Liććhavis, fell at their feet, and implored their favour for his son. As the eastern warder had for a long time been of service to them, they consented to give the courtesan to his son, in case he loved her. Thereupon the eastern warder's son, their permission being assured to him, was no longer alarmed, and made Utpalavarṇā his wife.

His father afterwards said to the western warder, "O friend, give your daughter to my son as his wife." The other replied, "What does your son want with another wife, seeing that he is already married." The eastern warder answered, "Inasmuch as we have already agreed thereto, give your daughter to him. As I have sufficient means, I will set the house of my son's wife on an excellent footing." So the western warder, in accordance with the agreement, gave his daughter to the eastern warder's son as his wife. About that time Ayushmant Maudgalyāyana [1] came to the eastern warder's house. And when he saw the warder's daughter-in-law, he cried, "O daughter, your fellow-wife is your mother. Your husband is your brother. But be not over troubled, and entertain no thoughts about hell."

When Utpalavarṇā had lived some time with her husband, there was born unto her a son. The daughter [of the western warder] used to set the babe in sport, before the door of the house. There came along the road a Brahman who, after looking at her, asked her in verse, how the boy was related to her. She answered him, also in verse—

"O Brahman, he is my brother, the son of my brother, my son [*i.e.*, step-son], and my brother-in-law. His father is my father [*i.e.*, step-father], my brother, and now my husband."

Overhearing this, Utpalavarṇā asked the maidservant what those two were saying. The maid replied, "What those two are saying is the truth and no lie."

"What then, is the truth ?" asked Utpalavarṇā.

"Your son," replied the maid, "whom I exposed at the east gate is now your husband. Your daughter, whom I exposed at the west gate, is now your fellow-wife."

Thereupon Utpalavarṇā reflected that formerly she

[1] Maudgalyāyanā "was the name of a pupil of Śākya-muni."

had been mother and fellow-wife, and her daughter had been her fellow-wife, and that her son was now her husband, wherefore, she must at any rate depart. So she veiled her head, and left the house.

As a caravan was just setting out for Rājagṛiha, she attached herself to it, and travelled along with it to Rājagṛiha, where she lived as before as a courtesan. An association of five hundred youths, who were going to a park one day, invited the Gandhāra woman to go there with them, on the payment of five hundred karshāpāṇas. There they ate and drank and enjoyed themselves with her.

Now Ayushmant Maudgalyāyana knew that the time for Utpalavarṇā to be converted was at hand, and he wandered up and down at a little distance from those young men. Then said the young men, "This worthy Maudgalyāyana is freed from the bonds of sin, but we are sunk in the slough of passion."

"In Vaiśālī," said Utpalavarṇā, "I beguiled the young grocer Anishṭaprāpta."

"Will you beguile this man also?" asked the youths.

She asked how much they would pay her in case she beguiled him. They promised her five hundred karshāpāṇas. And in return she bound herself to become the concubine of one of the members of the association if she failed. All this was agreed to. Then Utpalavarṇā betook herself to the spot where Mahāmaudgalyāyana was, and employed all kinds of feminine tricks and artifices. But Mahāmaudgalyāyana's senses remained unbeguiled. Then she reflected that a woman's touch is of the nature of poison, so she determined to embrace him, and thereby to bring him into her power. But when she tried to do so, Mahāmaudgalyāyana soared aloft with outstretched wings like a flamingo-king. And by the words which he spoke was Utpalavarṇā so affected that she besought him to instruct her in the doctrine. He did so, and she recognised the four truths.

XI.

KRISA GAUTAMI.[1]

A RICH householder of Vārāṇasī named Gautama, who travelled with goods to Takshaśilā, contracted a friendship there with another householder, and the two men made an agreement that their children should marry each other. To Gautama was born a daughter, who received the name of Kṛiśā Gautamī. After she had been taught to read, she had to apply herself to learning such work as women do. Now her father had been in the habit of associating with courtesans, so he entrusted his daughter's instruction to a woman of that class. The daughter began to study with her. After she had done so for some time she said, "As I have acquired what was to be learnt, I will go away." But the woman objected that she must first complete her studies properly; it was too soon for her to go away yet. The girl replied that she had already studied enough, and that she would go away. Then the woman took a paint-box and said that she would give herself a broken head if the girl was determined to go away. The girl begged her not to do that, and promised to remain. Then said the woman, "Kṛiśā, you believed that you had learnt everything, and yet you did not

[1] Kahgyur, xi., pp. 122–130. The principal theme of this tale occurs in the 25th chapter of the *Dsanglun*, but the Bhikshuṇī Utpalavarṇā is the heroine of the story. Kṛiśā Gautamī (Kisagotamī among the Southern Buddhists) has been made known by the work translated by Captain Rogers from the Burmese under the title of "Buddhagosha's Parables" (London, 1870, pp. 98, &c.), and has afforded a subject for comparisons with certain points in Greek tales to Prof. Rohde (see *Zeitschrift für das Gymnasialwesen*, 1876, Feb., p. 118).—S.

know this. Who would give herself a broken head for the sake of a stranger child? You know nothing then."

After the girl had tarried with her somewhat longer, she wanted to go away again. The woman declared that if that happened she would jump into the well. The girl besought her not to do that, and promised to stay. The woman said, "Kṛiśā, you believed that you had learnt everything, and you did not even know so much as this, that no one jumps into a well for the sake of a strange child. As you did not know that, you must stop here."

After the girl had stayed there some time longer, she again wanted to go away. The woman said that she need not wait long. She was going to bring in some milk, she said. The girl could drink it and then go away. The woman brought the milk, and in the girl's presence mixed oil and honey with it. Then she drank some of it, and having done so, rendered it loathsome, and told the girl to drink it. The girl refused to do so, whereupon the woman took to crying. When the neighbours heard this, they came together and asked her why she was crying. When the woman had explained the matter, the neighbours asked the girl why she would not drink the milk which had been prepared for her. The girl replied that she could not swallow what was loathsome. Thereupon the woman smote her breast repeatedly and said, "Wherefore should I give her what is loathsome to drink?" The neighbours seriously set to work to make the girl drink. But when she was going to drink, the woman seized her by the hand, slapped her face with the palm of her hand, and said, "O Kṛiśā, you believed that you had learnt all that was to be learnt. If that had been the case, you would certainly never have let that be given you to drink which you knew was loathsome. Consequently you know nothing." Having thus spoken, she drove the girl away.

After some time a merchant and five hundred traders

came to Madhyadeśa with merchandise. In the presence of these traders the merchant constantly spoke against women. Those traders had previously consorted with the courtesans of that place. But the courtesans now found that they and their leader only scoffed at women, and visited no courtesan's house. So they held counsel together, saying that whereas the traders who formerly came from Takshaśilā used to have converse with them, they were now entirely devoid of all passion. And so no man consorted with the women. Some of the courtesans said that they had heard that the merchant, who knew how to repress passion, blamed women severely, and that the traders, who were devoted to him, had therefore discontinued all converse with them. One of their number, an old woman, asked, "If I, by means of my daughter, effect a change in him, will ye make me your superior? And, in case she did not succeed, she promised to pay a penalty of five hundred kārshāpaṇas.

Thereupon the old woman hired a house in the neighbourhood of the traders, and provided it with a great quantity of domestic implements. The merchant's servants used to go there and borrow some of those implements. She said to them: "Who are ye, young men?"

They replied: "We serve the merchant from Takshaśilā."

She said: "O youths, my son also is a merchant, and he has travelled into another land with merchandise. As I suppose that his servants, like yourselves, are borrowing implements from other people, ye are at liberty to use all the utensils which are in this house, just as if they were your own."

So the servants made daily use of those utensils, and when the merchant had asked them whence they obtained them, and they had repeated to him the old woman's words, a friendly feeling was excited within him, and he said: "As she has shown you kindness, she shall be my mother." They told the old woman that their master prized her kindness highly, and regarded her as his mother. Thereupon she said that it would be desirable for her to become acquainted with him, and she asked them to invite the merchant to her house. There she received him with friendly words, saying that she found that he was like her son in appearance, and that he also bore the same name as her son, so that there was no difference between the two. Afterwards she told the wife of the master of the house to send for her daughter, whom she ordered to manifest her respect for her [adopted] brother. When the maiden appeared, and the merchant perceived her beauty, he desired to obtain her as his wife. The old woman said that there was only this drawback; that, as he was not regularly known to her, he might, if he married her daughter, leave her in the lurch. And so, for her security, she demanded that he should bring all his goods into her house. Agreeing to this, he brought his goods into her house. But the old woman immediately took them out of it by another door. When this was done, she promised to give him her daughter.

On the appointed day, and at the appointed hour, she invited the courtesans, adorned with all kinds of ornaments, to the wedding feast, during which they wandered to and fro. The merchant said: "Mother dear, are there only women here, and not a single man?" She yawned. One of the others secretly whispered into his ear: "O merchant, do you not perceive what is going on here? All these women are courtesans. How should there be any man present?" Then he perceived that he had really taken a courtesan to wife, and consequently that he had been duped. Moreover the girl demanded payment from him for her society. But he replied that the whole of his property had been taken away, and that he had no money besides.

When he had gone fast asleep, the old woman wrapped him up in a mat and deposited him in the middle of the market-place. When the daylight arrived, and many of the people who dwelt in the city began to come and go, he awoke, and, seeing how he had been treated, he gave way to despair. With eyes filled with tears, he wandered through the squares, the streets, and the roads of Vārāṇasī, and, plagued by hunger, in order to obtain food, he went to the spot where the day-labourers betook themselves. At that time the householder Gautama was building himself a house. As he was looking for day-labourers, the young merchant was brought up to him by one of the others. But the youth seemed to him too young and too little accustomed to work of that kind, so he ordered another man to be sought for. But the youth looked Gautama in the face with tearful eyes. Then Gautama asked him who he was, and whence he came. Full of grief at his pitiful condition, with tearful eyes and choking voice, he slowly said: "O father, as the result of former deeds did I prosperously arrive here from the northwards lying city of Takshaśilā. But now I know not whither I shall go, nor do I know how I shall get back there." When the householder Gautama perceived how cast down he was, and understood what he said, he felt kindly disposed towards him, and asked him if he knew many persons in Takshaśilā. Receiving an affirmative reply, he asked him if he knew such and such a householder. "O father, I know him, for he is my own father," answered the merchant. The householder Gautama was greatly pleased, and told the youth that he must not mourn or weep, adding, "As you shall be my son-in-law, this house shall belong to you." Then the youth took courage, and gave up being mournful. Gautama conferred upon him food, drink, clothes, and ornaments, a dwelling-house and a storehouse, and friendly words. And he said to his wife, "O good one, your son-in-law has come. As the wedding is about to take place, have all things in readiness." Thereupon he was going to fix the day and hour for the wedding, but the youth bade him wait a little longer, as he wished to get possession of his property first. Gautama wanted to prevent him from doing that, saying there was property enough in the house. But he replied: "What shall I do with the property?" As he wished to revenge himself upon the courtesan, he said: "O father, as this is so, I will not marry after the fashion of a man of low family." Thereupon he left Vārāṇasī.

As he wandered this way and that, he came to the bank of a river, and saw a corpse floating in the water. A raven, which was on the bank, and which wanted to feed on the corpse, could not reach it with its beak. Thereupon it rubbed its beak on a piece of wood, and the beak lengthened. Then the raven fed upon the corpse. Afterwards the raven rubbed its beak upon another piece of wood, and then the beak returned to its former length. The merchant took pieces of those two kinds of wood, and returned home.

He then took five hundred kārshāpaṇas and went to the house of that courtesan, and said to her: "O fair one, as I had no money, you turned me out of the house. Now, as I have money, come let us be friends." She, who cared for money, made friends with him. Meanwhile, however, the merchant rubbed the wood on her nose, which became very long. She called in all the doctors, and showed them her nose, but none of them could cure her. Given up by all the doctors, she betook herself to the merchant, and begged him to forgive her, and to cure her nose. He replied that he would do so as soon as she had restored him his property. She promised to do so in the course of the day. He rubbed her nose with the second piece of wood, the nose became as it had been before. Then she gave him back all the goods which he had brought with him. After that the merchant, with very great joy, took Kṛiśā Gautamī to wife.

The householder Gautama possessed some arable land in a hill district, and he bade his son-in-law go thither with his wife. When the time came for the wife to expect her confinement, her husband allowed her, at her request, to go to her parents' house, in order that she might there be cared for by her mother. After her confinement and the naming of her boy, she returned with him to her husband.

When the time of her second confinement drew near, she again expressed a desire to go to her parents' house. Her husband set off with her and the boy in a waggon, but when they had gone half-way she gave birth to a boy. When her husband saw that this was about to take place, he got out of the waggon, sat down under a tree, and fell asleep. While he was completely overcome by slumber, a snake bit him, and he died. When his wife in her turn alighted from the waggon, and went up to the tree, in order to bring her husband the joyful tidings that a son was born unto him, he, as he had given up the ghost, made no reply. She seized him by the hand, and found that he was dead. Then she began to weep. Meantime a thief carried off the oxen.

After weeping for a long time and becoming very mournful, she looked around on every side, pressed the newborn babe to her bosom, took the elder child by the hand, and set out on her way. As a heavy rain had unexpectedly fallen, and all lakes, ponds, and springs were full of water, and the road was flooded by the river, she reflected that if she were to cross the water with both the children at once, she and they might meet with a disaster, and therefore the children had better be taken over separately. So she seated the elder boy on the bank of the river, and took the younger one in her arms, walked across to the other side, and laid him down upon the bank. Then she went back for the elder boy. But while she was in the middle of the river, the younger boy was carried off by a jackal. Standing in the middle of the river, the mother waved her hands, trying to scare away the jackal. The elder boy thought that his mother was calling him, and sprang into the water. The bank was very steep, so he fell down and was killed. The mother hastened after the jackal, which let the child drop, and ran off. When she looked at it, she found that it was dead. So after she had wept over it, she threw it into the water. When she saw that her elder son was being carried along by the stream, she became still more distressed. She hastened after him, and found that he also was dead. Bereft of both husband and children, she gave way to despair, and sat down alone on the bank, with only the lower part of her body covered. There she listened to the howling of the wind, the roaring of the forest and of the waves, as well as the singing of various kinds of birds. Then wandering to and fro, with sobs and tears of woe, she lamented the loss of her husband and the two children.

As every action by gradual steps approaches maturity, so it came to pass that at that time her parents, along with their numerous domestics, were destroyed by a hurricane, only one man escaping with his life. When she, weeping and wailing, suddenly came upon that man, and saw him all aghast, she asked what was the matter. He smote his breast before her, and, sobbing and weeping, told her what had happened. When she had heard that, she again began to weep and wail, and asked what sin she had committed in her earlier existence, that she should have lost all at once her husband and her children, as well as all her relatives. And she came to the conclusion that she ought not to live any longer at home, seeing that her misery would only become greater there.

So she wandered about till she came to a hill village, where she took up her abode with an old woman who span cotton. And after recovering from her fatigue she took to spinning along with her.

There was in that village a young weaver who lived by his craft, and who was in the habit, from time to time, of buying cotton yarn from that old woman. One day, when she had served him with fine yarn, he asked her whence that came, seeing that she formerly span him only coarse yarn. She told him about the woman who was living in her house; thereupon he expressed a wish to take that woman as his wife, and to provide her with food and clothing and other necessaries of life. The old woman, after having received from him the money for the yarn and food, bade him wait for an answer; then, perfumed, and adorned with flowers, she went to Kṛiśā Gautamī and told her the whole story, praising the qualities of the weaver, saying that he asked her to be his wife, and advising her to accept his proposal. Although at first she opposed the idea, yet at last she gave in, and the marriage took place. Now the weaver was a rough, passionate man, who used constantly to beat her with his fist and with a stick; so she told the old woman that she had married her to a Rākshasa, and that she did not know what she should do, for he beat her every day with his hand and with a stick. The old woman comforted her, and said that he would beat her only so long as no son was born to him, but that later on she and her son would hold their own. When she was in the family way the weaver began to treat her kindly, but she treated him with contempt: with that, however, he put up.

One day the weaver, whom his friends had liberally treated with intoxicating beverages, came home dazed with drink. He found the door closed: his wife was just on the point of being confined, and when he called out to her to open the door, her pains prevented her from being able to do so, so he went away in great wrath. When her child was born she opened the door, and as soon as her husband came in she joyfully told him of the birth of their son. But he, whose rage was not yet appeased, being overcome by evil, declared that she, who had already despised him before the son's birth, would put him to death, in collusion with her son, after the son had grown up. Then he ordered her to light a fire, and set a cauldron over it, and to pour oil into the cauldron and make it boil, and then to fling the new-born babe into the oil and boil it. When she remonstrated with him, begging that he would not kill his own child, he beat her with a stick. Overcome by this cruelty, she threw the child into the boiling oil. When it was cooked he ordered her to take it out and eat its flesh. When she refused, he beat her most severely all over her body, whereupon she ate the child's flesh. When her husband's rage was appeased, and he was full of remorse and overcome by sleep, Kṛiśā Gautamī took as much food as she could carry, and went away.

She attached herself to some travellers from the north who had disposed of their goods in Vārāṇasī. Remarking her beauty, their caravan-leader conceived a passion for her, and asked her who she was and whither she was going. She replied, "My husband has been bitten by a snake; of my two sons, one has been carried off by a jackal, and the other has perished in the waters; and my father and my mother have been killed by a storm. I, who am now without any protector, am wandering at will, and I am going to journey along with this company of travellers." The caravan-leader made her his wife. Soon afterwards the travellers were suddenly attacked by robbers, in fighting with whom the caravan-leader was killed, and Kṛiśā Gautamī became the wife of the robber chief. But in his turn the robber found his death at the hands of the king of that country, and Kṛiśā Gautamī

P

was transferred to the king's zenana. The king died, and she was buried alive in his tomb, after having had great honour shown her by the women, the princes, the ministers, and a vast concourse of people. Some men from the north country, who were wont to rob graves, broke into this one also. The dust they raised entered into Kṛiśā Gautamī's nostrils, and made her sneeze. The grave-robbers were terrified, thinking that she was a Vetāla, and they fled; but Kṛiśā Gautamī escaped from the grave through the opening which they had made. Conscious of all her troubles, and affected by the absence of provisions, just as a violent storm arose, she went out of her mind. Covered with merely her underclothing, her hands and feet foul and rough, with long. locks and pallid complexion, she wandered about until she reached Śravastī.

There, at the sight of Bhagavant, she recovered her intellect. Bhagavant ordered Ananda to give her an over robe, and he taught her the doctrine, and admitted her into the ecclesiastical body, and he appointed her the chief of the Bhikshuṇīs who had embraced discipline.

XII.

SUSRONI.[1]

A MERCHANT who had married in Vārāṇasī determined to go to sea again with merchandise. His wife refused to stay behind. While they were on the voyage their ship was upset by a sea-monster. The husband perished, but the wife escaped on a plank, and was driven by the wind to Kaśerudvīpa, where dwelt the bird-king Suparṇa, who made her his wife. She bare him first a very beautiful boy, and then a young bird Suparṇa, who, after his father's death, was installed king of the birds. His mother insisted on his installing his elder brother as king in Vārāṇasī, so he carried off King Brahmadatta in his claws, and flung him into the sea; then he set on the throne in his place his own brother, arrayed in all splendour, and he warned the ministers that he would treat exactly like Brahmadatta any one of them who did the least thing wrong. The name of Brahmadatta was given likewise to the new king, who begged his brother to assist him from time to time.

After some time it happened that the king's elephant, which was parturient, was unable to bring forth its young. The ministers advised that it should be led into the zenana, in order that it might be relieved of its pains by

[1] Kah-gyur, xi. 93-99. When Utpalavarṇā appeared in the form of a Ćakravartin to the Buddha Śākya-muni on his return from the realm of the Thirty-three Gods, and Udayin recognised her by the lotus-fragrance which exhaled from her, the Buddha related this tale, with reference to the fact that Udayin had already recognised her in a previous existence by that fragrance.—S.

the asseverations of the king's wives. But although the elephant was introduced there, and the wives pronounced their asseverations, the pains did not come to an end, and the elephant uttered the most fearful cries. They were heard by a woman who was looking after some oxen near the palace, and who declared that by means of her asseveration the pains would be brought to an end. When the ministers had told this to the king, and he had ordered her to be brought into the zenana, she said, "If it is true that one husband is sufficient for me, and I have not two husbands, then as the result of this truth let the elephant be eased of its pains." Immediately after this utterance the elephant brought forth. When the king was informed of this, he declared that all his wives were of vicious habits, and ordered the herdswoman to be summoned. When she had replied in the affirmative to his question as to whether the elephant had been relieved of its pains in consequence of her asseveration, the king came to the conclusion that she must have a daughter like unto herself. This daughter, named Suśroṇī, he took as his wife; but fearing that, if he left her in the company of the other women of his court, she would undoubtedly contract bad habits, he begged the bird-king Suparṇa to convey her every day to Kaśerudvīpa, but to bring her back to him every night. Suparṇa agreed to this, and sent him every day wreaths of the odorous flower Timira, which grew at Kaśerudvīpa.

A Brahman youth who had gone into the forest for fuel was seen there by a Kinnarī, who hid him away in a rocky grot, where she used to enjoy his company. Whenever he left the cave, in order to fetch flowers and fruits, she closed its entrance with a great block of stone, which the Brahman youth was unable to remove. She bore him a son, who was called Āśuga (Swiftfoot), because he ran everywhere so swiftly.

As the father was always praising the merits of Vārāṇasī in his son's presence, the boy, when he learnt that it was his father's birthplace, asked him why he did not make his way thither. The father pointed out that there was a difficulty, the entrance of the cave being closed by the block of stone. Thereupon the son began to lift masses of stone, a larger one every day, until he had rendered himself capable of moving the block of stone. In order that his mother, who was in the habit of fetching fruits and flowers from the immediate neighbourhood, should be prevented from coming home too soon, he one day spat out all the fruits as soon as he had put them into his mouth, and declared that she must look for better fruits further away from the cave, for that those which had been plucked in its neighbourhood were uneatable. Next day the mother betook herself to a great distance, and Āśuga called upon his father to escape, for he had sent his mother far away. Then he pushed the rock on one side, and they two reached Vārāṇasī.

When the mother returned and found the cave empty she sat down and wept. Her friends consoled her, saying that, as her son was a man, he would not be in distress among men. The mother declared that, to prevent his being in distress while parted from her, she would give him something by means of which he could prolong his life. So she besought her friends, so soon as they should set eyes on him, to give him a lute, in order that he might support himself by means of it. Only he must be careful not to touch its uppermost string; for doing so would entail on him a great misfortune.

The Brahman had sent his son Āśuga to a Brahman as his pupil. One day when Āśuga had gone into the forest with the other young Brahmans to collect firewood he wandered far away, and was seen by his mother's friends, who asked him what news he had to give. When he had complained of hunger and thirst they asked him if he would not go to his mother, for she was weeping and wailing. He said that he could not hold converse with his mother, for she was so hot-tempered. Thereupon they gave him the lute, by means of which he would be able to keep himself alive. But they told him that, in order that no misfortune might arise, he was not to touch its uppermost string. Āśuga took the lute to where the Brahman youths were. When he had played and sung to them there, always without touching the top string, they asked him why he did not touch it. When he had told them the reason, and in spite of that they touched the top string, they all began to skip and dance. As this dancing made them late, it was only in the evening that they returned to their Paṇḍit, who asked them why they had remained out so long. When the youths had told the whole story the Paṇḍit asked the young Āśuga if he really understood how to play the lute and to sing. When he said that he did, he was thereupon obliged to play. And when at the instigation of the Paṇḍit he touched the top string, the Brahman and his wife began to skip and dance; moreover, the whole house skipped with a crash, and all the pots and crockery were broken to pieces. The Brahman in a rage seized the youth Āśuga by the neck and turned him out of the house.

After that Āśuga got his living by lute-playing and singing. Five hundred merchants who were putting to sea took him on board with them as a musician. When he was playing on board ship one day he touched the top string at the request of the merchants, whereupon the ship began to bound in the air and capsized, whereby the whole of the merchants lost their lives. But Āśuga, who got hold of a plank, was driven by a storm to Kaśerudvīpa.

There he took up his abode in a park where there were no other men. And there, having seen Suśroṇī, he held dalliance with her. In this fashion she was at the disposal of Āśuga by day and of King Brahmadatta by night. Now Āśuga besought her to take him with her to Vārāṇasī. She acceded to his request, asked him his name, and told him her own. Every day after that she carried with her, when mounted upon Suparṇa, more and more stones, until she had brought their weight to that of a man's body. Then she and Āśuga got on Suparṇa's back together. She told Āśuga to shut his eyes, saying that if he opened them a misfortune would occur. But when they drew near to Vārāṇasī, and Āśuga heard the voices and clamour of many people, he thought that he had reached the journey's end. So he opened his eyes; whereupon he immediately became blind. Suśroṇī left him in the park, and betook herself to King Brahmadatta's zenana.

Now when the king had come, and the trees were putting forth their leaves in the thick forest, and the voices were heard of geese, cranes, peacocks, parrots, mainas, kokilas, and pheasants, King Brahmadatta, surrounded by his women, betook himself with Suśroṇī to the park. There the Brahman youth Āśuga, scenting the odour of the Timira flower, was chanting a song after this fashion—

"Set in movement by the wind the odour of the Timira is perceptible. This is Kaśerudvīpa, where Suśroṇī dwells."

Hearing these words the king ordered his women to find out who had sung them. After Āśuga had been discovered and brought before the king, and had been obliged to repeat his song, the king asked him how far off Kaśerudvīpa was. He replied in a śloka—

"The waters of the ocean stretch well nigh a hundred yojanas from here to where lies Kaśerudvīpa, wherein Suśroṇī dwells."

The king answered likewise in a śloka—

"If it be said that thou hast looked in sinful fashion

on my dear Suśroṇī, say then what marks her body bears."

Aśuga replied in a śloka—

"On her thigh is the svastika. Her breast is spiral. Over her spread wreaths of Timira blossoms."

When in this way the king had become aware that Suśroṇī had sinned, he was of opinion that she was not necessary to him, and that he would give her to the blind man. In his anger he uttered this śloka—

"Suśroṇī is given to you, arrayed in all splendour. Let her mount on an ass, and get ye gone swiftly, exiled from this city."

Then he ordered Suśroṇī and the blind man to be driven out of the city, riding upon the same ass.

After wandering hither and thither they came at sunset to a hill town, and there they took up their quarters in an empty temple. That same evening there came five hundred robbers in order to plunder the town. But its inhabitants perceived this, and overcame the robbers. The robber chief, on whom they failed to lay hands, escaped into that same temple. The townsmen surrounded it, but the chief closed the door. When the townsmen asked who was dwelling there, Āśuga replied that some travellers were there. The townspeople threatened to make an end of him if he did not give up the robber. The robber chief said to Suśroṇī, "Why should you have to do with a blind man? We will turn him out and then live together." She agreed to this. The robber chief flung the blind man down from the wall, and the townspeople struck off his head.

Next day Suśroṇī and the robber chief reached the river Karada, and found no boat in which to cross it.[1] The robber chief bade her lay aside her finery, saying that she must swim across the river, and he would bring her things after her. She handed over to him all her

[1] Compare *Panchatantra*, iv. 7.—S.

clothes and ornaments, and went naked into the water. When she reached the middle of the stream, there arose in her mind the fear that he might run off with her things, and she uttered this śloka—

"The Karada is full of water. The fair one gave thee all her things. Fear has arisen within me. Deceive me not, O evil-doer!"

He likewise replied in a śloka—

"For the sake of one unknown hast thou slain one known of old, considering the man useless. Therefore is it difficult to put trust in thee. Me also mightest thou kill."

He went off with her things, but she crawled naked into the thick grass. There came by an old jackal carrying a piece of flesh.[1] Just at that spot a fish, driven on to the shore from the stream of the river Karada, was lying on the dry land. The jackal dropped the piece of flesh and made a dash at the fish. But the fish sprang back again into the stream, and the flesh was carried off by a vulture, so that the jackal, deprived of both, was left standing there mournfully, with drooping ears. Seeing that, Suśroṇī uttered the following śloka—

"The vulture has carried off the piece of flesh, the fish has slipped into the water. Wherefore grieves not the jackal, of both those things bereft?"

The jackal looked around on every side, and, seeing no one, uttered the following śloka—

"She who dances not before the robber, who herself has no joy in song, who now abides in the grass, who is she, who chides and scoffs at me?"

She replied, "I am Suśroṇī, uncle." The jackal reflected with vexation that this yoginī was mocking him, and said—

"Thy husband hast thou killed. Thy paramour has

[1] Compare *Panchatantra loc. cit.*, Benfey's remarks, I. 468, and Weber, *Indische Studien*, II. 339, &c.—S.

fled. Wherefore grievest thou not, yoginī, that thou art bereft of both?"

Suśroṇī replied, "When I have returned home I will take unto me an excellent husband. When I have obtained a husband, I shall not dishonour the house."

The jackal answered, "When the Ganges flows upwards, when the raven has the colour of curdled milk, then shalt thou be virtuous. When the snake and the ichneumon dwell in the same hole, and put up with each other, then shalt thou be virtuous. When a man, making clothes out of the hair of a tortoise, shall be able to provide himself thereby with a winter garment, then shalt thou be virtuous. When one shall have made a ladder out of the feet of flies, and climbed up it into heaven, then shalt thou be virtuous. When a bridge shall have been made out of the stalk of the jessamine, and an elephant shall have walked across it, then shalt thou be virtuous. When fire shall burst forth in the middle of the sea, and men shall enter therein, then shalt thou be virtuous. O Suśroṇī! now that I have scoffed at thee enough, I ask thee what reward wilt thou give me if I restore thee to thy former position?"[1]

She replied, "Uncle, if thou wilt do that, I will give thee a piece of meat every day."

"I will do it, see if I do not. Go into the water, immerse thyself in it up to thy neck, and remain there with thy face turned towards the east. I will go and petition the king."

So the jackal drew near to the royal palace, and made his request to the king, saying that it would be meet and fitting to send for Suśroṇī at once, seeing that she was piously and righteously performing penance. King Brahmadatta understood the language of the jackal, and

[1] Compare with this the variants which Reinhold Kohler has supplied to Laura Gonzenbach's *Sicilianische Märchen*, II., p. 242, especially the Bulgarian on p. 245.—S.

he ordered his ministers to send for Suśroṇī at once. The ministers made their appearance with clothes and ornaments, and the king restored her to her former position. Every day she gave the jackal a piece of meat. This she did for some long time. But at length she gave up doing so. Then the jackal came close to the royal palace, and threatened that if she failed to bring the gift, it would lay hold of her, and set her back again in the place she occupied before. She was alarmed, and continued to give it a piece of meat every day.

XIII.

THE OVER-REACHED ACTOR.[1]

THE Buddha Bhagavant was abiding in Rājagṛiha in Veṇuvana in Kalandakanivāsa. In Rājagṛiha lived the two Nāgarājas Girika and Sundara, through whose influence the five hundred warm springs in Rājagṛiha, the rivers, lakes, and pools received from the deity, from time to time, a rich copiousness of waters, whereby the grain thrived in the most excellent manner. As Bhagavant had brought under his influence the two Nāgarājas, Nanda and Upananda, they used to come to the slopes of Sumeru and manifest their respect to Bhagavant on the eighth, fourteenth, and fifteenth days of the month. Thereupon the two Nāgarājas, Girika and Sundara, considered that, as the two Nāgarājas, Nanda and Upananda. visited the Sumeru slopes on the eighth, fourteenth, and fifteenth of the month in order to show their respect for Bhagavant, they themselves who dwelt on the spot ought to testify their respect for Bhagavant. So they went to Bhagavant, paid honour with their heads to his feet, and seated themselves on the ground. Then Bhagavant confirmed them in refuge-seeking and in the basis of doctrine, whereby they felt themselves very much elevated. Thereupon they formed the intention of betaking themselves to the ocean. So they went to Bhagavant, paid him honour, and spoke to him thus: "O worthy of reverence, inasmuch as Bhagavant has led us to the search after refuge and the principles of the doctrine, we have become

[1] Kah-gyur vii. ff. 221-229.

so elevated that we would fain, if Bhagavant allows us, betake ourselves to the ocean." Bhagavant replied, "O Nāgarājas, as ye dwell in the land of Bimbisāra, king of Magadha, ye must ask him." They considered that there must be some reason why Bhagavant did not allow them to betake themselves to the ocean. When they appeared at night before Bhagavant in order to show him honour, they formed part of the retinue of the Gods'[1] dwelling. But when they came by day they had the appearance of ordinary householders.

At that time Bimbisāra, king of Magadha, went to Veṇuvana to Kalandakanivāsa. With Kshatriya pride the king halted on the way, and said to a man of low degree, "Ho, man, go and see who is paying honour to Bhagavant." The man of low degree obeyed the command of the king, went to the spot where Bhagavant was, and saw that there were two householders who were paying honour to Bhagavant. Of this he informed the king, remarking that those men dwelt no doubt in his territory. The king imagined that those two householders, as they dwelt in his territory, would be sure to rise up when he appeared, and he went to the place where Bhagavant was. The two Nāgārajas perceived him from afar, and said to Bhagavant, "O worthy of reverence, what ought to be done? Should we now pay honour to the excellent law or to the king?"

"O Nāgarājas, do ye pay honour to the excellent law. The Buddha-Bhagavants pay honour to the excellent law, and the Arhants also honour the law highly." This saying he repeated also in verse.

Then the two Nāgarājas omitted to rise in presence of the king, and the king waxed angry at seeing that the two householders who dwelt in his land did not stand up. After he had paid honour with his head to Bhagavant's feet, he sat down upon the ground and besought Bhagavant to instruct him in the doctrine. Bhagavant uttered the following verses:—

[1] See Childers' Dictionary of the Pali Language, under the word Vimána.—S.

"Not by him who is beside himself, who is excited by passion, can the excellent doctrine taught by the perfected Buddha be comprehended. But he who represses the commencement of sins, who lays aside anger, and who has given up passion, he can comprehend the excellent words."

The king thought that Bhagavant took the side of the two householders, and therefore would not teach him the doctrine; so he went away thence. When he had departed from Veṇuvana, he said to his servants, "So soon as those two householders go away from Bhagavant, tell them in the name of the king that they must not remain in the country." Having received this order from the king, the servants remained there, and communicated the king's order to the two Nāgarājas when they made their appearance. The two Nāgarājas perceived that their long fostered wish was going to be fulfilled. So they produced on the spot a mighty jet of water, and betook themselves into small çanals, and from the small canals into great canals, and from the great canals into small rivers, and from the small rivers into great rivers, and from the great rivers into the ocean. When they two reached the ocean, they were far more elevated than before.

At that same time the five hundred warm springs in Rājagṛiha, the rivers, lakes, and pools, inasmuch as the deity no longer sent them from time to time a fulness of water, began to dry up, and the crops began to perish. Then the king reflected that by the power of the Nāgarājas the water-courses used to be kept constantly full, and, as this was no longer the case, he considered that those two Nāgarājas were perhaps dead, or had been carried off or shut up by a snake charmer. He determined then to obtain information on this point from the omniscient Bhagavant. Bhagavant replied that the two Nāgarājas had not been destroyed, nor had they died, and that they had not taken themselves away secretly, nor had they been imprisoned by a snake charmer, but that they had been banished from the country by the king himself.

"Venerable sir, so far as I can remember, I have never seen, much less exiled, the two Nāgarājas Girika and Sundara."

"O great king, I will recall the fact to your memory."

Thereupon Bhagavant informed him that those two householders whom he had sent out of the country were precisely those two Nāgarājas, and recommended him, in order to obtain help for his land, to ask for their forgiveness. The king observed that he was not in a position to do this, as they had departed into the ocean. Then Bhagavant informed him that they were accustomed to come, in order to show him honour, on the eighth, fourteenth, and fifteenth days of the month. And that when he was teaching them the doctrine, the king might ask their forgiveness.

"Venerable sir, how should that be done? Ought I to touch the feet of them twain!"

"No, great king, that is what men of inferior degree do, who touch the hand of their superiors. But you should stretch out your right hand, and say to the two Nāgarājas: 'Forgive me!'"

So when the king met the two Nāgarājas in the presence of Bhagavant, he followed his instructions, and received the pardon he asked for.

Then he said: "O Nāgarājas, having accorded me forgiveness, return back to my country." They replied that they would do so then only when he had erected two temples, the one for Girika and the other for Sundara, and had provided them with the necessary attendants, and had founded a festival to be held every six months, at which they would appear in person and accept hospitality. The king obeyed these orders. He built the two temples, the one for Girika, and the other for Sundara, and he founded a festival to be held every six months. When this festival took place, vast multitudes of men came together from the six great cities.

One day there came an actor from the south, with the intention of discovering something whereby he might amuse the company, and obtain a large reward for himself. He hoped to attain both ends if he glorified the most excellent of men. Inasmuch then as the multitudes were full of faith in Bhagavant, he wished to take him as the subject of glorification, so he betook himself to Nanda and said:

"Venerable sir, when Bhagavant dwelling as the Bodisat in the Tushita region had arranged the five considerations respecting caste, race, country, time and wife, and had let the six Kāmāvachara gods three times perform the rites of purification, and in the form of an elephant had consciously entered the mother's womb, at that time the great earth quaked violently, and those regions of the world which enjoy the light neither of the sun nor of the moon, and therefore are filled with utter darkness, were illumined with the greatest brilliance; so that when the beings, which otherwise could not see their own hands when they stretched them out, saw each other by means of this light, they cried: "Honoured sirs, there are other beings besides ourselves born here." When after the lapse of ten months Bhagavant the Bodisat was born, leaving the mother's womb, then likewise did the great earth quake, and the bright radiance ensued. On the day on which Bhagavant the Bodisat was born, on that same day were born also sons of four great kings. In Śrāvastī truly to King Aranemi Brahmadatta there was born a son whom he called Prasenajit, because the whole world was filled with radiance at his birth. In Rājagṛiha there was born to King Mahāpadma a son whom he called Bimbisāra, because he was the son of Queen Bimbī, and at his birth the world was illumined as at the rise of the sun's disk. In Kauśāmbī there was born to King Śatānīka a son whom he named Udajana, because the world was illumined at his birth as if by the rising of the sun. In Videha there was born to King Anantanemi a son, whom he called Pradyota, because at his birth the world was greatly illumined. On the day on which Bhagavant the Bodisat was born, there were born also five hundred Śākya sons, Bhadrika, and so forth, and five hundred attendants, Chhanda, and so forth. Five hundred mares gave birth to five hundred colts, Kanthaka, and so forth, and five hundred treasures were conferred by the gods. The Brahmans versed in omens prophesied with respect to Bhagavant the Bodisat as follows: "If the Prince remains in the palace, he will become a Chakravartin, who will conquer the four regions of the world, a ruler in accordance with the law, a king having the seven treasures, those of the wheel, the elephant, the horse, the gem, the wife, the householder, and the general, a king to whom there shall be born a full thousand of heroic, extremely handsome sons, victorious over hosts of foes, and under whom the whole great earth up to the ocean shall live in peace of mind and in harmony with the law, free from harm or danger, without punishments or force of arms. But if, full of faith, with shorn hair and beard, and dressed in dark brown raiment, he leaves his home and joins the ecclesiastical body, then will he gain the renown in the world of a Tathāgata, an Arhant, and a fully consummated Buddha."

At the time when Bhagavant the Bodisat was born, it was known everywhere that on the shore of the river Bhagirathī, on the side of Himavant, not very far from the hermitage of the Rishi Kapila, a Śākya prince was born, and what sort of prophesies the Brahmans skilled in omens had uttered. When the kings of the earth heard thereof, they reflected that if they exalted the prince, they would gain thereby, and that if they honoured King Suddhodana, the prince would thereby be honoured; so they began to pay honour to King Suddhodana, and to send him in due season envoys and caskets of jewels. As King Suddhodana reflected that all things had attained their ends in consequence of the birth of his son, that son ought to receive the name of Sarvārthasiddha, and he called him by that name accordingly. When the prince had been taken to pay reverence to the Śākya-god, the Yaksha Śākyavardha, but was received with reverence by him, the Śākya-Mighty-One, he received the names of Śākyamuni and God of gods (Devātideva).

When Bhagavant the Bodisat had attained perfection in all sciences, and had enjoyed himself in youth, but then had looked upon old age, sickness, and death, and his mind had been agitated thereby, he retired into the forest and devoted himself for six years to penance. At that time were two hundred and fifty men sent every day, who made known the words of King Suddhodana and of Suprabuddha, and daily carried the words spoken by Bhagavant the Bodisat.

When Bhagavant the Bodisat had practised penance for the space of six years, and had attained to the knowledge that it was all of no avail, he desired to restore himself completely. So he took rice soup, and warm food in abundance, anointed his body with oil and melted butter, and bathed it with warm water. And when he came to the village of Senānī, the village maidens Nandā and Nandabalā gave him sixteen times purified milk mixed with honey, and the Nāgarāja Kālika extolled him. From the Svastika grass-dealers he received gold coloured grass. When he arrived at Bodhimaṇḍa, after he had prepared himself a couch of indestructible grass, and had taken up his seat upon it with crossed legs, and had made straight his body, and strengthened his memory, he said with emotion, "Until I shall have attained sinlessness will I not change my sitting position. How then Bhagavant the Bodisat, after he had, at the midnight hour by means of the wheel of mildness overcome Māra and the host of three hundred and sixty millions of demons, attained to the supreme perfection of insight—all this he pleased to relate to me in full."

Nanda asked, "What do you want it for?" The actor replied, "Venerable sir, I wish to compose a drama." Nanda said, "Wretched man, do you wish us to portray the Teacher for you? Begone, for I will tell you nothing." Then the actor betook himself to Upananda, but received from him the same answer, and the result was the same when he had recourse to Aśuga, Ravata, Chhanda, and Udayin. Thereupon the actor betook himself to where the company of Twelve Bhikshuṇīs was. First of all he had recourse to Sthūlanandā. When she had inquired what he wanted the information for, and he had replied that it was for a drama, she asked whether he would give her a recompense for her trouble. He promised that he would. Then as Sthūlanandā was very learned, and knew the Tripiṭaka thoroughly, she related everything to him in full out of the Abhinishkramaṇa-Sūtra, how Bhagavant the Bodisat, while dwelling in the Tushita region, appointed the five meditations with respect to caste, race, country, time, and wife, and having appointed these considerations, and having allowed the six Kāmāvachara gods to receive purification three times, he consciously entered the mother's womb, transformed into the shape of an elephant. Whereupon the great earth quaked greatly, and the intervals of the world in which the sun and moon are looked upon as great wonders, and the darkness is exceedingly great, inasmuch as no light is enjoyed there, were profusely illumined anew, so that the beings born therein, which had not been able to see their own hands when they stretched them out, looking upon one another by means of this light, exclaimed, "Honoured sirs, other beings also have been born here." Then she related to him all that had taken place up to the time, when at midnight Bhagavant the Bodisat overcame Māra and the attending three hundred and sixty millions of demons by the force of mildness, and attained to supreme insight.

The actor then composed his drama, and, as he knew that by means of it he could exalt the faith still higher, amid the masses of believers, he considered how he might create faith also among unbelievers. And, as he bore a grudge against the Six Bhikshus, and desired to find a cause of reproach against them, he betook himself to them. Now Āyushmant Chhanda had just prepared some food, but let it stand over. With the hope, however of partaking of sweet food, in case he met with any, he had washed his hands. With such food Āyushmant Udayin had supplied himself, so Chhanda sat down before him with crossed legs and begged him to think of him, saying, "I, the Bhikshu Chhanda, had prepared food, but I let it stand over, as I was fully satisfied. But now that I have found food, I desire to eat, and I beg you to leave me something." After taking two or three morsels of the food, Udayin said, "Take and go."

When the actor heard that, he thought that he might thereby convert even unbelievers to the faith. So he pitched a booth in Rajagṛiha on the day when the festival of the Nāgarājas Girika and Sundara was celebrated, and sounded a drum. And when a great crowd had collected, he exhibited in a drama the above-mentioned events in the life of Bhagavant, in harmony with the Abhinishkramaṇasūtra. Thereby the performers and the assembled crowds were confirmed in the faith. And they uttered sounds of approval, and he made a large profit.

In order that among the unbelievers also he might excite faith, he introduced one actor under the guise of Udayin, and another under that of Chhanda. And he filled a dish with ashes, on the top of which he placed two or three lumps of sugar. In front of him who played the part of Udayin, the other sat down cross-legged, and said, "Venerable Udayin, remember me. I am the Bhikshu Chhanda, and I have let my food stand over, for I was quite satisfied. But now that I have met with food, I want to eat, and I beg you will leave me something." Then he who played the part of Udayin ate up the two or three lumps of sugar, and upset the ashes which were in the dish over the head of him who played the part of Chhanda, and said, "Take and go." The crowd burst out laughing loudly, and even the unbelieving became believing, saying that it was a mad prank. And the actor made a large profit.

Now when men's talk had made the Six Bhikshus aware that the actor had taken them off they resolved to take counsel with the Bhikshuṇīs and make things unpleasant for him. So they betook themselves to the company of Twelve and asked them if they still retained any recollection of the play composed by them on the life of the Bodisat named Kuru. When they had gone out together into the park, and it was found that they had not forgotten even the least part of it, they supplied themselves with ornaments and raiment from the palace, and they set up a booth close to that of the actor. Then Upananda covered up his head with a cloth and beat the drum. A great crowd assembled, and in it was the actor, who thought that he was witnessing a divine drama, and was of opinion that it was performed by Gods, Nāgas, Yakshas, Gandharvas, Kinnaras, or Mahoragas.[1] So great was his astonishment.

[1] Mahoraga, "a great Nāga or serpent-demon, forming one of the classes inhabiting Pātāla."

When the Six went away, after finishing the performance and changing their clothes, the actor followed after them, in order to find out who they were, waiting for them at the door as they went out. When Udayin came forth, whose ears seemed to be smeared as though with orpiment, the actor asked him if he had been performing in the play. Udayin replied that they had wished to do him a hurt in that way, saying, "You wretch, who live by our art! as you have brought us on to the stage, we will go to every place where you perform, and we will annoy you. We have no need to provide ourselves with drums and strange properties."

The actor begged for pardon, for he got his living by his performances. Udayin demanded in return for this that the actor should give up to him the whole of his receipts. To which demand the actor yielded, from fear of farther interference.

XIV.

THE DUMB CRIPPLE.[1]

In long past days, King Brahmadatta lived in the city of Vārāṇasī. His wife's name was Brahmavatī, and a lake also bore the same name. Now the king was childless, and longed to have a son. With that intent he implored the gods in all manner of ways. At length his entreaties were heard, and a being of firm resolve, departing from hell, entered into the queen's womb. At her desire the king ordered presents to be given at all the gates of the city. Later on he had to go with her into the penance forest, and in the third place to embark with her on board a ship, which was constructed at her request, and placed in the above-named lake. There she gave birth to a fine boy, who was endowed with recollection of his previous existence. As he was born on the water, the name of Abja (water-born) was given to him.

As he rapidly grew up under the care of nurses and female attendants, he reflected that, if he were to be invested with sovereign power, this would not be a good thing, seeing that in consequence of a sixty years reign which he had accomplished in a previous state of existence, he had been born again in hell, and that he now ran the risk of going to hell a second time. So he determined to evade the sovereignty by means of an artifice, and he pretended to be a cripple. As the five hundred ministers' sons who were his playfellows, having all been

[1] Kah-gyur, vi. fol. 89–99.

born at the same time with him, were in the habit of running and jumping, King Brahmadatta reflected that his son, if he were not a cripple, would take part in those exercises. However, he determined to invest him with the sovereign power, although he was a cripple. When Prince Abja heard of this, he thought that it was very unkind of his father to do him such an injury, and he determined to pretend he was dumb. So he was commonly called "The Dumb Cripple."

When his father heard the five hundred sons of ministers speak, while his son remained dumb, he became exceedingly sad. When the ministers remarked this sadness of his, he explained to them that it was his son's dumbness which was troubling him. The ministers consulted the doctor, who declared that the prince was in perfect health, and was troubled by no complaint, and that he must be acted upon by threats. So King Brahmadatta sent for the executioners, and let them know privately that he was going to hand over the prince to them in the presence of a great assemblage, but that they were not to put him to death. In obedience to the king's commands, the executioners put the prince in a cart, and took him out of the city. When the prince saw the extent and the wealth of Vārāṇasī, he asked: "Is this city of Vārāṇasī deserted or inhabited?" The executioners took the prince back to his father, to whom they reported the words he had uttered. King Brahmadatta threw his arms around his son and said to him: "O youth, whom ought one to kill? Whom ought one to order to be killed? From whom ought life to be taken? To whom ought a gift to be granted, and what sort of a gift?" To these questions his son made no reply, but remained dumb. Then King Brahmadatta spake again to the executioners, saying, "I deliver unto you this prince, do ye carry him away." The executioners again, in obedience to the king's commands, set the prince in a cart and conveyed him out of the city. The prince saw four men carrying a corpse, and said, "Is this corpse that of a dead man or of a living man?" Again did the executioners take the prince back to his father, and repeat the words which he had uttered. King Brahmadatta folded his son in his arms, and put the same questions to him as before. But again did the son make no reply, persisting in his silence. The king then renewed his orders to the executioners to carry away the prince. When they had set him in a cart and conveyed him out of the city, the prince espied a great heap of grain, and said, "If this heap of grain were not continually devoured at its base, it would become great." Again did the executioners take the prince back to the king, and report the words which he had spoken. The king once more repeated the questions he had asked before, but his son left them unanswered. Then said King Brahmadatta to the executioners, "I deliver unto you the prince, go, bury him in a hole in the forest." In obedience to the king's commands, the executioners set the prince on a cart, took him into the forest, and there set to work to dig a hole. Then spake the prince the following śloka:

"Wherefore, O waggon-driver, dost thou deliberately dig a hole? Wherefore do ye dig a hole? Answer the question quickly."

The waggon-driver replied, "Because the king's son, dumb and a cripple from birth, does not speak, therefore will he soon, according to our commands, be put into the hole in the forest."

Then was the prince horrified at the thought that the cruel, red-handed, life-destroying executioners, men familiar with blows and deathstrokes, producers of fear by executions, should now proceed to kill him also, and he said, "If the king will grant me the fulfilment of one wish, I will go to the city on foot, and moreover I will speak." The executioners went to the king and told him all that had occurred. The king said, "If the prince wishes for the sovereignty, that also will I yield to him." Joyfully did he give orders to the ministers to clear the city with all speed of stones, and to provide incense, perfumes, flags, standards, and flowers of all kinds. The ministers carried out the king's commands, and many hundreds of thousands of people crowded together in order to witness the entry of the prince, and to hear him speak. The prince entered the city on foot, and when he came to where the king was, he showed him reverence, and said in ślokas—

"I am neither dumb nor crippled, I am neither dull nor senseless. With clear words am I able to speak, O prince of men. I am neither dumb nor crippled, I am neither dull nor senseless. Sound and clear and bright is my mind, O prince of men!"

When the king asked him why he had not spoken before, and why he had not used his legs, he replied—

"Hearken unto me, O king! In a former life I reigned as a king for sixty years, and then for sixty thousand years I suffered incessant tortures in hell. Remembering those terrible pangs, I do not wish to reign again, and therefore I beseech you, O my father, to allow me to renounce the world."

The father replied, "But, my son, it is for the sake of supremacy that the Rishis undertake penance and offer sacrifice. Wherefore will you, my son, give up that which is in your hands, and renounce the world?"

The prince replied that he did not wish to live in enjoyment, which is provocative of discord and contest, and that he preferred a life of penance; the former resembled the Kiṃpāka fruit, the latter possessed the Amṛita flavour. The king observed that the royal power guaranteed the enjoyment of all good things, and asked why he wished to give up the throne, and take to the ascetic life. The son replied that we ought to consider that as true pleasure from which pain ensues, and should in like manner esteem that as pain from which pleasure ensues, and that his father ought to allow him to go into the forest of penance. The king represented to him all the comforts of life in the palace, with incense, and odorous powders and flowers, with repose, free from all perils, on a soft couch, with awaking to the sound of music, with soft clothing, and savoury food and drink. On the other hand, he brought before his eyes the life of penance in the forest, the resting on leaves spread under a tree, amid all sorts of dangers, among wild gazelles, the awaking to the sound of the jackal's howl, the raiment of bark, the nourishment composed of roots and fruits, and the tepid, turbid water. The son replied that it would be better to live in the forest with raiment of bark, and roots and fruits for food, and wild gazelles as companions, that the wise prefer all this to a sovereignty, the characteristics of which are killing, binding, and smiting, and which is accompanied by danger with respect to the life to come; and that his father ought therefore to allow him to go into the forest of penance. The king said, "O son! answer these three questions of mine. Then you may renounce the world. When you saw the wealth and the extent of Vārāṇasī, you asked, 'Is Vārāṇasī deserted, or is the city inhabited?' For what reason did you say this?"

"Hear, O king, wherefore I said that. It was because, when you had condemned me to death without any cause, no one ventured to put the direct question as to how that came about."

"O son, you were right. But when you saw a corpse being carried along, you asked whether it was the body of a living or a dead person. For what reason did you ask that?"

"Hear, O king, the reason why. I said that because the corpse of him who has committed a crime is the corpse of one who is dead. But the corpse of him who has accomplished a good action is the corpse of one who is alive."

"O son, you were right. But when you saw the heap of grain you said, 'If this heap of grain were not continually consumed at its base, it would wax great.' Wherefore did you then say that?"

"Hear, O king, the reason why. I said that because the tillers of the soil, after they have borrowed corn, and have used it, are obliged to give a large heap of corn to the faithful after the labours of the field, so soon as the corn is ripe, and therefore do they consume it at its base. In like manner, when man has reached the path of the ten works of virtue, but continues on it no further, the roots of his earlier virtue are severed, and when they are severed, he passes from the path of bliss into perdition. For that reason have I thus spoken."

When the king heard these words of his son he embraced him with tearful eyes, and not only bade him behave according to his wish, but also allowed him to take all his young companions with him into the forest. There he who had hitherto been called the Dumb Cripple received the name of the Dumb Teacher. On the death of the Rishi under whom he had taken the vows he succeeded to his privileges, and he was able to manage so that his disciples, who had too great a quantity of mats, clothes, and utensils, at last followed his example, and contented themselves with that only which was most necessary.

XV.

RSHYASRINGA.[1]

In very remote times, in a forest region free from villages and richly provided with flowers, fruits, water, and roots, there lived a penance-performing Rishi, who fed upon roots, fruit, and water, and clothed himself with leaves and skins. As he had attained the five kinds of insight, the wild gazelles themselves were wont to dwell in the hermitage keeping him company. One day a gazelle doe came to a spot where he had lately been. And as the results of human actions are beyond mental comprehension it came to pass that she became pregnant. When the time came for her to bring forth, she went to that place and there gave birth to a boy. When she had smelt it, and perceived that it was a creature that did not resemble herself, she was terrified, and deserted it. When the Rishi came to that place and saw the child, he began to consider whose child it could be, and perceived that it was his own child. So he took it with him into his hermitage and there brought it up. When the boy had grown up, gazelle horns appeared on his head, on which account the Rishi gave him the name of Ṛshyaśringa (Gazelle-horn).

The Rishi fell ill, and was treated with fitting remedies, but the illness would not abate. When he saw that he must die, he spake shortly before his decease to the boy as follows:—

" O son, as from time to time many Rishis come to this

[1] Kah-gyur, iv. fol. 136, 137. A Buddhistic version of the well-known narrative in the Mahābhārata, i. 9999, &c., and the Rāmāyana, i. 8, &c.—S.

hermitage from all manner of regions, you must from love to me welcome them with the customary greeting, receive them in a friendly manner, invite them to repose on the couch, and set before them roots and fruits according to your means."

Then, according as it is said that the end of collection is diffusion, the end of the high is to fall, the end of coming together is separation, and the end of life is death, so he discharged his obligations to this law. The youth burnt the Rishi's corpse in the usual manner, and then, as he mourned, being depressed by grief at the loss of his father, he became possessed of the five kinds of insight.

One day, when he had gone to fetch water in a pitcher, the deity began to let rain fall. As he walked along with the pitcher, which was quite full of water, he let it fall, so that it broke. Rishis are very quickly moved to wrath. So spilling the little water there was left, he reproached the deity, saying, "As my full water pitcher has been broken in consequence of your bad behaviour, you shall not let rain fall for twelve years from this day." On account of this curse the deity let no rain fall. A great famine consequently arose in Vārāṇasī, and its inhabitants emigrated in all directions. The king sent for the diviners and said to them, "Honoured sirs, to whose power is it due that the deity sends no rain?" They replied, "To a Rishi's anger. If he can be disturbed in his penances the deity will again send rain. Otherwise it is not possible." The king sat absorbed in thought. His wives, the princes, and the ministers asked him, "Wherefore, O king, are you displeased?" He replied, "On account of a Rishi's anger the deity sends no rain. The diviners have declared that if the Rishi can be disturbed in his penances the deity will send rain again, but that otherwise it is impossible."

One of the king's daughters, Śāntā by name, said, "O king, if that be the case, be not disturbed. I will contrive so that the Rishi shall be completely distracted from this penance." The king said, "By what means?" She replied, "Let me and other women be taught mystic lore by the Brahmans. And let a hermitage, provided with flowers, fruits, and water, be prepared on a ferry-boat." The king allowed her and other women to be taught mystic lore by the Brahmans, and a hermitage to be constructed on a ferry-boat. Then she gave orders for the preparation of tempting objects, and fruits filled with wine, and other very bright fruits of various kinds. And she made herself look like a Rishi, dressed herself in bark and grass, and betook herself to that Rishi's hermitage, attended by the women to whom the Brahmans had taught mystic lore. His pupils said to the Rishi, "O teacher, many Rishis have come to the hermitage." He replied, "It is well that Rishis should have come; bring them in." When they had come in and he had looked at them, he said in verse, "Alas! a Rishi's appearance was never like this of old—a loosely flowing step, a face free from beard, a rising and falling breast." His mind a prey to doubt, he offered his visitors roots and fruit. They partook of them, and said to the Rishi, "Your fruits are harsh and acid. The fruits which are to be found in our hermitage on the water are Amṛita-like. Therefore do we invite you to our hermitage."

He accepted their invitation and went with them to the pleasure-ground on board the ferry-boat. There they spread before him stupefying substances, cocoa-nuts filled with wine, and other fruits. When he had become intoxicated with wine, and seduced by the alluring substances, he gave himself up to pleasure with the women, and his magic power vanished. The deity rejoicing in rain called the clouds together from every side and got the better of the Rishi. Śāntā said, "Now, do you know what the power is?" Having fettered the Rishi with amorous bonds she brought him to the king and said, "O king, this is the man."

As the deity now began to send rain a good harvest

ensued. The king gave Śāntā to the Rishi as his wife, together with her attendants. But when the Rishi, deserting her, began to indulge in love with other women, she also began to treat him with small respect, her good humour being destroyed by jealousy. One day, when during a wrangle with him, she hit him a blow on the head with a shoe, he said to himself—

"I, who used not to allow power to the thunder of the cloud, must now, being fettered by love bonds, allow myself to be set at nought by a woman!"

Thereupon he again devoted himself to ascetic exertion, and once more became possessed of the five kinds of insight.

XVI.

VISVANTARA.[1]

In long past times King Viśvāmitra reigned in the city of Viśvanāgara. As a king of the law, according to the law he ruled over that city, which was blest with wealth, plenty, prosperity, fruitfulness, and a large population, richly provided with rice, sugar-cane, oxen, and buffaloes, and free from disease, discord, quarrels, uproar, strife, and robbery. The king's faith was pure and his mind virtuous, he bethought himself of his own welfare and that of others, he was full of compassion, constant in magnanimity, and kindly towards mankind.

It came to pass that his wife conceived, and, after a space of eight or nine months, gave birth to a fine, well-formed, handsome boy, whose complexion was the colour of gold, his head canopy-like, his arms long, his forehead high-arched, his eyebrows interlacing, his nose aquiline, all his limbs and joints complete. When his birthday feast was celebrated after his birth, his kinsmen proceeded to give him a name. They said, "As the boy is King Viśvāmitra's son he shall be called Viśvantara. To the boy Viśvantara were given eight nurses, two for carrying, two for suckling, two for cleansing, and two for playing, who fed him on milk, curdled milk, butter, melted butter, butter-foam, and divers other excellent kinds of nutriment, so that he grew rapidly like a lotus in a pool. When he

[1] Kah-gyur iv. ff. 192–200. Printed as the Wessantara Játaka in Spence Hardy's Manual of Buddhism, p. 116.—S.

had grown up and learnt writing, counting, and hand-reckoning, he applied himself to all the arts and accomplishments which befit one of the Kshatriya class who has been consecrated to be a king, a ruler provided with riches, might, and heroism, a subduer of the whole orb. Such are riding on elephants and horses, driving in a car, handling of a sword and bow, advancing and retreating, flinging an iron hook, slinging, shooting missiles, striking, cutting, stabbing, seizing, marching, and the five methods of shooting. The young Viśvaṇtara, in whom dwelt pure faith and virtuous feelings, was considerate as to his own welfare and that of others, compassionate and addicted to magnanimity, kindly towards men, of a yielding and generous nature, bestowing presents freely and quite dispassionately, and assiduous in giving away. When men heard of this excessive generosity on his part, numberless crowds came to beg of him, whom he sent away with their expectations completely fulfilled.

One day the Bodisat Viśvaṇtara drove out of the excellent city to the park, in a splendid chariot, gleaming with jewels, gold, silver, steel, coral, lapis-lazuli, turquoises, rubies, and sapphires, constructed of sandalwood, covered with skins of lions, tigers, and bears, its four horses rushing along with the swiftness of the wind, resonant with bells of gold and silver. Some Brahmans versed in the Vedas met him and said, "O Kshatriya youth, may you be victorious!" And they added thereto, "Through the whole world are you renowned as one who gives all things away. Therefore it is meet that you should confer this chariot as a gift on the Brahmans." When they had thus spoken, the Bodisat Viśvaṇtara swiftly alighted from the chariot, and, while with joyful heart he gave the chariot to the Brahmans, he said, "As I have given away the chariot with the greatest pleasure, so may I, giving away the three worlds, become possessed of the greatest insight!"

Another time he was riding on the elephant Rājyavardhana,[1] which in whiteness equalled jasmine blossoms, white lotuses, snow, silver, and the clouds, which was of a remarkable size and provided with well-formed feet and trunk, and which strode along like the elephant Airāvaṇa, marked with the signs of distinguished gifts, and remarkable for its capacity. On it, followed by the troop of very devoted slaves, friends, and servants, like unto the moon surrounded by the starry host, he rode, as the spring was come, to the forest park, wherein the trees and the flowers were blooming, and the flamingoes, cranes, peacocks, parrots, mainas, cuckoos, and pheasants, were calling. There came up hastily unto Prince Viśvaṇtara, certain Brahmans who were engaged in discussion, and said to him, "Kshatriya prince, may you be victorious!" And they added thereto, "In the world with beings divine and not divine you are renowned as an All-giver. Therefore it is meet that you should give us this splendid elephant." When they had said this, the Bodisat swiftly alighted from the splendid elephant, and having presented that most splendid elephant to them with the utmost good humour, he said, "As I have given the elephant to the Brahmans with the greatest pleasure, so may I, after I have given away the three worlds, become possessed of perfect insight!"

When it became known that King Viśvāmitra's son, Viśvaṇtara, had given the splendid elephant, Rājyavardhana, to the Brahmans who were engaged in discussion, and King Viśvāmitra heard the news, he became angry, and he sent for Prince Viśvaṇtara, and ordered him to quit the country. Discarded by his father, Viśvaṇtara reflected that he, striving after completest insight, clothed with the armour of virtue out of good will towards the whole world, had given away even his elephant; that so long as he dwelt at home he had bestowed gifts according to his

[1] In the recension given by Hardy, the elephant is accredited with the power of producing rain. Has not the double meaning of the word *nāga* caused a characteristic of the Nāgas to be attributed in that case to the elephant?—S.

means; that dwelling in the penance-forest he had to strive intensely; that as he was not capable of refusing requests, he would rather quit his home and go into the penance-forest. Thereupon the Bodisat, after having pronounced a strong vow, went to his wife, Madrī, and told her everything. As soon as she had heard his words she joined the palms of her hands, and, with heart fearful of being parted from the loved one, she said to the Bodisat, "O lord, if this be so, I too will go into the penance-forest. Parted from you, O lord, I am not capable of living a single instant longer. And why? As the sky when it is deprived of the moon, as the earth when it is deprived of water, so is the wife who is deprived of her husband."

The Bodisat said, "There is no doubt that we must ultimately be parted, for such is the way of the world. You are accustomed to excellent food and drink, clothes and couches, and therefore you are of a very delicate constitution. In the penance forest it is necessary to sleep on grass and leaves, to feed on roots, flowers, and fruits, and to walk on a ground which is covered with millet and thorns and splinters, to keep constantly to one kind of food, to practise magnanimity towards all beings, and to offer hospitality to those who appear unexpectedly. As even there I shall undoubtedly bestow gifts according to my means, you must feel absolutely no regret on that account. Therefore you ought to think this over well for a time."

Madrī replied, "O lord, so long as I am able, I will follow after you." The Bodisat said, "If this be so, be mindful of your vow."

Then the Bodisat went to his father, paid him reverence with his head, and said, "O father, be pleased to forgive me my fault, the giving away of the elephant. As I am now going forth from the city into the forest, your treasury, O king, will not become empty." The king, losing his breath from grief at the parting, said with tremulous voice, "O son, give up making presents and remain here."

The Bodisat replied, "The earth and its mountains may perhaps be destined to overthrow; but I, O lord of the earth, cannot turn aside my mind from giving."

After saying these words he went away, mounted a chariot along with his son, daughter, and wife, and went forth from the good city; hundreds of thousands of the townspeople and country folks attending him with lamentation. A certain man who heard this wailing and lament, and saw such great crowds streaming towards the city-gate, asked another man, "Hey, friend, wherefore has so great a multitude set up such a lamentation?" "Honoured sir," was the reply, "do not you know in what way the king's own son has been sent away from here, because he persistently took pleasure in giving?"

When the prince, together with his wife and children, had reached the margin of the forest, all the people who formed his retinue raised a loud cry of lament. But so soon as it was heard, the Bodisat addressed the retinue which had come forth from the good city, and ordered it to turn back, saying—

"However long anything may be loved and held dear, yet separation from it is undoubtedly imminent. Friends and relatives must undoubtedly be severed from what is dearest to them, as from the trees of the hermitage wherein they have rested from the fatigues of the journey. Therefore, when ye reflect that all over the world men are powerless against separation from their friends, ye must for the sake of peace strengthen your unsteady minds by unfailing exertion."

When the Bodisat had journeyed three hundred yojanas, a Brahman came to him and said, "O Kshatriya prince, I have come three hundred yojanas because I have heard of your virtue. It is meet that you should give me the splendid chariot as a recompense for my fatigue."

Madrī could not bear this, and she addressed the Brahman in angry speech. "Alas! this Brahman, who even in the forest entreats the king's son for a gift, has a merciless heart. Does no pity arise within him when he sees the prince fallen from his royal splendour?" The Bodisat said, "Find no fault with the Brahman."

"Why not?"

"Madrī, if there were no people of that kind who long after riches there would also be no giving, and in that case how could we, inhabitants of the earth, become possessed of insight? As giving and the other Pāramitās (or virtues essential to a Buddhaship) rightly comprise the highest virtue, the Bodisats constantly attain to the highest insight."

Thereupon the Bodisat bestowed the chariot and horses on that Brahman with exceeding great joy, and said, "O Brahman, by means of this gift of the chariot, a present free from the blemish of grudging, may I be enabled to direct the car of the sinless law directed by the most excellent Rishi!" When Viśvaṇtara had with exceeding great joy bestowed on the Brahman the splendid chariot he took Prince Kṛishṇa on his shoulder, and Madrī took Princess Jālinī.[1] They went forth into the forest, and at length arrived at the forest of penance.

In that penance-forest Viśvaṇtara dwelt, after he had taken the vow which pleased his heart. One day, when Madrī had gone to collect roots and fruits in the penance-forest, a Brahman came to Viśvaṇtara, and said, "O prince of Kshatriya race, may you be victorious! As I have no slave, and wander about alone with my staff, therefore is it meet that you should give me your two children." As the Bodisat, Viśvaṇtara, after hearing these words, hesitated a little about giving his beloved children, the Brahman said to the Bodisat—

"O prince of Kshatriya race, as I have heard that you are the giver of all things, therefore do I ask why you still ponder over this request of mine. You are renowned all over the earth as the possessor of a compassion which

[1] In Hardy's Southern Recension, the boy is called Jāliya and the girl Krishnāyinā (Manual, p. 116).—S.

gives away all things: you are bound to act constantly in conformity with this renown."

After hearing these words the Bodisat said to the Brahman, "O great Brahman, if I had to give away my own life I should not hesitate for a single moment. How, then, should I think differently if I had to give away my children? O great Brahman, under these circumstances I have bethought me as to how the children, when given by me, if I do give away these two children who have grown up in the forest, will live full of sorrow on account of their separation from their mother. And inasmuch as many will blame me, in that with excessive mercilessness I have given away the children and not myself, therefore is it better that you, O Brahman, should take me."

Then said the Brahman to Viśvaṇtara, "O prince of Kshatriya race, descended from a great kingly family, as I have perceived how all over this earth your virtue is extolled, your goodness which takes pity on all beings—the presents, the hospitality, and the honour with which you welcome Śramaṇas, Brahmans, and strangers, and fulfil all the expectations of the poor and needy, the helpless and the hungry—it is not right that I, after having come to you, should remain without a present and deprived of the fruit of my journey, and that, with the knowledge that I have not obtained it, all the hopes which my mind had cherished should be brought to nought. Therefore is it meet that you, fulfilling my hopes, should give me the children. And why? One who gave away the earth, clothed with the ocean as with a garment, possessing the corn-fields as its incomparable eyes, the mighty hills as the upper parts of its body with breasts, and supporting towns and villages, would not be equal in might to you."

When the Bodisat Viśvaṇtara had heard these words of the Brahman, he laid aside the longing which clung to the children, saying to himself, "If I give the two children to the Brahman, Madrī and I will feel the pain of parting with the children. But if I do not give them to him, then I shall prove faithless to my vow, and the Brahman, disappointed in his hopes, will go away as he came. If he receives them, despairing grief for the loss of my children will be my lot upon earth. If I act otherwise, I break my promise and my vow disappears."

Then the Bodisat Viśvaṇtara determined to give up his beloved children, and he said, "Well, then, this takes place in order that, by means of a hundred kinds of penance, I, like a pillared transit bridge resembling the full moon with spotless visage, may save from the sea of troubles, containing manifold terrors, those who sink into its bottomless depths." After he had uttered these words with an untroubled countenance, his eyes filled with tears, and he gave his two children to the Brahman, and said, "As I am to obtain a very great recompense in return for the gift of the children, I shall save the world from the ocean of revolution."

Immediately after the surrender of the children, the earth quaked in a sixfold manner. When the ascetics who dwelt in the forest, terrified by the earthquake, asked one another by whose power the earth had been shaken in so intolerable a manner, and wished to know who it was who possessed such power, an old ascetic of the Vaśishṭha race, who was versed in the meanings of signs, made the matter known to them, saying, "The earth has doubtless been set in movement because Viśvaṇtara, in order that he may completely redeem men reduced to despair by trouble, has given up his two bright-eyed, beloved children, who dwelt in the penance-forest, partaking of fruit and water."

Now, when the two children saw that their father was about to give them away, they touched Viśvaṇtara's feet, uttering mournful cries, and joining the palms of their hands, and saying, "O father, will you give us away in the absence of our mother? Be content to give us up after we have seen her." Then the Bodisat gave way under the grief which had laid hold of his mind, and his face was wet with tears as he embraced his two children and said, "O children, in my heart there is no unkindness, but only merciful compassion. As I have manifested virtue for the salvation of the whole world, I give you away, whereby I may attain unto complete insight, and, having myself obtained rest, may save the worlds which lie, deprived of support, in the ocean of woes."

When the children perceived that their father's resolve was firm to give them up, they paid honour to his feet with their heads, laid their palms together, and said with soft complaint, "If you have severed the cord, we have this to say: grant us forbearance. O father, be pleased to utter the words. Every fault which we, as children, have committed against you, our superior, or any words at any time uttered by us, which displeased you, or anything in which, not obeying you, we have wrongly left aught undone—grant us forgiveness of these things, regarding them as the faults of children."

After they had thus spoken, and had paid reverence to their father, and three times encompassed him, they went forth from the hermitage, ever looking back with tearful eyes, keeping in their hearts those things which they had to say to their superior. The Bodisat consoled them with compassionate words, and then, desiring to attain to the highest insight, he betook himself to a hut made of leaves in the forest of penance.

Scarcely had the children gone away when the system of the three thousand worlds quaked six times. Many thousands of gods filled the air with sounds of shouting and rejoicing, and cried, "Oh the great deed of surrender! Truly is he worthy of being wondered at, whose mind remains constant even after the surrender of both his children."

Meanwhile Madrī had set off for the hermitage, carrying roots and fruits, and when the earth shook, she hurried on all the faster towards the hermitage. A certain deity, who perceived that she might hinder the surrender which the Bodisat proposed to make for the salvation of the world, assumed the form of a lioness, and barred her way. Then Madrī said to this wife of the King of the Beasts, "O wife of the King of the Beasts, full of wantonness, wherefore do you bar my way? In order that I may remain truly irreproachable, make way for me that I may pass swiftly on. Moreover, you are the wife of the King of the Beasts, and I am the spouse of the Lion of Princes, so that we are of similar rank. Therefore, O Queen of the Beasts, leave the road clear for me."

When Madrī had thus spoken, the deity, who had assumed the form of the lioness, turned aside from the way. Madrī reflected for a moment, recognising inauspicious omens, for the air resounded with wailing notes, and the beings inhabiting the forest gave forth sorrowful sounds, and she came to the conclusion that some disaster had certainly taken place in the hermitage, and said, "As my eye twitches, as the birds utter cries, as fear comes upon me, both my children have certainly been given away; as the earth quakes, as my heart trembles, as my body grows weak, my two children have certainly been given away."

With a hundred thousand similar thoughts of woe she hastened towards the hermitage. Entering therein she looked mournfully around, and, not seeing the children, she sadly with trembling heart followed the traces left on the ground of the hermitage. "Here the boy Kṛishṇa and his sister were wont to play with the young gazelles; here is the house which they twain made out of earth; these are the playthings of the two children. As they are not to be seen, it is possible that they may have gone unseen by me into the hut of foliage and may be sleeping there." Thus thinking and hoping to see the children, she laid aside the roots and fruits, and with tearful eyes embraced her husband's feet, asking, "O lord, whither have the boy and girl gone?" Viśvantara replied, "A Brahman came to me full of hope. To him have I given the two children. Thereat rejoice." When he had spoken these words, Madrī fell to the ground like a gazelle pierced by a poisoned arrow, and struggled like a fish taken out of the water. Like a crane robbed of her young ones she uttered sad cries. Like a cow, whose calf has died, she gave forth many a sound of wailing. Then she said, "Shaped like young lotuses, with hands whose flesh is as tender as a young lotus leaf,[1] my two children are suffering, are undergoing pain, wherever they have gone. Slender as young gazelles, gazelle-eyed, delighting in the lairs of the gazelles, what sufferings are my children now undergoing in the power of strangers? With tearful eyes and sad sobbing, enduring cruel sufferings, now that they are no longer seen by me, they live downtrodden among needy men. They who were nourished at my breast, who used to eat roots, flowers, and fruits, they who, experiencing indulgence, were ever wont to enjoy themselves to the full, those two children of mine now undergo great sufferings. Severed from their mother and their family, deserted by the cruelty of their relatives, thrown together with sinful men, my two children are now undergoing great suffering. Constantly tormented by hunger and thirst, made slaves by those into whose power they have fallen, they will doubtless experience the pangs of despair. Surely I have committed some terrible sin in a previous existence, in severing hundreds of beings from their dearest ones. Therefore do I now lament like a cow which has lost its calf. If there exists any exorcism, by which I can gain over all beings, so shall my two children, after having been made slaves, be by it rendered free."

Then Madrī, looking upon the thick-foliaged trees which the children had planted and tended, embraced them tenderly, and said, "The children fetched water in small pitchers, and dropped water on the leaves. You, O trees, did the children suckle, as though ye had been possessed

[1] Properly "lotus-arrow." According to Maximowicz, the young lotus leaves are reed-like or arrow-like in appearance.—S.

of souls." Further on, when she saw the young gazelles with which the children used to play, standing in the hermitage, she sadly said, gently wailing, "With the desire of seeing their playfellows do the young gazelles visit the spot, searching among the plants, offering companionship with my never-ending woe." Afterwards, when the footprints on the road along which the children had gone became interrupted, and she saw that their footprints did not lie in a straight line, but in all sorts of directions, she was seized by bitter anguish, and cried, "As the footprints point to dragging along and some of them to swiftness of pace, you must surely have driven them on with blows, O most merciless Brahman. How have my children fared with tender feet, their throats breathing with difficulty, their voices reduced to weakness, their pretty lower lips trembling, like gazelles timidly looking around?"

Observing how she bore herself and uttered complaints, the Bodisat exerted himself to exhort his wife with a series of such and such words about instability, and said: "Not for the sake of renown, nor out of anger, have I given away your two children; for the salvation of all beings have I given the children, whom it was hard to give. By giving up the objects which it is hardest to give up, children and wife, may one, like the great souls, attain to the completest insight. O Madrī, as I cling closely to giving, I have given for the redemption of the world the children whom it was hard to give. My purpose is to sacrifice all things, to give myself, my wife, my children, and my treasures."

When after a time Madrī had recovered her strength of mind, she said to the Bodisat: "I will in nothing be a hindrance to you. Let your mind be constant. If you wish to give me too, give me without hesitation. As soon as, O courageous one, you have attained to that, for the sake of which you give up that which is connected with difficulty, save all beings from revolution."

When the King of the Gods, Śakra, perceived this marvellous endurance on the part of the Bodisat, and the striving of Madrī, and their deeds very hard to be accomplished, he descended from heaven, surrounded by the company of the thirty-three gods, into the hermitage and lighted it up with great brilliance. Remaining in the air, he said to the Bodisat: "Inasmuch as after this fashion, O mighty one, in the foolish world, the mind of which is bound fast by knots of ignorance, in the world which is fettered by the bonds of a mind which pays homage to enjoyment, you alone, superior to passion, have given up the children in whom you delighted, you have certainly attained to this degree through stainless and joyless tranquillity."

After gratifying the Bodisat with these words, the King of the Gods, Śakra, said to himself: "As this man, when alone and without support, might be driven into a corner, I will ask him for Madrī." So he took the form of a Brahman, came to the Bodisat, and said to him: "Give me as a slave this lovely sister, fair in all her limbs, unblamed by her husband, prized by her race." Then in anger spake Madrī to the Brahman: "O shameless and full of craving, do you long after her who is not lustful like you, O refuse of Brahmans, but takes her delight according to the upright law." Then the Bodisat, Viśvaṇtara, began to look upon her with compassionate heart, and Madrī said to him: "I have no anxiety on my own account, I have no care for myself; my only anxiety is as to how you are to exist when remaining alone." Then said the Bodisat to Madrī: "As I seek after the height which surmounts endless anguish, no complaint must be uttered by me, O Madrī, upon this earth. Do you, therefore, follow after this Brahman without complaining. I will remain in the hermitage, living after the manner of the gazelles."

When he had uttered these words, he said to himself with joyous and exceedingly contented mind: "This gift here in this forest is my best gift. After I have here absolutely given away Madrī too, she shall by no means be recalled." Then he took Madrī by the hand, and said to that Brahman: "Receive, O most excellent Brahman, this my dear wife, loving of heart, obedient to orders, charming in speech, demeaning herself as one of lofty race."

When, in order to attain to supreme insight, he had given away his beautiful wife, the earth quaked six times to its extremities like a boat on the water. And when Madrī had passed into the power of the Brahman, overcome by pain at being severed from her husband, her son, and her daughter, with faltering breath and in a voice which huskiness detained within her throat, she spoke thus: "What crime have I committed in my previous existence that now, like a cow whose calf is dead, I am lamenting in an uninhabited forest?" Then the King of the Gods, Śakra, laid aside his Brahman's form, assumed his proper shape, and said to Madrī: "O fortunate one, I am not a Brahman, nor am I a man at all. I am the King of the Gods, Śakra, the subduer of the Asuras. As I am pleased that you have manifested the most excellent morality, say what desire you would now wish to have satisfied by me."

Rendered happy by these words, Madrī prostrated herself before Śakra, and said: "O thou of the thousand eyes, may the lord of the three and thirty set my children free from thraldom and let them find their way to their grandfather." After these words had been spoken the Prince of the Gods entered the hermitage and addressed the Bodisat. Taking Madrī by the left hand, he thus spake to the Bodisat: "I give you Madrī for your service. You must not give her to any one. If you give away what has been entrusted to you, fault will be found with you."

Afterwards the King of the Gods, Śakra, deluded the Brahman who had carried off the boy and girl, so that under the impression that it was another city, he entered the selfsame city from which they had departed, and there set to work to sell the children. When the ministers saw this they told the king, saying, "O king, your grandchildren, Kṛishṇa and Jālinī, have been brought into this good city in order to be sold, by an extremely worthless Brahman." When the king heard these words, he said indignantly, "Bring the children here, forthwith."

When this command had been attended to by the ministers, and the townspeople had hastened to appear before the king, one of the ministers brought the children before him. When the king saw his grandchildren brought before him destitute of clothing and with foul bodies, he fell from his throne to the ground, and the assembly of ministers, and the women, and all who were present began to weep. Then the king said to the ministers: "Let the bright-eyed one, who, even when dwelling in the forest, delights in giving, be summoned hither at once, together with his wife."

After this the King of the Gods, Śakra, having paid reverence to the Bodisat, returned to his own habitation.

Now, when King Viśvāmitra was dead, the Brahmans, the ministers, the towns-people, and the country people, went to the hermitage and with entreaties invited the Bodisat to come to the city. There they installed him as king. Thereafter King Viśvantara was known by the name of Viśvatyāga (all-giver). And after he had made presents of various kinds to the Sramaṇas, Brahmans, the poor and needy, his friends and relations, his acquaintances and servants, he uttered these ślokas: "In order to obtain supreme insight have I fearlessly bestowed gifts on Kshatriyas, Brahmans, Vaiśyas, Sūdras, Chandalas, and Pukkasas, with gold and silver, oxen and horses, jewelled earrings, and labouring slaves. For giving is the most excellent of virtues. With a heart free from passion have I given away my wife and children, and obtained thereby power over men in this and the other world."

As King Viśvāmitra had, for Viśvantara's sake, bestowed great treasures on the Brahman Jujaka, who had thereby attained to great wealth, Jujaka's friends and relations, and those who were dear to him, came to him and said: "Your property and wealth and high fortune all depend upon Viśvaṇtara." He replied: "What have I to do with Prince Viśvaṇtara? As I was born in the first caste, I have obtained the recompense of the world, and therefore have I become so wealthy."

XVII.

THE FULFILLED PROPHECY.[1]

In long past times King Sarjarasin[2] reigned in Vārāṇasī, over that great, rich, prosperous, blissful, and populous city. He took to wife the daughter of another king, and lived with her. She became with child, and after the lapse of eight or nine months, when the sun was high at midday, she gave birth to a very fine boy. When the boy's birth-feast was held, and it was asked what name should be given to him, the ministers said: "O king, as the boy was born at the time when the sun [sūrya] is highest, let him be named Sūryanemi. When he had received that name, he was entrusted to eight nurses, two for carrying, two for suckling, two for cleansing, and two for playing. These eight nurses nourished him with milk, curdled milk, butter, melted butter, butter-foam, and other excellent kinds of food, and he grew apace like a lotus in a pool. When he had grown up he learnt writing, reckoning, drawing, and hand-reckoning, and the arts and accomplishments which befitted a prince of the Kshatriya race, destined to be a king. King Sarjarasin's first wife was named Dharmikā, and his prime minister, in whom the king placed the greatest confidence, Goshṭhila.

After some time Dharmikā again became with child. The diviners declared that a son would be born, who would take the king's life, and usurp royal power, setting the diadem on his own head. After a time King Sarjarasin

[1] Kah-gyur, iv. ff. 233–236.

[2] In Tibetan, Sartsi-ldan, which is evidently a corrupt form.—S. Professor Schiefner has in one instance altered the name from Sarjarasin to Archismant.

fell ill, and when his illness could not be cured, although remedies of all kinds were applied, he reflected, after he had learnt the state of his body, that it would be necessary to take precautions in order that Sūryanemi, after becoming king on his decease, should not cause Dharmikā to be put to death. So he determined to entrust her to his minister, Goshṭhila, whom he had supplied with valuable property. Having sent for him, he said to him: "Dharmikā is my first wife, you are my first minister. As I am aware of my position, and I am undoubtedly about to lose my life, you must out of love for me take care that Sūryanemi does not put Dharmikā to death."

The minister gave him a consoling promise. When Sarjarasin had died and his body had been burned with all pomp, Sūryanemi was consecrated as king. He gave orders to his ministers to put Dharmikā to death. Goshṭhila remonstrated against this, saying: "O king, is it just to put her to death rashly? Who can tell whether she will bear a son or a daughter? If a son is born, he shall be put to death." King Sūryanemi ordered him to act in accordance with this saying, and to keep watch over the queen. So Goshṭhila took her to his own house, where, after eight or nine days, she gave birth to a son. That same day a fisherman's wife gave birth to a girl. Immediately after the confinement Goshṭhila, who had gained over the fisherman's wife with money, exchanged the children, and told the king that Dharmikā had been delivered of a girl. The boy was suckled and brought up by the fisherwoman. When he had grown up he learnt reading and writing, and as he took to making verses, he was called the verse-writing fisher-lad.

Goshṭhila informed Dharmikā that she had a son who was a poet, and she felt a desire to see him. The minister tried to dissuade her from that, but she could not overcome her longing. Goshṭhila saw how dangerous the matter was, and perceived that some precaution must be taken, and he sent the lad to the queen with a fish.

When the youth entered the palace the king became aware that this poetic fisher-lad was he of whom of the diviners had predicted that he would take the king's life, place the diadem on his own head, and usurp the regal power. So he ordered the ministers to lay hands on him in order that he might not escape. The youth heard of this as the order passed from mouth to mouth, so he ran this way and that way until he came to the house of an old woman who hid him away. From thence, after his body had been anointed with oil of mustard and sesame, and laid upon a bier as if it had been a corpse, he was carried out to the cemetery and deposited there. A man who was looking for fruits and flowers there saw him get up and run away. The men who were sent in pursuit of him asked this man if he had seen a person of such and such a height, and such and such an appearance, going that way. He told them in what direction the youth had gone, and they followed after him.

The youth reached a hill-town, entered into the house of a dyer, and told him his story. So when his pursuers began to search the town, the dyer placed the youth in a clothes chest, which he set upon an ass, and so took him out of the town to a bath-house, where he left him. The youth stood up, looked around on all four sides and went away. But there also he was seen by a man, who disclosed the fact to his pursuers, and showed them the road which he had taken. The youth came to another village, and entered the house of a shoemaker, to whom he told his story, and whom he asked to make him a pair of shoes, the toes of which should be where the heels generally are. The shoemaker declared he had never made shoes of that kind. The youth replied in verse:—

"Manifold is the mind, numerous are gifts. They cannot be weighed in the same scale. So make me, O shoemaker, what I have ordered, with the heels in front."

According to these instructions, the shoemaker made him shoes of that kind. As the town was surrounded by a wall, the youth put on the shoes, crept out through a cistern, and got away. His pursuers, following the traces left by his shoes, were led back by them to the village, and they perceived that he had escaped. He took to the water, and was conveyed by the Nāgas to their residence.

As the news of this passed from mouth to mouth, King Sūryanemi learnt that the Nāgas had received the youth into their dwelling-place. Thereupon he ordered his ministers to summon into his presence all the snake-charmers who lived in his realm. When they had done this, the king said to the snake-charmers, "Honoured sirs, go and question the Nāgas in such and such a Nāga residence." In compliance with the king's orders, the snake-charmers all betook themselves thither.

Now a Yaksha named Pingala, who lived upon flesh and blood, dwelt in a certain wilderness. As the wild beasts, not to speak of human beings, had deserted this wilderness from fear of him, it was called the Pingala wilderness. When the snake-charmers made their preparations for the purpose of endangering the Nāgas by spells, the youth became frightened, and, knowing no other way of escape, fled into the Pingala-wilderness. The Nāgas took counsel together, and decided that it would not be right if they were not to save the youth from the Pingala-wilderness, and that it would do them a hurt if he were to be killed by Pingala; but they did not know what to do. However, the Nāga king told them to give information to the snake-charmers. The Nāgas said to them, "Honoured ones, he on whose account ye have troubled us has been put to death by our contrivance, for he has fled into the Pingala-wilderness." The snake-charmers reported the matter to the king, who gave orders to continue the search after the youth. Meanwhile the youth took to wandering about in the Pingala-wilderness.

The Yaksha Pingala was sitting at a certain spot surrounded by his dogs. When he and his dogs saw the youth from afar, he reflected that he had heard that the youth would kill him, and he thought that he had come for that purpose. So he set the dogs on the youth. But the youth outstripped them and climbed up a tree. Pingala and the dogs lay in wait for him at the foot of the tree. Pingala asked him if he had not heard that a demon named Pingala dwelt in the Pingala wilderness, and put to death all who came thither. And he summoned him to come down, seeing that he must die. The youth replied, "So long as I live I shall remain here." As soon as the Yaksha Pingala, who had placed himself in the shade with his ascetic's cloth,[1] had gone to sleep, the youth threw down on him a part of his clothes. The dogs thought that it was the youth who had fallen down, so they ate up the Yaksha Pingala and went away.

The youth slowly descended from the tree, and, after wandering to and fro, remembered that he had an uncle, who had retired from the world among the Rishis, and he determined to go to him. He lived in a hill district, in a grove which was well provided with excellent roots, flowers, fruit, and water, with clumps of various trees, and with the song of different kinds of birds. By means of inquiries the youth gradually made his way thither, and he informed his uncle of his relationship to him, and took up his abode with him. But even there the king's men searched for him, and they were on the point of laying hands on him, when he jumped down a precipice. As he sprang into the air, a man seized hold of his head-dress, and the head-dress remained in the man's hands. As the pursuers supposed that he was dead, they determined to go away. So they took the head-dress, and went to the king, and said to him, "O king, the fisher-lad poet is dead, here is his head-dress." And the king provided them with good things.

[1] The equivalent of the Sanskrit *yogapaṭṭa*. See Böhtlingk-Roth.—S. "The cloth thrown over the back and knees of an ascetic during meditation."

After a while a deity, who dwelt in the Rishi-grove, said to that Rishi, "Do not you take any interest, then, in your nephew, who is reduced to despair, subjected to intolerable woes?" The Rishi replied, "If I keep him in mind no more, may I die upon the spot!" The Rishi was in possession of spells and magic formulas, and knew one spell by which a man might be turned into a woman and back again into a man. This spell he taught to his nephew, and said to him, "Now, go away, and be fearless and free from anxiety." The youth, by means of the spell, assumed the form of an incomparably beautiful woman, and betook himself to Vārāṇasī. While abiding in the king's park he was seen by the keeper, who was astounded, and set off instantly and informed King Sūryanemi, saying, "O king, a woman of supreme beauty and youth is dwelling in the park." The king ordered him to fetch the woman. By the powerful dispensation of fortune the woman was brought to the palace, and King Sūryanemi became violently enamoured of her. But when an opportunity occurred, the youth put the king to death in a solitary spot. Then he reversed the spell and became a man again. Afterwards he set the crown on his head, and, after making the minister Goshṭhila acquainted with the matter, assumed the regal power. A deity said in a śloka, "He whose head has not been cut off, he is not dead. He gets up again and completes his work. Like unto the poet, when he found his opportunity and slew the son of Sarjarasin."

XVIII.

THE TWO BROTHERS.[1]

In long past times, a king came to the throne in the palace of a country well provided with riches, prosperity, good harvests, and numerous inhabitants. Some time afterwards his wife became with child, and, after the lapse of eight or nine months, gave birth to a very handsome boy, complete in limbs and joints, whose skin was the colour of gold, whose head stood out like a canopy, and who had long arms, a broad forehead, interlacing eyebrows, and a high-arched nose. At his birth there occurred many thousands of happy events. When his birth-feast was held, and the question arose as to giving him a name, the ministers said, "O king, as many thousands of happy events have taken place at his birth, let him be called Kshemanˑkara.[2] This name was given to him, and he was entrusted to eight nurses, two to carry him, two to suckle him, two to cleanse him, and two to play with him. These nurses brought him up on various milk products and other excellent forms of nourishment, so that he shot up like a lotus in a pool.

The king's wife again became with child, and after the lapse of eight or nine months a boy was born, at whose birth many thousands of unfortunate events took place, on which account there was given to him the name of Pāpanˑkara.[3] He also thrived apace and grew up.

[1] Kah-gyur, iv. ff. 186–189.

[2] Kshemanˑkara, "promoting well-being, causing peace and security, propitious," &c.

[3] The opposite of Kshemanˑkara, from *pāpa*, bad.

The young Kshemaṅkara, who was of a friendly and merciful nature, and compassionate towards all living creatures, loved to give, taking his delight in bestowing, and conferred gifts upon the Śramaṇas and Brahmans, the poor and the needy who begged of him. His father said to him, "O son, do not be constantly making presents. If you give away so freely, where are we to find the necessary riches?"

Now, in accordance with the nature of things, many men take delight in gifts and giving, and when they thus delight themselves their fame is extolled in words and verses, and celebrated in all parts of the world. The king of another country, who had heard of the great virtues of the prince, wished to give him his daughter. The prince's father was highly pleased, and wanted to go to meet her. But Kshemaṅkara said, "Until I have acquired wealth I will not marry. Allow me, O father, to go to sea." He replied, "Do so." When he set forth for the sea with his merchandise, his brother, Pāpaṅkara, said to himself—

"As he is now liked and loved by many men, he will be still more liked and loved by many men when he shall have equipped a sea-ship and have returned home. And as there will be an opportunity of his being invested with the regal power during our father's lifetime, therefore I, too, instead of remaining here to see whose turn will come, will go to sea along with him, and will take away his life out there, and then I shall be invested with the heirship even against my father's will." With these thoughts in his mind he went to his father, and said to him, "O father, as Kshemaṅkara is going to sea I will go with him." His father said, "Do so."

Now Kshemaṅkara ordered proclamation to be made throughout the land as follows: "Listen, O honourable merchants inhabiting the city. As Prince Kshemaṅkara is going to sea with merchandise, and as he among you who is inclined to go to sea under Prince Kshemaṅkara's guidance will be freed from tolls, taxes, and freight-money, therefore get ready the goods which are to be taken to sea." Many hundreds of merchants got ready goods to be taken to the sea. Then Kshеman·kara, as the leading trader, accompanied by his brother Pāpan·kara, after performing ceremonies for the sake of obtaining a successful result, surrounded by many hundreds of merchants, taking with him in waggons, carts, chests, and hampers, and on camels, oxen, and asses, quantities of goods to be transported by sea, set out on his way. Visiting lands, towns, villages, commercial emporiums, and estates, he came by degrees to the sea-coast. There he purchased a ship for five hundred kārshāpaṇas, and after making proclamation three times, set out on the ocean, taking with him five hundred servants, diggers, cleansers, fishermen, mariners, and pilots. When on board ship he said to his brother Pāpan·kara: "Should a shipwreck take place in the middle of the ocean, then throw your arms round my neck without hesitation." Pāpan·kara replied, "Good, I will do so."

After a time the ship arrived with a favourable wind at the Island of Jewels, and the steersman said: "Listen, O honourable merchants of Jambudvīpa! as ye have heard that the Island of Jewels is a mine of diamonds, lapis lazuli, turquoises, emeralds, and divers other precious stones, therefore have we come hither. Now then, take yourselves as many jewels as ye wish."

They searched for them with joy and desire, and they filled the ship full, as though with rice, pease, sesame, and the like. Now, as Bodisats are wise and sharp-witted, Prince Kshеman·kara made fast to his girdle some large jewels of great value. On the way back, when not far from shore, the ship was rendered useless in consequence of an injury inflicted by a sea monster. Therefore Pāpan·kara threw his arms round the neck of Kshеman·kara, who by great exertions brought him ashore. Exhausted by the burden, Kshеman·kara fell asleep. As he lay sleeping, Pāpan·kara caught sight of the jewels fastened to his girdle, and thought: "Ought I to return with empty hands while he comes back with such jewels?" Then he took away the jewels from his soundly sleeping brother, put both his eyes out with a thorn, and left him sightless on the ocean shore.

By a fortunate chance some oxherds who were tending their cattle came to that spot. When they saw the prince, they said, "Ho, friend, who are you?" He told them everything that had occurred. When they had heard his story they were filled with compassion, and they led him to the house of the chief herdsman. There he took to playing on the lute. The chief herdsman's wife, who was charmed by his youth and beauty, heard the sound of his lute and tried to allure him. But he, thinking of a course of life acquired by good deeds, closed his ears and did not stir. As there is nothing which they may not do who are seized by desire, she said to her husband: "This blind man is trying to tempt me, will you put up with such people?" The prince reflected that, of all kinds of anger, the worst is the anger of a wife, and perceived that there was nothing left for him, in order not to be smitten thereby, but to go away. So he left the house, and along all manner of streets, market places, and by-roads, he gained himself a living by his music.

On the death of his father his brother, Pāpan·kara, came to the throne. And after a time he himself arrived at the town of that neighbouring king who had formerly wished to give him his daughter in marriage. She had by this time grown up, but when there came to woo her the sons of kings, ministers, and purohitas, dwelling in many lands, her father said: "O daughter, Prince Ksheman·kara, for whom I had intended you, went to sea and there died in consequence of a misfortune. As suitors have now arrived, and as those who do not obtain you will be discontented, the question arises, what is to be done?" She replied: "O father, if this be the case, let orders be given to have the city swept and garnished; I will choose a husband for myself."

Then the king ordered proclamation to be made in the different lands and cities that his daughter was going to choose herself a husband. He also gave orders that his own city should be cleared of stones, potsherds, and rubble, sprinkled with sandalwood water, and perfumed with odours, and that canopies, standards, and flags, should be set up, and numerous silken hangings displayed, together with flowers of many kinds, giving the appearance of a grove of the gods, and that joy-inspiring proclamation should be made to this effect: "O honourable dwellers in town and country, and crowds of men assembled from various lands, give ear! To-morrow the king's daughter will choose herself a husband. So do ye assemble as is fitting."

Next morning the king's daughter, adorned with many ornaments and surrounded by numerous maidens, came to a grove made bright with flowers by the deity of the grove, rendered extremely beautiful by the dispensation of great good fortune. And when several thousand men had assembled in the midst of the city, she came into the assembly in order to choose herself a husband. Somewhat removed sat Ksheman·kara playing on the lute.

As men by their deeds are reciprocally connected, and the force of effect is constrained by the great power of cause, so it came to pass that the king's daughter, when her feelings were moved by the sound of the lute, became closely attached to Ksheman·kara's playing, and she threw him the crown of flowers, crying, "This man is my husband."

The assembled people were discontented, and some of them in bitterness of heart began to find fault with her, saying, "What sense is there in this, that the royal princess, who has so much beauty, and who is so supremely young and accomplished, should slight the sons of kings, ministers, and purohitas, who have come from many lands, besides excellent householders, and should choose a blind man to be her husband?"

With reluctance and discontent did the officials convey the tidings to the king, saying, "O king, the princess has completed the choice of a husband." The king said, "What manner of man has she chosen?" They replied, "O king, a blind man." The king also was displeased when he heard this, and he sent for his daughter and said, "O daughter, wherefore have you chosen such a man as your husband, in spite of there being extremely young, rich and handsome sons of kings, proprietors, merchants, caravan leaders, ministers, and purohitas?" She replied, "O father, this is the man I want." The king said, "O daughter, if that be so, then go to him. Wherefore do you delay?" She went to him and said, "I have chosen you as my husband." He replied, "Therein you have not acted well. Perhaps you have thought, 'as such is the case and this man is blind, I can give myself to another.'" She replied, "I am not one who does such things." He said, "What proof is there of this?" She replied, commencing an asseveration—

"If it be true, and my asseveration is righteous, that I have been in love only with Prince Kshemaṅ·kara and with you, but with none else, then through the power of this truth and my asseveration shall one of your two eyes become sound as before."

So soon as this asseveration was uttered, one of his eyes came again just as it was before. Then he said, "I am Kshemaṅ·kara. My brother Pāpaṅ·kara reduced me to the state I was in." She said, "What proof is there that you are Prince Kshemaṅ·kara?" Then he too began to asseverate, saying—

"If it be true, and my asseveration righteous, that although Pāpaṅ·kara put out my eyes, I do not in the least bear him malice, then in consequence of the truth and affirmation may my other eye become sound as before."

So soon as he had pronounced this asseveration, his other eye also became as it had been originally. Then the royal princess betook herself to the king, along with Kshemanּkara, who was no longer imperfect in any part of his body, and said, "O father, this is Kshemanּkara himself." As the king was incredulous, she told him how everything had come about. The king was exceedingly astonished, but with great joy did he give his daughter to Kshemanּkara as his wife. Then he set forth with a great army for that city, and drove Pāpanּkara from power, and set Kshemanּkara as king upon his father's throne.

XIX.

THE PUNISHMENT OF AVARICE.[1]

In long past times a hunter wounded an elephant with a poisoned arrow. Perceiving that he had hit it, he followed after the arrow and killed the elephant. Five hundred robbers who had plundered a hill-town were led by an evil star to that spot, where they perceived the elephant. As it was just then a time of hunger with them, they said, "Now that we have found this meat, let two hundred and fifty of us cut the flesh off the elephant and roast it, while two hundred and fifty go to fetch water."

Then those among them who had cut the flesh off the elephant and cooked it, said among themselves, "Honoured sirs, now that we have accomplished such a task and collected so much stolen property, wherefore should we give away part of it to the others? Let us eat as much of the meat as we please, and then poison the rest. The others will eat the poisoned meat and die, and then the stolen goods will be ours."

So after they had eaten their fill of the meat, they poisoned what remained over. Those who had gone to fetch water, likewise, when they had drunk as much water as they wanted, poisoned what was left. So when they came back, and those who had eaten the flesh drank the water, and those who had drunk the water ate the flesh, they all of them died.

Now there came to that spot a jackal, fettered by the ties

[1] Kah-gyur iii. f. 103. The end of this may be compared with *Panchatantra*, ii. 3. The beginning is a well-known theme. See Liebrecht on "Die vergifteten Gefährten" in *Orient und Occident*, i. 656.—S.

of time, and it saw all those dead bodies. With a joy that sprang from greediness it thought, "As an extremely large amount of booty has accrued to me, I will take each part of it in its turn." So it seized the bow with its jaws, and began to knaw at the knots of the bowstring. The string snapped, and the end of the bow struck the jackal in the roof of the mouth so hard, that it died. The jackal uttered this śloka—

"It is good to accumulate, but not to accumulate immoderately. See how the jackal, infatuated by greed after the accumulated, was killed by the bow."

XX.

THE MAGICIAN'S PUPIL.[1]

In long past times, King Brahmadatta lived in Vārāṇasī. There also a Chaṇḍāla[2] lived, who was versed in spells and magic lore, and who, employing the Gāndhāra-Mantra, was wont to obtain by spells from the Gandhamādana mountain[3] such fruits and flowers as were not in season, and to present them to king Brahmadatta. The King who was highly pleased thereby, made him presents. Now there was a Brahman youth who longed after a knowledge of spells. And in his search after them, in accordance with what he heard spoken thereof, he came from his own country to Vārāṇasī. After he had recovered from the fatigues of his journey, he betook himself to the Brahman who was versed in spells and magic lore. And when he came before him, he said—

"I wish to serve the Paṇḍit."

"Why?"

"For the sake of learning magic."

The Chaṇḍāla replied in verse, "Magic lore is communicated to no man. It dies with its possessor. Or it is vouchsafed to him who has knowledge and means and renders service."

The youth said, "O Paṇḍit, if such is the case, and I

[1] Kah-gyur, iv. f. 171.

[2] *Caṇḍāla*, "the generic name for a man of the lowest and most despised of the mixed tribes, born from Sudra father and Brāhman mother."

[3] *Gandhamādana*, "intoxicating with fragrance. . . . Name of a particular mountain, forming the division between Ilā-vrita and Bhadrāśva, or to the east of Meru, renowned for its fragrant forests."

have to render service, I ask for how long a time must that be."

"When you have served twelve years," was the reply, "it will be seen whether I shall communicate it to you or not."

As the youth had a great craving after magic lore, he agreed to this, and after he had with the greatest joy testified his respect, he entered upon his service.

It happened once that the Chaṇḍāla came home drunk, and the Brahman youth said to himself, "As the master has drunk so much more than is befitting, I will lie down to sleep beside him." The Chaṇḍāla took to tossing about on his bed, and as he did so one side of the bed gave way. The noise this made awoke the Brahman youth, who said to himself: "As the master is so restless in his sleep, I will support the bed with my back." Accordingly he propped up the bed with his back, and patiently held out all night [in spite of much discomfort,][1] thinking that if he moved his body, or uttered a word, the teacher would hear the noise he made, and would awake, and be unable to go to sleep again.

When the Chaṇḍāla awoke of his own accord, and saw the youth, he asked who was there. The youth replied, "O teacher, it is I, the companion of your fortunes," and he told him all that had occurred. The Chaṇḍāla was greatly delighted, and said, "O son, as I am exceedingly pleased, I will teach you the art of magic."

As Brahmans are of a conceited nature, the youth could not restrain himself, but must needs immediately make a trial of his magic art on the spot, and then depart. So he employed his magic power, and soared into the sky. When he came to Gandhamādana, he there plucked fruits and flowers which were out of season on earth, and gave them to the king's purohita, who gave them to King Brahmadatra. The king asked where he had got them. The purohita replied—

[1] This passage has been slightly modified.

"There is a Brahman youth here from a distant country. He it is who gave them to me. As he is extremely well versed in spells and magic lore, and as the Brahman is of a better nature than the Chaṇḍāla, who is despised by the whole world, the question arises of what is to be done with the Chaṇḍāla. Be pleased to take away his employment from the Chaṇḍāla, and to confer it upon the Brahman youth."

The king replied, "Do so." Accordingly the Chaṇḍāla was deprived of his employment by the purohita, who conferred it upon the Brahman youth. But in consequence of the youth's ingratitude his magic power deserted him.

XXI.

HOW A WOMAN REQUITES LOVE.[1]

IN lost past times, in a palace in a land every way blest, there reigned a king to whom his wife bore four sons, named Śākha, Gulma, Anugulma, and Viśākha. After having all grown up, and taken to themselves as wives kings' daughters from other lands, they began to behave disrespectfully to the king. The king banished them, and they departed, along with their wives, and came to a desert place, where their means of sustenance ran short. So they made an agreement among themselves to put their wives to death one after another, and by feeding on their flesh to make their own way through the desert. Viśākha, however, was of opinion that it would be better to sacrifice his own life than to take away another's, and instead of waiting to see who was to die he determined to escape along with his wife. So he fled away with her. But after a time she said, being exhausted by the want of food and drink, and by the fatigue of the journey, "O lord, I am dying." Viśākha thought that it would be sad if she were to die now, after he had saved her from the hands of the Rākshasas (or cannibals). So he sliced some flesh off his hams and gave it to her to eat, and then he opened the veins of both his arms and gave her the blood to drink. In this way they made their way to a mountain, on which they supported themselves with roots and berries.

At the foot of this mountain ran a river, into which a

[1] Kah-gyur, vol. iv. ff. 183–191. See Benfey, *Panchatantra*, i. 436, &c. —S.

man happened to fall, whose hands and feet had been cut off. Carried away by the stream he uttered cries of despair. Viśākha, who was gathering roots and berries somewhere thereabouts, heard his cries for help. His mind being stirred with compassion he climbed the mountain, and began looking about on all sides. As soon as he saw the man being swept away by the waters, he ran swiftly down from the mountain, sprang into the river, seized the man, and conveyed him ashore. Affected by the sight of his misery he said to him, "O son, whence do you come?" When the man had told him the whole story, Viśākha spoke words of solace to him, satisfied his hunger with roots and berries, and then handed him over to his wife, thanks to whose care he recovered entirely. With this care there was associated pleasure, which induced her to pay him frequent visits, passing the time in varied talk.

It is part of the nature of things that Bodisats are not remarkably addicted to the passion of love, and so it happened that Viśākha indulged only from time to time in amorous pleasure. As, in consequence of the Bodisat's power, trees, roots, and berries possessed a special force, living upon them excited the desires of the wife, and she began to allure the man who had no hands or feet. The cripple was unwilling to respond to her advances, pointing out that he, when as good as dead, had been saved and restored to life by her husband; and that if he were to behave in such a way he would be putting himself into a position like unto that of a murderer. But as she repeatedly tempted him, and it was hard for him to master passion, he finally acceded to her request.

Although in the fruition of love passion increased, yet he reflected that, as she was now so possessed by passion, and as of all enmities that of the woman is the worst, he was going to ruin. In accordance with these ideas, he began to take counsel with her, saying, "If your husband finds out that we have lived together, he will undoubtedly do you some injury and put me to death." She was of opinion that these words were true, and that precautions must be taken. As women are adroit, even without being taught, she wrapped a cloth round her head and lay down on a rock to sleep. When Viśākha saw her sleeping there, as he returned home with roots and berries, he asked her, "Good wife, what is the matter with you?" She replied, "O lord, as my head aches, I feel very unwell." Viśākha said, "What can be done?" As she had seen wolf's-milk [1] growing in a ravine, she said, "O lord, when I once before suffered from this pain in the head, the physician ordered me wolf's-milk, by means of which I was cured." Viśākha replied, "I will seek for wolf's-milk." She said, "As it grows in this ravine, I will let you down with a rope and you shall fetch it up." As august beings are simple and upright, he suspected no guile, and said, "Let us do so; you hold the rope and I will fetch the wolf's-milk." When he had let himself down with the rope, she let go of the rope with her hand, whereby he also lost hold of it and fell into the water at the bottom.

As the Bodisat was destined to long life and the exercise of regal power, he did not die, but was carried along by the stream, and so he reached a royal city. The king of that city had died without leaving any heirs, and the ministers and the towns-people and the country-folk were holding counsel as to whom, seeing there was no king, they should invest with the sovereignty. They chose men well versed in omens, and they ordered them to seek out a man provided with virtuous merit, in order that they might invest him with the sovereignty. As the deeds which were to secure sovereignty for Viśākha were now approaching maturity, he emerged from the water and sat down on a spot which, through the power of the Bodisat, appeared as though decked with ornaments. To this spot came the diviners, and when they saw the august being

[1] The Tibetan word appears to answer to the Sanskrit *sudhā* ["the milk-hedge plant, the plant *Aletris hyacinthoides*," &c.]—S.

provided with the marks of sovereignty, they betook themselves to the ministers, full of joy and bliss, and told them that they had found in their researches a being provided with much virtuous merit, whom the sovereignty would befit. Thereupon the ministers caused the road and the city to be cleansed, and prosperously conducted him into the city, and installed him as king on the fitting day, at the fitting hour, under the fitting constellation.

As he had no wife, the ministers, the purohitas, and the kings of other lands, as well as other people, proprietors, merchants, and caravan leaders, all brought their daughters to that city, adorned with all sorts of ornaments, in order that they might be received into the palace. But the king, who had been so shamefully treated by his wife, did not consent to that. The ministers said, "O king, it is not customary for kings to be without wives, princes, ministers, and inhabitants of town and country; so be pleased to nominate a spouse. Kings and grandees living in all manner of districts, and grandees from foreign lands, have their daughters in readiness to be exhibited to you." But he was not to be induced to consent thereto, and he reviled women without ceasing.

Now as all things good for fruition derive their force and completeness from the power of the virtuous merits of beings, it came to pass that, after the Bodisat was thrown down from the mountain through the misdeed of his wife, the roots and berries of that mountain shrivelled and lost their power. Thereupon the woman, fearing to perish in the hour of hunger, having taken the cripple on her back, betook herself to the villages, and asked for alms in the streets, market-places, cross-roads, and by-roads. When she was questioned she always replied, "My husband has never found fault with me." And as a wife, with whom her husband has never found fault, is wont to be highly respected in the world, she obtained alms wherever she went. When she arrived at the capital, and the inhabitants heard of her, they were seized with astonishment. Some of them went forth full of wonder to see her. And the dwellers in the city took to asking if that king, who always had something to say against all women, ought not to look upon this excellent female wanderer, whose husband had never found fault with her, and who carried on her back the handless and footless cripple. When the purohita had made the king acquainted with these sayings the king thought the matter over, and gave orders that this woman should be summoned, as he wished to see her. When she had been sent for, and he had seen her, he laughingly uttered this verse—

"Thou who hast eaten the flesh of my loins, who hast drunk my blood, and hast taken the cripple on thy back, wilt thou not now be blamed by thy husband?

"After having, for the sake of wolf's-milk, flung me down the precipice, after having taken the cripple on thy back, wilt thou not now be blamed by thy husband?"

She stood still with drooping countenance and heart full of shame. When the ministers had asked the king about this matter, and he had given them a full account of all that had taken place, they drove the woman out of the city with contumely.

XXII.

THE FLIGHT OF THE BEASTS.[1]

At a long distant period there stood on the shore of a lake a vilva[2] forest. In this forest dwelt six hares.[3] Now a vilva tree in that forest fell into the lake, thereby producing a great noise. When the six hares heard this noise, they began, as they had but small bodies, to run away full of fear. The jackals saw them running, and asked, "O honoured ones, wherefore do ye run?" The hares replied, "There was a great noise." Thereupon the jackals also took to flight. When the monkeys saw them running they asked, "O honoured ones, wherefore do ye run?" The jackals replied, "There was a great noise." Thereupon the monkeys also took to flight. When the gazelles saw them running they asked, "O honoured ones, wherefore do ye run?" The monkeys replied, "There was a great noise." Thereupon the gazelles also took to flight. When the boars saw them running they asked, "O honoured ones, wherefore do ye run?" The gazelles replied, "There was a noise." Thereupon the boars also took to flight. When the buffaloes saw them running they asked, "O honoured ones, wherefore do ye run?" The boars replied, "There was a noise." Thereupon the buffaloes also took to flight. When the rhinoceroses saw them running they asked, "O honoured ones, wherefore do ye run?" The buffaloes replied, "There was a noise."

[1] Kah-gyur, vii. 194.

[2] *Vilva*, "the tree *Ægle Marmelos* (commonly called Bel)."

[3] The number six is chosen, because it has reference to the group of Bhikshus, known as the Six.—S.

Thereupon the rhinoceroses also took to flight. When the elephants saw them running they asked, "O honoured ones, wherefore do ye run?" The rhinoceroses replied, "There was a noise." Thereupon the elephants also took to flight. When the bears saw them running they asked, "O honoured ones, wherefore do ye run?" The elephants replied, "There was a noise." Thereupon the bears also took to flight. When the hyænas saw them running they asked, "O honoured ones, wherefore do ye run?" The bears replied, "There was a noise." Thereupon the hyænas also took to flight. When the panthers saw them running they asked, "O honoured ones, wherefore do ye run?" The hyænas replied, "There was a noise." Thereupon the panthers also took to flight. When the tigers saw them running they asked, "O honoured ones, wherefore do ye run?" The panthers replied, "There was a noise." Thereupon the tigers also took to flight. When the lions saw them running they asked, "O honoured ones, wherefore do ye run?" The tigers replied, "There was a loud noise." Thereupon the lions also took to flight. At the foot of the mountain there dwelt a maned lion, which likewise seemed to wear a diadem. When it saw the lions running it asked, "O honoured ones, wherefore do ye all run, although each of you is strong in claws and strong in teeth?" The lions replied, "There was a loud noise." "O honoured ones, whence did the noise come?" it asked. "We do not know," they replied. Then said that lion, "O honoured ones, do not run. Inquiry must be made as to where the noise came from." It asked the tigers, "Who told you about it?" The tigers replied, "The panthers." It asked the panthers, "Who was it told you?" The panthers replied, "The hyænas." It asked the hyænas, "Who was it told you?" The hyænas replied, "The bears." It asked the bears, "Who was it told you?" The bears replied, "The elephants." It asked the elephants, "Who was it told you?" The elephants replied, "The rhinoceroses." It asked the rhinoceroses, "Who was it told you?" The rhinoceroses replied, "The buffaloes." It asked the buffaloes, "Who was it told you?" The buffaloes replied, "The boars." It asked the boars, "Who was it told you?" The boars replied, "The gazelles." It asked the gazelles, "Who was it told you?" The gazelles replied, "The monkeys." It asked the monkeys, "Who was it told you?" The monkeys replied, "The jackals." It asked the jackals, "Who was it told you?" The jackals replied, "The hares." It asked the hares, "Who was it told you?" The hares replied, "We saw the terrible thing with our own eyes. Come, we will show you whence the noise came." So they guided the lion, and showed it the vilva forest, saying, "That is where the noise came from." Inasmuch as the noise was caused by the fall of a vilva tree out of that forest into the lake, the lion said: "O honoured ones, be not afraid, for that was only an empty sound." Consequently they were all tranquillised. And a deity uttered this verse: "Let not men believe in words. They ought to see everything for themselves. Observe how, through the fall of a vilva, the forest lost its beasts."

XXIII.

THE FIVE LOVERS.[1]

A MERCHANT had a wife with whom four of the city stipendiaries and their superior officer fell in love, and they all sent go-betweens to her. She listened to what they said, and appointed a time for a meeting. But when they asked where the meeting-place was to be, she directed them to a fig-tree which stood not far from the city, the head of which soared aloft towards the sky, the branches of which were widespread, and the foliage of which was thick. Up this tree they were to climb, and there to await her. She herself awaited an opportunity of going out of the house. But her husband became suspicious, beat her, and bound her to a pillar. She had told one of the four lovers that he was to climb on to a branch on the eastern side of the tree, and she would come by daybreak. He did so joyfully. The second one, likewise by her instruction, climbed on to a branch on the south side of the tree, the third mounted on the western side, and the fourth on the north side, and the superior officer clambered on to a branch in the middle of the tree. They spent the whole night on the tree in expectation, terrified by the wind, all by themselves. For the woman did not come although the day dawned. Then he who was waiting on the eastern branch uttered this verse: "The sun has risen, from the village comes the ploughman. The fig-tree must learn that the false do not come."

He who was waiting on the southern branch said: "The

[1] Kah-gyur, ix. ff. 67–69.

woman who was to come is truly false. This sun full of splendour is now about to rise."

He who was on the eastern side said: "Wilt thou come, excellent one? Being asked this, she replied, 'Yes.'"

Then he who sat on the western branch uttered this verse: "As the sun has risen on the right hand, the ploughers go forth from the village. As I knew not the appointed time, I have not closed my eyes during the night."

After a while he who sat on the northern branch said: "The wind has shaken me the whole night long. He who goes after strange women suffers thus and in other ways."

Then said the superior officer: "If the wind has shaken you well, I shall not complain. The fig-tree, in nought to blame, complains that its branches are broken."

The deity who dwelt in the tree, seeing that they were tricked, said: "You will complain, and the four others too. When the Vaiśākha month[1] comes, the tree which men have maimed recovers."

Having given up their hopes with respect to the woman, the men came down from the tree and went homewards. But the woman had been released by her husband, and she betook herself secretly to that tree. When they saw her they asked her why she had deceived them. She told them the whole story. They said, "So you are now come to light!" As she reflected that she could not have to do with five men after the fashion of dogs, she said that she would yield herself to him among them who should bring her the most beautiful flowers. Now there was in the royal castle a keeper of the king's lotuses, whose nose and ears had been cut off. To him they betook themselves. But they thought that they would certainly get nothing from him by way of purchase, though they might if they flattered him. So one of them said: "As the bulrush

[1] "The first of the twelve months constituting the Hindū solar year (answering to April-May)."

grows again after being cut, so may your nose grow again. Give flowers to him who prays."

The second said: "As the kuśa grass grows again after being mown, so may your nose grow again. Give lotuses to him who prays."

The third said: "As the Dūrvā grass[1] and the Vīraṇa[2] grow again even when cut down, so may your nose grow again. Give flowers to him who prays."

The fourth said: "As hair and beard, although shorn, yet grow again, so may your nose grow again. Give flowers to him who prays."

The fifth said: "The lotus-cravers have all talked nonsense to you. Whether you give lotuses, or do not give them, your nose will never grown again."

The watchman said to himself: "Those four men have talked to me useless stuff. But the fifth has kept steadily to the truth. To him will I give the lotuses."

So he gave him as many lotuses as he wanted. That man went joyfully with them to the woman, whose enjoyment now fell to his share.

[1] "Bent grass, panic grass, commonly Panicum Dactylon."
[2] Andropogon muricatus.—S.

XXIV.

THE VIRTUOUS ANIMALS.[1]

In the long past times there lived in a dense forest four animals: a partridge,[2] a hare, a monkey, and an elephant. As they had become attached to each other, they lived together in harmony and full content, and spent their time joyfully, without fear or strife. But after some time it occurred to them that although, actuated by a reciprocal attachment, they lived without strife in full content, yet as they did not know which of their number they ought most to esteem, honour, and revere, they must for that purpose investigate their several ages. So they began to take counsel with one another, in order to find out which of them was the oldest. Then the partridge pointed out a fig-tree, and said: "O honoured ones, at what periods of its growth has each of us seen this fig-tree?" The elephant said: "When I came this way with our herd I saw this tree of the size of my body." The monkey said: "When I came this way with our troop, I saw that its size was the same as my own." Then said the animals: "You are older than the elephant." The hare said: "When the tree had only two leaves, I licked the dew-drops off them

[1] Kah-gyur, iii. ff. 189–193. Here we have the Tittira Jātaka, which is also printed in Fausböll's Jātaka (London, 1875), p. 218. [See "Buddhist Birth Stories" Translated by T. W. Rhys-Davids. London, 1880, p. 310, No. 37.] In the latter only the partridge, the monkey, and the elephant take part in the question as to age, the hare does not occur. The same is the case in the Chinese recension in "Les Avadānas trad., par Stanislas Julien," ii. p. 17.—S.

[2] In the German version the bird is called a "Haselhuhn." For the sake of convenience, the name given in the "Tittira Jātaka" has been adopted here.

with my tongue." Then the animals said: "You are older than both the others." The partridge said: "So ye have seen the fig-tree when it was of a certain size?" They said that they had. "But I," it continued, "having eaten seed, let fall that from which this tree has sprung." The animals said: "If that is so, you are the oldest among us." Thereupon the elephant began to pay honour to all the others, and the monkey to the hare and the partridge, and the hare to the partridge. In this way they showed each other reverence according to their respective ages.

In the dense forest they were wont to wander to and fro, and when they came to open spaces and broken ground, the monkey used to ride on the elephant, and the hare on the monkey, and the partridge on the hare. Now when their feelings of mutual attachment and reverence had still more increased, there occurred to them this thought, that as their attachment and reverence had increased, they ought to strive a little after other virtues as well. In reply to the question as to what was to be done, the partridge said, "One should abstain from putting living creatures to death." The other said, "What like are those among us who put living creatures to death?"

The partridge replied, "There are leaves, flowers, and fruits, which are endowed with life, as well as those which are devoid of it. In future we will enjoy those which are lifeless, giving up those which possess life." So they took to giving up what possessed life, and partaking of what was lifeless. Then they thought, "Since we have renounced the putting to death of what is living, but not as yet the acquisition of the unbestowed, therefore will we also renounce the acquisition of the unobtained." "What like are those among us who acquire the unbestowed?" said the others. The partridge said, "There are in our possession, roots, leaves, flowers, and fruits, but there are also such as are unpossessed; therefore will we in future give up those which we possess, and feed only on the unpossessed." So they took to giving up what was possessed, and feeding on the previously unpossessed.

Then they thought, "We have now renounced the acquisition of the unbestowed, but not as yet illicit intercourse." "In what does our illicit intercourse consist?" The partridge said, "As we enter into allowable unions and also unallowable, we must henceforth enter into allowable unions alone, and not unallowable." So they followed the lawful paths and gave up those which were unlawful. Then they thought, "We have now renounced unlawful love, but not as yet falsehood. Well, we will also renounce falsehood." "Wherein then consists our falsehood?" asked the others. The partridge said, "Whereas we have been in the habit of speaking all at random, we will in future speak at random no more, but will utter only well-considered words at the right time." So they no longer spoke at random, but uttered merely well-considered words at the right time. Then they thought, "We have renounced falsehood, but not as yet shameless intoxication, by means of intoxicating drinks. Well, we will also renounce shameless intoxication by means of intoxicating drinks." "What like are those among us who shamelessly intoxicate themselves with intoxicating drinks?" The partridge said, "As there are fruits which intoxicate, and also such as do not, we will in future, giving up the intoxicating fruits, partake of those only which are not intoxicating." So they began to partake of only the non-intoxicating fruits, giving up those which intoxicate.

Now when they were duly set fast in the five vows, the partridge said, "O honoured ones, as we are now duly set fast in the five vows, we will confirm others also in the five vows." The others said, "We will do so. But whom shall each of us confirm in them?" The monkey said, "I will confirm all monkeys therein." Then said the hare, "I will confirm therein all hares and furry beasts." The elephant said, "This being the case, I will confirm therein all elephants, lions, tigers, and bears." The partridge said, "This being the case, I will also now confirm in the five vows all the as yet unconverted birds and creatures, footless, two-footed, and four-footed." Then they confirmed in the five vows all the living creatures of the animal world, as many as there were of them in the Kāśi land.

As they did each other no harm, and lived in the dense forest according to their knowledge and pleasure, their influence brought it about that the deity sent rain from time to time, and the earth was constantly provided with seeds, flowers, and fruit-trees.

Now, when the king saw that men were living without doing each other any harm, and that the earth was constantly provided with seeds, flowers, and fruit-trees, he said, "As I rule according to law, this is due to my influence." His wives, and the princes, ministers, warriors, towns-people, and country-folk, were of opinion that it was due to their influence. When the king perceived that they all considered it as due to their influence he was astonished, and he sent for the diviners and asked about it, but they knew nothing of the matter.

Not far from Vārāṇasī there was a grove in which there dwelt a Rishi, endowed with the five kinds of higher knowledge. He practised divination for the men who dwelt in Vārāṇasī and paid honour to him. To this Rishi the king betook himself, touching his feet and saying, "O great Rishi, as all the living beings in my realm belonging to the animal world, without doing one another any harm, live according to their knowledge and pleasure, and the deity sends rain at the right season, and the earth is constantly provided with seeds, flowers, and fruit-trees, therefore I have supposed that, as I rule according to the law, this is due to my power. But as my wives, and the princes, ministers, warriors, towns-people, and country-folk, are of opinion that it is all due to their power, I am greatly puzzled. Therefore it is meet that you should dispel the doubt as to whose power it is due."

The Rishi replied, "O great king, it is not your power which has brought this about, nor yet that of your wives, princes, ministers, warriors, towns-people, or country-folk. But there are four living creatures in your realm whose power has done so." The king said, "If this be so, I will go to see them." The Rishi said, "Wherefore do you wish to see them? Rather adopt the course of life which they have adopted, and live according to it."

"What course of life have they adopted?"

"That of the five vows."

"O great Rishi, what is the nature of these five vows?"

"O great king, they are these: Not to take the life of any living creature; not to steal the property of others; not to enter into unlawful unions; not to lie; not to drink intoxicating liquors."

"O great Rishi," said the king, "if this be so, I also will observe these five vows, and live in accordance with them."

Thereupon the king began to observe those five vows, and to behave accordingly. As the king observed the five vows, and lived in accordance with them, his wives did the same, and the princes, ministers, warriors, towns-people, and country-folk, accepted the five vows, and took to behaving in conformity with them. When the tributary kings heard that King Brahmadatta, together with his wives, princes, ministers, warriors, towns-people, and country-folk, had undertaken the five vows, and were living in conformity with them, they also, along with their wives, princes, ministers, warriors, towns-people, and country-folk, accepted the five vows and observed them. The greater part of the inhabitants of Jambudvīpa accepted the five vows, and began to observe them. Whosoever then died in Jambudvīpa, after his body perished, was born again in the Tushita region of the thirty-three gods.

When the king of the gods, Śakra, saw the circle of the gods so enlarged, he uttered this verse—

"The partridge's disciples, dwelling in the penance-forest with esteem and reverence, have instructed the world in the doctrine."

Bhagavant said, "O Bhikshus, what think ye? I myself was the partridge of that period, the hare of that period was Śāriputra, the monkey Maudgalyāyana, and the elephant Ananda."

XXV.

THE ICHNEUMON, THE MOUSE, AND THE SNAKE.[1]

A VERY long time ago, it once rained unseasonably seven days long, and an ichneumon took refuge in a mouse-hole. Into the same hole came, after wandering to and fro, a snake, alarmed by the rain. Now the ichneumon was preparing to kill the mouse, but the snake said, "O honoured ones, as we have all suffered from the agony of intolerable woe, therefore we ought to remain here without exposing each other to danger and free from disturbance." The snake was named Nandasena, the ichneumon Nanda, and the mouse Gaṇgādatta.

Nandasena and Nanda said to Gaṇgādatta, "Go stealthily, and try to find some food for us." As the mouse was honest and well-disposed, it zealously began to look for food for those two, but could not find any. Nanda said to Nandasena, "If Gaṇgādatta comes back without food, I shall eat Gaṇgādatta." But Nandasena thought, "Even during the anguish of intolerable woe did this ichneumon intend to kill that mouse; there is no need to say, then, what will happen if the mouse returns without bringing food. I had better give it notice beforehand."

So the snake informed the mouse, saying, "Nanda has spoken thus: 'If Gaṇgādatta comes back without bringing food, I will eat Gaṇgādatta.'" Gaṇgādatta, who, after seeking for food, had found none, thought, "Without doubt he will devour me," and said to Nandasena, "As one who is weakened and oppressed by hunger becomes merciless, therefore say to the ungrateful creature that Gaṇgādatta will return no more."

[1] Kah-gyur, iv. ff. 213, 214.]

XXVI.

THE GRATEFUL ANIMALS AND THE UNGRATEFUL MAN.[1]

In long past times King Brahmadatta came to the throne in Vārāṇasī. A man, who had gone with his axe and wood-basket into the forest to fetch wood, was frightened by a lion while looking for wood, and in running away fell into a pit. Into it fell likewise the lion which was intending to devour him. A mouse, which had been frightened by a snake, ran away from it, and a falcon pursued the mouse, in order to devour it. They all four fell into the pit, and they all entertained the evil design of putting each other to death. But the lion said, "O honoured ones, ye are all comrades of mine. As things are so, and we are suffering intolerable pain from woe, it is now no time for us to expose one another to danger. Therefore sit quietly without disturbing yourselves."

By the dispensation of destiny a hunter, who was looking for gazelles, came to that spot, and while he was looking at that pit, all those creatures exclaimed in confused words, "Ho, friend, rescue us!" Understanding what they said, the hunter drew out first of all the lion. It touched his feet and said, "I shall prove grateful to you. But do not draw out that black-headed one who forgets accepted benefits." Having thus spoken, the lion departed. The hunter then proceeded to extricate them all by degrees from the pit.

One day the hunter came again to that spot when the lion had killed a gazelle. The lion recognised the man,

[1] Kah-gyur, iv. ff. 212*, 213*. This story is very intimately connected with that contributed by me to Benfey's Panchatantra i. 194. See also ii. 128.—S.

and touched his feet, and gave him the gazelle. At another time King Brahmadatta had gone into the park with his spouse, and, after enjoying himself there, had lain down to sleep. Left at their ease, the women took off their clothes and exposed them to the air. And they laid aside their ornaments in divers places and roamed about, or sat, reposed, and slept in the grove. When one of the wives had laid aside her ornaments at a certain spot, and had gone to sleep, the falcon carried them off, and gratefully presented them to the hunter. When the king awoke from his sleep he went swiftly to Vārāṇasī. And away went quickly also the wives, princes, ministers, towns-people, and country-folk. The wife, who looked for her ornaments but could not find them, said to the king, "O king, my ornaments are lost in the park." The king gave orders to his ministers, saying, "O honoured ones, as the ornaments are lost, find out who has carried them off."

When they began to make inquiries, the black-headed man, who had visited the hunter from time to time and knew that he was in possession of the ornaments, came with ungrateful heart and told the king. Then the king was very angry. And the king's men summoned the hunter, and said to him, "Ho, friend, you stole the ornaments out of the park." The hunter was terrified and related what had taken place. The ornaments were restored to the king. But the hunter was bound and cast into prison.

Then the mouse went to the snake and said, "By the contrivance of the black-headed sinner has our benefactor been bound and cast into prison." The snake said, "O hunter, I will bite the king to-day. Then do you heal him with this spell and this remedy. If that is done, no doubt the king will set you at liberty, and will confer upon you gifts and good things." The hunter said, "Good, so be it!" The snake bit the king, and the hunter came and healed him with the spell and the remedy. Then the king joyfully released him from the prison, and bestowed upon him gifts and good things.

XXVII.

THE UNGRATEFUL LION.[1]

In long past times the Bodisat, his accumulations [2] as yet incomplete, was born again among birds as a woodpecker, dwelling in a villageless solitude in a hill district, rich in mountain streams, fruits, and flowers. In the same district there lived a king of the beasts, a lion, which was in the habit of killing and devouring gazelles at its pleasure. One day it had been eating meat; a bone stuck fast between its teeth, and the lion, which had never known fear or anxiety, now that toothache was plaguing its body, was quite prostrated and could eat nothing.

By good fortune a woodpecker, which was wont to fly from one tree-top to another, came to the place where the king of the beasts was. When it saw the lion so tormented by pain, it said, "Uncle, wherefore are you cast down?" The lion replied, "Nephew, I am tortured by pain." "What sort of pain?" asked the woodpecker. When the lion had told the whole story, the woodpecker said, "Uncle, I will treat your case. As you are the lion and the king of all four-footed beasts, and can be of service, therefore you must from time to time be of service to me." The lion replied, "I will act in accordance with your words."

The woodpecker thought, "I will manage so that the lion shall not perceive what I am doing to it, and shall

[1] Kah-gyur iv. f. 181.

[2] *Aniyatarâśi.* See Childers on the word *râsi.* By this word may be represented the mass of the merits obtained by means of earlier deeds. —S.

find it out only after recovering." Anxious to assist the lion, the woodpecker remained there observing its way of going on. The violence of the pain having abated, the king of the beasts passed into a happier mood, and went to sleep with its jaws apart on a great, broad, flat rock. The woodpecker drew near to the king of the beasts, and thought that, as it found the lion in so convenient a position, this was the proper moment for treating it. After making a careful examination, the woodpecker, by means of a continued fluttering of its wings, extracted the bone which had stuck between the lion's teeth. And the lion sat up, with eyes opening after surmounted slumber. Then the woodpecker, knowing that the king of the beasts was freed from pain and discomfort, came up to it in high glee, and said, "O uncle, here is the bone which caused the pain." The king of the beasts was greatly astonished and said, "O nephew, as I wish to recompense you for this service, come to me from time to time in order that I may be of use to you." The woodpecker replied, "Good, I will do so," and flew away.

At another time, while the king of the beasts was devouring flesh, the woodpecker, which had been seized by a falcon, and had only just escaped from death, appeared before the king of the beasts in a state of suffering from hunger. Having described its need, it said to the lion, "O uncle, I am tormented with hunger, so give me a piece of flesh." The lion replied in a verse—

"Having torn to pieces a living creature, I am now savage and a misdoer. Are not you, who passed between my teeth, thankful for remaining alive?"

The woodpecker answered likewise in verse—

"Profitless are forms seen in dreams and accumulations flung into the ocean. Profitless are intercourse with a bad man, and benefits conferred on the ungrateful."

XXVIII.

THE TRICKED ELEPHANT.[1]

LONG ago there lived a herd of elephants in a certain district. One of their number fell in love with a female elephant. But she was warmly attached to another young male elephant, to whom she said, "Should not we take to flight when he goes forth to the chase?"

"Is there any means by which we may escape?" asked the young elephant.

"I know of a means," she replied.

Then she said to the other elephant, "Let us go into the pool to bathe."

He went into the pool. Then she said, "Let us see which of us two can remain under water the longest."

As soon as he, who was liberally endowed with stupidity, had gone under water along with her, she emerged and fled away together with the young elephant. When the other elephant had remained a long time under water, he also emerged. But as the female elephant was not to be seen, he thought that he was in danger of being surpassed by her, so he determined to go under water again. When he had gone again under water, he propped himself up at the bottom with his tusks.

When, after some time, being out of breath, he lifted his head out of the water and saw that the female elephant was not there, he took to tramping about wildly in the tank, and thereby inflicted unjustifiable injury on fishes, frogs, tortoises, and many other creatures. Then a deity uttered this verse—

"What a huge lump of flesh devoid of intelligence! Because another has carried off the female, therefore he inflicts injury upon others."

[1] Kah-gyur, iv. f. 256.

XXIX.

THE WOLF AND THE SHEEP.[1]

IN long past times there lived a householder in a certain hill-village. His shepherd went afield to tend his flocks. As the shepherd returned to the village at sunset from tending them, an old ewe which lagged somewhat behind was seized by a wolf.

"Aunt, aunt," said the wolf, "is it well with you? Aunt, aunt, do you seem to find yourself comfortable all alone in the forest?"

Moreover the wolf said, "Do you think, O sheep, whom I have addressed by the name of aunt, that you will escape after having pinched my tail, and also plucked hairs out of my tail?"

The sheep replied, "How could I pinch your tail, seeing that it is behind you, and I have been going in front of you?"

But the wolf said, "Which way then did you come, seeing that my tail spreads all over the four parts of the world, together with the ocean and the hill-villages?"

The sheep rejoined: "As I had heard beforehand from my kinsmen that your tail, O best one, spreads everywhere, I came through the air."

The wolf replied, "O mother, if you came through the air, you must have scared away the herd of gazelles which I meant to feed upon."

Having thus spoken, the malefactor made a spring, tore off the sheep's head, and having killed the sheep, devoured its flesh.

[1] Kah-gyur, iv. f. 287.

XXX.

OXEN AS WITNESSES.[1]

In a certain hill district there lived a householder, to whom, after his marriage, a daughter was born. He was a tiller of the soil, and ploughed his corn-field himself.

The orphan son of a householder, who was bringing a load of wood from the forest, happened to draw near to that corn-field one day. And he threw down the wood he was carrying, rested awhile, and then said, "O uncle, why do you plough yourself? You must certainly have village affairs to look after. Why, then, do you work like a forester in the forest?"

"O nephew, I have neither sons nor brothers."

"O uncle, give me the plough. Do you take rest, and I will plough for you."

With these words he began to plough.

After a time the householder came bringing rice-soup, and invited him to eat. When the meal was finished the householder's son said, "O uncle, I do not know your house. Go away now, and I will continue ploughing; but come to meet me in the evening."

The householder went away, and the youth went on ploughing for a time. Then he turned out the two oxen to graze by the side of the corn-field. In the evening he took a load of grass, and set off to go to the village. The householder came to meet him, and brought him to his house. The youth took the oxen to their stall, shook down straw, and placed grass before them. The householder thought that the youth would be useful to him, and

[1] Kah-gyur, vi. ff. 228–231.

that he would give him his daughter to wife. So he said to him, " O nephew, do everything satisfactorily, and I will give you my daughter to wife."

He began to build a house there. One of his oxen ran into a rice-field, and he could not drive it out, so he reviled it, and then flung a log at it, whereby one of its horns was broken off. In consequence of this, the ox received the name of Hornbreak.

Another time, the ox ran again into the field, and he could not drive it back, so he reviled it, and then flung a sickle at it, whereby its tail was cut off; on account of which it received the name of Stumptail. These two names were afterwards contracted into that of Breakstump.

After some time the youth said to the householder, " Uncle, fulfil what you have promised." The householder said to his wife, " Good wife, make all the preparations for a wedding. I am going to give my daughter in marriage." The wife said, " O lord, as our daughter has not been promised to any one, how can she be given in marriage ? "

He replied, " I shall give her in marriage."

" To whom ? "

" To this householder's son."

The wife said, " Shall I give my daughter in marriage to this fortuneless one, forsooth, who has grown up like white pepper ? I shall marry her there where I find food and clothing."

The husband rejoined, " Good wife, the youth has done me excellent service. If he goes away, I shall be obliged to plough my land myself."

The wife replied, " I cannot give my daughter to this paltry fellow."

Then the householder said to himself, " If I tell the youth that I am not going to give him my daughter, he will go away this very day, and I shall be reduced to great straits." So he tried putting him off from time to time. When the youth again called upon him to fulfil his promise he replied, " O nephew, first of all make an end of the rice-harvest, for I shall have to prepare rice-soup for a very large circle of relatives."

When that was done, the youth called upon him to celebrate the wedding. The householder replied, "O nephew, as sugar-cane will be wanted, first of all make an end of the sugar-cane harvest."

The youth did so, and then renewed his demand. The householder said, "O nephew, as bread will be needed, first of all make an end of the wheat-harvest."

The youth did so, and anew demanded the fulfilment of the promise. The householder said, "As the early rice has come to an end, make preparations for one more harvest."

The youth thought, "As these things cannot be done at that time, and he is playing with me, I will go into one of the great assemblies of the people, and compel him to give me an answer. If he will not give me his daughter, I will bring it about so that I shall receive her in a friendly way out of the king's palace."

So he went into a large assembly of the people, and said, "O uncle, celebrate the wedding." The householder reviled him, and said, "O friends, I certainly will not give my daughter to this man, who works for me as a day-labourer." The young man thought, "As I have received from him neither money nor his daughter, I will do him some small injury and then go away."

After ploughing with the oxen all day he beat them with the goad, fastened them to a dry tree in the sun, and then went away."

Now it was part of the nature of things, not long after the creation of the world, that even brute beasts could speak. And so the two oxen said to him, "O man, you have constantly been for us, as it were, a father and a mother, and have always treated us with kindness. Why have you now beaten us with the goad, after ploughing with us through the day, and why are you going away, after fastening us to a dry tree in the sun? O man, have we wronged you in any way?"

"Ye have not wronged me in the least, but your master has wronged me."

"In what way?"

"He promised me his daughter, but he has not given her to me."

"Why do not you go to the palace of the king?"

"I have no witnesses."

"You just go; we will be witnesses."

"Will ye speak with the language of men?"

"No. But this is how you must make your asseveration. You must tie us up in our stalls for seven days, and give us neither grass nor water; and on the seventh day you must let us go free to a spot where grass and water are plentiful. And you must appear before the king, and say to him, 'If I am speaking the truth, may these oxen neither eat grass nor drink water.'"

The householder's son went to the palace of the king, and said, "O king, that proprietor has promised me his daughter, but he has not yet given her to me to wife."

The king said, "Have you any witnesses?"

"Yes, O king."

"Are they human beings or not?"

"No, they are not human beings, but oxen."

"Can they speak the language of men?"

"No, but my words will in this way be proved to be true. I will tie up these oxen in their stalls during seven days, and leave them without grass or water. But on the seventh day I will let them go free to a place where grass and water are plentiful. Then the oxen, in order to prove the truth of my words, will neither eat grass nor drink water so long as the king refuses to believe me."

The king said to his ministers, "O honoured ones, let the matter be so arranged."

The ministers ordered the oxen to be tied up in their stalls. Breakstump asked, "Does the sun rise in the West? why are not we set free?"

The others said, "We have promised the householder's

son, that if he keeps us tied up in our stall, for seven days without giving us grass and water, and lets us go free on the seventh day in a spot which is rich in grass and water, and if he makes asseveration before the king that if he speaks the truth these oxen will neither eat grass nor drink water, then we will neither eat grass nor drink water so long as the king refuses to believe him."

Breakstump said, "If I were set free I should eat even stones, not to speak of grass."

The oxen said, "The householder's son has always acted towards us like a father and a mother. So do not behave in that manner."

Breakstump said, "It is indeed true that he has behaved towards us like a father and a mother; still, as he has given me the name of Breakstump, I will not consent, but would much rather that his belly should burst."

The householder's son visited the oxen from time to time, and asked, "O oxen, how do ye fare?" They replied, "We fare well, but you do not."

"Why not?"

"Breakstump here has declared that if he be let loose he will devour the very stones, not to speak of grass."

"Then ought I to give in?"

"Do not do that, but bore Breakstump's nose. Then, when he wants to eat grass or drink water, we will seize his nose with our horns and hold it up in the air. At the same time you must say, 'They are pointing to the sun, because they wish to show that the sun, as the fifth guardian of the world, is a witness.'"

So the youth set to work to bore the nose of the ox. Breakstump said, "Honoured ones, see how scandalously he is treating me!" They replied, "Hold your peace, he wishes to embellish you."

On the seventh day the king, after calling his ministers together, had these oxen driven to a spot rich in grass and water. Breakstump was about to pluck a mouthful of grass, when the other oxen seized his nose with their horns and looked up towards the sun. The king asked his ministers, "O honoured ones, wherefore look these oxen towards the sun?" Then one of the ministers said, "That is done because they wish to show that not they alone are witnesses, but the sun, the fifth guardian of the world, is also a witness." The king wondered and said to the ministers, "O honoured ones, as the beasts have thus borne witness, do ye take care that the householder gives his daughter to this young man."

Overcome by the householder-son, the householder bestowed upon him his daughter.

XXXI.

THE STUBBORN AND THE WILLING OXEN.[1]

LONG ago two merchants, with five hundred waggons apiece, were journeying along a forest road, where at one time there was too little grass, at another too little water, and sometimes there was nothing at all to be had. So when the merchants, who, as well as their oxen, were in a state of great exhaustion, saw from the forest road a region in which meadows and water were plentiful, they unharnessed their oxen, and they bathed and drank much water. Now when the oxen, which had been greatly exhausted by the want of grass and water, had drunk water and eaten their fill of grass and recovered their strength, the leading one among the first set said to its comrades, "O honoured ones, as we have been completely exhausted by the want of grass and water, and this place is full of water and pasture, if ye are so inclined, we will remain here."

But the leading ox of the other troop spoke to them in this wise, "O honoured ones, as men are strong and have the mastery over even the difficult to be subdued, and we should only suffer damage at their hands, let us endure the burden which shall be laid upon us."

When it had thus spoken, the first chief ox said angrily to its troop, "O honoured ones, who has seen the further side of the moon? Let those oxen submit to their burden. We will not endure ours."

So when the merchants began to load their oxen, and the first set of animals held stubbornly back, the mer-

[1] Kah-gyur iv. ff. 248*, 249.

chants beat them and lacerated them with thorny rods, and yoked them dripping with blood to the waggons. But the others submitted to the yoke without resisting, so no harm came to them. Thereupon a deity uttered this śloka:

"See how the steers which the ox misguided, bleeding and wounded, suffer hunger and thirst. See how those which the ox rightly advised, after leaving the forest, quaff cooling water."

XXXII.

THE ASS AS A SINGER.[1]

WHEN in long-past times the Bodisat, in consequence of his aggregation of merits remaining incomplete, had been born in a herd of horned cattle as a bull, he used to go out of the city in the evenings to a bean-field belonging to the king, and there take his food. But by day he lived in the city. There an ass joined him. It said one day, "O uncle, your flesh and your blood and your hide thrive, and yet I have never seen you change your abode."

The bull answered, "O nephew, I feed at eventide in the king's bean-field."

The ass said, "Uncle, I will go with you too."

The bull objected, "O nephew, as you are wont to let your voice resound, we might run a risk."

The ass replied, "O uncle, let us go, I will not raise my voice."

After they two had broken through the enclosure of the bean-field and reached the interior, the ass uttered no sound until it had eaten its fill. Then it said, "Uncle, shall not I sing a little?"

The bull replied, "Wait an instant, until I have gone away. Then do just as you please."

The bull ran off, and the ass lifted up its voice. As soon as the king's people heard that, they seized the ass, and in order to punish it, as in their opinion it had devoured the whole produce of the king's bean-field, they cut off its ears, fastened a pestle to its neck, and then set it free.

[1] Kah-gyur, iv. f. 293. Cf. *Panchatantra*, v. 7, and Benfey's remarks on the passage, i. 494.—S.

As it wandered to and fro, the bull saw it, and pronounced this verse—

"Excellently hast thou sung forsooth, and therefore obtained thy recompense. In consequence of thy song I also well-nigh lost my ears.

"He who knows not how to keep his word, to him may easily happen some such thing as this; to wander to and fro, adorned with a club and destitute of ears."

The ass also gave utterance to a verse, "Keep silence thou with broken teeth, be silent then, O old bull; for three men are searching for thee with clubs in their hands."

XXXIII.

THE JACKAL AS CALUMNIATOR.[1]

A.

In long-past times there lived in a certain forest a pregnant lioness. Now it is the custom of lionesses to lay up stores of flesh for the time when they shall bring forth their young. The lioness, having followed after a herd of cattle, struck down a cow which had calved, and which, while taking care of her calf, lagged behind the rest of the herd. The lioness killed the cow, and dragged it off to her lair; the calf, which wanted to suck her mother's teats, following after her. The lioness was at first inclined to kill the calf too, but reflected that it would serve as a playfellow for her cub so soon as she brought it into the world. She gave birth to a male cub, which she suckled along with the calf.

After they had both grown up, the lioness fell ill, and before her death spoke thus, "O children, as ye have both sucked the same dugs, behave as brothers. The world is full of evil calumniators. Take heed, when I am dead, that ye do not listen to such persons."

The lion, which ate the good flesh of the gazelles he killed, and drank his fill of their blood, grew big; and so did the bull, which fed on the good grass guarded by the lion, and enjoyed clear water. The lion, as the king of

[1] Kah-gyur, vi. ff. 239–243. Benfey has called attention, in his Introduction to the *Panchatantra*, to the story in the Siddhi-Kûr of the fox which sets the lion and the bull at variance, and brings about the destruction of both. The story occurs as the twentieth tale in B Jülg's "Mongolischer Märchen-Sammlung," Innsbruck, 1868, pp. 171–176. ["Mongolische Märchen," pp. 35–40.]—S.

beasts, was followed about by an old, very greedy, remainder-devouring jackal. When the lion had killed gazelles, and having devoured their good flesh and drunk their good blood, tranquilly rested, none of the rest of the smaller beasts dared to draw nigh. Only the old jackal used to approach, in order to enjoy what remained over of the good flesh and blood, thanks to which his hide, his flesh, and his blood all thrived.

One day, when the lion had eaten the good flesh of gazelles and drunk their good blood, he hastened to his lair, where he played with the bull. In the meantime the smaller beasts devoured the remains. The jackal thought, "First, I will go to see whither the lion has gone." Having followed after the lion, the jackal saw him playing together with the bull, and came to the conclusion that the bull was the adversary of his maw, and that therefore he must set those two comrades at variance. So with drooping ears he appeared before the bull. The bull said, "O uncle, has any hot wind arisen?"

The jackal replied, "O nephew, a very glowing wind has arisen."

"What is it then that has happened?"

"The lion has asked, 'Whither has gone the bull which belongs to my stores of flesh? If I find no other flesh, I shall devour that bull.'"

The bull replied, "O uncle, our dying mother said to us twain, 'O children, as ye have both sucked the same dugs, be brothers. The world is full of evil calumniators. Take heed that ye listen to none of them after my death.' As she has left behind her such a legacy as this, do not talk in that way."

The jackal said, "O nephew, as you will not listen to my well-meant words, you will go to perdition."

The bull asked, "O uncle, what then will be the course of events?"

The jackal replied, "O nephew, the lion will come forth from his lair, and will stretch himself, and after he has stretched himself he will yawn, and after he has yawned he will look round on all four sides, and after he has looked round on all four sides, he will roar three times, and when he has come to where you are, he will think, 'This creature will kill me;' be sure of that."

Afterwards the jackal betook himself with drooping ears to the lion. The lion asked, "Uncle, has a hot wind arisen?"

The jackal replied, "O nephew, a very glowing wind has arisen."

"What has happened then?"

"The bull has said, 'Whither has my lion-grass gone? As his mother killed my mother, I will slit up his belly.'"

The lion said, "O uncle, our mother, before she died, thus spoke to us twain, 'As ye two have sucked the same dugs, be brothers. The world is full of evil calumniators. Take heed that ye do not listen to any of them.' As she has left such a legacy behind, do not speak in such a manner."

The jackal replied, "O nephew, if you do not now listen to my well-meant words, you will go to perdition."

The lion said, "O uncle, what will take place?"

The jackal replied, "O nephew, the bull will come forth from the meadow, and will stretch himself, and when he has stretched himself he will bellow, and when he has bellowed he will tear up the ground, and when he has torn up the ground he will come snorting into your presence and will think, 'This one will kill me;' know all this."

Although those two animals were constantly in the habit of acting in this way according to their natures, they had never taken any notice of the fact. So when one day after this the lion, the king of beasts, came forth from his lair, after stretching and yawning and looking around on all four sides, and roaring three times, he appeared in presence of the bull. Likewise the bull had come out from the pen, and had stretched himself, and bellowed, and torn up the ground and snorted, and then it appeared in presence of the lion. Although they had both been accustomed to act in this way according to their natures, they had never taken any notice of the fact. But they noticed it now that the seed of discord was sown. The bull thought, "He will kill me," and the lion thought just the same. The lion seized the bull's breast with his claws, the bull slit up the lion's belly with his horns. And so they both perished.

A deity uttered the following verse: "Men who pay regard to what is good, ought not to hold converse with bad men. See how the jackal set at variance the lion and the bull who had been friends."

B.

In long-past times there lived in a forest a lioness with her cub and a tigress with her cub. While the lioness was absent one day, her cub, while wandering about, came into the neighbourhood of the tigress. When the tigress saw it, she was going to kill it, but she changed her mind, seeing that the young lion might be a playfellow for her own cub, and so she began to give it suck. The lioness, on her return from her outing, not finding her young one, set to work to look for it, and at length saw the tigress suckling it. When the tigress perceived the lioness, she was frightened and began to run away. But the lioness cried out to the tigress, "O sister, run not away. Let us dwell together, so that, when I go out, you can take care of my young one, and when you go out, I will take care of yours." So they took to dwelling together, and they called the lion cub Sudaṇshṭhra, and the tiger cub Subāhu. And the two cubs grew up.

After a time the lioness and the tigress fell ill, and when the time for their departure came, they said to the two young beasts, "O children, as ye have both sucked the same dugs, be ye brothers. The world is full of evil calumniators, take heed after our death not to listen to any of them."

Now the young lion was wont to kill gazelles, and to devour their good flesh and lap their good blood, and then, having done this, to betake himself at once to his lair. But the young tiger, when he went out, underwent great fatigue in killing gazelles, and having devoured their flesh and lapped their blood, returned home after a long absence. One day the tiger devoured the remains of a meal which he had hidden away, and then returned quickly home. The lion asked, "How is it that you, who never came back before till after a long time, have returned to-day so soon?" The tiger replied, "I have eaten the stores which I had set aside." The lion asked, "Do you lay up stores, then?" The tiger said that it did. The lion said, "When I have slain gazelles and eaten their good flesh and lapped their good blood, I am wont to go away without troubling myself further." The tiger replied, "You are strong. I cannot do like that." The lion said, "Let us go together." So they took to going out together.

Now an old, very malicious, remainder-devouring jackal, was in the habit of following after this lion, the king of the beasts. The jackal considered that the tiger was the antagonist of his maw, and that he must set those two animals at variance. So he came into the presence of the lion with drooping ears. The lion said, "O uncle, has any hot wind arisen?"

The jackal replied, "O nephew, a very scorching wind has arisen."

"What has happened then?"

"This tiger has said, 'Where has my lion-grass gone? As he leaves me to feed on remnants, I will assuredly kill him.'"

The lion replied, "O uncle, our two mothers said to us just before they died, 'O children, as ye two have sucked the same dugs, be brothers. The world is full of evil calumniators. Take heed that after we are both dead, ye do not listen to any one among them.' As they have left such a legacy behind them, do not you speak in that way."

The jackal said, "As you will not listen to my well-meant words, you will come to ruin."

The lion said, "O uncle, what will be the course of events?"

The jackal replied, "O nephew, the tiger will come forth from his lair, and will stretch himself, and after stretching he will yawn, and after yawning he will look round on all four sides, and after looking round on all four sides he will roar three times, and then come into your presence and think, 'He will kill me.' Be sure of this."

Afterwards the jackal went with drooping ears to the tiger. The tiger asked, "O uncle, has some hot wind arisen?"

The jackal replied, "O nephew, a very scorching wind has arisen."

"What has happened then?"

"This lion has said, 'Where has my tiger-grass gone? I will assuredly kill him.'"

The tiger said, "O uncle, our two mothers said to us, just before they died, 'O children, as ye have sucked the same breast, be brothers. The world is full of evil calumniators. Take heed that ye do not listen to any of them. As they have left us this legacy, do not you speak in that way."

The jackal replied, "O nephew, as you will not listen to my well-meant words, you will go to ruin."

"O uncle, what then will be the course of events?"

"O nephew, this lion will come forth from his lair and will stretch himself, and after stretching he will yawn, and after yawning he will look round on all four sides, and after looking round on all four sides, he will roar three times, and then come into your presence, and think, 'He will kill me.' Be sure of all this."

Now although both of them were in the habit of acting in this way, according to their natures, they had never taken any notice of that. But one day the lion, the king of beasts, came forth from his lair and stretched himself, and yawned, and looked round on all four sides, and roared three times, and then went into the presence of the tiger. The tiger also came forth from his lair, and stretched himself and yawned, and looked round on all four sides, and then went into the presence of the lion. Although both of them had always been in the habit of doing all this, yet they had never taken any notice of the fact. But now that the seed of discord was sown, they did notice it. Just as the lion thought that the tiger wanted to kill him, so also the tiger thought that the lion wanted to kill him. But then the lion thought, "I am strong, but the tiger is not. As he cannot then master me, I will investigate the matter further." So he uttered this śloka—

"O Subāhu, to strive with Sudaṇshṭhra, possessor of complete excellence, agility, and force, is not right."

The tiger also replied in a śloka, "O Sudaṇshṭhra, to strive with Subāhu, possessor of complete excellence, agility, and force, is not right."

The lion asked, "Who spoke to you about this?"

The tiger replied, "The jackal."

Then the tiger asked, "Who spoke to you about this?"

The lion replied, "The jackal."

Then the lion thought, "This creature wanted to set us two at variance," and struck the jackal dead with a slap in the face. Then a deity uttered this śloka—

"Friends ought not to be abandoned on account of the words of others, but the words of others ought to be tested. No reliance ought to be placed upon calumniators, who seek opportunities for sowing discord. See how the jackal, who desired to set friends at variance by means of lies, was put to death as a calumniator, while the friends were happy and rejoiced."

XXXIV.

THE TWO OTTERS AND THE JACKAL.[1]

In long-past times there lived on the bank of a river two otters, which from time to time used to enter the water and bring fish ashore. But while the otters were on the dry land, the fish used to get back into the water.

Finding there was nothing left, the otters took counsel together one day, and determined that in future one of them should go into the water while the other remained on land, and that they should share the spoil in common. So one of them went into the water while the other remained on land. The one which went into the water frightened the fish, and drove them ashore, while the one which remained on land killed them; the fish also which remained in the water were killed by the otter which had gone into the water.

Now when the heap of fish had become great, one of the otters said, "Divide the heap."

The other replied, "I will not divide it."

"Why not?"

"I should not like to make a mistake."

Then the other said, "For the matter of that, I too might make a mistake."

While they stood there absorbed in thought, the jackal Mukhara came up to them and said, "O nephews, why are you so absorbed in thought?"

"O uncle, we have caught some fish."

"Why do not you divide them?"

"O uncle, for fear of acting unrighteously."

[1] Kah-gyur, ff. 94*, 95.

Then Mukhara said to himself, "As they both hesitate I will undertake the division."

After looking at a tortoise which regularly waited upon the two otters, he went to one of them and said, "O nephew, what have you done in this matter?"

"O uncle, I dived into the water, and after diving into it, I frightened the fish, which were driven on land and killed by my companion here."

"O nephew, however little was to be got by going into the water, yet Mukhara would certainly go into the water. The otter who has to be on the dry land is exposed to danger from fissures, tree-stumps, thorns, wild beasts, and men. Besides, if he were not to kill the fish, of what use would your frightening them be? In short, as the whole catch is entirely the other otter's work, you must take what he gives you and raise no objection."

The otter did not utter a word in reply, smitten to the heart and overawed by the jackal.

Then the jackal went to the other otter, and said, "O nephew, what was your share in this matter?"

"O uncle, I kept on the dry land, and killed the fish which were driven ashore."

"O nephew, however little was to be got by going upon dry land, yet Mukhara would always keep to the dry land. The otter who has to go into the water is in danger from waves and waters, from tortoises, alligators, and crocodiles. Besides, if he had not frightened the fish, how could you have killed them? In short, all the take of the fishing is the other otter's work; and therefore you must be content with what your companion gives you." The otter, heart-smitten and overawed by the jackal's words, sat there without saying a word. Then Mukhara said, "O nephew, there is a means of accomplishing the division without injustice, by means of the utterance of a śloka."

Then the two otters said despondingly, "O uncle, undertake the division."

So Mukhara divided the heap into three parts, one containing the heads of the fish, and another their tails, and the third the rest of their bodies. And he uttered this verse:—

"The goer on land receives the tails, and the goer into the depths the heads; he who is conversant with the law receives the middle parts."

Moreover, Mukhara said to himself, "Having deluded these two, I will secure the booty." So he seized the middle part of a large fish, and went off to his mother. She joyfully addressed him in a śloka,

"Mukhara, whence dost thou come that thou hast brought a large fish without head or tail? whence dost thou come so highly blessed?"

"Even as the king's cat," he replied, "that knows neither right nor wrong, in that fools strive with one another, gains thereby, so shall we obtain food in plenty."

The mother also uttered this śloka, "O Mukhara, fine and fair exceedingly art thou who hast been too much for the otters. They twain are content, and thou hast secured a rich booty."

XXXV.

THE JACKAL SAVES THE LION.[1]

In lost past times, when the Bodisat remained in an incomplete state of merit-accumulation, he lived in a certain hill district as a lion, king of the beasts. In the neighbourhood of the hill there dwelt five hundred jackals, which followed after him and devoured what he left. When the lion had killed any animal, and had eaten of its good flesh and drunk of its good blood, he used to leave it lying on the ground and go away. This state of things lasted a long time.

Once when the lion, king of beasts, was hunting beasts at night, he fell into a well, and all the five hundred jackals, with one exception, dispersed in divers directions. Only one of the jackals paid any attention to the lion, sitting by the edge of the well, and thinking in what way he could draw the lion out. While running to and fro in the neighbourhood of the well, he saw a small lake at no great distance. Having observed it, he dug a canal on one side, and filled the well with water from the lake, so that the lion was able to get out. A deity uttered this verse:—

"The mighty as well as the rest must make themselves friends. See how the jackal rescued the lion from out of an old well."

[1] Kah-ygur, iv. f. 244*.

XXXVI.

THE BLUE JACKAL.[1]

In times long past there was a very greedy jackal, which used to roam in the forest, and even in places uninhabited by men. At length he made his way into the house of a dyer, and fell into an indigo vat. After he had escaped he lay down to sleep on a neighbouring dunghill. Having tossed about thereon, so that his body became ever so unshapely, he jumped into the water. When he had come out, and had been exposed to the rays of the sun, he acquired the colour of cyanite.

When the other jackals saw him, they dispersed and stood afar off, and asked, "Who are you? where do you come from?"

He replied, "My name is Śataga, and I have been appointed king of the fourfooted beasts by Śakra, the king of the gods."

The jackals considered that, as his body was of a colour never before seen, this must be true, and they made all the fourfooted beasts acquainted with the fact. The lions thought, "If some one is exalted above us and made the king of the beasts, we must go and carry this news to the chief of our band." So they told the news to the maned chief of their band, who dwelt in a certain hill district. He ordered the other beasts to go forth and find out whether any animal had seen this chieftain of the fourfooted. So they betook themselves to where the jackal was, and made

[1] Kah-gyur, iv. f. 255. Cf. Panchatantra, i. 10, and Benfey's remarks thereon, pp. 224-5; Hitopadeśa, iii. 7; A. Weber, *Indische Studien*, iii., 349, 366.—S.

inquiries. And they perceived the jackal, like unto nothing ever seen before, surrounded by all the fourfooted creatures except the lions. Then they returned to their chief and told him what they had seen. And he, when he had listened to them, betook himself, surrounded by the band of lions, to where the jackal was. The jackal, surrounded by many quadrupeds, rode along on an elephant, with the lions around him, and then the tigers and other quadrupeds. The jackals formed a circle round him at a greater distance.

Now the jackal's mother dwelt in a certain mountain ravine. Her son sent a jackal to her, and invited her to come, now that he had obtained the sovereign power. She asked what was the nature of his surroundings.

The messenger replied, "The inner circle is formed of lions, tigers, and elephants, but the outer of jackals."

She said, "So much for things not following their proper order." She also said in verse :—

"I live here comfortably in the mountain ravine, and amid cool waters enjoy my good fortune; so long as he utters no jackal's cry, the elephant will let him retain his prosperity."

The messenger jackal said to the jackals, "This king of the fourfooted is only another jackal. I have seen his mother who dwells in such and such a mountain ravine."

They replied, "In that case we will test him and see whether he is a jackal or not."

Now it is according to the nature of things that jackals, if they hear a jackal howl without howling themselves, lose their hair.

So the jackal, when he heard the other jackals lift up their voices, said to himself, "If I utter no cry, my hair will certainly fall off. But if I get off the elephant and then begin to howl, he will kill me. So I will lift up my voice where I am."

So soon as, sitting on the elephant, he began to lift up

his voice, the elephant perceived that it was a jackal that was riding on his back, so he flung him off and trampled him under foot. A deity uttered this verse:—

"He who keeps at a distance those who should be near, and brings near those who should be at a distance, will be cast down, as the jackal was by the elephant."

XXXVII.

THE JACKAL HANGED BY THE OX.[1]

In long-past times, there lived in a certain hill-town a householder, who possessed an ox marked with signs. Śramanas, Brahmans, kinsmen, the poor, the helpless, the needy, and the sick provided it with sustenance, and it could wander about at its pleasure. One day, as it was roaming about, it got into a certain swamp. Towards sunset came the householder, who had heard of this, and was looking for it. As he could not get it out at the moment, he determined to do so next morning. But the ox said, "Fling me a noose, and then go away. If a jackal comes, I will pick up the noose with my horns and throw it over him. The householder flung a noose in front of the ox and went away.

In the course of the night up came a jackal, and said, "Who is it that is tearing up these lotus roots and white lotuses?"

The ox replied, "It is I. Here I am, stuck fast in the swamp."

The jackal thought it had found a feast, and prepared to do the ox an injury. The ox said, "Get away from here; harm and disgrace might come upon you." But as there was no driving away the jackal, and he was still bent upon injuring as before, the ox uttered this verse—

"No lotus roots do I tear up, nor white lotuses either. If thou wishest for food mount upon my back, there wilt thou find food."

[1] Kah-gyur, iv. f. 293.

Full of gluttony, the jackal got on the back of the ox. But the ox flung the noose with its horn, caught the jackal round the neck, and let him hang in the air. The ox uttered this verse—

"Art thou Jakara the dancing-master, or art thou one who is learning to dance? In the forest are no fees paid; arts are taught in cities."

The jackal also uttered a verse in reply—

"Not the dancing-master Jakara am I, nor one who is learning to dance. As Śakara has provided a ladder, I betake myself to Brahma's world."

The ox rejoined likewise in verse—

"Śakara has not provided a ladder; still less is there any question about going to Brahma's world. As thou hast been laid in the fetters of contrivance, thou wilt never see thyself saved."

XXXVIII.

THE JACKAL IN THE ELEPHANT'S FOOTPRINTS.[1]

An elephant came long ago to the Himalayas to drink water. In its track followed a jackal, which saw the elephant's footprints, and began to measure its own stride with them.

"These footprints are mine," it said to itself.

Then springing forwards it set its foot in one of the footprints, and tripped over a broken piece of wood.[2]

A deity uttered this verse—

"In a word, O fool, thy footprints and those of the elephant are not alike. Give up this useless attempt. Thou wilt only derive weariness therefrom."

[1] Kah-gyur, iv. f. 222.

[2] Of the Kāndakīllaka or *Symplocos racemosa*. See Böhtlingk-Roth.—S.

XXXIX.

THE GUILTY DOGS.[1]

In long-past times, King Brahmadatta came to the throne in Vārāṇasī, at a period when the land was blessed with riches, profusion, prosperity, and crops, and had a large population. Now there were two dogs, Gaṇḍa and Upagaṇḍa by name, which used to gnaw the king's horse-gear. Once when King Brahmadatta was going to take the field against the Liććhavis, he ordered his ministers to inspect the horse-gear. When they had done this, and found that it was all torn and tattered, they said to the king, "O king, the dogs have gnawed the horse-gear to pieces."

The king said, "Honoured sirs, if this is the case, I give up the dogs altogether."

Thereupon some of them were killed and others ran away. A dog, which came from another country, seeing them running off, asked them what had frightened them so much. They gave a full account of all that had occurred. It said, "Why do not you implore the king?"

They replied, "We who are running away have no power of imploring the king, and the others have been rendered mute."

It said, "Wait awhile, I will implore the king in your behalf."

Encouraged by him they turned back; and after they had made a halt they expressed their prayer in a verse, uttered at a distance from which they could be heard, saying—

[1] Kah-gyur, iv. f. 212.

"These two dogs, Gaṇḍa and Upagaṇḍa, full of force and health, living in the king's stronghold, ought to be put to death. We are not deserving of death. O king, it is not right to let the innocent be put to death."

Having heard this, the king said next day to his ministers, "Honoured sirs, find out those who implored me yesterday in verse."

The ministers gave orders to the body-guards, saying, "Find out those who implored the king yesterday in verse."

The guards said, "It was the dogs of the land that did so."

The king said, "Honoured sirs, find out whether the horse-gear was devoured by Gaṇḍa and Upagaṇḍa, or by other dogs."

The ministers assembled, and began to take counsel together, saying, "Honoured sirs, the king has ordered us to find out about the dogs. How shall we manage it?"

Then some of them said, "There is only one way of finding out. What need is there to seek out others? The dogs must be given a hair-pellet and made to vomit."

When the pellet of hair had been given to the dogs, and they had been made to vomit, Gaṇḍa and Upagaṇḍa brought up fragments of leather. When the king had been informed of this, he delivered those dogs over to death. But he rendered the others free from fear.

XL.

THE HYPOCRITICAL CAT.[1]

In long-past times there was a chieftain of a company of mice who had a retinue of five hundred mice. And there was also a cat named Agnija. In his youth he had been wont to kill all the mice in the neighbourhood of his dwelling-place. But afterwards, when he had grown old, and no longer had the power of catching mice, he thought: "In former times, when I was young, I was able to catch mice by force. But now that I can do so no more, I must use some trick in order to make a meal off them." So he began to watch the mice by stealth. By means of such watching he found out that there were five hundred mice in the troop.

At a spot not far distant from the mouse-hole, he took to performing fictitious acts of penance, and the mice, as they ran to and fro, saw him standing there with pious mien. So they cried out to him from a distance, "Uncle, what are you doing?"

The cat replied, "As in my youth I have perpetrated many vicious actions, I am now doing penance in order to make up for them."

The mice fancied that he had given up his sinful life, and there grew up within them confidence nourished by faith.

Now as they returned into their hole every day after making their rounds, the cat always seized on and devoured the mouse which came last. Seeing that the troop was constantly dwindling, the chief thought: "There must be

[1] Kah-gyur, iv. ff. 247, 248.

some cause for the fact that my mice are diminishing in number, and this cat is thriving apace." So he began to observe the cat closely. And when he saw that the cat was fat and well covered with hair, he thought: "There is no doubt that this cat has killed the mice. Therefore must I bring the matter to the light of day."

Now as he kept careful watch from a hiding-place, he saw how the cat ate up the mouse which went last. Then from afar off he pronounced this verse—

"As the uncle's body waxes bigger, but my troop on the contrary becomes smaller, and as he who eats roots and berries will not become fat and well covered with hair, this is not a genuine penance, but one performed only for the sake of gain. Because the number of the mice diminished have you, O Agnija, thrived."

XLI.

THE GAZELLE AND THE HUNTER.[1]

In long-past times, when the Bodisat was in a state of indefinite merit-aggregation, he was the prince of a band of five hundred gazelles. Now a hunter had prepared a great many traps, nets, and springs, for the purpose of catching gazelles. As the gazelle prince carelessly enjoyed life, wandering about the forest with a troop of five hundred gazelles, he was caught in a net one day while heading the troop of gazelles. When the other gazelles saw him caught in the net, they all fled away, except one doe which remained beside the prince. Although the gazelle prince struggled hard, he was not able to tear the net. When the doe saw that, as she ran to and fro, she said, "As the hunter has prepared this net, exert thyself, O blessed one, exert thyself, O head of the gazelles."

He replied, "Although I press my hoofs firmly against the ground, yet as the net which binds me is strong, and my feet are sorely wounded, I cannot tear the net. What then is to be done?"

Presently came the hunter towards that spot, dressed in brown clothes and bearing a bow and arrows. The doe saw the hunter draw nigh in order to kill the gazelle prince. Having seen him, she hurriedly exclaimed in verse—

"As this is the hunter who prepared this net, exert thyself, O highly blessed gazelle prince, exert thyself."

He replied, also in verse—

"Although I set my hoofs hard against the ground, yet

[1] Kah-gyur, iv. ff. 244*-245*.

as the net which binds me is strong, and my feet are sorely wounded, I am not able to tear the net. What, then, is to be done?"

Then the doe approached the hunter with courageous heart, and coming up to him uttered this śloka—

"O hunter, draw thy sword and first kill me, and then kill the gazelle prince."

When the hunter asked her with astonishment what she had to do with the gazelle prince, she replied, "He is my husband." The hunter replied in a verse—

"I will kill neither thee nor the gazelle prince. Thou shalt keep company with thy beloved spouse."

She answered, likewise in a verse—

"As I, O hunter, take pleasure in my dear spouse, so mayst thou, O hunter, enjoy thyself with all that belongs to thee."

The hunter, whose astonishment became still greater, went away together with the gazelles, whom he left at liberty.

XLII.

THE MONKEYS SAVED FROM DEATH.[1]

In long-past times there lived in a hill-place a troop of five hundred monkeys, which, when the corn was ripe, devoured the crops. The men who lived in that place assembled and began to take counsel together, saying—

"Honoured sirs, what shall we do, seeing that the monkeys endanger the corn?"

Some of them held that the monkeys must be killed. But how were they to set about doing that? All the trees which stood around the place must be cut down, one Tinduka[2] tree only being allowed to stand. And a hedge of thorns must be drawn around, and the monkeys must be killed inside the enclosure, when they climbed the tree in search of food. Accordingly all the trees growing around that place were cut down, only one Tinduka tree being allowed to stand; and that tree was surrounded by a hedge of thorns, and a watchman was set there, with orders to give notice as soon as the monkeys assembled.

Now one day when the Tinduka tree had put forth flowers and fruits, and these had grown ripe, the monkeys said to their chief—

"O chief, as the Tinduka tree is ripe, let us go to it and eat."

Thereupon the chief, with a troop of five hundred monkeys, climbed the Tinduka tree, and they began to devour the fruit. The watchman brought word to the

[1] Kah-gyur, ii. ff. 115–116. This story is given in Spence Hardy's "Manual of Buddhism" (London, 1853, p. 113), under the title of "The Tinduka Játaka."—S.

[2] Diospyros embryopteris.—S.

men who dwelt in that place, saying, "Honoured sirs, all the monkeys have climbed up the Tinduka tree and are feeding. Do ye do what ought to be done."

Then in all haste the troop of men who dwelt there, with clenched fists, and armed with bows and arrows and battle-axes, betook themselves to the Tinduka tree and began to cut it down. Fear came upon the monkeys, and they sprang to and fro on the tree. But the chief sat still and did nothing. The monkeys said to him, "O chief, wherefore do you sit there tranquilly, while we are running to and fro in the pangs of intolerable misery?" He replied in a verse—

"The busy and the idle are like unto each other. The ends of the tree are many; let food be taken by him who is intent upon his life."

At that time one of the monkey-chief's young ones, a captive in the village, was sitting absorbed in thought, leaning his cheek upon his hand. A good monkey came that way, saw the young monkey thus absorbed in thought, and said—

"O friend, why do you sit there thus absorbed in thought, leaning your cheek upon your hand?"

The young monkey replied—

"How could I not be absorbed in thought, since the whole troop of the men who live in the village have taken the field in order to put my relatives to death?"

"Why do you not behave with courage?"

"How can a captive behave with courage?"

"I will set you free from your bonds."

So soon as the young monkey was set free, he set the village on fire. When it began to burn, and clamour and uproar arose, the inhabitants heard it and said—

"Honoured sirs, while we and the monkeys are at a distance, a great calamity has occurred. As the village is burning, we will put out the fire and then come back."

So they hastened to put out the fire; but the monkeys came down from the Tinduka tree and ran away.

XLIII.

INCREDULITY PUNISHED.[1]

In long-past times, in a spot well provided with flowers and fruits, in the neighbourhood of a hill-town, there lived two chiefs of monkey troops, each of which was composed of five hundred monkeys. One of the two chiefs dreamed one night that he was placed alive in a caldron, together with a retinue of five hundred monkeys. At this he was greatly alarmed, and he gave way to lamentation. Before the break of day he arose and called the monkeys together, and began to relate to them his dreams.

"Honoured sirs, last night I dreamed an evil dream, in consequence whereof we will leave this place."

The monkeys said, "Let us do so and set forth."

As Bodisats have dreams which are full of significance, the august being said to the chief of the other band of monkeys, "As I have dreamed such a dream, it is to be hoped that you will move somewhere else."

The other chief answered incredulously, "Do dreams then turn out true? If you want to go, in that case go. But as I possess a widely extended domain, I shall not go."

When the first monkey-chief saw that the other did not believe in him, he himself, together with his band, went away.

One day after this, as a servant-maid was roasting barley on the earth in one of the houses of the hill-town, a

[1] Kah-gyur, iv. 246.

wandering sheep came by bad luck that way, and began to eat the grain. The maid struck the sheep with a firebrand, and the sheep ran blazing into the king's elephant stable. From its flames the elephant stable caught fire, and many elephants were scorched. The king sent for the doctor, and asked how the elephants which had been scorched by the fire ought to be treated. The doctor prescribed monkeys cooked in barley-meal. Accordingly orders were given to the hunters, who caught all the monkeys residing in the neighbourhood. These monkeys, whose flesh had increased in the course of time, the doctor threw into the caldron alive.

A deity uttered this verse : "It is not good to dwell in a town or a village in which discord exists. On account of discord between the sheep and the servant-maid, the monkeys perished."

XLIV.

THE WISE AND THE FOOLISH MONKEY CHIEFS.[1]

In long-past times there lived in a certain country two monkey chiefs, each ruling over a band of five hundred monkeys. As one of them wandered about with his band he gradually came to a hill-village. A kimpāka tree grew there, the branches of which were bowed down to the ground by the fruit, so the monkeys said to the chief of their band: "O chief, as the tree is very rich in fruit, and the fruit weighs its branches down to the ground, let us after our fatigues enjoy the fruit."

After looking at the tree, the chief of the band said in a verse: "Although the tree stands near the village, yet have the children not partaken of the fruit. From that it may be concluded that the fruit of this tree is not conducive to enjoyment."

After he had thus spoken, they went away.

Following after him, the leader of the other band also gradually drew near to that village. And when the monkeys saw the kimpāka tree, they said to the leader of their band: "O leader, as there is fruit on this tree, and we are fatigued, we would like to enjoy the fruit and gain strength."

He replied, "Good; do so."

The monkeys partook of the fruit, and unfortunately suffered agonies in consequence.

[1] Kah-gyur, iv. f. 247.

XLV.

THE MONKEYS AND THE MOON.[1]

In long-past times there lived a band of monkeys in a forest. As they rambled about they saw the reflection of the moon in a well, and the leader of the band said: "O friends, the moon has fallen into the well. The world is now without a moon. Ought not we to draw it out?"

The monkeys said, "Good; we will draw it out."

So they began to hold counsel as to how they were to draw it out. Some of them said, "Do not you know? The monkeys must form a chain, and so draw the moon out."

So they formed a chain, the first monkey hanging on to the branch of a tree, and the second to the first monkey's tail, and a third one in its turn to the tail of the second one. When in this way they were all hanging on to one another, the branch began to bend a good deal. The water became troubled, the reflection of the moon disappeared, the branch broke, and all the monkeys fell into the well and were disagreeably damaged.

A deity uttered this verse: "When the foolish have a foolish leader, they all go to ruin, like the monkeys which wanted to draw the moon up from the well."

[1] Kah-gyur, iv. f. 249. Cf. A. Weber in the "Monatsberichten der K. Akademie der Wiss. zu Berlin," 1860, p. 69, and "Indische Streifen," i. 246 (Berlin, 1868). —S.

XLVI.

THE PEACOCK AS BRIDEGROOM.[1]

In long-past times lived the flamingo-king, Rāshṭrapāla. The birds which dwelt in the different countries, having heard that his daughter was going to choose herself a husband, assembled themselves together, each hoping that he would be her spouse.

When she had looked at the peacock, she said, "He shall be my husband."

Thereupon the other birds told him that she had chosen him as her spouse. He expanded his tail and began to dance.

Rāshṭrapāla saw him, and asked, "Why does he dance?"

The others replied, "It is because he is to be your daughter's husband."

He said, "To him I will not give my daughter, for he is shameless and bold."

When the peacock heard of this, he went to Rāshṭrapāla, and asked in a śloka: "Wherefore dost thou refuse to give me thy daughter, although I have a lovely voice, a beautiful colour, wings set with eyes, and a neck like unto lapis lazuli?"

Rāshṭrapāla replied, "Although thou hast a lovely voice, a beautiful colour, wings set with eyes, and a neck like unto lapis lazuli, yet I will not give her to thee, for thou art afflicted with impudence."

[1] Kah-gyur, iii. f. 90.

XLVII.

THE CROW WITH THE GOLDEN CAP.[1]

It happened long ago, that a crow uttered agreeable sounds in the presence of a woman, whose husband had undertaken a long journey.

The woman said, "Ho there, O crow! if my husband returns home safe and sound, I will give you a golden cap."

After a time her husband returned home safe and sound, when the crow appeared before her with an eye to the golden cap, and uttered agreeable sounds. She gave it a golden cap.

The crow put it on, and fled hither and thither.

But on account of the golden cap a falcon tore off the crow's head.

A deity uttered this verse: "A possession, which has no necessary cause, will be taken away. The gold on the crow's head was looked after by a robber."

[1] Kah-gyur, iv. f. 221.

XLVIII.

THE REVENGEFUL CROW.[1]

In long-past times the men of Rājagriha and their king determined, on account of some occurrence or other, to establish two cemeteries, and to bury men in one of them and women in the other. It happened once that a hermaphrodite died and could find room neither in the one cemetery nor in the other. In a certain locality in Rājagriha there was a park full of roots, fruits, splendid flowers, and various singing-birds. There a Rishi dwelt with shaven head, who fed upon roots, fruits, and water, and was clothed in a hide and the bark of trees. A ricinus shrub grew there in a three-cornered field, and there the body of the hermaphrodite was left. Perceiving the smell of the body, a jackal came and began to devour its flesh. Now a crow had built her nest on the top of the ricinus tree, and was nestling in it. It occurred to her to flatter the jackal, in order that he might give her the remains of the feast, so she began to sing his praises in a verse: "As I testify my reverence for thee, who art provided with the neck of a lion and the back of a bull, so deign to be gracious to me for the benefit of the asker."

The jackal looked up and said, likewise in verse: "O most excellent of birds, wanderer through the air, lighter-up of all places, now like unto a gem dwelling upon the summit of a splendid tree."

The crow continued, "As I have descended in order to

[1] Kah-gyur, iv. f. 231.

look upon one so highly blest, and as I pay honour to thee as the king of the beasts, deign to be gracious in behalf of the asker."

The jackal said, "O crow, whose neck is like unto the neck of the peacock; O most excellent of pleasure-bringers, fair to see, descend in order to feed at will."

The crow flew down, and, in the company of the jackal, began to devour the dead body.

When the Rishi saw that, he said in a verse: "Alas! from afar off have I seen thee, shamelessly nestling in the shadow of the most wretched of trees, and devouring the most wretched of corpses."

When the crow heard that, she indignantly uttered this verse: "What is it to this baldpate that the lion and the peacock, feeding here upon excellent flesh, prolong their existence by means of strangers' gifts?"

The Rishi was affronted in his turn and uttered this verse: "See here the union of the shameless. The most wretched of birds is the crow, the most wretched of beasts is the jackal, the most wretched of trees is the ricinus tree, the most wretched of men is the hermaphrodite, the most wretched of fields is the three-cornered one."

Then an exceedingly great anger sprang up within the mind of the crow, and she betook herself to the Rishi's kitchen, and began to look about her. Seeing nothing there, she broke the pots and pitchers, and then flew away. When the Rishi came into his kitchen, and found the pots and pitchers broken, he knew that it was none but the bad crow who had done that, and he said in a verse: "To her who, without being told, has with shameless malice broken the things in the kitchen, shall in future, whether for praise or for blame, not even the smallest word be spoken. The wise ever obtain repose only by means of this, that they keep silence."

XLIX.

THE UNITED PHEASANTS.[1]

In long-past time there lived on the sea-coast two pheasants, named Dharmika and Adharmika, whose bodies were united in their growth. Once while Adharmika was asleep, Dharmika kept awake, and saw an amṛita fruit driven ashore by the waters. He took it out and considered whether he should wake the other or eat the fruit by himself. Reflecting that if he ate it, the body they shared in common would be nourished thereby, he did not wake the other.

When the other awoke of his own accord, and perceived that Dharmika's breath smelt of amṛita fruit, he said, "What is it your breath smells of?"

"Amṛita fruit," replied Dharmika.

"Where did you get it?" asked Adharmika.

Dharmika replied, "I found an amṛita fruit while you were asleep, and I ate it without waking you, because I considered that our common body would be nourished thereby."

Adharmika said, "As you have not acted rightly therein, I also will bide my time."

On another occasion, when Dharmika had gone to sleep and Adharmika was awake, the latter perceived a poisonous fruit which the waves had brought ashore. He ate it, and both of the birds became insensible. Affected by the poisonous fruit, Adharmika said, "Wherever I may be

[1] Kah-gyur, iv. ff. 232, 233; and Cf. Benfey's *Panchatantra*, i., iii., ii., 360.—S

born again, there may I be thy antagonist, O enemy and slayer!"

Dharmika said, "Wherever I may be born again, may I show you kindness!"[1]

[1] This is a variant of the fourteenth story of the fifth book of the *Panchatantra*, in which figures a bird named Bharanda, having one body but two beaks. The first beak devours an ambrosia-like fruit, which it refuses to share with its companion. The aggrieved beak, out of spite, eats a poisonous fruit and the bird dies. With this may be compared the following passage, quoted from the Mundaka Upanishad by Prof. Monier Williams (Indian Wisdom, p. 42), "Two birds (the Paramātman and Jīvātman, or supreme and individual souls), always united, of the same name, occupy the same tree (abide in the same body). One of them (the Jīvātman) enjoys the sweet fruit of the fig (or fruit of acts), the other looks on as a witness. Dwelling on the same tree (with the supreme soul), the deluded (individual) soul, immersed (in worldly relations), is grieved by the want of power; but when it perceives the Ruler, separate (from worldly relations) and his glory, then its grief ceases. When the beholder sees the golden-coloured maker (of the world), the lord, the soul, the source of Brahmā, then, having become wise, shaking off virtue and vice, without taint of any kind, he obtains the highest identity."

L.

THREE TALES ABOUT ARTISTS.[1]

1. THE IVORY CARVER AND THE PAINTER.[2]

THERE lived an ivory carver in Madhyadeśa who, after he had carved a few grains of rice made of ivory, travelled with them to the Yavana land, and there took up his abode in the house of a painter. In the absence of the husband, he said to the wife, "Wife of my friend, cook this rice and serve it up to me."

The woman began to cook the rice, but her store of wood came to an end, and yet the rice remained uncooked. When the painter came home, he asked, "Good wife, what is the meaning of that?"

She told him the whole story. The man looked at the rice, perceived that the separate grains were carved out of ivory, and said to his wife, while setting her right:

"Good wife, the water is salt. He must bring us fresh water; the rice will then get cooked."

[1] In S. Beal's "Romantic Legend of Sākya Buddha," pp. 93–96, it is related how the son of a man of quality in Vārāṇasī, in order to obtain the hand of a blacksmith's daughter, applied himself to making fine needles, and made such progress in the art that he included, among the needles which he showed to the smith, one which could float on the surface of water. This tale occurs in a somewhat different shape in the Mākandikāvadāna in the Divyāvadāna, p. 239 of the St. Petersburg MS. A Brahman's son in a hill-place, entering the house of a smith in order to collect alms, falls in love with the smith's daughter, but learns that her father will give her to that man only who can equal or surpass him in art. The Brahman youth applied himself to the art of making needles, and then came to the smith's house, and offered him needles for sale. All the seven needles which he produced as a test of his skill are of such a nature that they float upon water, even the largest among them not being excepted.—S.

[2] Kah-gyur, ii. f. 285.

"The wife said to the ivory carver, "Fetch us fresh water." Now the painter had painted a picture of a pond hard by, with a dead dog's body beside it. The ivory carver took a water jug, and went towards the place where he imagined there was a pond. When he saw the dead dog he held his nose, and then he tried to get the water. But he only smashed his jug, and came to the conclusion that he had been fooled.

2. The Mechanician and the Painter.[1]

In olden times there was a painter in Madhyadeśa, who travelled on business to the Yavana land, and took up his abode there in the house of a mechanician. In order to wait upon the wearied traveller, the mechanician sent an artificial maiden whom he had framed.[2] She washed his feet, and then stood still. He called to her to draw near. But she made no reply. As he was of the opinion that the mechanic had no doubt sent her to him for his enjoyment, he seized her by the hand and tried to draw her towards him. Thereupon, however, the artificial maiden collapsed, and turned into a heap of chips. Being thus befooled, he said to himself, "I have been made a fool of here in private. But in return I will make a fool of the mechanician in the midst of the king's retinue."

So he painted his own likeness on the door, just as if he had hanged himself, and then he hid behind the door. When the time had gone by at which he was wont to rise, the mechanician came to see why the painter had not made his appearance, and imagined he saw him hanging there. While he was considering what could be the painter's reason for depriving himself of life, he saw

[1] Kah-gyur ii. f. 283.

[2] On an artificial elephant which could move by means of machinery, see Mahākātyāyana and Tshaṇḍapradyota (Mém. de l'Acad. des Sciences, viie., Série, T. xxii., No. 7, p. 36). In the Jyotishkāvadāna, p. 108, artificial fishes which can be set in motion by machinery, appear under a crystal floor. The entering guest takes this for water, and is about therefore to take off his shoes. —S.

that the artificial maiden had collapsed and turned into a heap of chips. Thereupon he fancied that the painter had hanged himself out of vexation at having been made a fool of.

Now it was the custom in the Yavana land, that whenever any one died suddenly in any house, the funeral could not take place until information thereof had been given to the king. So the mechanician went to the king and told him that a painter from Madhyadeśa had put up at his house, and that he had sent an artificial maiden to wait upon him, and that the painter had seized her by the hand and tried to draw her towards him, whereupon she had turned into a heap of chips; and that the painter, out of vexation at being made a fool of, had hanged himself. And he besought the king to have the corpse inspected, in order that he might be able to bury it.

The king ordered his officials to undertake the inspection. When the officials reached the spot, and began to consider how they should get the hanged man down, some of them recommended that the rope should be cut, and accordingly an axe was fetched. But when they were about to cut the rope, they perceived that what was before them was only a door, and that the mechanician had been made a fool of. Then the painter came forth from his hiding-place and said, "O inmate of this house, you made a fool of me in private. But I have made a fool of you in the midst of the royal retinue."

3. THE COMPETITION BETWEEN THE TWO ARTISTS.[1]

In olden times a dispute arose between two painters in a hill-place, each of the two affirming that he was superior in art to the other. They went before the king, and fell at his feet. Then each of them explained how he was a better artist than the other. As the king could not settle their dispute, he pointed to the entrance hall, and

[1] Kah-gyur, ii. f. 283.

ordered each of them to paint one of its walls. When their work was finished, he would be in a position to decide which of them was the better artist.

They set to work, divided from one another by a curtain. One of them painted a picture, and completed it in six months. But the other in six months covered the surface of his wall with mosaic work. Having finished his picture, the first artist came before the king and said, "O king, my picture is finished, may it please you to set eyes upon it."

When the king, attended by his ministers, had passed through the doorway and gazed upon the picture, he was well pleased and said, "The painting is excellent." Then the other artist fell at his feet and said, "Now vouchsafe to look at my picture." When he had drawn the curtain aside, and the king saw several figures standing well out, he marvelled greatly and said, "Of the two paintings this is the most excellent." Then the artist drew the curtain once more in front of his work, and fell at the king's feet and said, "O king, this is no painting. I have decorated the wall in mosaic."

Thereupon the king's astonishment waxed still greater, and he said, "This is the one who is the best artist."

INDEX

THE END.

Treasure of Books

Under One Roof

Demand Any Rare Book at

www.facsimilepublisher.com

Demand Any Rare Book at:

www.facsimilepublisher.com

if not available, give information,
our team will search and update you.

Promote Knowledge:

If you have any rare book
which is not available at
www.facsimilepublisher.com,
offer it to other readers so that others can also be
benefitted with your cooperation.
The book will be printed with your courtesy.

Print & Publish:

If you wish to get your book printed or published,
we have the service for you.

Customization on Demand:

We offer customization of books
as per the demand of the customer.

Published by

Facsimile Publisher
Ashok Vihar, Delhi-110052 (India)
Website: www.facsimilepublisher.com

Distributed by

Gyan Books Pvt. Ltd.
5, Ansari Road, Daryaganj, New Delhi-110002 (India)
E-mail: books@gyanbooks.com, Website: www.gyanbooks.com

2 222000 007645